EXPLORER'S GUIDE

ARKANSAS

D0913822

EXPLORER'S GUIDE

SECOND EDITION

ARKANSAS

JANA WOOD

THE COUNTRYMAN PRESS
A division of W. W. Norton & Company
Independent Publishers Since 1923

Manufacturing by Versa Press
Series book design by Chris Welch
Production manager: Devon Zahn

The Countryman Press
www.countrymanpress.com

A division of W. W. Norton & Company, Inc.
500 Fifth Avenue, New York, NY 10110
www.wwnorton.com

978-1-68268-257-9 (pbk.)

10 9 8 7 6 5 4 3 2 1

This book is dedicated to the kind and caring people of Arkansas who welcomed me with open arms and shared their passion and special place in the world with me. I hope to see you again very soon, and until then, I am sharing your stories with a few new friends.

EXPLORE WITH US!

Welcome to the second edition of *Arkansas: An Explorer's Guide*, and an expedition through 53,187 square miles of natural diversity that varies from the swampy lowlands of the Delta to the eroded domes of the Ozark Mountains. As an Arkansas native who has relished spending 20 years traveling the state professionally (10 of them specifically scouting locations and escorting tours for out-of-state businesses), it is my goal to provide you with an insider's guide to the state's lodging, dining, and attractions that not only includes those businesses that specifically cater to tourists, but also the sacred mom-and-pop diners, bed & breakfasts, and off-the-grid shops and galleries. Arkansans favor these so much we are tempted to keep them to ourselves to ensure they don't outgrow us and move on to the big city. You will find vibrant cities and quaint villages replete with upscale dining, interesting museums, scenic drives, exciting theme parks, unique historical sites, challenging golf courses, pampering resorts, and luxurious spas to soothe your body and rejuvenate your spirit. From the rib shacks tucked in the fields of the earthy Delta to the dining rooms of lodges perched on the shoulders of the Boston Mountains, you will find detailed listings for bed & breakfasts and resorts; restaurants; attractions; state, local, and federal parks; shopping; events; and more than a few opportunities to share only with special friends. Think of this guide as a backseat passenger on your adventure, here to provide directions and guidance, and fill you in on the legend and lore along the way.

WHAT'S WHERE In the beginning of this book, you'll find a few pages that highlight the basics, special features, and some helpful tips to know when traveling the Natural State. For a quick reference on everything from crystal mines to dude ranches, this section will show you where to start.

PRICES Please don't hold us (or the listed innkeepers) responsible for the rates listed as we go to press for 2018. Changes are inevitable. Most of the lodging options listed here are privately owned, and most emphasis is placed on resorts, campgrounds, cabins, and bed & breakfasts. Franchise and chain operations are not included; my goal is to take you along the back roads, not the highways, and show you the people and places that make our state unique.

SMOKING Arkansas law bans smoking in public places and any establishment that serves minors. Adults are also prohibited from smoking in vehicles in which young children are passengers.

RESTAURANTS There are separate sections for Eating Out and Dining Out, with the former devoted to casual dining and the latter reserved for a more gourmand experience. You will find most restaurants in Arkansas require neither reservations nor fancy attire.

LODGING PRICES The prices listed range from low-season to high-season rates. On summer weekends and holidays, prices can double. Prices do not include local taxes.

$	Under $100
$$	$101–200
$$$	$201–300
$$$$	over $300

DINING PRICES The prices listed do not include drinks, tax, or gratuity (which is normally 15 percent of your total bill). Prices generally include an entrée plus an appetizer, salad, or dessert signature to the restaurant.

$	Under $10
$$	$10–19
$$$	$20–29
$$$$	Over $30

Please send any comments or corrections to:

Explorer's Guide Editor
The Countryman Press
500 Fifth Avenue
New York, NY 10110

KEY TO SYMBOLS

- *Child-friendly.* The kid-friendly crayon symbol appears next to listings with special appeal to young people.
- &. **Handicapped access.** The wheelchair symbol appears next to listings that are partially or fully handicap accessible.
- **Pets.** The dog paw symbol appears next to lodgings that accept pets. In general, you can expect to pay a fee for letting Duke the dog or Luna the cat come along. Make sure to tell the owners upon your reservation that you plan to bring an animal.
- Y **Bars and nightlife.** The martini glass symbol appears next to restaurants with bars or drinking establishments.
- **Special value.** The blue ribbon symbol appears next to lodging and restaurants that give you an exceptional deal for your money.

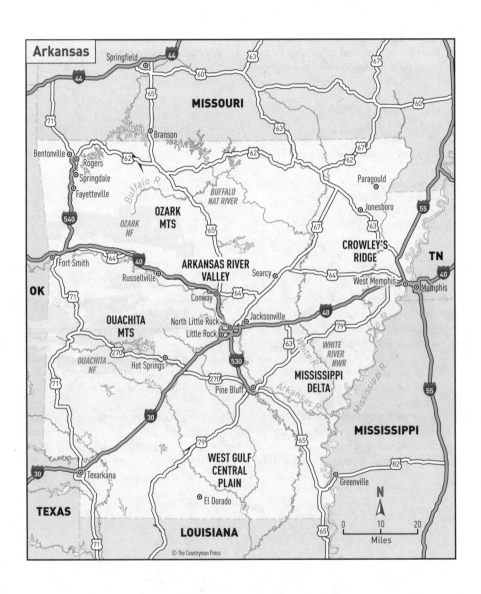

CONTENTS

MAPS

ACKNOWLEDGMENTS

Welcome to the second edition of Explorer's Guide Arkansas. There have been a lot of developments in Arkansas since the first edition was published. Everything in this guide has been thoroughly updated to include new offerings sprinkled throughout the state to ensure you don't miss a thing while you are here.

Most notably, the quaint hamlet of Bentonville has transformed since the November 11, 2011, opening of the Crystal Bridges Museum of American Art. The artist's rendering referenced in this guide's debut is now 271,000 square feet of galleries and meeting spaces featuring acclaimed artistic treasures and a world-class restaurant. Special thanks to Blair Cromwell of the Bentonville Convention and Visitors Bureau for her gracious hospitality, support, and expertise about her community. I emerged from my tour with a passion for this charming town and deep admiration for the artisans who operate its businesses. You will find this inspiration extends beyond the town and through the Northwest Corridor of the state. Nearby Fort Smith has gained international recognition for its public art exhibitions featuring murals with realistic figures that stand six stories tall.

In Fort Smith, Meredith Baldwin not only invested her time in an interview but also supplied the architectural renderings and photos for the US Marshals Museum planned for Fort Smith. Claude Legris of the Fort Smith Convention and Visitors Bureau turned me on to one of my new favorites—The Unexpected—a spectacular series of murals painted by international artists around the historic downtown area and an attendant street festival. Claire Koberg, the chief organizer of the project, proved an invaluable resource about the festival, its art, and its artists.

Róisín Cameron, senior editor for The Countryman Press, was an advocate for this update, and provided the encouragement and guidance that is essential to a successful revision. I am extremely grateful to her for this opportunity to share the growth seen in my state in the years since our first edition. Michael Tizzano and Kathryn Flynn shepherded this update through a rigorous edit to ensure its accuracy. In fact, I haven't felt this confident in my writing since the death of my own personal editor—my sister, Kelley—in 2012. I have missed her terribly in the years that have passed, but it wasn't until reviewing these edits that I realized how much her absence was reflected in my writing. Michael and Kathryn nurtured this guide with the deft-but-gentle hands of those experienced in the mechanics of editing, while coaxing the author to flesh out the story to its fullest.

No guide to Arkansas is adequate without the inclusion of the growth that has taken place is our Northwest Corridor. It is home to some of our most impressive offerings, many of which opened or expanded since Crystal Bridges broke ground.

Special thanks to friend and fabulous photographer Casey Crocker, who helped me choose the best photos that the Arkansas Department of Parks and Tourism has to offer to supplement my own when needed.

Finally, no project would be complete without acknowledging my numero uno, my son, Jason Greenbaum. I was always close to my boys, Joshua and Jason, and in the years since Josh's passing, Jason helped me rebuild my life with a new normal. My smart, compassionate, determined, resilient, and loving son inspired the strength I needed to not only carry on despite a tragic loss, but also to reclaim my love for life. Jason's love reminds me that I am surrounded by splendor in the Natural State. I also must remember my Joshua, whose love no doubt provided divine inspiration to find the words to convey this beauty to you.

PREFACE

I was prompted in writing this book to spend six months traveling more than 10,000 miles through 62 of Arkansas's 75 counties, canvassing communities to include local recommendations—and a firsthand observation of their recommendations whenever possible—supplemented by an ample number of suggested pit stops I uncovered along the rural roads that connect them. I took the same approach while drafting the update, packing up the car and hitting the road to gather the reliable intel only acquired by an immersive traveler on a quest to uncover an authentically Arkansas experience.

Determined to incorporate the perspective of a newbie, I invited friends along for the ride to provide their thoughts and impressions and help me supply you with objective reviews of the state's hospitality and all of its offerings. After all, we live in a world where the Internet now supplies us with too much information at times, and I have frequently referred to it as a level playing field because a geek in a garage can look as impressive as an international conglomerate. It is not my intention to replicate another all-inclusive listing of hotels and restaurants. There are plenty out there for you, starting with the state's mega-monster website, Arkansas.com. No, there are far too many options in the state for that approach, and it doesn't leave pages available to include those places I want to show you that aren't located in any town; they just collect their mail there. It also doesn't allow me to profile some of the smaller towns that may only have one attraction, but it is a really great one. Historically, Explorer's Guide readers are explorers first, right? So I think you will gain a better appreciation for the state, and ultimately more enjoyment while you are here, if I venture off the tourism radar (and off road when necessary). I have opted to present a comprehensive, though not all-inclusive, listing of attractions, lodging, and dining options, and an all-inclusive guide to places I want you to see, people I want you to meet, and things I want you to do while you are here.

In addition to updating the listings included in the first edition, I specifically wanted to revise this guide to expand my coverage of Bentonville and Fort Smith. Northwest Arkansas transformed following the November 11, 2011, opening of Crystal Bridges Museum of American Art. The museum and its acquisitions gained national attention prior to its debut, and its impact on this charming community is impressive. I love my state, and it is impossible for me to choose a favorite town, much like it is impossible

THE BUBBLE BY HARRIET WHITNEY FRISHMUTH ON DISPLAY AT CRYSTAL BRIDGES MUSEUM OF AMERICAN ART for a mom to choose a favorite child. However, if you could only visit one city in Arkansas, I would recommend Bentonville. The controversy generated when Helen Walton acquired George Washington's portrait and located it in a small town in middle America compels me to share the result of her endeavor. Every restaurant, shop, attraction, and bike path reflect the impact of Walton's vision.

I also wanted to expand the Fort Smith story. On September 24, 2019, the official US Marshals Museum opens in conjunction with the 230th anniversary of the esteemed law enforcement agency. The aerial view of the final structure is designed to resemble a marshal's badge, and prior to its opening visitors can take a virtual walk-through of the site from its footprint along the Arkansas River. Fort Smith has also embraced the arts in public spaces with a series of murals painted by artists from around the world. Increased national interest in this town has expanded its hospitality offerings in preparation for the visitors to come.

No destination paid for inclusion within these pages. In fact, at least one hotelier in Hot Springs comped our lodging on more than one occasion, fully aware that I would not be covering chain hotels in the book.

INTRODUCTION

So far, more than half of my career has been spent introducing folks from off (Arkansas-speak for non-Arkansans) to the richness and diversity of my state's landscape and culture. For nearly a decade I freelanced as a film production crew member for visiting film companies: motion picture makers, documentarians, and broadcast commercial producers. They sought out our state for one of three reasons: their client was here, they needed our 5 percent rebate, or they needed to film our state Capitol. Its distinction as one of few that can pass as the nation's Capitol inspired its use as a location for *Under Siege* in 1987, when fictional terrorists hit the building with a magical movie missile that actually did leave a blackened stain on the dome, providing fodder for the local op-ed page for months. It was last used in the filming of *The Brotherhood* in the early 1990s, when the crew left motorcycle skid marks on the marble stairway leading to the legislative chamber. As a production coordinator, I met the directors and producers at the airport when they arrived and shared heartfelt goodbyes on its tarmac when they left. My crews came from the East and West Coasts, Florida, and our neighboring states. Creative types come in all shapes and sizes, and there are more varieties of lifestyle out there than I realized, but the overwhelming majority of them used one word to sum up their experience in Arkansas: surprising. They were amazed at the diversity of our terrain and our natural beauty—even in our metropolitan areas— and astounded by the affordability and quality of our food, lodgings, and services. But what impressed them most was the graciousness and hospitality of our residents.

Years later, in another life, I escorted travel writers and editors researching stories on Arkansas destinations for their media outlets. It was my job to discuss with a journalist an assignment or area of interest, and then coordinate an itinerary and escort him or her during a tour of Arkansas. Many of them were quite jaded as travelers; their worldwide travels included all of the A-list vacation spots in the States and abroad, with first-class accommodations provided at no charge in many cases. And yet, as before, when asked to choose one word to describe their visit to our state, 90 percent of the people I asked said "surprising." In 2008, the Arkansas Department of Parks and Tourism commissioned ERA Longwoods, a national tourism consulting company, to conduct a $250,000 study of our tourism industry. The results of that study were most surprising to Longwoods' experts. Most significantly, the company said they had encountered something they had never seen before: a location burdened by a preconceived negative image that was completely dispelled following a visit to the location. We like to think of ourselves as a boutique destination, showcasing Mother Nature's splendor alongside upscale spas, Euro-Ozarko bistros, and independent art galleries. But a case can also be made that we are America's Amazon, as our state remains virgin, unexplored territory for a majority of our country's travelers. It is my hope that this guide will ensure that your visit to Arkansas is not surprising because I have armed you for your journey with insight into our culture, a native's guide to good eats and cozy shelter, and imagery to whet your appetite for our scenic vistas. Unless otherwise noted, the destinations listed in this guide are open year-round.

In 1987, the state changed its nickname from the Land of Opportunity to the Natural State in deference to the uniqueness and abundance of our natural resources.

Arkansas is home to the only public diamond mine in the world, the first federally protected river, the first national park (technically), and it boasts one of the few state park systems offering free interpretive services and programs. There are 52 state parks within the state's 53,000 square miles, ensuring we are never more than an hour from homage to our heritage. Samuel Davies, the system's first director, instilled in park staff and his family a commitment to not only preserve, protect, and perpetuate Arkansas resources through a state park system, but also to ensure that they remained economically accessible to the state's population. The mantle was carried by grandson Richard Davies until his retirement in 2015, and the state's ability to ride the tide of change without eroding the environment is testament to its success nurturing conservation in Arkansas.

Hunters and birders lobby side by side to protect our forests, a partnership resulting in habitat that protects a number of endangered species—most recently and notably, the ivory-billed woodpecker. Our 600,000 acres of lakes are considered among the purest in the country, delighting divers and photographers beneath the surface and skiers, paddlers, and fishermen above. Our clean air refreshes the mind and body of the earthbound and fuels the flight of avian migration on the Mississippi Flyway and hang gliders along the River Valley.

Arkansas's state park system promotes six natural divisions in the state: the Ozark Mountains, the Mississippi Alluvial Plain (Arkansas's Delta), Crowley's Ridge, the Ouachita Mountains, the Arkansas River Valley, and the West Gulf Coastal Plain. Each region is distinct environmentally, and most communities in the state developed their economies by tapping into their natural resources.

From the oil fields of southern Arkansas to the cotton fields of the Delta to the sparkling gemstones of the Ouachitas, the state's marriage to Mother Nature encouraged us to embrace forward progress in harmony with our place on the planet. Our fidelity to our commitment leaves Arkansas perfectly poised to enchant the modern traveler whose eco-morality now values, yea prizes, our Natural State.

It's easy to look at a topographical map of Arkansas and draw a diagonal line across the center of the state, dividing it into two distinct regions—the highlands in the northwest and the lowlands in the southeastern half of the state. A closer look at the geology of these areas reveals three distinct divisions within the two that not only shaped the land but also the people and their culture in distinctly different ways. The highlands are characterized by two mountain regions: the Ozark Plateau and the Ouachita Mountains, with the Arkansas River Valley between them. The Mississippi Alluvial Plain and Crowley's Ridge within, and the West Gulf Coastal Plain compose the geological divisions of the lowlands in southeast Arkansas. I have never found myself into geology, and until writing the first edition of this guide I would have taken your bet that I never would be. But taking that closer look into the geology of my home state helped me to see it in a new light, and I have a new appreciation for the possibilities that await when you travel Arkansas. You can visit, say, Village Creek State Park in Wynne and have a blast for a week riding your horse through 25 miles of golden hickory and beech trees without ever noticing the point at which you cross over The Trail of Tears. On the one hand, you would have still enjoyed your vacation, and likely you would greatly appreciate the park's Horse Hilton, considered the best in a four-state area. But that would also be a shame, because Village Creek is one of few places in the country where you can actually stand on the ground Native Americans walked during their historic exodus. But if you know the geological history of Crowley's Ridge—the park's natural region—before you go, you will not only mark the moment you cross the tragic trail, you might even recognize the botanical banners flagging water and the path ahead. Sometimes a tree is more than just a tree.

HORSEBACK RIDING AT VILLAGE CREEK STATE PARK   ARKANSAS DEPARTMENT OF PARKS & TOURISM

You will find within these pages the where and the when of Arkansas, and also the why. In some cases, such as the West Gulf Coastal Plain, lodging is divided because the region is very large and attraction driven, so it is organized to help you lay your head at night in the vicinity of the place you plan to play during the day.

The Ozarks Plateau is characterized by its flat-topped mountains, heavily eroded over millions of years by the many mighty rivers that originate here. You will find three distinct regions within it, each with its own topography, history, and culture: the Springfield Plateau, the Salem Plateau, and the Boston Mountains. The communities that formed on the Springfield Plateau capitalized on its extensive, level prairies, advancing transportation to their area and ultimately their economies. Today, these communities unite as the Northwest Corridor, one of the most progressive sectors of the state with an economy that continuously shows growth, even when national trends decline. This is where you will find the state's newest airport, XNA; Fort Smith; and the belle of this edition of this guide, Bentonville.

Just north and east of the Springfield Plateau is the Salem Plateau, at an elevation of 1,560 feet. Eureka Springs lies on the cusp between the two plateaus, giving it its mountainous character. The Salem Plateau also had fairly level hilltops, described as barrens, with rocky soil not easily adaptable for agriculture, and towns and villages here struggled for traction against the rugged terrain.

That all changed in the late nineteenth century, when interest developed in the healing waters of Eureka Springs. The home of numerous cold-water springs soon became a hot destination for tourists, as the little village's business community developed to support the temporary residents that came in droves during the high-season months of spring, summer, and fall. You will find Eureka Springs has preserved the quirky charm that created its special sense of place in the late 1800s, as well as the majority of its architecture; the entire downtown is on the National Historic Register.

As you travel east across the Salem Plateau, the rivers that originate in the west grow in size and importance in the development of the towns that formed along their shores. Mountain Home is the largest, due to its location between the two reservoirs (Bull Shoals Lake and Lake Norfork) created by the US Army Corps of Engineers' damming projects on the White and Norfork Rivers. When cold waters released from the dams damaged the ecosystem beneath them, the Corps built trout hatcheries as an alternative for local communities. Trout fishing on the White River is now world famous, and resorts and guide services are major contributors to local economies. As I mentioned before, my job duties once included escorting writers researching travel stories around Arkansas, usually with the state, local chamber, or civic-minded destination footing the bill. Most of them felt their time in the state was too short to see and do everything of interest to them. But there was only one time when the writer actually took a vacation day to extend his stay, and he was fishing the White River.

The highest of the three regions, the Boston Plateau, skirts the other two along the southern border of the Ozark Plateau, parallel to and north of I-40. More commonly known as the Boston Mountains, this plateau's rugged topography and its inherently narrow and winding roads made for arduous travel, and the communities that developed here are small, and few and far between. This is the land of the Ozark Mountaineer, isolated by the lack of a solid transportation system and forced to adapt to that isolation with self-sufficiency. The largest community in the Boston Mountains is Clinton, which lies in the wide valley of the Little Red River. Thirty miles from Clinton, as the crow flies, the Ozark Folk Center State Park will allow you to immerse yourself in the Ozark Mountain way of life through living histories, music and craft demonstrations, and the carefree feel of a simpler way of life.

At the southern perimeter of the Ozark Plateau, the Arkansas River Valley is a roughly 40-mile-wide trough between the Ouachita and Ozark mountain ranges. This region has the flat-topped mountains of the Ozarks in the north, the rolling ridges of the Ouachitas in the south, with the Arkansas River and its wide bottomlands of fertile soil between. The combination of rich farmland and river transportation was a winning one for communities that prospered along the river's banks. Arkansas's winemakers began tending their vines in the River Valley over a hundred years ago. On the state's western border with Oklahoma, Fort Smith, the state's second-largest city, was the last trading post before entering the western plains. Arkansas's frontier heritage is here, marked at the Fort Smith National Historic Site, and in 2019 the US Marshals Museum will open as its most prestigious local attraction. You will find not only the first state park along the Arkansas River Valley, on Petit Jean Mountain, but also the system's single greatest capital investment in the $33 million lodge atop Mount Magazine.

The long, narrow ridges of the Ouachita Mountains run east to west across the central portion of the state and harbor natural treasures of national significance. In 1832, President Andrew Jackson set aside Arkansas land for federal protection of the geothermal waters that boiled naturally beneath its surface, technically making it America's first national park. Hot Springs National Park can also lay claim as the nation's first spa, dating back to the days of Hernando de Soto. We'll talk more about this when we get to the Hot Springs section. By the 1920s, the healing waters of Hot Springs were reportedly protected by both the National Park Service and Al Capone, who declared the streets of the spa city a no combat zone when he and the boys were in town. The town became a smaller, mid-America version of Vegas, with thoroughbred racing at Oaklawn Park, casinos, and elegant bathhouses, but set in a lush national forest rather than a desert. Hot Springs is even more charming today, despite the fact it is no longer under Mafia protection. Oaklawn's season is extended, thanks to modern technology and simulcasting, and you can play the ponies there year-round now. The addition of electronic gaming, following many years of prohibition, hearkens back to the town's colorful past. The story is told at the new Gangster Museum, the only facility in the country willing to talk.

The Ouachitas are also one of a few places in the world with substantial enough quartz deposits to warrant commercial mining. Though their exact size is unknown, the deposits beneath the earth's crust at Mount Ida are considered world-class for both their size and quality. But the individual crystals themselves are also prized for their colorless, nearly clear terminals, the mineral's manifestation of the pure waters of western Arkansas. You will find Mount Ida quartz displayed in Europe and on the ground of several private and two public mines in this small town 30 minutes west of Hot Springs.

Roughly a third of the lowlands of Arkansas fall within the Mississippi Alluvial Plain, more commonly known as the

GEOTHERMAL WATERS FLOW IN DOWNTOWN HOT SPRINGS

Delta. Oddly enough, it is technically not a delta or flood plain, which refers to an area often inundated when a river or stream overflows. The relatively flat alluvial plain was created by millions of years of deposits and encompasses a far larger area representing the region where the flood plain shifted during geological time. This distinctive and unique corridor of geology extending down the heart of the United States is clearly visible to astronauts in orbit and in satellite imagery on cloudless days in summer months. Arkansas's Delta is both wild, with huge tracts of remote, nearly virgin woods, and cultivated, with thousands of acres of farmland. Its rich and fertile soil makes it one of the most productive agricultural regions in the world. Its fields are filled with lush crops of cotton and rice, soybeans and corn. Its agricultural history predates European settlement of the state; Hernando de Soto examined fields tended by Quapaw tribes during a Delta tour in the winter of 1541. With a climate perfectly suited for cotton, plantation farmers built huge spreads throughout the Delta, employing slave labor. Historic battle sites and Civil War markers have replaced the plantations prevalent in the 1800s, with only Lakeport Plantation in south Arkansas remaining as an example of the antebellum showplaces that once stood on the shores of the Mississippi River.

This is a land that has known both feast and famine, and its people have learned to appreciate nature's bounty and fear its wrath. Their ability to endure is evident in levees that hold back the mighty river, irrigation channels that nurture their fields, and museums that recount their struggle. These are the levees Johnny Cash, as well as countless bluesmen, sing about in their songs about life in the Delta. Cash's boyhood home and the restored colony at Dyess have attracted thousands of visitors from around the world looking for the humble beginnings that inspired the legendary man in black.

LAKEPORT PLANTATION IN LAKE VILLAGE   ARKANSAS DEPARTMENT OF PARKS & TOURISM

Completely surrounded by the Delta is the smallest geological region in Arkansas, Crowley's Ridge. Covered with dense vegetation, it rises 200 feet above the landscape, high ground that provided shelter from the floods below. Early Native Americans were the first to seek safe passage on the ridge, and you can follow the footsteps of their successors on the Trail of Tears at Village Creek State Park. We know now that the particular type of fragile loess soil on the ridge is only found in one other place on earth (the other location is Croatia), but to the ridge's first settlers it was simply safe and fertile ground on which they could build families and towns. The Delta's largest city, Jonesboro, is at the northern end of the ridge. The city is the center of culture and education in east Arkansas and active in the preservation of the natural and cultural history of the entire region.

The West Gulf Coastal Plain, the last of Arkansas's natural regions, is famous for its geology, as it encompasses the only diamond mine in North America as well as being the center of our oil industry. The Gulf Coastal Plain is also the focus of much of the timber industry in the state. Crater of Diamonds State Park makes national news regularly for the diamonds recovered from its public fields. The park averages two diamonds a day found by treasure seekers who pay a small fee to keep the diamonds, minerals, and gemstones they find scattered over its 37 acres. Looking for the diamonds is so easy a baby could do it, and it was a favorite activity for my kids until they were well into their teens. Finding them is not so easy; I haven't found one yet. But the experience is a blast and I go every year and come back with a bucket full of jasper, agate, quartz, and other minerals that are plentiful at the park.

We also have our own black gold, Texas tea, in the fields around El Dorado in southeast Arkansas. An oil boom in the 1920s brought instant wealth and wild times to the town. The beautifully restored downtown now sets the stage for summer reenactments of the Showdown at Sunset, a legendary gunfight that took place on the courthouse steps in its wilder days. The downtown was declared a National Historic District in 2004 and is a popular shopping destination for the entire state.

The Little Rock/North Little Rock area is the geographic center of the state; parts of it fall in the Ouachitas, the Delta, and the West Gulf Coastal Plain. I have included it in the last region for a number of reasons, both philosophical in nature as well as organizational. An important factor was a teacher's reference guide on the natural divisions that was updated in 2008 and definitively placed Little Rock in the Coastal Plain. If you're reading this and you live in Little Rock and always considered yourself a resident of the Delta, you still are. That is your tourism region, not your geological one. Show your physiographic pride in the West Gulf Coastal Plain.

An understanding of the natural regions should help you understand and appreciate the diverse communities and cultures in the Natural State. We can seem more than a little schizophrenic to the casual observer, even to each other. The geology of our state blessed each community with its own unique and rich natural resources and also created the natural barriers that isolated each of them from the rest of the state. We didn't come together to present a unified image of Arkansas to the rest of the world until the mid-1970s.

That was also about the time that Jim Gann became Arkansas's first state park interpreter at Logoly State Park, and the state began to formally explain our unique natural gifts to visitors. It is also when Richard Davies took over the helm as director of Arkansas's state parks system, and we began to verbalize a cohesive story of national interest. And while Henri de Tonti may have established Arkansas's first hub

HISTORIC GUNFIGHT RECREATED AT SHOWDOWN AT SUNSET IN EL DORADO   ARKANSAS DEPARTMENT OF PARKS & TOURISM

of hospitality at Arkansas Post in 1686, the state's tourism industry was born in the mid-1970s, when our leadership began to reflect a lifetime of passion and respect for Arkansas's extraordinary natural resources.

Today's parks are partially funded by a conservation tax that provides perpetual funding for maintenance, interpretation, and security that drew strong support from Arkansans, some of whom have literally grown up in these parks. Nearly 100 years after the inception of the system, hundreds of thousands of Arkansans have fished state park lakes, toured their historic buildings, and camped under the shelter of their trees. Always economically challenged, our education system has relied on Arkansas's state parks to fill the void in our kids' educations when municipal monies ran light, and the parks responded by ramping up the quantity and quality of interpretive programming to a nationally recognized level. They are a great place for you, too, to start exploring Arkansas.

WHAT'S WHERE IN ARKANSAS

ANTIQUES Antiquing is hugely popular in Arkansas, with more than 200 shops and flea markets that offer everything from authentic period pieces to primitive farm implements. The **Antique Warehouse of Arkansas** in Botkinburg is a must-see, and you might want to pack a lunch for your exploration of this 90,000-square-foot complex of timeless treasures. Its location on US 65 will take you by dozens of smaller shops and roadside markets worthy of a true bargain hunter's time. Just southeast of Little Rock, you will find **Old Gin Antiques** in the small town of Keo. It has garnered regional and national attention for the quality and quantity of pieces in its inventory. If you prefer the serendipitous shopping experience of flea markets, **Bargains Galore** on US 64 is an annual event held in August that spreads over 160 miles of the two-lane highway from Beebe to the Oklahoma border and was designated a Travel Treasure by *Southern Traveler* magazine. Launched nearly 20 years ago, the event draws dealers and collectors from throughout the South every year.

ARKANSAS.COM The state's tourism division publishes a ginormous clearinghouse of travel-related information on the website at **arkansas.com**. The home page includes direct links to handy travel planning tools like a trip-building program that delivers a thorough itinerary based on the destinations you pull from the site's database. Maps are posted for each region, as well as specific routes of interest, such as noted hiking and biking trails, plus an interactive map that allows you to select the features highlighted, such as state parks or waterways. The site organizes the information by interest, geography, and the calendar, which gives you a variety of ways to explore the state from the comfort of your own home before you travel. The City Listings section includes lodging, dining, and attraction offerings in the majority of cities and towns in the state and is an invaluable resource when planning a road trip in Arkansas. You can search the Calendar of Events section by travel dates, city names, and selected keywords to link to festivals and special events happening throughout the state.

ARKANSAS WELCOME CENTERS One of the more important tips to know when traveling in Arkansas is the location of the closest Arkansas Welcome Center to your chosen destination. Thirteen are located at the major gateways to the state, and another is housed within the Department of Parks and Tourism offices on the grounds of the state Capitol in **Little Rock**. Each is staffed with travel consultants well versed in Arkansas's scenery, lodging, events, and history; they are also well stocked with free maps and literature about the state's destinations and attractions. Over a million people a year use their expertise for local lodging and dining recommendations, driving directions, and attractions in their area and the entire state. In 2005, Parks and Tourism joined with the state's Department of Transportation and began replacing the more heavily trafficked locations with larger, native stone and pine structures with state-of-the-art technology and engaging local exhibits that give you an excellent overview of the area's points of interest while checking your e-mail or booking your room. Most are open daily, excluding holidays, from 8–5.

The centers in **Helena–West Helena** and **Red River** close at 4 p.m. During the extended days of summer, you will find them there until 6 p.m. Cities hosting welcome centers include **Siloam Springs**, **Bentonville**, **Harrison**, **Mammoth Spring**, **Corning**, **Blytheville**, **Van Buren/Fort Smith**, **West Memphis**, **Helena–West Helena**, **Little Rock**, **Texarkana**, **Red River**, **El Dorado**, and **Lake Village**.

BBQ You could literally travel from one end of the state to the other, sampling the slow-smoked, hickory flavor of slab ribs and pulled brisket, and not taste the same recipe twice. Hot and spicy, sweet and tangy, off-the-bone with fresh white bread, layered with beans and coleslaw over flaky baked potatoes, or spread over hand-rolled tamales and smothered in cheese, Arkansas has almost as many versions of BBQ as it does places that serve it. Every town, and many otherwise deserted roadways between, has at least one local landmark surrounded by diners waiting for a seat at one of its handful of tables. Perhaps the most famous in the state is the presidentially preferred **McClard's BBQ** in Hot Springs, naming Bill Clinton among its devotees. Nearby Arkadelphia is home to my personal pick, **Allen's Barbeque**, which serves its fire-kissed fare from a trailer wedged in a Y in the roadway to Crater of Diamonds State Park. But it would be blasphemous to disregard the Delta from the Q question, particularly in Arkansas, where the BBQ shacks boast recipes perfected decades ago and served by third- and fourth-generation family members. Here, you will find the epitome of the Southern BBQ shack you might drive past without noticing if not for the throngs of cars and tantalizing smoky aromas. The **Cross-Eyed Pig** in Little Rock is known for its ribs.

Craig's Brothers Café in DeValls Bluff has been a destination of choice in east Arkansas since the 1940s. **Jones Bar-B-Q Diner** in Marianna is believed to be the oldest continuously operated African American–owned business in the South, and it was declared an American Classic by the James Beard Foundation in 2012.

BIKING Street cycling and mountain biking are gaining ground in popularity with travelers to the Natural State. One big darn reason is the **Big Dam Bridge** in central Arkansas, spanning the Arkansas River and connecting the cities of Little Rock and North Little Rock with the nation's longest bridge built specifically for pedestrian/bicycle traffic. Just down the river, near the Clinton Library, the **Junction Bridge** has been renovated into a pedestrian and bicycle bridge and is believed to be the only converted lift span bridge in the country. Visitors ride elevators up to and down from the 360-foot lift span as they cross the entire 1,800 feet of the bridge. Events like the **Joe Martin Stage Race** in Fayetteville annually draw amateur and professional cyclists and have earned a spot on the National Racing Calendar for the sport. Arkansas is one of the top three destinations in the country for mountain bikers, home to five **Epic Rides** designated by the International Mountain Bicycling Association (IMBA). This places the state tied for second with Colorado and just behind California, which has seven official routes. The IMBA also named Bentonville, Fayetteville, and Hot Springs as Ride Centers due to their world-class facilities and welcoming hospitality. In fact, the entire region of northwest Arkansas was distinguished as the first **Regional Ride Center** noted by the IMBA.

BILL CLINTON From his birthplace home in the city of Hope to his presidential library in Little Rock, you can follow the footsteps of the nation's 42nd president from the Ouachitas to the White House. Four communities—Fayetteville, Hope, Hot Springs, and Little Rock—offer numerous locales that provide a glimpse of Clinton's personal and political past in the state. In Fayetteville, the **Clinton House Museum**, the house where Bill and Hillary Clinton married, is convenient to the University of Arkansas, where he taught law during the couple's newlywed days. Clinton's childhood in Hot Springs is marked in a former family home, the church and high school he attended, as well as the YMCA where Clinton and his high school band, The Three Kings, frequently played.

BIRDS AND BUTTERFLIES Arkansas's location along the **Mississippi Flyway**, plus numerous expanses of unblemished natural habitat, provides birdwatchers with a resource that contains 400 species, including rarely seen coastal birds venturing through on their annual migration. In 2005, the Big Woods of eastern Arkansas was the site of all sightings when Gene Sparling and David

Luneau generated worldwide interest with their grainy footage of an ivory-billed woodpecker, previously believed to be extinct, flying through the swampy bottomland. While the formal search for the bird has now subsided, avid bird-watchers still man blinds in the bottom-land forest, drawn to the 310 species regularly observed in the state in the appropriate season, including the brown-headed nuthatch, Bachman's sparrow, and Henslow's sparrow. Arkansas's butterfly population includes more than 150 species as well as a few transient visitors during the annual migration season, which lasts from March through early December. A butterfly festival is held in early June at **Mount Magazine State Park**, easily the most popular location for observation, with more than 90 species spending their summers here. In southwest Arkansas, the **Rick Evans Grand-view Prairie Wildlife Management Area**, the nation's largest contiguous tract of

CROWLEY'S RIDGE NATURE CENTER ARKANSAS DEPARTMENT OF PARKS & TOURISM

publicly held blackland prairie, attracts a diverse selection of species to a butterfly garden on its grounds. The unique plant life found on Crowley's Ridge draws the fluttering creatures to the grounds of **Forrest L. Wood Crowley's Ridge Nature Center** in Jonesboro, where elevated walkways enhance your perspective.

BLUEGRASS The small, Ozark Mountain town of **Mountain View** is the Folk Music Capital of the World, where traditional folk instruments like the fiddle, dulcimer, and mandolin celebrate the genre daily with performances on the stage of the **Ozark Folk Center** and the square of its historic downtown. Eureka Springs is home to an annual bluegrass festival that fills its winding streets with amateur and professional musicians drawn to the eclectic community and its funky venues. Every show during the weeklong event is free, making it one of the state's most popular music festivals for families. Located in the beautiful Ouachita Mountains near Waldron, **Turkey Track Bluegrass Park** hosts one of the largest bluegrass festivals west of the Mississippi River, holding two festivals in June and October every year.

BLUES Roads lined with soft tufts of cotton are among the first harbingers of fall for the thousands of people making their way through east Arkansas for the **King Biscuit Blues Festival**. For more than 30 years, this annual event has been held every October on Cherry Street in historic downtown Helena, which has its own place of significance in the history of blues. Legendary artists like B. B. King, Bonnie Raitt, Keb' Mo', Dr. John, Greg Allman, Buddy Guy, and Taj Mahal have graced its Main Stage, while its six city blocks have been lined with up-and-comers. The **Delta Cultural Center** is also here. It offers interactive exhibits that tell the story of the Delta's role in the development of the genre and is also home to the longest-running daily blues radio show in the United States.

Bubba's Blues Corner nearby stocks an amazing collection of records, CDs, tapes, and memorabilia that intrigues both amateurs and aficionados.

BREWERIES AND DISTILLERIES The clean, clear waters of the state are showcased in the beers brewed by craftsmen throughout Arkansas. In 2016, the state was home to 30 breweries, with nine in Little Rock, 10 on Fayetteville's **Ale Trail**, and the remainder scattered throughout the state. Pub crawls and brewery tours attract locals and visitors and are frequently paired with gallery walks, music festivals, and exhibitions. Crafted spirits are constantly evolving in Arkansas, with local distillers bottling more than moonshine in them thar hills. Bourbons, vodkas, and hard ciders are just a few of the spirits you can sample during your visit or purchase for your bar at home. Tours and demonstrations are also offered at many of these fine establishments, spotlighting the science behind the magic in the bottle.

CAVES The subterranean splendor of the Ozarks is easily explored in guided tours in show caves such as **Hurricane River Cave, Cosmic Caverns, War Eagle Cavern**, and **Blanchard Springs Caverns**. These locations also offer guided wild caving tours for the physically fit. Hikers exploring the mountains near the Buffalo National River may also encounter wild caves such as the **Lost Valley Trail Cave**, which houses a 35-foot waterfall. Some wild caves in the Ozark Mountains require permits or guides for entry. Hikers may also come across cave openings with grated entries designed to protect endangered species whose year-round homes are in the caves.

Additional information on the caves and obtaining permits is available from the Harrison office of the **Buffalo National River** (870-741-5443).

CIVIL WAR Arkansas's role in the Civil War is diversely depicted throughout the

CAVING AT DEVIL'S DEN STATE PARK

Civil War history guided by area experts. State parks mark three battle sites that were part of the Union Army's Red River campaign at **Poison Spring**, **Marks' Mills**, and **Jenkins' Ferry**. The **Old State House Museum** was one of two of the state's Confederate Capitols. The 1836 **Hempstead County Courthouse** at Historic Washington State Park near Hope is also open to the public and is just one part of the park's interpretation of daily life in Arkansas during the era.

DRIVE-IN MOVIES Arkansas's temperate climate is perfect for outdoor recreation and entertainment, so you will find a number of communities in the state where you can still experience the magic of watching a movie under the stars. Mountain View's **Stone Drive-In** and the **112 Drive-In** in Fayetteville are traditional, old-fashioned venues with concession stands serving up buttery popcorn, cheesy nachos, and nostalgia nightly.

EQUESTRIANS Arkansas's reputation with equestrians has been on the rise for a number of years, and if you like to pack your own pony when you travel, **Village Creek State Park** on Crowley's Ridge offers you and your steed all of the luxury you would find in the Bluegrass State on the loess-covered hills of the ridge. Its facilities have earned it the nickname

state in battlefields with self-guided tours, annual reenactments, and more modern, interactive displays within historic structures. Battlefields at **Prairie Grove** and Pea Ridge alternate as the annual site for reenactments of the deadly battles that occurred there in 1862. **Pea Ridge National Military Park**'s 4,300 acres offers visitors a 7-mile, self-guided tour daily. The battlefield at the state park in Prairie Grove is nationally recognized as the most intact Civil War battlefield in the country. **Arkansas Post**'s proximity to the Mississippi River in southeastern Arkansas made it a critical site for both Union and Confederate forces. The museum there today offers interpretive displays and programming on the post's history with both sides and the battles that led to its fall to Maj. Gen. William T. Sherman and his troops in January 1863. The last major Confederate offensive in the state was also fought near the banks of the Mississippi River at Helena in east Arkansas. Several sites, including the **Confederate Cemetery**, are part of a Delta heritage tour on the city's

THE BATTLE OF PRAIRIE GROVE REENACTMENT ARKANSAS DEPARTMENT OF PARKS & TOURISM

Horse Hilton, but its paths alongside the Trail of Tears draw riders back every year. Experienced and novice riders alike seek the sage wisdom of Arvell Bass, Arkansas's horse whisperer, at **Stone Creek Ranch** in Mountain Home. Brilliant cutting horses aid his tutorial process, which ranges from locating the equine emergency brake to cutting a cow from its herd. Near Jasper, **Horseshoe Canyon Ranch** saddles horses in one of the most scenic settings in the Ozark Mountains.

FALL COLOR Arkansas travelers eagerly await the advent of autumn and the flourish of fall color that paints our state in a Technicolor display reminiscent of Dorothy's landing in Oz. The Arkansas Department of Parks and Tourism has a network of color spotters in every region of the state who supply weekly updates that are compiled into one report that is posted on **Arkansas .com** every Thursday evening. The reports describe foliage changes in these three regions: northwest/north central Arkansas (Ozarks), central Arkansas/Ouachita Mountains, and southern/eastern Arkansas, though specific areas and highways are cited when notable.

There are a number of variables that affect the intensity of fall's display as well as its timing. As a rule, significant color change begins in the Ozarks of northern Arkansas in late September or early October. The trees in central Arkansas and the Ouachita Mountains of west-central Arkansas reflect a noticeable change by early to mid-October, and the color finally reaches the southern and eastern forests during mid-October. There is usually a period of a week or so when the fall foliage in a particular area is at its best. Normally, the peak of color occurs around two or three weeks after color changes begin, meaning late October for the Ozarks, late October or early November for central and western Arkansas, and early to mid-November for the southern and eastern sections. The

state's scenic byways wind lazily through the striking canopy, past roadside stands brimming with the season's harvest, and through communities celebrating nature's bounty. While the rugged slopes of the Ozarks provide an abundance of panoramic perches for soaking in the splendor of the season, the ethereal golden glow of the unique vegetation on Crowley's Ridge in eastern Arkansas remains my personal favorite.

FESTIVALS The friendly folk who populate the state take great pride in their communities and great pleasure in showcasing their distinct destinations in festivals that are held all over the state throughout the year. You can pay homage to watermelons, strawberries, peaches, raccoons, crawdads, trout, elk, butterflies, birds, ducks, or toads. Immerse yourself in the sultry strains of the **King Biscuit Blues Festival** in Helena or the refreshing waters of the **Cardboard Boat Festival** in Heber Springs. The award-winning thoroughbred facilities at Oaklawn Park in Hot Springs are spotlighted in spring during its **Racing Festival of the South**. The highlight of the weeklong celebration, the **Arkansas Derby**, attracts prominent Kentucky Derby contenders and is now considered a major prep race for the Run for the Roses. You can race horses, dogs, toads, outhouses, and tillers, and if you really want to get your thrill on, try spending Labor Day in Clinton, Arkansas, at the **National Chuckwagon Race Championships**.

Arkansas's temperate climes extend the season for outdoor music festivals, and the tranquil banks of our pristine rivers have hosted artisans of both sight and sound for decades. The shores of the White River in Newport entice national country and rock acts, as well as tens of thousands of people, to **Portfest**—a large water carnival that includes fishing and horseshoe tournaments and handmade crafts. The **King Biscuit Blues Festival** in Helena sprawls along the levee of the mighty Mississippi River, the perfect proving ground for the genre born in the heart of the Delta. As for the state's namesake—the Arkansas River—Fort Smith, Little Rock, and Pine Bluff are just a few of the cities hosting large riverside music festivals annually. The granddaddy of the three, **Riverfest**, features several stages spanning both sides of the river, drawing over a quarter of a million people every May. Newcomer **Bikes, Blues, and BBQ** in northwest Arkansas draws hundreds of thousands of bikers, as well as those who simply want to enjoy good food and music in the hip college town of Fayetteville.

FISHING If you think you need saltwater or a deep-sea rig to land a trophy fish, think again. The Natural State claims no fewer than five world records in the sport, all landed within a few hours of each other in the northern half of the state. The small town of **Greers Ferry** in north-central Arkansas boasts two: a 27-pound hybrid striped bass and a 22-pound, 11-ounce walleye. **Bull Shoals Lake** was the site where a skilled Arkansas angler caught the mini but mighty Ozark bass, weighing in at 1 pound. Without a doubt, though, a guided float-fishing trip down an Arkansas river is an idyllic and iconic experience that electrifies fishermen in a most relaxing way. The ever-changing tapestry of Arkansas's rustic landscape is a hypnotic backdrop as your mind visualizes the lunker swimming just beneath the river's crystal, reflective surface. You'll want to fish for bass on the **Spring River**; an 11-pound, 13-ounce shadow bass caught on the Spring holds the world record for the species. There are several tributaries that are fruitful for trout. Arkansas's aggressive and cooperative natural resource management partnership with the Corps of Engineers has resulted in an abundant population of trout that thrive in many of its rivers. A 40-pound, 4-ounce brown trout, caught on the **Little Red River** in the Ozark Mountains, holds the world record for browns. Arkansas.com is an excellent resource for researching and planning your trip. Fishing reports (they will tell you what the fish are biting and when) are posted for waterways throughout the state, along with videos and photos of fish tails (tales).

FOUR-WHEELING Riding ATVs and other motorized vehicles is a rapidly growing recreational use of the national forests in the state. **Brock Creek**, **Huckleberry Mountain**, and **Mill Creek Trails** in the Ozark National Forest are most popular in northern Arkansas. The entire forest includes over 1,100 miles of designated routes available for off-highway vehicle use. Riders are responsible for obtaining a copy of the most recent Motor Vehicle Use Map to show the legally designated routes. The map is reprinted each year and is available online at www.aokforests.com or at any Ozark National Forest office. The gently folding hills of the Ouachita National Forest in western Arkansas are also popular with four-wheelers.

GOLF If you have your green jacket, you will probably be scheduling a round at the **Alotian**, founded in part and inspired by the late and legendary Jack Stephens. The Alotian in Little Rock is one of the newest and most exclusive golf clubs in the South, maybe even the country. It is also reported to rival the natural beauty of Augusta with its lush greens and constantly changing elevations. And while the majority of us may never play there, it has drawn the attention of nationally renowned golfers such as Tiger Woods to the state. And just as a rising tide floats all boats, Arkansas courses reflect a sophistication many golfers find surprising, set in natural beauty usually found only at high-end resorts or members-only clubs. A coalition of courses that meet strict standards of quality for their course and facility formed the **Natural State Golf Trail** a few years ago, and now numbers 15 courses in 13 locations accessible to you while on vacation in the state (www.naturalstategolftrail.com). You will even find an Andy Dye-designed course, the **Ridges at Village Creek State Park.**

HANG GLIDING On a clear day in the Arkansas River Valley, the winds that bluster along the river's path give flight to eagles, falcons, hawks, and humans. Both **Mount Magazine** and **Mount Nebo State Park** offer launch pads adjacent to cabins to accommodate those that do and those that are just fine watching from over here in the hot tub. But even the most acrophobic will find the hang gliders' flight mesmerizing as their path takes them past sights only the daring can see.

HOGS At over 100 years of age, the **University of Arkansas**'s Fayetteville campus is considered the flagship of the state's collegiate programs. Its mascot, the Razorback, is sacred to most Arkansans; many will tell you that if you cut them, they'll bleed Razorback red. We are also convinced that most people do the same, whether they are willing to admit it or not. The university's public facilities include **Barnhill Arena**, which houses the nation's first on-campus museum dedicated solely to female athletes at the collegiate level. **Bud Walton Arena**, home of the Razorback basketball team, is the fifth-largest on-campus basketball facility in the country; it displays Razorback highlights and memorabilia in a museum on its concourse. The **Tommy Boyer Hall of Champions Museum** in Bud Walton Arena and the **Jerry Jones/Jim Lindsey Hall of Champions Museum** in the **Frank Broyles Athletic Center** also display a century of Arkansas sports memories.

HUNTING Several million acres of public land make Arkansas prime ground for hunters, and big game hunting is popular in the state. With a herd of white-tailed deer estimated at 1 million, plus black bear and elk, the Natural State's reputation with hunters predates its European settlement. Liberal regulations for big game hunting seasons are set for archery, crossbow, muzzleloaders, and modern guns. Arkansas is also famed for its small game, and duck hunting along the famous Mississippi Flyway in the Arkansas Delta is prime fare.

For hunting seasons, regulations, licenses, permits, and guides, visit the **Arkansas Game and Fish Commission** at www.agfc.com.

LAKES More than 600,000 surface acres of lakes provide year-round waterborne recreational opportunities for visitors to the Natural State. Damming projects created many of the larger lakes found in northern Arkansas, such as **Bull Shoals, Greers Ferry**, and **Norfork**. In the Ouachitas, the **Diamond Lakes of Catherine, DeGray, Greeson, Hamilton**, and **Ouachita** are among the most popular in the state with recreational boaters. In the River Valley, **Lake Dardanelle, Blue Mountain, Cove**, and **Ozark Lakes** are popular recreation areas.

The lakes of southern Arkansas— **Chicot, DeQueen, Gillham**, and **Millwood**—are more popular for their fishing.

MOTORCYCLING Arkansas's scenic roadways bank along a verdant landscape that beckons motorcyclists year-round to explore historic sites, luxurious resorts, and national forests rich with wildlife and lush vegetation. Biker-friendly towns include **Hot Springs, Eureka Springs, Harrison**, and **Mountain View**, each hosting large rallies and events every year. **Bikes, Blues, & BBQ** in Fayetteville is one of the fastest-growing rallies in the country, as every year more bikers embrace the town's cosmopolitan personality surrounded by unspoiled natural beauty.

MUSEUMS Former Arkansas Governor Winthrop Rockefeller's contribution to the state's museum system is evident

LOCAL HERITAGE AND HISTORY ARE PRESERVED AT PEEL MANSION MUSEUM AND HERITAGE GARDENS

both in its art museums and its state history museums. The **Winthrop Rockefeller Legacy Gallery** on Petit Jean Mountain is the only museum in the country strictly dedicated to the life and achievements of a Rockefeller. Just an hour away, in Little Rock, the **Arkansas Arts Center** offers numerous galleries and exhibits that display the works of European masters. The state's newest and most prestigious art museum is Bentonville's **Crystal Bridges Museum of American Art**, founded by Walmart heiress Alice Walton, with a collection that includes several national art treasures.

NATIONAL FORESTS The **Ozark National Forest** sprawls through the Ozark Mountains of northern Arkansas and features miles of hiking trails, including the 165-mile Ozark Highlands National Recreation Trail, which runs from Clarksville in northwestern Arkansas to Ozone. Though its 22,000 acres of grounds make it one of the smaller national forests in the country, the campgrounds at **St. Francis National Forest** in

east Arkansas are my personal favorite in the state. Situated strategically for privacy, many are set on small peninsulas that make you feel like you are the only campers in the forest but still not too far from the Blues Festival in Helena, the casinos in Lula, or Beale Street in Memphis if you need urban relief from this pastoral setting.

OPERA One of the oldest summer festivals in the country, **Opera in the Ozarks** at Inspiration Point is a series of three fully staged operas performed annually in June and July. *Money* magazine rates it in the top 10 in the world, with an open venue that resembles the Santa Fe Opera.

PASSION PLAY In 2009, *The Great Passion Play* in Eureka Springs celebrated its 40th anniversary and updated its scripts to include text from different New Testament passages, focusing on more of the miracles performed by Christ in the days immediately prior to, and following, the crucifixion. Elaborate costumes and sets, as well as a large multigenerational cast, create a sense of pageantry for their performances. Performances are held from late April through October.

PIE Arkansas has great pie. Icebox pies, fried pies, meringue pies, peanut butter, and snickerdoodle all vie for counter space with Mom's apple pie. Truth is, you don't have to go far to find a pie that literally inspires folks from off (non-Arkansans) to take its picture. But if you are a true pie person, one who believes that the right slice of pie can cure anything that ails you, then DeValls Bluff, just east of Little Rock, is a must-see, or must-eat, for you. You will have to judge between **Ms. Lena's** and **The Family Pie Shop** as to which might just make the best pies on the planet. Just to be certain, though, as you pass through Keo on your way east, a quick stop at **Charlotte's Eats & Sweets** in town will ensure that you have a proper basis for comparison.

RAILROADS Just as the waterways of eastern Arkansas were critical to the settlement of that sector of the state, the railroad was equally essential to the development of communities in the Ozark Mountains.

Passenger excursions are still offered aboard the **Arkansas & Missouri Railroad**, which bridges the communities of Winslow, Van Buren, and Fort Smith. The **Eureka Springs & North Arkansas Railway** also offers a variety of trips and is well known for the food served in the Eurekan Dining Car.

The **Arkansas Railroad Museum** in Pine Bluff displays samples of rolling stock, railroad memorabilia, and model trains, and will give you a historic overview of its contribution to the state's economic and cultural advancement.

RIVERS Over 9,000 miles of stream traverse the Arkansas landscape, tumbling through the mountains of the Ozarks and

FLATWATER KAYAKING IN THE DELTA ARKANSAS DEPARTMENT OF PARKS & TOURISM

Ouachitas and meandering along the flatlands of the Delta.

The nation's first federally protected river, the **Buffalo**, is in the Ozarks, and it is also one of the state's most popular for canoeing. Also in northern Arkansas, the **Kings**, **White**, **Little Red**, and **Spring Rivers** are popular with paddlers and fishermen alike.

White-water kayaking on the **Cossatot River** in southwest Arkansas is considered to be the most challenging in the state, with the rapids showcased in the River Valley on **Mulberry**, **Big Piney**, and **Illinois Bayou** running close behind. The **Caddo**, **Little Missouri**, and **Ouachita Rivers** offer a more leisurely float for families and beginners. The wild environs of the cypress-lined **Cache River** in eastern Arkansas have been compared to the Amazon River in South America and brought flat-water kayaking into the national limelight in 2005, when a kayaker spotted the ivory-billed woodpecker while paddling the Big Woods area that borders the river.

SPOOKY SITES The 1882 **Crescent Hotel** in Eureka Springs is considered to be the most haunted hotel in the country. More than 70,000 sightings have been logged on the hotel's site; footage captured by the acclaimed *Ghost Hunters* camera crew launched their fall season in 2006, the first to capture spectral images visible on film. Ghost tours are also offered of the hamlet's historic downtown and the 1906 **Basin Park Hotel**. The towns of **Gurdon** and **Crossett** have attracted attention from nationally recognized paranormal researchers investigating ethereal lights that hover over specific sections of railroad tracks, swaying back and forth as they move down the track without casting light below. The Gurdon event has been broadcast on national television and is regularly photographed by tourists. Though there is debate as to whether or not it is the result of supernatural intention or scientific anomaly, it is generally accepted as "real" and is a present-day phenomenon that you can see yourself on dark and overcast nights. The lights are not visible from the highway; you will have to hike a couple of miles to see them. **Haunted Tours of Little Rock** explores the capital city's sites from a funeral car and includes Mount Holly Cemetery, private homes, and government buildings reported to be home to spirits dating back to the state's origins.

TROLLEYS Trolley service is available in downtown **Little Rock** and **North Little Rock**, providing connecting service between the Argenta entertainment district of the north shore, the River Market district on the southern shore, and the Clinton Library and Heifer Global Education Center.

VERMIN In addition to the flora and fauna found in our forests, you will also meet up with a few unsavory characters when playing in the woods. Hot summers and high humidity create the perfect breeding ground for mosquitoes, chiggers, and ticks. You will want to use a strong repellent in spring, summer, and fall, and check yourself frequently for offenders, quickly removing any ticks you find. Though rare, cases of West Nile virus, Lyme disease, and Rocky Mountain spotted fever have been reported. All of that virgin forestland is a haven for elk and bear, and also timber rattlers, cottonmouths, and water moccasins. Forewarned is forearmed: wear insect repellent and watch your step. The majority of snakes in the state are nonpoisonous, but it is recommended that, if bitten, you assume the snake is poisonous if you are unsure. Most severe snakebite injuries are the result of mishandling the injury rather than the venom itself.

VROOOM, VROOOM Take I-167 (Batesville Boulevard) to north-central Arkansas and the "dirt tracks of Batesville," the home of the **Mark Martin Museum**

(1-800-566-5561; www.markmartin museum.com), 1601 Batesville Boulevard, Batesville. Mark Martin may have retired from the NASCAR circuit, but his legacy still draws crowds to the foothills of the Ozark Mountains. Martin's 40 years of racing are immortalized in this state-of-the-art museum displaying the cars, races, and accolades that made him famous. Martin was inducted in the NASCAR Hall of Fame in 2017.

WINERIES As the oldest and largest grape juice/wine producing state in the southern US, Arkansas's viticultural history dates back 120 years. The state's most prominent vintners are located in the Altus region in northwest Arkansas, with some of the wineries now run by the fourth- and fifth-generation descendants of the original families. Four wineries— **Chateau Aux Arc**, **Mount Bethel**, **Post Familie**, and **Wiederkehr**—are located in Altus and offer free tours and tastings for visitors. Nearby Paris is home to the **Cowie** winery and the **Arkansas Historic Wine Museum,** the only museum in the nation dedicated to a state's wine history. The new cask on the block is in Eureka Springs, where **Keels Creek Winery** offers retail sales, a tasting room, and an art gallery.

ARKANSAS STATE PARKS

ARKANSAS STATE PARKS

No matter where you go in the Natural State, you are never far from an Arkansas State Park. You can collect sparkling gemstones at the Crater of Diamonds and sail sparkling waters at Lake Ouachita. You can watch eagles fly from a barge on the water and watch hang gliders soar from the deck of a lodge. You can sleep in a historic schoolhouse, rent an RV or a yurt, or pitch your tent under the stars beside one of our pristine rivers. Your guides are botanists and biologists, conservationists and preservationists, historians and artisans, all interpreters at Arkansas State Parks. Funded by a perpetual state tax, Arkansas's state park system is one of the few in the country that provides degreed interpreters to enhance visitor experience every day the parks are open.

The birth of the park system is a good example of the state taking lemons and making lemonade. In 1921, the Fort Smith Lumber Co. enlisted the support of Dr. T. W. Hardison in brokering a deal with the federal government to convert company-owned land in the Arkansas River Valley into a national park. In a two-hour meeting with Stephen Mather, director of the national park system, Hardison described the area and its recreational value to the state, and showed photographs of the beauty of Seven Hollows, Petit Jean Mountain, and Cedar Falls. At the meeting's end, Mather determined the area too small for a national park and not unique enough on a national level to carry the national designation. He recommended that Hardison partner with Arkansas to create a state park. Hardison's mission was accomplished in 1923, when legislation was passed setting aside the land for Arkansas's first state park on Petit Jean Mountain.

A decade later, the nation struggled with the burden of the unemployment of millions, and less than three weeks after President Franklin D. Roosevelt took office, he signed legislation creating the Civilian Conservation Corps.

Arkansas's state park system, still in its infancy, was the primary beneficiary of efforts in the state as the work program created roads, trails, lodges and cabins, campgrounds, amphitheaters, bathhouses, picnic pavilions, and beaches at six locations in four different regions of the state. Petit Jean, Mount Nebo, Crowley's Ridge, Devil's Den, and Lake Catherine, charter parks in the newly created system, now preserve and protect Arkansas's CCC history, as well as their own.

Areas of Emphasis

While each park is individual and uniquely portrays its natural resources or place in history, they can be classified as one (or more!) of the following types: adventure, mountain, history, or lakes and rivers.

If you are an adrenaline junkie, you will find no shortage of heart-thumping, jaw-dropping, mind-blowing alternatives at Arkansas's mountain parks. Hang gliders find near-perfect conditions flying off peaks at two parks in the River Valley. **Mount Magazine State Park**, home of the state's tallest mountain (2,753 feet), has a launch pad located between two cabins, so you can watch pilots fly off the mountain from your hot tub. Nearby **Mount Nebo State Park** hosts two events annually, in April and August.

THE DAVIES LEGACY

I n 1937, the State Parks Commission received its first budget and authorization to hire a superintendent. The commission selected Samuel G. Davies, the former construction superintendent for the CCC stationed at Petit Jean State Park. Davies and his son Ladd worked side by side for much of the Petit Jean project, including the design and construction of the Cedar Creek Bridge (rededicated as the Davies Bridge in 1988). In 1976, when he was named Arkansas State Parks director, Richard W. Davies became the third generation of the family to serve the state as guardian of its natural resources. Richard grew up on Petit Jean Mountain; the first state park was a second home to him. The men he most admired had devoted decades to the care and conservation of what they believed to be Arkansas's most valuable treasures, the state parks. The stories told around his family table were park stories, and he shared those stories with an ever-growing staff; their shared vision would motivate the people of Arkansas, one of the poorest states in the country, to take unprecedented steps that would catapult the system from relative obscurity to national prominence.

By the 1980s, Arkansas's state parks were the top tourist draw in the state, with 42 locations and a seat on the governor's Cabinet. Through the 1980s and 1990s, better training and regulated uniforms for staff were added, marketing efforts improved, and visitation was up, disguising the financial straits that stalked the parks. Despite their apparent success, many of the aging facilities were beginning to decline from increased use as well as the revenue demands caused by legislative initiatives that added new properties without funding to support their operation. The parks found themselves to be a low priority for legislative funding, and by 1993 a coalition of state conservation agencies and land managers was formed to ask the people of Arkansas for help. They proposed the adoption of a conservation tax to provide perpetual funding for its members, which included Arkansas's Game and Fish Commission, Department of Heritage, and Keep Arkansas Beautiful Commission. The proposal called for a 1/8-cent tax to be levied on lodging and attractions, with the revenue generated funneled back into operations, maintenance and repair, and capital improvements. The agencies also assured voters they would not use the money to acquire new lands that would further deplete their resources.

The matter was finally put before Arkansas voters in 1996 following an aggressive campaign that included 16 stops along the Arkansas River by then-governor Mike Huckabee and his wife to focus the state's attention on the issue. In November of 1996, Act 75 was passed, providing substantial and perpetual funding for the preservation and protection of the state's natural and cultural heritage. During the first three years that the state collected the Conservation Tax, it generated nearly $65.4 million in additional funds for state parks. Today's state parks are the envy of the nation, immaculately maintained and staffed by degreed professionals with a common goal of helping visitors develop an emotional and intellectual connection to the park they represent.

If your idea of adventure is wet and wild, Arkansas's premier white-water experience is at **Cossatot State Park**, and when water levels are high, these Class IV and V rapids attract the state's expert paddlers. Or, if you want a little more glide with your ride, flat-water kayaking through bald cypress trees at **Pinnacle Mountain State Park** may be more your speed. **Davidsonville Historic State Park** offers two 8-mile floats that also let you really get a feel for the life and times of the early 1800s. Interpreters at **Cane Creek State Park** have created a kayak trail that is unforgettable; you will paddle from the starkly beautiful remains of the bald cypress forest in the Delta into acres of delicate lily pads of the West Gulf Coastal Plain. If you are into geocaching, you can grab a find along the way.

The system's newest park is the **Mississippi River State Park**, developed through a special use permit from the US Forest Service. Accessed via two national scenic byways (the Great River Road and Crowley's Ridge Parkway), MRSP is nestled in the lush St. Francis National Forest in eastern Arkansas. The park visitor center is staffed by US Forest Service personnel and Arkansas State Parks rangers and interpreters. Its exhibits interpret the Mississippi River, Crowley's Ridge, and the Delta. The facility also includes a large multipurpose area for group events.

Sailing, skiing, fishing, and recreational boating are popular pastimes on Arkansas's crystal clear lakes. But the pure waters are equally appreciated from beneath their surface by snorkelers at three state parks. **DeGray Lake Resort** conducts almost daily guided tours of the lake during summer months. Underwater Discovery is a weekly snorkeling experience showcasing the fish that inhabit **Lake Ouachita State Park**. Snorkeling is also allowed in the pools of the Cossatot River when water levels are low.

Nine state parks feature well-developed and maintained trails for your cycling pleasure. If you are considered sport or expert class, you will appreciate access to the 31-mile Bear Creek Cycle Trail, formerly reserved for motorcycles and ATVs. Obviously challenging for foot-pedalers, this trail will give you firsthand experience with the rugged terrain of the Ouachita Mountains. You can ride historic trails at **Village Creek, Hobbs, and Mount Nebo State Parks**. **Devil's Den State Park** hosts two major events that pack the park each year: the Ozark Mountain Bike Festival, which is usually the first weekend in April, and the Northwest Mountain Bike Championships, usually held two weeks after Labor Day.

Mount Magazine, with its rugged bluffs, deep canyons, and natural diversity, is the highest relief between the Rockies and the Appalachians and the state parks system's most dramatic location for technical climbing. Traditional and sport climbing as well as rappelling are allowed in a designated area on the mountain's south bluff overlooking the Petit Jean River Valley. This 1,500-foot wide stretch of sandstone boasts over 100 routes up to 80 feet high, ranging from 5.5 to 5.12c in difficulty, with plenty in the 5.10 and under range. For scenic in the city, try Pinnacle Mountain, just minutes west of Little Rock. The park's dominant natural feature and namesake, the 1,011-foot peak has several faces suitable for technical climbing. A number of routes ranging in difficulty up to 5.8 have been mapped on the south and east faces by local climbing clubs.

The Ozark Plateau is known not only for the scenic vistas above the ground, but also the panoramic perspective found beneath it. Caves in the Ozarks are like cars in Los Angeles—everyone has at least one. At **Devil's Den State Park**, you can explore the unique sandstone crevice area on your own or as part of a strenuous guided tour offered weekly by park interpreters. You will step back in time in Rock House Cave on Petit Jean Mountain, where pictographs are symbolic reminders of the Native Americans who first climbed this mountain 10,000 years ago.

History is an important chapter in most of the stories creatively told in the parks, whether it is Native American, Civil War, or natural history. Some of the parks are crafty about it, like slipping vegetables to toddlers. Thirteen museums use dioramas, interactive displays, and interpretive programming to bring their locations to life. At **Mammoth Spring State Park**, you can stroll through the oldest railroad station in Arkansas, the circa 1886 Frisco Depot. This restored, turn-of-the century Victorian depot is populated with custom-sculpted, lifelike figures that portray the train crew, depot crew, and train passengers of the early 1900s.

In the south Arkansas town of Smackover (yes, Smackover), the **Arkansas Museum of Natural Resources** takes you, by elevator, on a journey inside the earth where you can see the formation of the oil strata. **El Dorado**'s wild and colorful history is re-created in a replica of a 1920s oil boomtown, complete with rutted streets. At **Jacksonport State**

Park, the restored courthouse museum houses exhibits themed *If These Walls Could Talk,* incorporating first-person dialogue audio, court records, and vintage photos to tell the town's story. Nearby, on the river's shore, a restored sternwheel paddleboat, the Mary Woods No. 2, re-creates the life of a paddleboat crew in the late 1930s.

Two state parks are living museums, with flesh-and-blood characters demonstrating daily life during a specific time period. **Historic Washington State Park** is an entire town of 30 restored nineteenth-century structures, including the courthouse, which serves as its visitor center, and a restaurant that serves some of the best Southern cooking you will find in the state. In the mountains of north-central Arkansas, the **Ozark Folk Center** is a village within a town captured in time. It is a hands-down, no-contest favorite with travel writers as one of the most unique attractions in the country. Many stories of the folk center begin with, "If you can only do one thing when you are in the Ozarks, visit the Ozark Folk Center."

At **Toltec State Park,** you can tour the mounds and an earthen embankment that are the remains of a large ceremonial and governmental complex that was inhabited here from A.D. 600 to 1050. Or you can have a more hands-on experience at a primitive pottery workshop at **Parkin Archeological Park.** Many scholars believe Parkin to be the American village of Casqui that Hernando de Soto chronicled during his 1541 expedition. The head pots recovered at this archaeological site are on display in the park museum and considered to be the most perfectly preserved in the country. Both parks are National Historic Landmarks and operate research stations with the Arkansas Archeological Survey, giving you an opportunity to see firsthand the result of careful excavation and laboratory analysis.

At every park you will find events and programs designed to enhance your experience, all of them well within any vacation budget. In fact, a lot of them are free or for the cost of your materials. From interpreter-led guided hikes exploring the park and the medicinal and edible foliage along the trail, to using handheld GPS units to find

JACKSONPORT STATE PARK ON THE WHITE RIVER

CAPTURED IN TIME IN MOUNTAIN VIEW

Ozark Folk Center (870-269-3851; www.ozarkfolkcenter.com), 1032 Park Avenue, Mountain View. In picturesque Mountain View, the Folk Music Capital of the World, you will find the only park in the country dedicated to the preservation and explanation of the Ozark Mountain way of life. The idea for the Ozark Folk Center originated with the success of the Arkansas Folk Festival that started here in 1963, and the folk center manages to capture the feel of those festival days on a daily basis between the months of April and October. The Ozark Mountain people were known for their ability to survive off the land with their own two hands, with little influence from the outside world, crafting their tools and their toys and making their own kind of music. Start your trip back in time at the Crafts Village (open April 15 through September 30, Wednesday through Saturday 10–5 and Tuesday through Sunday 10–5 in October), touring the shops of 24 artisans demonstrating basketry, blacksmithing, printing, broom making, quilting, woodcarving, pottery, and several other pioneer skills. Their products are useful, and they are also works of art. Did you know that there are over 20 different uses for a broom? Of course, if you buy one or have one made for you, you won't want to let it touch a floor.

The Crafts Village is also where you are likely to find Tina Marie Wilcox, master gardener of the lush folk center grounds and also known as Widder Wilcox, an Ozark Mountain widow who shares her knowledge of mountain yarbs and their uses. Wilcox's character is a composite personality, rather than a depiction of a real person, but she will completely take you in if you haven't met her before the presentation. You might believe she is the uneducated, backwoods character she portrays, rather than a nationally acclaimed herbalist, on the International Herb Association's Board of Directors, a member of the Herb Society of America, the Arkansas Native Plant Society, and the American Botanical Council. Widder Wilcox's engaging

hidden geocaches, you will find park staff provide a number of creative ways for you to get more out of your visit.

Interpretation—It's Not Translation

It's funny, when many people read a park brochure and see a reference to the park's interpretive services, they think it means language translation for foreign nationals. In Arkansas, you will find it means a degreed professional, certified by the National Association of Interpreters, whose sole goal is to help you get the most out of your visit to their park. Arkansas is one of a few states in which all of the interpreters are certified, and a number of them are recognized nationally for their knowledge and achievements.

They are experts on the natural resources, the local heritage, and in designing creative ways for you to make an intellectual and emotional connection to their parks. This is a godsend for parents looking for ways to unplug their children from their sedentary worlds. But interpretive programming is not just for kids; most parents wish their kids would take a nice Dutch oven cooking workshop and help out in the kitchen. For $25, you will learn the art of cooking with cast iron, and the workshop includes both a meal and a Dutch oven of your own.

Arkansas's interpretive staff is absolutely passionate about their mission. Many of them are members of reenactment troupes that travel the country demonstrating a particular era in which they specialize. Historic Washington State Park is probably the most frequent site of these performances, with humorous testimony of local scandals portrayed in the town's courtroom. Be prepared to do your civic duty, as park visitors

chat with you, perhaps on the deck by the schoolhouse, will endear her to you and the toddlers, teenagers, and senior citizens who happen to join you. It will also make you formidable competition on *Survivor*, able to feed and clothe yourself with just foliage from the forest. Or at least educate you about a good idea of a few herbs you can grow at home, and not just for use in the kitchen.

Of course, it's the music that gives the Ozark Folk Center and Mountain View its charm, and the park's 1,025-seat theater (open April through October, Thursday through Saturday, shows start at 7 p.m.) hosts folk music concerts and gospel sings that will give a glimpse into the music that has serenaded the lives of the Ozark Mountain people for generations. You will also find folk musicians performing on the grounds of the Crafts Village during the day. Check the park's website for details on the celebrity concert series that includes nationally known acts like Kathy Mattea.

The **Cabins at Dry Creek** are nestled in the woods, but not too far away from the restaurant where you can enjoy an Ozarks version of good old Southern cooking. The rustic cabins feature a number of modern amenities, including wireless Internet and cable television. The modest decor is in keeping with the place and the era it portrays, and the ironwork in the bathrooms was forged in Mountain View at the acclaimed Stone County Ironworks. Homemade apple preserves are available for sale at the counter, and you might want to take two. The lodge is open year-round, but the restaurant is only open mid-April through early November, Monday through Saturday 8–7, Sunday 8–2 p.m.

Each spring, the park also conducts an **Ozark Folk School**, offering instruction in traditional Ozark crafts, music, and gardening. **Elderhostels**—an educational week of programs, classes, lectures, etc. for those 55 years of age or older—are scheduled throughout the season with folk themes ranging from "Hill Culture" to "Crafts and Songs."

are frequently called upon to serve on the jury. Prairie Grove Battlefield State Park in northwest Arkansas is the site of the state's largest battle reenactment (every other year) that commemorates the historic Civil War battle that occurred there. Prairie Grove alternates annually as host for the event with the national site at Pea Ridge.

✳ Arkansasstateparks.com

You will find very specific information about each of Arkansas's state parks, their facilities, programs, and events on the state park website. The Park Finder map will show you where the parks are located, and then you are just a click away from details about the park. Each park has a mini-site that describes its history and unique features. Trail descriptions and maps are posted here, most in a downloadable format easy to print before you leave home. Fees and rates specific to the park are posted, like kayak rental rates, museum hours, and ticket prices.

If you need some help filling your time, the site has a section called Plan a Trip for inspiration. The itineraries are set up by region and by areas of interest. There is also a section called See & Do that will let you figure out what you want to do first, and then find the park that fits the bill.

Once you have made up your mind about where you want to go and what you want to do, you can book your room, cabin, or campsite online. You'll also find some clever ideas for camping here, particularly if equipment, or setting it up, is a problem. You can rent a complete RV at **Bull Shoals-White River** ($80/day), **Lake Charles** or **Millwood** ($70/day); and **Cane Creek State Park** ($70/day). This economical rate entitles you to temporary ownership of a 29-foot trailer with heat and air-conditioning, private bath with shower, deck with gas grill, refrigerator, microwave, stove, and television. Cooking and eating utensils are included, but your linens are not furnished. The RV comfortably sleeps eight and is permanently set up at a park campsite, so you have nothing to worry about except what to cook for dinner or where to wet your hook.

For $50 a day, you can rent one of two tepees permanently set up on campsites overlooking Lake Bailey, the Petit Jean State Park's 100-acre lake that is perfect for fishing and pedal boating. Each tepee sleeps up to six people and comes with foam sleeping pads, a battery-powered lantern, propane cook stove, ice chest, canoe, and personal floatation devices. A picnic table and grill are located just outside each tepee for easy meal preparation and enjoyment overlooking the lake. **DeGray Lake Resort State Park** offers tepee camping with a twist: the yurt. A yurt is a large, round, high-walled tent with electricity, wood floors, screened windows, and a door that can be locked. It is equipped with cots, a lantern, stove, and ice chest. It can sleep six easily, but bring your own linens.

THE MISSISSIPPI ALLUVIAL PLAIN (ARKANSAS DELTA)

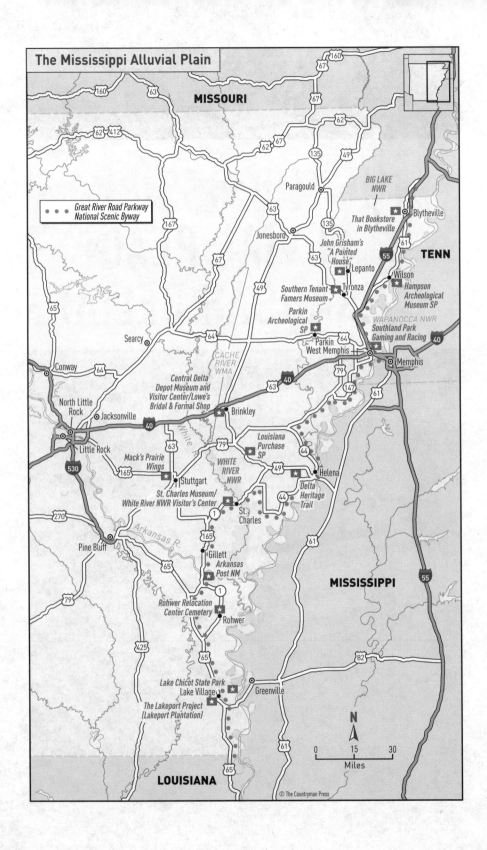

The Mississippi Alluvial Plain

MISSOURI

TENN

MISSISSIPPI

LOUISIANA

Great River Road Parkway
National Scenic Byway

Paragould

BIG LAKE NWR

That Bookstore in Blytheville

Blytheville

Jonesboro

John Grisham's "A Painted House"

Lepanto

Wilson

Southern Tenant Famers Museum

Tyronza

Hampson Archeological Museum SP

Parkin Archeological SP

WAPANOCCA NWR

Parkin

West Memphis

Southland Park Gaming and Racing

Memphis

Searcy

CACHE RIVER WMA

Conway

Central Delta Depot Museum and Visitor Center/Lowe's Bridal & Formal Shop

Brinkley

North Little Rock

Jacksonville

Louisiana Purchase SP

Little Rock

Mack's Prairie Wings

WHITE RIVER NWR

Helena

Stuttgart

Delta Heritage Trail

St. Charles Museum/White River NWR Visitor's Center

St. Charles

Arkansas R.

Pine Bluff

Gillett

Arkansas Post NM

Rohwer Relocation Center Cemetery

Rohwer

Lake Chicot State Park

Lake Village

Greenville

The Lakeport Project (Lakeport Plantation)

N

0   15   30
Miles

© The Countryman Press

THE MISSISSIPPI ALLUVIAL PLAIN (ARKANSAS DELTA)

The Delta is not just a destination, it's a journey. Its fields full of cotton, sprawling homes with wraparound porches, voices that seem to drawl even when they are laughing—all seem to whisper seductively to you, "Slow down, stay a while, sip some sweet tea." A land of rivers, the Delta covers the eastern third of Arkansas. Major Delta cities include Blytheville, West Memphis, Brinkley, Clarendon, Stuttgart, and Lake Village. Crowley's Ridge, one of Arkansas's six geological regions, is completely surrounded by Delta farmland, with Helena–West Helena straddling the southern end of the ridge and extending to the Mississippi River. Its location on the raised ground above the plain made it a strategically important location during the Civil War; consequently, it is included in a separate chapter on Crowley's Ridge.

When the Gulf of Mexico receded from the Delta millions of years ago, its geological deposits were removed by rivers and replaced by deep layers of sand, silt, and clay, eventually building up one of the most fertile agricultural areas in the country. Natural vegetation includes cypress and tupelo trees that live in lakes and swamps that are permanently flooded. Oak, hickory, and pecan trees grow well here, and you will often find pecans for sale at roadside stands along the Delta's long two-lane roads.

The Delta is a wildlife paradise (most migratory birds like ducks and geese winter somewhere in the Delta of Arkansas, Mississippi, or Louisiana), and Arkansas is favored by hunters for the mass quantities found here for most of the winter. During hunting season in the Delta, you could find yourself savoring fresh seafood and hand-cut Angus steak, and you might be the only party dining in the restaurant that is not clad in camouflage. Arkansas's portion of the Delta is chock-full of exclusive lodges and hunting clubs that require an invitation and a GPS for admission. You will also find that many public lodges have raised their standards to compete with private facilities and have broadened their services to accommodate the needs of wildlife watchers the remainder of the year. The vast expanse of habitat in the Delta includes tracts that have proven enormously productive in the protection and recovery of many endangered species, creating tantalizing viewing opportunities for serious enthusiasts. In 2005, the Big Woods near Brinkley became the center of the universe for birders worldwide when federal officials confirmed reported sightings of an ivory-billed woodpecker, a bird believed to be extinct for more than half a century. Though the bird was never officially located, there continue to be rumors of "Elvis" sightings more than a decade after the formal search ended.

The region runs more than 250 miles along the Mississippi River on the eastern side of the state. Its width ranges from 12 miles wide at its most narrow point in Desha County to its widest near Little Rock. This second edition has been revised to break up the Delta section into two parts: Upper Delta and Lower Delta. I-40 connects the state's capital in Little Rock/North Little Rock to Memphis and separates the Delta into two fairly equal sections. Those that came before you spoke up with this request, and it is implemented for all of you now. You will also want to check out this guide's section about Crowley's Ridge. It is a natural region of its own embedded within the Delta and many of its destinations are easy add-ons to your tour of the area.

PADDLE THE MIGHTY MISSISSIPPI FROM HELENA

AREA CODE Phone lines in the Delta respond to the 870 area code.

GUIDANCE Arkansas Delta Byways Tourist Association (870-972-2803; www .deltabyways.com) is the regional tourist association for the entire Delta. In addition, the following local chambers of commerce will be helpful in finding out about local events in their specific county or town.

Greater Blytheville Area Chamber of Commerce (870-762-2012; www.greater blytheville.com). This gateway city is also a good place to pick up a copy of your Great River Road map, and maybe a crop brochure for the drive.

Brinkley Chamber of Commerce (870-734-2262; www.brinkleyar.com). This area is ivory-billed woodpecker territory and also where brides come from all over the South to buy their wedding dresses at Low's Bridal and Formal in the old railroad hotel downtown. Low's will sell over 10,000 dresses annually, making it the third largest in the country.

West Memphis Area Chamber of Commerce (870-735-1134; www.wmcoc.com).

GETTING THERE *By auto:* From the east or west, **I-40** bisects Arkansas's Delta at the midway point in West Memphis. From the north, enter Arkansas on **US 49** in Piggott, following it south to Jonesboro, where you will want to get on **The Great River Road (AR 1)**, which runs the length of most of the Delta from Jonesboro to McGehee. **US 65** connects at McGehee, exiting southern Arkansas at Eudora.

By air: **Memphis International Airport** (901-922-8000; www.mscaa.com), 2491 Winchester Road, Memphis, Tennessee This international airport is a major hub in the country, offering direct flights from all major metropolitan areas. United, Delta, and American all maintain regular routes to and from this airport. About 90 minutes away is the **Little Rock National Airport** (501-372-3439; www.lrn-airport.com), 1 Airport Drive, Little Rock. Airlines that service the Little Rock Airport include Allegiant Air, American Airlines, Delta, Frontier Airlines, Southwest, United, and Via Air.

✳ Wandering Around

EXPLORING BY CAR The **Great River Road–Arkansas National Scenic Byway** is part of a 10-state driving route along both sides of the Mississippi River, from its headwaters at Lake Itasca in Minnesota to the Gulf of Mexico in Louisiana. In Arkansas, the historical roadway travels through 10 eastern counties that either border the river or are associated with it historically.

In 1932, the US Secretary of the Interior urged the forming of the Mississippi River Parkway Planning Commission. More than a decade later, a feasibility study was completed by the Bureau of Public Roads and the National Park Service. The study recommended that, rather than constructing a new parkway, a scenic drive could be created by designating, upgrading, and linking existing roads. By the late 1950s, the green-and-white pilot's wheel logo began appearing in each of the 10 states, linking them to form the Great River Road (GRR).

Arkansas was the fifth of the 10 Great River Road states to attain National Scenic Byway status in 2002. This designation allowed states to compete for federal grants to expand the roadways and add amenities such as signage, scenic overlooks, interpretive centers, restrooms, parking areas, and more. Designated routes must possess at least one of six intrinsic qualities—archaeological, cultural, historic, natural, recreational, or scenic—to be named a national scenic byway. Arkansas's section of the GRR has been documented to include all six qualities, with a primary focus on history and culture, including how Delta land and lives were shaped by the river.

PRO TIP: It is a good idea to travel with a first aid kit no matter where you go, particularly when traveling by foot, bike, or car. It is a really good idea when traveling in the Delta. Cell service is based on population density, and the large agricultural tracts of the Delta cause every provider to lose service at some point. Towns and services like gas stations can be 30 to 45 miles apart, depending upon the road you are on. If you rely on a GPS, you can also count on it dropping service in route, and a missed turn can be easily overlooked when traveling through acres of farmland. Plan for an outage and take an alternate navigational tool (like a map) with your route marked in advance.

THE GREAT RIVER ROAD RUNS THE LENGTH OF EASTERN ARKANSAS   ARKANSAS DEPARTMENT OF PARKS & TOURISM

You can order a free state highway map and specific guides to each region of the state online at www.arkansas.com/travel-tools/vacation-kit.

✳ Towns and Villages

UPPER DELTA

Blytheville is a northern gateway to the Delta, one of 13 communities in the state to have an Arkansas Welcome Center (870-762-2512; I-55) staffed with travel consultants to answer your questions about their part of the state. Blytheville was originally established in the 1880s as a lumber mill town, and also served as a center for the cotton-growing industry and a Strategic Air Command (SAC) airbase. The airbase was phased out years ago, but Blytheville has emerged as a steel production center, and agribusiness is strong. The downtown area is alive with interesting shops, including That Book Store, a favorite stop of Arkansas native and award-winning novelist John Grisham. Catch a show at the Ritz Civic Center, a restored opera house on Main Street that stages live shows throughout the year, and Blytheville's Heritage Museum, which explores the past with exhibits and photos. Arkansas Northeastern College schedules cultural events throughout the year.

Brinkley, on I-40, at about the midway point between Little Rock and Memphis, is a small town with a big place in history. Brinkley is near the Louisiana Purchase State Park, marking the point from which all property surveys west of the Mississippi River are measured. Founded during the construction of the first railroad across Arkansas, the town is named for one of its builders, Hugh Brinkley, and eventually became a crossroads and center of commerce. For a glimpse into its rail history, visit the beautifully restored 1912 Central Delta Depot Museum and Visitor Center in the downtown district. Antiques and gift shops plus travel accommodations are available. Just north of Brinkley, the Fargo Agricultural School Museum preserves items from an early twentieth-century African American school started by Floyd Brown of the Tuskegee Institute. Fishing opportunities are plentiful nearby, including Marion McCollum/ Greenlee Lake. The Arkansas Game and Fish lake is 300 acres, with two barrier-free fishing piers, two boat docks/launches, and plenty of bluegill, bass, and channel catfish. The region also boasts great waterfowl hunting in nearby public management areas.

LOWER DELTA

Lake Village is located at the southernmost end of the Delta, approximately 125 miles southeast of Little Rock. Lake Village is sited along the shores of Lake Chicot, a 20-mile-long oxbow lake created years ago when the Mississippi River breached its levee. When the waters receded, what remained was the largest natural lake in the state. Fishing for crappie, bass, bluegill, and catfish is popular on the lake, as are water sports and birding. Also on the water, Lake Chicot State Park offers cabins, campgrounds, a marina, and recreational access to the lake.

The park's visitor center displays exhibits on area history and natural resources and has free brochures detailing self-guided Mississippi River levee and Civil War tours. County and private campgrounds are also located on the lakeshore, while the downtown Jack R. Rhodes Lakefront Park provides a swimming area, walking path, small amphitheater, boat ramp, and picnic pavilions.

Just north of downtown, a marker records the site where Charles Lindbergh landed in April 1923 after completing history's first night flight. And you won't want to miss historic Lakeport Plantation, the meticulously restored Greek Revival home now a part of Arkansas State University's Heritage Sites. Other area attractions include exhibits at the Lake Chicot Pumping Plant, a $90 million facility built to protect the lake's water quality; the Museum of Chicot County; and the Guachoya Cultural Arts Center. The Paul Michael Company offers shoppers a wide variety of home decor items ranging from traditional to modern.

St. Charles is situated along the banks of the White River. The town was incorporated in 1879, but one of its most significant events took place in 1862. On June 17 of that year, Confederate marksmen positioned along the banks of the White attacked four Union gunboats. Using guns from several Confederate warships, the marksmen began firing on the ships as they closed in on the town. One of the shots hit the steam drum of the USS *Mound City*, killing over 100 of the soldiers onboard. It would become known as the deadliest shot of the Civil War. A monument downtown marks those who died during the incident. The monument, which honors both Union and Confederates, is listed on the National Register of Historic Places as the only one known of its kind. The town is also home to the St. Charles Museum, one of the most charming museums in the state. Located in the mayor's office and tenderly tended by same, the museum recounts the history of the town, including Civil War artifacts and a diorama depicting the Battle at St. Charles. The Dale Bumpers White River National Wildlife Refuge Visitor Center is a high-tech museum and education center located on the White River Refuge. The refuge runs along the White River for approximately 90 miles, is one of the largest hardwood bottomland preserves in the United States, and is a delight for outdoor enthusiasts.

Stuttgart has two claims to fame: rice and mass quantities of ducks. Commercial rice production was pioneered in the Arkansas Grand Prairie in 1904 and led to Arkansas's status as the top rice-producing state in the nation. Rice fields and irrigation reservoirs entice ducks and geese migrating on the Mississippi Flyway to linger, making the area nationally renowned among waterfowl hunters. The World's Championship Duck Calling Contest and Wings Over the Prairie Festival are celebrated here on Thanksgiving weekend every year. The award-winning Museum of the Arkansas Grand Prairie depicts the natural history of the prairie and tells the story of the pioneers who settled and farmed it. Tour the Arts Center of the Grand Prairie for a look at the works of regional and local artists.

✳ To See

MUSEUMS

UPPER DELTA

✐ ♿ **Blytheville Heritage Museum** (870-763-2525), 210 West Main Street, Blytheville. Open seasonally Monday through Friday 9–noon and 1–4 p.m.; Saturday and Sunday by appointment. This little museum is located in the Kress Building, which is listed on the National Historic Register. Displays focus on the cotton industry and regional Native American culture. Call for hours of operation.

✐ **Central Delta Depot & Museum** (870-589-2124), 100 West Cypress Street, Brinkley. Open Monday through Friday 9–5, Saturday 9–4; closed Sunday. Just off Main Street and located in a beautifully restored 1912 Union Railroad Depot, this museum's exhibits focus on the Louisiana Purchase survey of 1815, area railroads, and other facets of local history. The building is on the National Register and serves as the visitor center for Brinkley and nearby Louisiana Purchase Historic State Park. Colorful murals depicting the nearby swampland are a vibrant backdrop for panels that recount the story of the survey of the Louisiana Purchase. Geocachers, this is one of the 10 Arkansas sites included on the Great River Road geocaching program. Also located on the museum grounds is the 100-year-old Arkansas Midland-MoPac depot from Monroe, Arkansas, and a furnished sharecropper house.

&. **Southern Tenant Farmers Museum** (870-487-2909; stfm.astate.edu), 117 South Main Street, Tyronza. Free admission. Open Monday through Friday 9–3, Saturday noon–3. Closed major holidays. The historic Mitchell-East Building and adjacent former bank have been renovated by Arkansas State University and now include photographic exhibits and artifacts focusing on the farm labor movement in the South and the tenant farming system of agriculture. During the early 1930s, the building housed the businesses of H. L. Mitchell and Clay East, two of the principal founders of the Southern Tenant Farmers' Union (STFU). This national union—established July 13, 1934, in Tyronza by 11 whites and 7 blacks—conducted much of its business at the Mitchell-East Building.

The STFU, which included women and blacks in leadership positions alongside white males, is regarded as a forerunner of the 1960s civil rights movement. It achieved its peak membership during the late 1930s, when its leadership claimed about 35,000 members in Arkansas, Missouri, Tennessee, Mississippi, and Oklahoma.

Opened in October of 2006, this museum focuses on the tenant farming system of agriculture in the South and the farm labor movement that arose in response to this system. It is considered a significant civil rights site in part because, unlike others in the day, this union included both black and white members, and both women and men served in leadership positions.

The building facade has been restored to its 1930s appearance, while the interior includes exhibition space, a reception area, a gift shop, and a classroom. The museum layers many exhibits to interpret tenant farmer life in the turbulent 1930s.

LOWER DELTA

✐&. **Desha County Museum** (870-382-4222; www.dumasar.net), US 165 E, Dumas. Open Monday through Friday 10–3, Sunday 2–4 p.m. The 10 buildings—an agricultural building; three log houses, including a c. 1840 dogtrot; and plantation commissary housing—are furnished with artifacts of the Delta, early medical and dental equipment, and early twentieth-century artifacts. The newest addition to the Desha County Museum is the African American Pickens Plantation Baptist Church—an excellent example of vernacular Delta architecture.

✐&. **Plantation Agriculture Museum** (501-961-1409; www.arkansasstateparks.com /plantationagriculturemuseum), US 165 and AR 161. Open Tuesday through Saturday 8–5, Sunday 1–5 p.m. Gallery pass and site walking tours are $3 per adult; children 6–12 are $2 each; family passes are $10. This is the place for the definitive picture of cotton agriculture in Arkansas, from statehood in 1836 through World War II, when agricultural practices quickly became mechanized. You can walk through the restored 1920s cotton gin and see how cotton was grown, picked, and processed. A part of the exhibit is a cotton wagon with harnessed mules (full size), located under the weigh-scale shed in front of the cotton gin building. The one-of-a-kind structure includes equipment from the original owner's early 1900s cotton gin and is built so that you can view the full-sized gin from every angle. The site includes two Munger gin stands, a rotating two-bale press, a Fairbanks engine, and a line shaft pulley system.

&. ❀ **St. Charles Museum,** 608 Broadway Street, St. Charles. Free admission. Open 10–4. This little museum is well worth the stop. Be nice, as your guide will likely be

DELTA'S ABUNDANCE IS CELEBRATED AT STUTTGART MUSEUM

Museum of the Arkansas Grand Prairie (870-673-7001; www.grandprairiemuseum.org), 921 East Fourth Street, Stuttgart. Open Tuesday through Friday 8–4:30, Saturday 10–4; closed Sunday and Monday. This impressive museum is the result of volunteers who wanted to depict the history of agriculture in the area, its acclaim as a duck hunter's paradise, and the pioneers who farmed the Grand Prairie. Even if you are not a hunter, you will enjoy the waterfowlers exhibit and library with its impressive and colorful display of taxidermy. East Arkansas's agriculture contribution to the nation's food chain is portrayed in exhibits on the state's rice-milling history, a crop-dusting film in the mini-theater, and a fish-farm exhibit. It's all housed in a 20,000-square-foot building with five outbuildings. You can tour the 1895 *Freepress*, Stuttgart's first English newspaper, and kick the tires of Stuttgart's first store-bought hand-cranked fire truck. The Prairie School House is a replica of the Independence school located 3.5 miles northeast of Stuttgart—a colony of Mennonites from the Midwest established the school in the 1880s. The church is a two-thirds scale replica of the Lutheran church built by founder Rev. Adam Buerkle. And for a taste of everyday life, the Prairie House is a replica of an early prairie house with artifacts common to families in the late 1800s and early 1900s. The nationally recognized *Waterfowl Wing* displays depict an early morning duck hunt and identify species of ducks and their calls. Highlights of the museum's collection include an impressive selection of decoys, guns, and a duck blind; a one-of-a-kind Coat of Many Feathers; an 800-year-old duck effigy pottery by Native Americans; 500 award-winning game calls; carvings of waterfowl; an antique decoy collection; market hunter guns; and waterfowl art.

the town's mayor, Mayor Patrick, a Delta darling version of Larry "Bud" Melman of David Letterman fame. You will love his passion for the Civil War artifacts displayed, and he can tell you as much about regional history in the Delta as any reference book you might find. St. Charles is where Confederate troops fired the deadliest shot of the Civil War, and the story is told in a detailed diorama. Photos and ephemera mark the Civilian Conservation Corps time in the area. A monument outside the mayor's office also marks the historic battle.

CULTURAL SITES

UPPER DELTA

Historic Dyess Colony: Johnny Cash Boyhood Home (870-764-2274; dyesscash.astate.edu), Dyess. Open Monday through Saturday; tours being at 9 a.m., with the final tour starting at 3 p.m. Admission includes both buildings. $10 general admission, $8 senior rate, $8 for groups of 10 or more, $5 student rate (children 5–18 or with a university ID), $5 field trip rate, free for children under 5 and ASU students. One of the most popular attractions in the Delta is the boyhood home of The Man in Black, Johnny Cash. President Franklin D. Roosevelt's 1934 New Deal for the nation's economic recovery included the establishment of the Dyess Colony in northeast Arkansas. Cash's family was one of 500 impoverished Arkansas farm families given 10 acres and a house on which to build a new future. Several historic buildings have been restored and are open to visitors, including a visitor center, administration building, and the Cash family home. The visitor center is located at the former site of the theater and soda shop and includes a gift shop, orientation video, and exhibits. The Dyess Colony Administration building displays exhibits that tell the story of the establishment of the colony, the lives of those who lived there, and the influence life in the colony had on Cash and his music. The interior of the Cash home has been re-created from the memories of his family members.

LOWER DELTA

♂ ♿ **Toltec Mounds Archeological State Park** (501-961-9442; www.arkansasstateparks .com/toltecmounds), Scott. Open Monday through Saturday 8–5, Sunday, noon–5. You can choose either a gallery pass or a walking tour of the site for $4 per adult, $3 per child (6–12), or $14 per family. You can call ahead to make reservations and get the gallery pass plus a tram tour of the site for $6 per adult, $5 per child, or $22 per family. The mounds are Arkansas's tallest American Indian mounds, and one of two of the state park system's National Historic Landmark Sites that preserve and interpret prehistoric Native American mound sites. Walk through the remains of a world that existed here from A.D. 600 to 1050. Toltec sports a 2,240-square-foot educational pavilion adjacent to the visitor information center, providing a place for park staff to conduct programs indoors. Open year-round, the facility provides restrooms, is heated for cold weather use, and has fans to cool it during warm weather months. The center also includes a meeting room.

♂ ♿ **Scott Plantation Settlement** (501-351-5737; www.scottconnections.org), Alexander Road off US 165, Scott. Free admission. Open Thursday through Sunday, February through November. Call for hours. This collection of historic buildings depicts a typical Arkansas plantation and includes a hand-hewn cypress corncrib, an 1840s log cabin, a wash house, several tenant houses, and a blacksmith shop. Toward the front of the settlement is a Civil War marker explaining the Battle of Ashley's Mills, part of the campaign conducted by Union Gen. Frederick Steele that led to the fall of Little Rock in 1863.

✳ To Do

WILD PLACES ♂ ♿ **Big Lake National Wildlife Refuge** (870-564-2429; fws.gov/ biglake). This National Wildlife Refuge includes 11,000-acres of Delta lowlands in extreme northeast Arkansas and offers excellent nature watching year-round. This is the place to fish. Mallard Lake is where the state record largemouth bass was caught. Some 5,000 acres of the refuge constitute a National Natural Landmark, and another 2,100 acres are designated part of the Wilderness Preservation System. Over 2,600 acres are open waters, and the remainder is bottomland marsh. Established in 1915, the refuge is home to over 225 species of birds, includes an eagle sanctuary, and is an important area for migrating/wintering waterfowl and neotropical birds in the Lower Mississippi River ecosystem. You'll have to bring your own boat, but boat ramps are available. A small information center is located in the refuge headquarters 2 miles east of Manila on AR 18. The refuge has developed into an important habitat for endangered species and played an important role in recovering the bald eagle from its endangered species status.

Cache River National Wildlife Refuge (870-347-2614; cacheriver.fws.gov), Clarendon. The refuge offers small game, waterfowl, and big game hunting; fishing; wildlife observation; and photography. This habitat includes 33,000 acres of bottomland forest and associated sloughs and oxbow lakes, 4,300 acres of croplands, and 7,500 acres of reforested areas. There are large concentrations of wintering waterfowl during the winter. The refuge is recognized as a Wetland of International Importance by the

Ramsar Convention and as the most important wintering area for mallards by the North American Waterfowl Management Plan.

Wapanocca National Wildlife Refuge (870-343-2595; www.fws.gov/wapanocca), 8 miles north of Marion. This huge wetlands area includes forested portions, some farmland, and the 600-acre Wapanocca Lake. Prior to establishment of the refuge, it was the site of the Wapanocca Outing Club, which was formed in 1886 and was one of the nation's oldest and most prestigious hunting clubs. The club was managed for waterfowl, and most of the lake was set aside as a waterfowl sanctuary. The area is great for bird-watching, hunting, and fishing for panfish and bass. The driving trail provides a glimpse of what the Arkansas Delta was like in the late 19th and early 20th centuries from the comfort of your car. The refuge is located 4 miles west of the Mississippi River and is protected from the river by a levee. Functioning within the Lower Mississippi River ecosystem, the land is managed for migrating and wintering waterfowl and migrating neotropical birds, also providing critical nesting habitat for those species.

STATE PARKS

UPPER DELTA

⚓ ♿ **Louisiana Purchase State Park** (870-64-3474; www.arkansasstateparks.com) is located just outside Brinkley, off US 49, 21 miles south of I-40. Open Monday through Sunday 6 a.m.–9 p.m. Free admission. An elevated boardwalk, suspended above a headwater swamp in east Arkansas, invites you to experience the untamed, marshy environs of Louisiana Purchase State Park, and you won't even get your feet wet.

Interpretive panels along the boardwalk recount the story of the largest land acquisition in American history—the Louisiana Purchase. In 1803, the US government purchased over 800,000 square miles of land west of the Mississippi River from France. Named Louisiana after the French King Louis XIV, the territory stretched from the Gulf of Mexico to Canada and encompassed much of the present-day western US, including Arkansas. It allowed the US government to open up lands in the west for settlement, secured its borders against foreign threat, and gave Americans the right to deposit goods duty-free at port cities (mainly New Orleans). More than a decade passed before President James Madison ordered an official survey of the entire Louisiana Territory. On October 27, 1815, one survey party headed north from the confluence of the Arkansas and Mississippi Rivers, while a second party traveled west from the junction of the St. Francis and Mississippi Rivers. Your journey ends at the granite monument that marks the point where their paths crossed nearly a century ago, designating the initial point

MONUMENT MARKS EXACT STARTING POINT OF LOUISIANA PURCHASE SURVEY

from which future surveys would originate. Sunlight breaks through the dense canopy of the tupelo forest tracing the imaginary baseline, surreally reinforcing the significance of the site.

Randolph County Museum (870-892-4056; www.randolphcomuseum.org) 106 East Everett Street, Pocahontas. Open Monday through Friday 10–4, Saturday 9–1. From its perch at the northern tip of the state, Pocahontas is home to many of the state's "firsts." Just to name a few . . . the first post office, the first ferry boat, the first steamboat, and the oldest standing building and house in the state. These firsts and many more are remembered at this charming community-driven museum on Pocahontas' town square. Among the museum's treasures is a representative from the early mass production of the "Wonder Horse," which was invented by Pocahontas native William (Bill) Baltz in 1939. The wooden horse, attached to its frame with big heavy springs, was soon mass produced to satisfy demand from children throughout the country. The rich heritage of the area is documented through photographs and artifacts, and described by area volunteers who are frequently personally connected to the stories they share. While admission to the museum is free, they welcome donations to support their ongoing operations.

LOWER DELTA

🖉 ♿ **Lake Chicot State Park** (1-800-264-2430; www.arkansasstateparks.com/lake chicot), 2542 AR 257, Lake Village. This park is the recreational gateway to the state's

VISITOR CENTER AT LAKE CHICOT STATE PARK

largest natural lake, annually luring thousands of visitors to its shores. The 20-mile-long oxbow lake, formed hundreds of years ago when the Mississippi River diverted course, is also the largest of its kind in the country. Bass, bream, crappie, and catfish are prolific in the protected waters of the upper end of the lake, and wildlife is abundant in the forests that surround it. Lake Chicot's location along the Mississippi Flyway makes it a preferred perch for birding year-round. The park's 122 campsites are nestled in a pecan grove, with a swimming pool, picnic tables, pavilions, laundry, and playground nearby. Cabins with kitchens (many with lake-view patio and fishing dock) are serene settings for lakeside dining and soaking up the splendor of a Delta sunset. The park rents bikes, boats, and Jet Skis for independent exploration, and also has guided lake and levee tours led by experienced staff interpreters. Interpretive programs at the park highlight area history and natural resources, including Dutch oven cooking workshops, living history presentations, and reenactments.

⚓ ♿ **Lower White River Museum State Park** (870-256-3711; www.arkansasstateparks .com/lowerwhiterivermuseum), 2009 West Main Street, Des Arc. Open Monday through Saturday 8–5 and Sunday 1–5; closed New Year's Day, Christmas Eve, and Christmas Day. Admission $3.25 adults, $2 for children ages 6–12, and $10 for families (parents and children through age 18); free the first Sunday of each month (excluding special events). The 722-mile-long White River begins in northwest Arkansas, winding its way through the Ozark Plateau for over 450 miles before reaching Arkansas's Delta region. As it makes its way across that natural border in Newport, the river's crooked course begins to straighten, making it more navigable for barges and steamboats. Consequently, the Lower White River, as it became known, became a vital transportation route for the first settlers to brave the Arkansas frontier. This park tells the story of the river's influence on settlements established along its banks and their subsequent commerce rooted in hunting and fishing, which expanded into agriculture, shelling, and timber. Visitors are greeted by life-sized figures of Capt. James C. McManus; Miss Sallie Davis, a schoolteacher from Memphis; surveyor John Garretson; and Henry, a slave. The characters introduce themselves via audio using dialogue taken from oral history records and slave narratives. An interactive display for young museum visitors features an 8-by-12½-foot map of Arkansas with the Arkansas and White Rivers highlighted on it. Red dots show where towns are located along the Lower White. The park hosts several special events throughout the year, including quilting workshops, acrylic and sand painting classes, a crafts and quilt show, beginner's gourd workshop, and instruction in Dutch oven cooking. Next door, a replica of a late 1800s dogtrot log cabin is set up in traditional style, with the kitchen in one side and living quarters in the other, separated by an open-air breezeway. Outbuildings used as a washhouse and either a smokehouse or a potato house complete the complex.

TOURS **Delta Heritage Tours** (870-338-8972), 514 Walnut Street, Helena–West Helena, Phillips County. You just have to use the county name when you talk about the Delta. At least for this tour, if for no other stops you make. And be prepared to tell folks where your people come from, too. Say hi to Mr. John, Miss Munnie, and Granny Dee, and don't be offended when you are called ma'am or sir; that's not your age, that's just good old Southern upbringing. One of the most genteel and informative tours you will ever take, it includes historic homes, Battle of Helena sites, the tranquil, terraced Confederate Cemetery, and the Delta Cultural Center. If you are into agritourism, your tour can also include a crawfish farm and agricultural sites in the area at your request. But mind your manners and call ahead.

✳ Lodging

UPPER DELTA

Mallard Pointe Lodge (870-589-2266; www.mallardpointelodge.com), 1097 Hallum Cemetery Road, Brinkley. Rates are based on season, activity, and number of people in your group, so call for an exact quote for your needs. Located on the border of Dagmar Wildlife Management Area, the lodge has guides available for duck hunting, deer hunting, or game bird hunting (pheasant, quail, and dove). Other offerings include shooting range; trap and skeet shooting; home-cooked breakfast and dinners; gaming, pool tables, and big-screen televisions; whirlpool tubs and five-jet body massage showers; and king and double rooms. Mallard Pointe has two spacious lodges that both offer a great place to unwind after a hunt. The main lodge, which sleeps 32, is 11,000 square feet, while the new Buck Lodge spans 10,000 square feet and can sleep up to 25 guests. Not just for hunting—the lodge is available for corporate retreats, wedding receptions, or family reunions. The conference room seats up to 100 with a state-of-the-art audiovisual system that has an 8-foot-by-8-foot screen (compatible connections allow you to connect your computer or portable CD/DVD players for business presentations or watching movies at night). With a range of private, semiprivate, and bunk rooms, in addition to meeting space for 100, Mallard Pointe is the right destination for a group of any size. $$.

LOWER DELTA

🏨 **Delta Resort & Spa** (1-877-463-3582; www.deltaconferencecenter.com), 8624 Bucksducks Road, McGehee. All Delta Resort & Spa two-bedroom suite rates are based on single through quad occupancy. Guest rooms are based on single and double occupancy. Three-night minimum restrictions may apply during certain event weekends, peak weekends, and holidays. This 130-room complex sits on 2,000 acres of hardwoods adjacent to a shooting sports and conference center. Nestled among some of the best duck-hunting grounds in the world, the hotel was designed with the outdoor enthusiast in mind. King and queen suites include flat-screen televisions, fiber-optic Wi-Fi connectivity, plush bedding, fine linens, toiletries, and ample room for gear. Suites also feature a living area, convenient mini-fridge, and coffeemaker. Elevated Southern cuisine is served on-site at the 43 Grill & Bar. Continental breakfast is served daily in the lobby of Bucksducks Lodge from 5–10 a.m. A professional massage therapist is available by appointment. Duck Pro Outfitters is on location to provide for all of your hunting and shooting needs. $$$.

🏨 **Palaver Place Bed & Breakfast/Lodge** (870-998-7206), 10498 Loomis Landing, DeValls Bluff. Rates are based on season and the size of your group. Call for more information. Built one room at a time, this bed & breakfast offers unique architecture, a relaxed atmosphere, and warm hospitality; each room accommodates from two to seven people and has a private bath. A swimming pool, hot tubs, indoor/outdoor bar, game room with billiard table, and big screen TV will keep you entertained when you aren't out seeing the sights in east Arkansas. A library with Internet access will allow you to check in with the world if you must. Take in the great outdoors of east Arkansas on nature walks, fishing, and hiking; during duck-hunting season, guided hunting trips are available. Or hang around the lodge and play lawn croquet or view collectibles, antiques, and artwork by the owner. Canoeing facilities are on hand if you don't have your own. Conference room available; a 10,000 square-foot lodge accommodates 22 people. $–$$.

🏨 **Popa Duck Lodge** (870-282-8888; www.popaducklodge.com), 132 Sixth Street, St. Charles. This 14,000-square-foot lodge, near the White River Refuge, has queen-sized beds and a great room with big-screen television, pool and game tables, and table soccer. You will be treated to three home-cooked meals daily, served buffet-style. Professional guide services are available through the lodge. Small and large groups welcome; dog kennels provided. The lodge is also available for family reunions, business meetings, and wedding receptions. Pet friendly. $–$$.

🐾 **The Schoolhouse Lodge** (870-830-0151; www.theschoolhouselodge .net), 1178 AR 276, Stuttgart. This lodge was formerly the Bayou Meto School and is listed on the Arkansas Register of Historic Places. It has six bedrooms with private baths, a full kitchen, great room, fireplace, boot room, and spacious deck. The innkeepers will gladly cater to your special requests, including catered meals, and fill you in on area events going on during your stay. Guided hunting and fishing packages are also available. The lodge can sleep up to 15 people. Additional services for guests include personal shopping, catered meals, servers for receptions, daily housekeeping service, and custom invitations. Pet friendly. Summer rates are $45 per person with a $240 minimum. Waterfowl season rates are $65 per person with a $260 per night minimum. $–$$.

✳ Where to Eat

EATING OUT

UPPER DELTA

Cottage Mall & Café (870-734-1313; www .cottagemall.com), 322 West Cypress, Brinkley. Open Tuesday through Saturday 11–2. Brinkley's downtown area features quaint storefronts stocked with everything from vintage pieces to current trends. The Cottage Mall & Café, just off the main drag, allows you to shop for a little bit of everything while the kitchen prepares your lunch. All menu items are moderately priced at less than $10 per person. The house specialty is a homemade chicken salad served with a fluffy croissant. They also offer a selection of sandwiches, pasta, soups, salads, and desserts. Great fudge! Catering services are also available. $.

Ed's Country Catfish House (870-762-2603), 2075 South Division, Blytheville. Open Tuesday through Saturday 4–9:30; Sunday 11–8:30. Ed's serves an all-you-can-eat buffet every night, featuring different menu items daily. Buffet items include catfish, shrimp, chicken, crab legs, and ribs. $–$$.

Lavada's Sale Barn Café (870-248-2060), 706 Townsend Drive, Pocahontas. OK, so here's a tip that is seldom shared by locals in Arkansas: if you are a carnivore, you may be surprised to learn that cow sale barns are great places to get top-notch steaks, bacon, pork chops, and any other type of meat that passes through an auction house. It makes sense if you stop and think about it. What cattle rancher is going to pay for a lousy steak or hamburger or slab of bacon? Lavada's was formerly known as Brenda's Sale Barn Café, and has been serving both breakfast and lunch to some of the more discriminating meat eaters in the area for decades. Biscuits and gravy, hash browns, and pancakes round out the hearty breakfast menu. Very fresh steaks, burgers, and pork chops make up the midday menu with slow-cooked fresh vegetables, hand-cut fries, and freshly made desserts completing the meal.

PRO TIP: There is good Southern chocolate gravy, there is bad chocolate gravy, and there is chocolate gravy so good it will make your eyes roll back in your head. Lavada's may make the best Southern chocolate gravy in the Delta. It is the one you will compare all others to in the future. $–$$.

LOWER DELTA

Country Village Bar-B-Que (870-628-3181), US 425 South, Star City. Days and hours are seasonal; call ahead.

This restaurant is part of the Country Village, a compound of shops, restaurants, and a taxidermy shop near Star City. This is a great place to get a little civilization when you are visiting Cane Creek State Park. They serve BBQ pork, beef, and chicken. Burgers and sandwiches are also available. $–$$.

Craig's Brothers Café (870-998-2616), US 70, DeValls Bluff. Open Tuesday through Saturday 11–6, Sunday noon–6. People drive from miles around to eat at this tiny, no-frills restaurant on US 70. Plan to wait for a seat at the Formica tables if you are dining prime time. A true Southern BBQ shack that dates back to the 1940s, Craig's serves BBQ sandwiches and plates, ribs, and burgers. Known for their slow-smoked meats, fiery sauces, and savory coleslaw, their moderately priced menu will run you less than $10 per person, including drink. You will want to drive across the highway to the Family Pie Shop for dessert. $.

Family Pie Shop (870-998-2279), US 70, DeValls Bluff. Located directly across the street from Craig's Brothers Café, this unassuming building is known to locals as Mary's Place. Mary specializes in coconut, chocolate, sweet potato, and egg custard pies, as well as flaky, crescent-shaped fried pies filled with fruit, an Arkansas delicacy. The Family Pie Shop has been featured in *USA Today*, *New York Times*, and *Roadfood* by Jane and Michael Stern. $.

Ms. Lena's Pies (870-998-1204), AR 33 South, DeValls Bluff. Open Saturdays only; call for hours. It's probably not 2 miles from The Family Pie Shop to Ms. Lena's, so you can forget working up an appetite between the two. A secret family recipe makes these fried pies special. Local favorites include peach, apple, apricot, chocolate, and coconut that are made fresh every Saturday. Ms. Lena also makes a few specialty flavors such as cherry, Mounds, and pecan on alternate Saturdays. Special orders can be made any day of the week—just call. Ms.

Lena's Pies have been featured in *Southern Living* magazine. $.

La Petit Cajun Bistro (870-673-1833), 1919 South Main Street, Stuttgart. Open for dinner Tuesday through Sunday. Hours are based on the season, but generally the Bistro is open from 5–9 p.m. The restaurant extends its hours during duck season. Plan on spending about $25 per person, including your appetizer. This outstanding restaurant packs them in when the hunters are in town, and if you aren't wearing camo you may feel overdressed. Most duck lodges in Stuttgart employ in-house chefs who use the finest ingredients to plate high-end meals for their guests. It is saying a lot when a local restaurant entices these experienced travelers to venture off their private reserves to dine out during their stay. Authentic Cajun cuisine, steaks, and fresh seafood make up the mouth-watering menu. $–$$.

Leo's White River Café (870-747-5413), 716 Madison Street, Clarendon. Open Monday through Saturday 8–2. Leo's serves a very inexpensive home-cooked breakfast and lunch. A buffet is also available for lunch. Breakfast will set you back about $6, lunch will run you about $7. $.

&. **Pickens Restaurant & Commissary** (870-382-5266), 122 Pickens Road, Dumas. Open Monday through Friday 11–2. Located on the Pickens Farm just south of Dumas, this eatery serves plate lunches featuring traditional Southern fare like pork chops, baked chicken, and fried catfish. A few of the restaurant's signature dishes include skillet-fried potatoes and onions, squash dressing, fresh vegetables, and chicken salad. The restaurant's popular homemade desserts include coconut cream, chocolate, and pecan pies. The adjacent commissary stocks staples such as canned greens and toilet paper, hunting and fishing gear, T-shirts, and gift items, and it has an old-fashioned candy counter. $–$$.

Rhoda's Famous Hot Tamales (870-265-3108), 714 Saint Mary Street, Lake

Village. Rhoda Adams is a gifted cook with the ability to inject soulfulness into every dish she prepares. Diners rave about her tamales, her cheese dip, her brunch, her basic breakfast, her sandwiches, and pretty much everything that comes out of the kitchen. Her restaurant feels like her kitchen, and she feels like someone who has been lovingly preparing meals for you for years. The restaurant is named for her tamales, and they inspire fans to travel great distances for the sole purpose of satisfying their tamale craving. Iconic Southern favorites include fried chicken and catfish. $.

&. **St. Charles Community Store** (870-282-3311; www.stcharlescommunitystore .net), AR 1, St. Charles. Open daily 11–8. A wonderful little restaurant near the White River Refuge serves standard slap-your-mama Southern cooking and a breakfast and lunch buffet daily. A catfish buffet is offered every Friday and Saturday night, and crawfish is featured every Saturday night. Breakfast and lunch menus average $7 per person; the dinner buffet is $10 with a drink. $.

DINING OUT

UPPER DELTA

&. **Dondie's White River Princess Restaurant** (870-256-3311), 101 East Curran Street, Des Arc. Open Thursday, Friday, and Saturday nights only; first Sunday of the month for lunch. Located on the shore of the White River in downtown Des Arc, Dondie's has a wide variety of menu items to sate any palate or appetite. The buffet features huge, crispy catfish fillets, boiled shrimp, and chicken strips. You can dine onboard without ever leaving shore. Dondie's was built to resemble the steamboats that once docked at Des Arc as they traveled up and down the White River. The restaurant has won numerous awards and has been featured on television and in magazines for its outstanding catfish and hospitality. Dondie's also has a wide selection of menu items, including award-winning prime rib, rib-eye and sirloin steaks, Riverbend Chicken, and frog legs. Save room for dessert; these homemade delights are worth a trip to the gym. $$–$$$.

&. **Uncle John's Restaurant** (870-823-5319), 118 Main Street, Crawfordsville. Open Tuesday through Thursday 9–8:30, Friday 9–9, and Saturday 5–9. Uncle John's serves homemade lasagna, ravioli, their special tangy spaghetti sauce, and other Italian favorites using Uncle John Marconi's old family recipes. Dessert lovers won't want to miss Uncle John's famous bread pudding. The mural on the west wall, painted by local artist Joann Bloodworth, depicts what Crawfordsville might be like if dropped into the mountains and hillsides of Tuscany, Italy. It includes likenesses of many of the town's residents. $–$$$.

LOWER DELTA

&. **Cow Pen Restaurant** (870-265-9992; www.thecowpen.com), 5198 East Highway 82, Lake Village. Open Tuesday through Thursday 5–9, Friday and Saturday 5–9:30, and Sunday for brunch from 11–2. In 1967, Floyd Owens converted an old cattle inspection station into a restaurant and named it The Cow Pen. Gene and Juanita Grassi took over the restaurant in 1987, expanding its reputation as one of southeast Arkansas's best eateries. The Cow Pen became known for its steaks, seafood, Mexican dishes, and cheese dip, winning numerous culinary awards through the years. The Grassis retired in 2007, turning the eatery over to the Faulks family. Sadly, six months later the restaurant was destroyed by fire. On November 26, 2008, the Cow Pen reopened at the foot of the new Mississippi River bridge on Arkansas Highway 82. The new location is bigger than the original, poised to capitalize on the expanded traffic expected at its location where Arkansas, Tennessee, and Mississippi meet. $$–$$$$.

♿ **The Village Steakhouse** (870-628-5053), Country Village, US 425 South, Star City. This simply named restaurant is one of the hot spots in Star City. Dine on prime rib, steaks, chicken, and seafood in the relaxing atmosphere of the Country Village. Save room for one of the restaurant's homemade desserts. $$–$$$$.

🍸 ♿ **Traylor's River Road Grill** (870-946-2441), 513 East Ninth, DeWitt. Open Tuesday through Thursday 10–2 for lunch, 5–9 for dinner; Friday and Saturday 10–2 and 5–10. The menu at Traylor's runs the gamut from hamburgers to lobster; steaks are the house specialty. An outdoor patio is available for alfresco dining and for smokers. $$–$$$.

* Entertainment

UPPER DELTA

The Ken Theatre (870-731-0300), 103 West Second Street, McCrory. Call for a schedule of performances and ticket information. McCrory's former movie house, The Ken Theatre, has been restored and now serves as a regional performing arts center. In addition to hosting movies, concerts, and theatrical performances, they also hold classes in dance, production, and chorus.

Southland Park Gaming and Racing (1-800-467-6182; www.southlandgreyhound.com), 1550 North Ingram Boulevard, West Memphis. Open year-round, Monday through Friday 8 a.m.–4 a.m., 24 hours on weekends. Free admission and free parking. Southland offers live greyhound racing and simulcast greyhound and thoroughbred racing. An electronic gaming arena features instant racing machines and electronic poker games. Four different restaurants offer international cuisine, casual, and fine dining. Featuring interactive entertainment weekdays (live trivia, Guitar Hero, and karaoke) and live music weekends.

* Selective Shopping

UPPER DELTA

Black River Beads and Pottery (870-248-0450; www.blackriverbeads.com), 213 East Broadway Street, Pocahontas. An on-site glass-blowing studio allows you to customize your piece when the artists are on the premises creating sparkling glass beads, one-of-a-kind glassware, and objets d'art. Hand-thrown pottery and mixed media art pieces complete the inventory. This little shop has been featured in national trade publications for the quality of its products and in national travel articles as a recommended destination. The store's hours are Monday–Thursday 10–5, Friday 10–4, Sunday noon–5.

Falling Star Farms (870-202-9595) 4068 Highway 166 North, Maynard. Falling Star Farms is not the typical roadside stand with bushels of fresh fruits and vegetables in rows under a tent. No, this is a full-blown store with sustainable produce grown on the local farm, as well as fresh eggs and a house-made line of jellies, preserves, and fruit butters. The hours vary with the season; it is a good idea to call before you go.

Sisters' at the Crossing (870-763-2520; www.sistersbly.com), 223 West Main Street, Blytheville. Sisters' at the Crossing is located in a restored historic 1900s dry goods store, inspiring a sense of nostalgia with its location and its inventory. Antiques and collectibles are displayed with more modern unique gifts and interior design pieces, drawing in collectors, stylists, and tourists visiting the city. On Tuesday, Thursday, Friday, and Saturday, the on-site Southern Grace Tea Room serves lunch from 11–2.

That Bookstore in Blytheville (870-763-3333; www.thatbookstoreinblytheville.com), 316 West Main Street, Blytheville. Open Monday through Saturday 10–6. The store's 2,400 square feet with more than 25,000 titles in stock invites visitors to browse while sipping a cup of coffee. You can relax in a rocking chair next to a woodstove, engage in conversation about the book you've just read, or enjoy a spontaneous reading of the new favorite children's book of the day. A handpicked selection of popular titles, including autographed books by contemporary authors, has made this a mid-America landmark, complete with its own coffee blend, Special Edition. Best-selling novelist John Grisham drops in occasionally for book signings. The guest book is a set of wooden chairs with authors' signatures. The back room also hosts reading groups, musical performances, and author signings and readings.

Whitton Farms (870-815-9519; squareup.com/store/whitton-farms), 5157 West State Highway 118, Tyronza. Open Monday through Saturday 9–6. For more than 15 years, Jill and Keith Forrester have continued their family's farming tradition that began in the early 1900s, when Leona Wells Forrester moved to Whitton, Arkansas. Leona's son, Jess, eventually took on the role of expanding the farm, increasing the humble plot of land purchased by Leona many times over. Jess retired in 1996, passing soon after. In 2002, his son, Keith, brought his wife, Jill, back to the house that Jess built. However, Jill and Keith planned to take the farm in a new direction, growing fresh produce, herbs, and flowers. They plowed right into the specialty crop farming niche and after 12 years were named Farm Family of the Year in 2014 by both their county and the northeast Arkansas region. The Forresters not only stock the on-site store with their harvest, but also their farm-to-table restaurant, the Trolley Market Stop in Memphis, Tennessee. In Tyronza, you can shop on the farm for fresh fruits and vegetables, cut flowers, arrangements, and wreaths. Take a tour of the fields of flowers and produce with Jill or Keith for $12. The price includes a tasty farm-fresh picnic lunch in the pecan grove with options for meat eaters and vegetarians.

LOWER DELTA

Amish and Country Store (870-538-9990; www.amishandcountrystore.com), 3040 Highway 65 North, Dermott. This family owned and operated shop stocks over 200 Amish and Mennonite handmade products. Jellies and jams, soaps, breads, pickles, cheeses, furniture and more highlight the craftsmanship of these artisans and the quality of their local ingredients. Time-tested techniques and recipes shared through the generations are surprisingly modest in price. Open Monday through Friday 8–5; Saturday 8–4.

James Hayes Art Glass Co. (870-692-9203; www.hayesartglass.com), 2900 Ridgeway Road, Pine Bluff. James Hayes studied glassblowing in Murano, Italy; Columbus, Ohio; and the Pilchuck Glass School near Seattle, Washington, before returning to his home state. His gallery serves to display examples of his work from which you can choose for inspiration for a custom piece created specially for you. In addition to numerous local and regional awards and recognition, Hayes created a Christmas ornament for the Clinton White House. The website provides details on special events, Hayes' exhibitions, new designs, and directions to the showroom.

Mack's Prairie Wings (1-800-229-0296; www.macksprairiewings.com), 2335 US 63 North, Stuttgart. Open Monday through Friday 9–5:30, Saturday 9–5, Sunday 10–6. Billed as "America's Premiere Waterfowl Outfitter," Mack's inventory includes ammunition, game calls, archery supplies, duck boats, ATV/truck hunting blinds, hunting gear, decoys, home decor, footwear, hunting clothing, gifts, gun accessories, hunting knives, hunting optics, hunting dog supplies, casual clothing, and tree stands. It's like a Tiffany's for boys.

POTTERY SHOPPING AT MILLER'S MUD MILL   ARKANSAS DEPARTMENT OF PARKS & TOURISM

Miller's Mud Mill (870-382-5277; www.millersmudmill.com), US 65 South, Brookhaven Shopping Center, Dumas. Open Monday through Friday 10–5. Fine wheel-turned pottery featuring vibrant colors and unique shapes is available. Gail Miller's trademark mug is a smooth, symmetrical vessel offset with a primitive hand formed with a rough glob of clay fixed on the side.

Paul Michael Company (870-265-3872; www.paulmichaelhome.com), 3696 US 65 and US 82 South, Lake Village. Open Monday through Saturday 9–5, Sunday 1–5. Paul Michael cleverly matched a decline in the US dollar and an environmental movement toward recycling to create a signature line of home furnishings and decor he believes will stand the test of time to age into the antiques of tomorrow. The majority of pieces are constructed from either architectural salvage or reclaimed wood personally collected by Paul over the years. Paul Michael Company has 35,000 square feet of fine decorative accessories, seasonal items, furniture, and rugs, including a famous Scratch & Dent room that rewards bargain hunters for their elbow grease. Inventory changes continuously.

✶ Special Events

July: **T Tauri Film Festival & Movie Camp** (870-251-1189; www.ttauri.org), 195 Peel Road, Locust Grove. Workshop tuition $75–100. Screenings: some free; others $3 adults, $2 seniors and youth. This is a really cool annual event featuring movies made by filmmakers under the age of 18 from around the nation. The juried event features judges of the same age. Organizers offer a number of filmmaking workshops ranging from two to five days in duration. Workshop topics include documentary filmmaking, narrative filmmaking, and animation.

October: **King Biscuit Blues Festival** (870-338-6583; www.kingbiscuitfestival .com). The first weekend of every

October, the normally quiet Delta town of Helena becomes a thriving community of blues musicians and their fans, shopping tents stocked with handmade crafts and art, samplings from a wide variety of food vendors, and music that celebrates Arkansas's Delta blues heritage. Now the largest blues festival in the South, it has grown exponentially since its humble beginnings, when the primary venue was the back of a flatbed pickup in front of the old train depot. The main stage is set up on the levee, parallel with historic Cherry Street. What began in 1986 as a one-day event with a crowd of 500 was, by the late 1990s, a three-day event with more than 100,000 people attending. The festival has remained free and draws blues enthusiasts from around the world. Book your room early, as vacancies are few and far between. In addition to the requisite BBQ competition mandatory for most southern festivals, you can try Pasquali's Famous Tamales, alligator on a stick, or the oxygen bar if you need a breather. As you walk the length of Cherry Street, the soulful sounds of blues musicians playing on street corners and in doorways drift through the air. A blues awards program on the first day (Thursday) recognizes performances prior to the festival. Nationally known headliners close out the festival on Saturday night. The King Biscuit Blues Festival originally took its name from the *King Biscuit Time* radio program, the longest-running radio program in the country. In 2005, the name was changed by the festival's organizer, the Sonny Boy Blues Society, because the New York firm that purchased the rights to the King Biscuit name wanted too much money for its use. An agreement was reached in 2010, allowing the name to revert to the King Biscuit Blues Festival.

November: **World's Championship Duck Calling Contest** and **Wings Over the Prairie Festival** (870-673-1602; www.stuttgartarkansas.org), Main Street, Stuttgart. Most events are free. This is

PAUL MICHAEL COMPANY SHOWROOM

MAIN STAGE AT KING BISCUIT BLUES FESTIVAL IN HELENA   ARKANSAS DEPARTMENT OF PARKS & TOURISM

one of the premier events for duck hunters every season. The annual festival features duck-calling contests, arts and crafts, commercial exhibits, off-road vehicles, carnival and midway, Great 10K Duck Race, World Championship Duck Gumbo Cook-Off, Queen Mallard and Junior Queen Mallard pageants, and youth duck-calling classes.

November to December: **Lights of the Delta** (870-762-9788, www

.lightsofthedelta.com), Arkansas Aeroplex, downtown Blytheville. Enjoy the Mid-South's largest holiday festival with over 6 million lights in a drive-through setting. Experience hayrides every night, new displays, pictures with Santa on weekends, and hot chocolate, toys, and ornaments at the souvenir stand. Don't miss the Lights; it's a great way to spark the spirit of the season. Admission: $10 per vehicle and up.

CROWLEY'S RIDGE

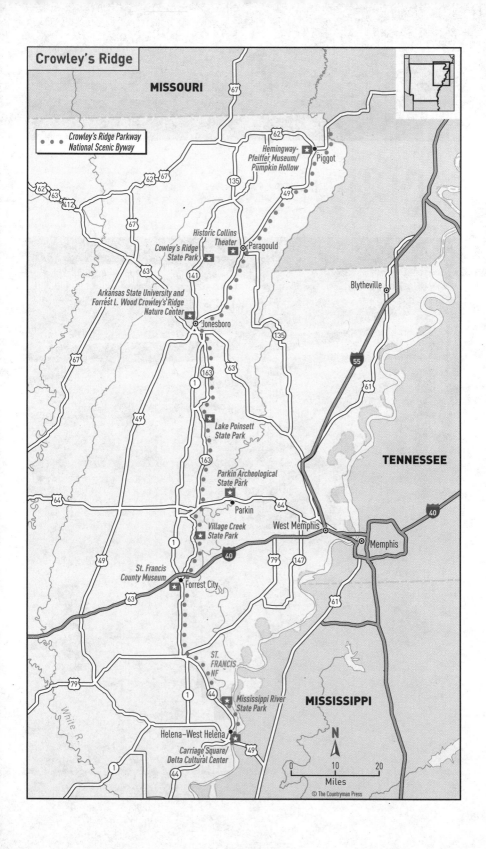

Crowley's Ridge

MISSOURI

• • • Crowley's Ridge Parkway
National Scenic Byway

Hemingway-
Pfeiffer Museum/
Pumpkin Hollow
Piggot

Historic Collins
Theater
Paragould

Cowley's Ridge
State Park

Arkansas State University and
Forrest L. Wood Crowley's Ridge
Nature Center
Jonesboro

Blytheville

Lake Poinsett
State Park

TENNESSEE

Parkin Archeological
State Park
Parkin

Village Creek
State Park

West Memphis

Memphis

St. Francis
County Museum
Forrest City

ST.
FRANCIS
NF

MISSISSIPPI

Mississippi River
State Park

Helena–West Helena

Carriage Square/
Delta Cultural Center

N

0   10   20
Miles

© The Countryman Press

CROWLEY'S RIDGE

At less than 400 square miles, this geological oddity accounts for less than 1 percent of the state's total land mass, but the unexpected appearance of these gently rolling hills makes a large impression as they seemingly tower in the distance from the flat tableland of Arkansas's Delta. Crowley's Ridge is the only geographical phenomenon ridge formation in North America and one of only two similar geological ridge formations in the world (the other being in Siberia). It rises to an elevation of 550 feet at its northernmost point and ranges from about 12 miles wide in the north to a half wide in the south, where it meets the Mississippi River. The most popular theory of its formation posits that it was carved by the flows of the Mississippi and Ohio Rivers thousands of years ago. Composed primarily of loess (pronounced "luss"), a windblown sediment, Crowley's terrain ripples like drifts of snow artistically arranged by Mother Nature herself. The higher ground of the Ridge was a welcome relief for the state's first European settlers, having slogged their wagons through the swampy lowlands that surround it.

Benjamin Crowley served his country during the War of 1812, receiving a land grant for 160 acres of land west of the Mississippi River as payment for his service. In 1821, Crowley and his family left Henderson Valley, Kentucky, to claim their new home. While en route, Crowley learned that his land sunk during the 1811–12 New Madrid earthquakes; he would have to find new land and file a petition for its substitution. Crowley crossed the Mississippi River in Missouri, entering Arkansas west of the Black River. His quest stalled briefly along the Spring River near the present boundary between Lawrence and Randolph Counties. He planted one crop before continuing east until he reached the hill country north of the town now known as Walcott. The numerous clear springs, plentiful game, and rich soil of the land running to the Cache River bottoms below inspired him to stake his claim along the sheltered hills of what is now called Crowley's Ridge. Crowley's settlement escaped the destruction of the floods of the 1820s, and soon other farmers climbed the ridge to build their homes safely out of flood range. As the community grew and the trees that protected the Ridge's fragile soil from erosion were harvested for homes and fields, deep gullies began to cut through its sloping hills. In 1936, the Civilian Conservation Corps planted pine trees and kudzu along the ridge in an effort to stymie its erosion. The first tendrils of kudzu appear just south of Jonesboro, becoming more prominent as you travel south to Helena–West Helena, where the hills of the parkway are blanketed with the hearty vines.

Helena's easily defensible position on the high ground where the Ridge meets the Mississippi River made it an important location during the Civil War, and historical sites remain a significant draw for visitors. The town's place in history was further enhanced on November 12, 1941, when radio station KFFA began broadcasting *King Biscuit Time* featuring local performers of a style called blues, a genre developed by black musicians in the South. The program that revolutionized music in the United States at the time still broadcasts Monday through Friday from the Delta Cultural Center in historic downtown Helena.

Modern explorers find the clear waters and diverse wildlife that attracted Benjamin Crowley to the ridge in the 1800s remains abundant today. Its forests are teeming with white-tailed deer and wild turkey, largely due to the protection of the state's land management agencies. Deer are not only plentiful, but also particularly large—it is rumored they know park boundaries and taunt hunters from their safe harbor. Millions of raptors, songbirds, and shorebirds migrate to the Mississippi Flyway each spring and fall, attracting birders from throughout the country. Can't blame the birds. In spring, the large, lemony yellow blossoms of the tulip poplars herald the season in explosive fashion. Who wouldn't want to perch on one of those branches? Fall color on Crowley's Ridge must be seen to be truly believed. On sunny days, the forests are luminous with such varied and vivid hues of umber, gold, and saffron it is as if they are lit from within. Scarlet halos of sumac pool beneath the autumnal oak and beech canopy, blazing like bonfires along the parkway.

Preservation is more than a mission to the people who live here; it is fundamental to their daily way of life. Perhaps it is their close connection to the fickle shores of the Mississippi River, or maybe it comes from a couple centuries of building permanent structures on these delicate hills of loess. This is a place where folks don't take more than they need, and area history is proudly displayed in local museums staffed by community volunteers. Their commitment to the fragile environment of Crowley's Ridge protects it from the reckless destruction of the progression of man and ensures its endurance for centuries to come.

AREA CODE Communities along Crowley's Ridge fall under the 870 area code.

GUIDANCE **Arkansas Department of Parks and Tourism** (501-682-7777 or 1-800-NATURAL; www.arkansas.com), 1 Capitol Mall, Little Rock. The state's tourism division provides a plethora of valuable resources to travelers considering a vacation in Arkansas. Crowley's Ridge also falls under the purview of one of the state's most creative and effective regional tourist associations—Arkansas Delta Byways (870-972-2803; www.deltabyways.com), P.O. Box 2050, State University. This savvy group's tourism arsenal includes a self-guided Civil Rights Trail, a "Birding the Byways" brochure, and a hugely popular crops guide to help city folk recognize the difference between a field of cotton and a field of rice.

Several chambers of commerce and visitor centers strategically located throughout the Ridge serve as modern-day guides for travelers along this scenic byway. For additional information about events, dining, lodging, and individual town services, the following will prove helpful on the way.

Phillips County Chamber of Commerce (870-338-8327; www.phillipscountychamber.org), Helena–West Helena.

Forrest City Area Chamber of Commerce (870-633-1651; www.forrestcitychamber.com), 203 North Izard, Forrest City.

Jonesboro Regional Chamber of Commerce (870-932-6691; www.jonesborochamber.org), 1709 East Nettleton, Jonesboro. Open Monday through Friday 9–5.

Paragould-Greene County Chamber of Commerce (870-236-7684, www.paragould.org), Paragould.

Piggott Area Chamber of Commerce (870-598-3167), Piggott.

GETTING THERE *By auto:* The simplest route to Crowley's Ridge, from east or west, is by way of I-40, which crosses the lower third of the ridge at Forrest City. The southern end is accessed by following AR 1 south. The northern route to the upper Ridge departs Forrest City on AR 284. From Campbell, Missouri, in the north, follow US 62 south across the St. Francis River into the Arkansas border town of the same name.

By air: There are two clear choices for air travel to eastern Arkansas, both requiring additional travel by auto. **Little Rock National Airport** (501-372-3439; www.lrn-airport

.com), 1 Airport Drive, Little Rock, is located in the state's capital city and the heart of the state. However, many travelers to eastern Arkansas find the **Memphis International Airport** (901-922-8000; www.mscaa.com), 2491 Winchester Road, Suite 113, Memphis, Tennessee more cost effective and convenient.

MEDICAL EMERGENCIES **Helena Regional Medical Center** (870-816-3940; www.helenarmc.com), 1801 Martin Luther King Drive, Helena, is a full-service facility.

St. Bernards Medical Center (870-972-4100; www.stbernards.info), 225 East Jackson Avenue, Jonesboro. St. Bernards serves as an acute care hospital and referral center for 23 counties in Arkansas and Missouri.

✳ Wandering Around

EXPLORING BY CAR **Crowley's Ridge Parkway**, Arkansas's first National Scenic Byway, merges six US highways, nine Arkansas highways, and 11.5 miles of well-maintained gravel road through a national forest as it traverses the spine of the Ridge. The parkway stretches 198 miles over half a million acres in Arkansas, encompassing eight counties and 11 communities from St. Francis (Clay County) to Helena–West Helena (Phillips County). An additional 14.2 miles run through Missouri. The unique topography and variety of floral species provide the most beautiful and dramatic scenery in east Arkansas, rivaling even the Ozarks in fall. **Mississippi River State Park** opened in 2009 along what may be the Parkway's most scenic segment as it passes through the St. Francis National Forest on its path to the mighty Mississippi. In the higher elevations, the canopy-covered road leads to vistas incongruous with the flatlands of the Delta. The low road leads to the wildlife of the wetlands.

EXPLORING BY FOOT **Military Road Trail** (870-238-2406; www.arkansasstateparks.com/villagecreek), 201 CR 754, Wynne. Village Creek State Park boasts 7 miles of hiking and 25 miles of multiuse trails that showcase the unique terrain of Crowley's Ridge as they meander through nearly 7,000 acres of forest encompassed by the park. The moderate 2.25-mile trail preserves the most dramatic remaining Arkansas portion of the Trail of Tears. Originally called the Memphis to Little Rock Road, its completion in 1820 made it the first improved road between Memphis and Arkansas's capital city. It eventually became a major route in the removal of the Creek, Chickasaw, Choctaw, and Cherokee Indians. Self-guided trail brochures, available at the visitor center, provide the navigation for this two-hour trek that is both scenic and stirring. It doesn't take much imagination to get a sense of those times in this place. Every time it rains, the fragility of the loess soil of Crowley's Ridge reinforces the ruts originally made by covered wagons over a century ago. The resultant bluffs that now line the trail are sliced sporadically by stair steps to the abandoned homesteads of the Ridge's original settlers. In spring, some of these walkways are still lined with jonquils planted by hands of those long since gone. One of the trailheads for the Military Road Trail is adjacent to Lake Austell's picnic area; the second is at the intersection of Village Creek, the creek, and Old Military Road, the road.

EXPLORING BY RIVER The **St. Francis River** begins in southeast Missouri, paralleling the eastern border of Crowley's Ridge, as it meanders its way some 300 miles through the Natural State before converging with the Mississippi just north of Helena. Historic landmarks and natural Delta beauty abound from start to finish. A county-owned park marks the site of **Chalk Bluff Civil War Battlefield** (1863) a short distance from where the river enters the state, north of the town of St. Francis. Access to the river is available at St. Francis. One of the most interesting sections of the river extends some 30 miles along its course, east of Jonesboro. The massive New Madrid earthquake of 1812 created the **St. Francis Sunken Lands**. The river, and thousands of acres along it, dropped a few feet to create a wetlands region. An Arkansas Game and Fish Commission wildlife management area preserves almost 17,000 acres of the sunken lands.

Farther south, the river flows adjacent to the ancient Native American village at **Parkin Archeological State Park** (US 64), and, on the lower reaches of the river, the **St. Francis National Forest**. There are no outfitters on the river and you will have to shuttle your own canoe, but it is a peaceful float with little traffic.

The **L'Anguille River** originates in Poinsett County, flowing south until it converges with the St. Francis River at Marianna. Its name means "eel" in French, and it is referenced in explorers' journals dating back to 1723. Access is at highway crossings and outside Marianna (US 79). The L'Anguille River also borders parts of the **St. Francis National Forest** as it meanders the 300 miles south toward its confluence with the St. Francis. Fishing and waterfowl hunting are favorites along this lazy Delta stream. Once again, you will have to tote your own canoe, but you will be richly rewarded for your efforts, as the final leg of your journey flows along the scenic shores of **Mississippi River State Park**. If you're wanting to canoe and camp, this park's primitive campsites

FISHING ON BEAR CREEK LAKE

are my first choice in all of Arkansas. Each is within view of the water and many are intimately placed on peninsulas, enhancing the feeling of privacy for your stay.

❋ Towns and Villages

Forrest City. On the western slopes of Crowley's Ridge, Forrest City has long been a popular exit from I-40 for travelers seeking recreation, historic sites, and accommodations. Village Creek State Park is nearby, offering 7,000 acres of woodlands, streams, lakes, cabins, and camping. It is also the site of the state's newly built Ridges at Village Creek, a 27-hole golf course designed by Andy Dye and constructed by Oliphant Golf. Located on 600 acres adjacent to Village Creek State Park, the 7,449-yard, par 72 course's cart paths and tees may offer the perfect vantage point for truly appreciating the wonder of the terrain of Crowley's Ridge. The St. Francis County Museum, in the downtown area, is filled with memorabilia from the past, including some of the most significant prehistoric artifacts discovered on the ridge.

Jonesboro. The largest city on the Ridge and in northeast Arkansas spans the broad plateau near the northernmost section of Crowley's Ridge. The Forrest L. Wood Crowley's Ridge Nature Center, operated by the Arkansas Game and Fish Commission, is the perfect place for a thorough introduction to the formation of Crowley's Ridge, as well as to take in a bird's-eye view of its unique plant life and terrain from the walkways that lace the grounds. Jonesboro also is home to Arkansas State University, which houses several major attractions, including the Arkansas State Museum, an athletic complex, a convocation center, the Fowler Center, and the Bradbury Art Gallery. Arkansas Delta Byways, regional tourist association for the area, headquarters at the college and serves as a think tank for tourism development for all of eastern Arkansas. Dr. Ruth Hawkins, executive director of the association, is credited as the driving force behind both national scenic byway designations in the Delta. An art deco–inspired courthouse in the historic downtown district is an architectural draw amid numerous fine art galleries and retail shopping.

Marianna is home to Arkansas's latest, and last, state park—Mississippi River State Park. The town square is regarded by many as the most beautiful on the Ridge, featuring a park area, gazebo, Confederate monument, and local courthouse. The Lee County Museum is also convenient to the square, and the Huxtable Pumping Station, the world's largest, monitors the mighty Mississippi River just north of town.

Paragould. Sometimes it just pays to be in the right place at the right time. Paragould has managed to be the right place during many times. In 1930, residents were awakened by a long, loud noise and arose to find an eerie glow in the sky. A meteorite hit just 4 miles from town, leaving two galactic stone fragments—75 pounds and 820 pounds—as souvenirs of its unearthly origins. Less than a decade later, two men fishing the banks of Hurricane Creek unearthed a 3-foot bone from the sandy shore. For a three-week period, the men continued their amateur archaeological excavation, eventually unearthing the bones of a 10,000-year-old mastodon. The town's name is a hybrid formed from the surnames of two rival railroad men critical to the town's founding: Jay Gold and J. W. Paramore.

Piggott. Named in honor of Dr. James A. Piggott, whose petition successfully secured the post office for the area, this picturesque town at the northern tip of Crowley's Ridge is probably best known for its connection to American literary icon Ernest Hemingway, who was married to Piggott native Pauline Pfeiffer while in Paris on assignment for *Vogue* in 1927. Hemingway claimed the barn behind Pauline's parents' house and penned portions of *A Farewell to Arms*, as well as other short stories, in between quail hunting and visiting with Pauline's parents. The Hemingway-Pfeiffer Museum and Educational Center now occupies the former family home; the Matilda and Karl Pfeiffer Museum next door displays a world-class mineral collection for rock hounds on the Ridge.

Wynne. Incorporated after the completion of the St. Louis, Iron Mountain, and Southern Railroad, Wynne was the first stop on the route between Bald Knob and Memphis. Modern-day visitors to the area recount the town's history at the Cross County Museum adjacent to the parkway, and horse lovers come from a four-state area to take advantage of the exquisite equine facilities recently constructed at Village Creek State Park near town. The addition of a 27-hole golf course adjacent to the park has attracted the attention of duffers from throughout the South, and even around the country. The park is the site for a number of events in the region, most notably May's annual Pickin' in the Park, which draws thousands of amateur and semi-pro bluegrass musicians to the grounds for a week of impromptu campfire jam sessions.

✲ To See

MUSEUMS ✐ ♿ **St. Francis County Museum** (870-261-1744), 603 Front Street, Forrest City. Open Tuesday through Saturday 10–5. Free admission. This museum, which also serves as an official national parkway visitor center, is housed in the historic 1906 Rush-Gates Home and is just one of the town's buildings listed on the National Historic Register. Native American pottery and other prehistoric artifacts from the J. O. Rush Relic Collection are exhibited during the museum's normal business hours and by special appointment. Dr. Rush's office is reconstructed here, and the eclectic inventory includes geology and fossils from Crowley's Ridge, local lore and memorabilia, and

ST. FRANCIS COUNTY MUSEUM

ERNEST HEMINGWAY WROTE PASSAGES OF *A FAREWELL TO ARMS* IN PIGGOTT

items that reflect African American history. Don't let the old-fashioned outhouse in the yard alarm you; thoroughly modern water closets are available inside.

⌀ ♿ **Phillips County Museum** (870-338-7790), 623 Pecan Street, Helena. Open Tuesday through Saturday 10–4. Located in the heart of Helena, the museum's portraits of the town's seven Confederate generals remind visitors of the town's significance as a Civil War site and its loyalty to the Confederacy despite being a critical Union stronghold in the South. Ephemera from the era, including letters drafted by Robert E. Lee, provide first-person testimonial of the determination amid devastation that ruled the day. The Mississippi's most prestigious author, Mark Twain, helped establish the museum over a hundred years ago; Thomas Edison's ancestors recently contributed artifacts documenting his scientific discoveries, including actual experiments. Free.

⌀ ♿ **Arkansas State University Museum** (870-972-2074; museum.astate.edu), Dean B. Ellis Library, State University. Open Tuesday 9–7, Wednesday through Saturday 9–5, Sunday 1–5. This museum now occupies 25,000 square feet in the west wing of the Dean B. Ellis Library on the campus of Arkansas State University in Jonesboro. The museum started with a single glass case of archaeological facts in the university's Wilson Hall in 1936 and gained its museum accreditation from the American Association of Museums in 1967. Over 70,000 exhibits cover a broad range of fields of study, of which 24,000 record over 500 million years of change on Crowley's Ridge. Fossil specimens dating from the Paleozoic through the Cenozoic Eras were carefully assembled by Dr. Wittlake, a paleobotanist and the former museum director. Archaeologists and amateurs alike have harvested abundant mastodon finds, as well as giant beaver, sloth, and bison remains. All of these are represented in the museum's collections, along with a nearly complete Paleolama skeleton. Free.

⌀ ♿ **Hemingway-Pfeiffer Museum and Educational Center** (870-598-3487; www.hemingway.astate.edu), 1021 West Cherry Street, Piggott. Open Monday through Saturday 9–5. Tours are offered by appointment, and on a drop-in basis every hour on the hour Monday through Friday 9–3 and Saturday 1–3. Guests can visit the family home of Paul and Mary Pfeiffer, prominent citizens of northeast Arkansas and Ernest

Hemingway's in-laws, as well as the barn/studio where Hemingway wrote portions of *A Farewell to Arms* (he fled to California to finish the book—away from the skeeters and heat of summertime in Piggott). Hemingway visited the area frequently and commemorated one of his visits in the short story "A Day's Wait" in 1933. One of my all-time favorite quotes is from a letter Mary wrote to Hemingway when he divorced her daughter, Pauline. Always the epitome of Southern grace, Pauline references their future with forgiveness, "May we meet again in fairer climes on farther shores." Or maybe she was just wishing the mosquitoes on him. Hemingway-related books are among the unique gifts available in the museum store. Free admission.

   ♿ **Matilda & Karl Pfeiffer Museum & Study Center** (870-598-3228; www.pfeiffer foundation.com), 1071 Heritage Park Drive, Piggott. Open Tuesday through Friday 9–4, Saturday 11–4. This early 1930s Tudor Revival home is situated on 11 acres of natural gardens. Rock hounds relish the 1,400 specimens, many of them rare or one of a kind, in the museum's vast mineral collection. Striking smoky fissures in quartz with pyrite, chunky tomato spessartine, and the funky fuchsia of rhodochrosite on quartz are just a few of the rocks that ROCK! Native American artifacts, collected locally, and a library of over 1,600 volumes round out the museum's permanent displays. Film buffs might recognize the location from scenes filmed there for the 1956 movie *A Face in the Crowd*. The center is next door to the Hemingway-Pfeiffer museum. Groups of 10 or more require reservations. Free.

CULTURAL SITES Historic cemeteries are prolific here because early settlers, including those who lived in the lowlands, buried their dead on the higher ground of Crowley's Ridge. Many of the headstones have unusual grave markings and insightful epitaphs.

   ♿ **Chalk Bluff Battlefield Park** (870-598-2667), CR 368, St. Francis. The town of Chalk Bluff was the site of several Civil War skirmishes, the most significant of which was the May 1–2, 1863, action as Gen. John S. Marmaduke retreated from an unsuccessful raid into Missouri. The town is long gone, but that battle and the town's history are interpreted through markers placed along a walking trail. The park is listed on the National Register and is handicapped accessible.

   Parker Homestead (870-578-2699 or 870-578-9251; www.parkerhomestead.com), 6944 Homestead Road, Harrisburg. Saturday 10–5, Sunday noon–5. This fascinating living-history museum consists of 12 log buildings as well as several other structures, most of which are believed to have been constructed during the late 1800s and early 1900s. Roberts' Chapel is considered the oldest structure in the village; check out the carving just inside the large window as you exit the chapel. Originally a two-room house, the story goes that a woman lived there alone while her men were off fighting the War of Northern Aggression. Union soldiers came through and confiscated her only means of transportation—a little mare. She had the last laugh in the end when she was awakened that evening by the mare's return. (This may also be the state's first unconfirmed and unofficial example of a homing horse.) The village also includes Clark's Cabin, the Loom House, the Broom Shop, the General Store, the Barn, the Blacksmith, the Way Station, the Grist Mill, the Sorghum Mill, the E. Sloan Heritage School, the Smokehouse, and the Post Office and Print Shop. Admission $7 adults, $5 seniors and under 12.

   Delta Cultural Center (870-338-4350; www.deltaculturalcenter.com), 141 Cherry Street, Helena. Open Tuesday through Saturday 9–5. The museum is also open on national Monday holidays throughout the year; closed Thanksgiving, Christmas Eve, Christmas Day, and New Year's Day. Historic downtown Helena was blessed when "Sonny Boy" Williamson chose to broadcast his blues radio program from this Cherry Street location. Williamson still broadcasts *King Biscuit Time* weekly from Blues

TRY THE SIMPLE LIFE AT WITTEN FARMS   ARKANSAS DEPARTMENT OF PARKS & TOURISM

Corner, and exhibits, guided tours, and educational programs detail the rich blues heritage of the city.

The center is divided into two locations: the depot and the visitor center. *A Heritage of Determination*, the featured exhibit on the depot's ground floor, recounts the history of the Delta from its earliest inhabitants, into early settlement, and through great Mississippi River floods. Upstairs, *Civil War in the Delta* gives visitors insight into Union occupation and the Battle of Helena. The visitor center, just one block north, features a *Delta Sounds* music exhibit, the radio studio, a museum store, and temporary exhibit space. Free.

🎣 ♿ **Parkin Archeological State Park** (870-755-2500; www.arkansasstateparks .com/parkinarcheological), P.O. Box 1110, Parkin. Open Monday through Saturday 8–5, Sunday 1–5. Just 6 miles east of Crowley's Ridge, this National Historic Landmark provides a glimpse into life in this Native American village between the years 1400 and 1650, known as the Mississippian Period. The park is believed to be located on the site where the province of Casqui once stood. Referenced in accounts filed by the 1541 de Soto expedition, Casqui was described as the capital of the mound-building cultures in the region. Spanish artifacts have also been recovered at the park, and Parkin's de Soto exhibit is one of the highlights on display. Park visitors are allowed to observe modern archaeologists at work when excavations are underway. The Northern Ohio School, a historic one-room schoolhouse, picnic area, playground, and standard pavilion invite visitors to stay a while and immerse themselves in days gone by. Replicas of the Casqui head pots unearthed at Parkin are among the unique items for sale in the park's gift shop. An enclosed pavilion and a meeting room in the visitor center are available for groups and special events. Admission $3.50 adults; $2.50 ages 6–12; $12 family; special rates for groups and schools are available by calling the park in advance.

COWPOKES WELCOME

Horseback Riding 🐾 **Village Creek State Park** (870-238-9406; www.arkansasstateparks .com/villagecreek), 201 County Road 754, Wynne. Open seven days a week year-round. This 7,600-acre park boasts the finest equestrian facilities in a four-state region. Fondly referred to as the Horse Hilton, this 80-horse barn opened in 2006 and pampers horses with warm showers while captivating riders with its scenic, historic trails and entertaining visitors with unique annual events. Covered stalls and ceiling fans set the 66 bays at Village Creek apart from other facilities; 30 campsites with water and electricity nearby allow owners to keep a close eye on their mounts. Vicki Trimble, a former interpreter at the park and force behind the project and its design, patterned the facility after Land Between the Lakes, a prominent horse camp in Kentucky. Over 25 miles of horse trails meander through the park before crossing over the Trail of Tears as it departs the park. Village Creek is one of the few places left where the public can still walk (and horse trails cross over) the Trail of Tears. The tragic story of the massive relocation of Native Americans is told in interpretive panels, complete with complementary audio tracks, placed at the trailhead and sporadically along its path. Crowley Ridge's extraordinary topography is spotlighted throughout the picturesque trails that meander through the park. Opportunities for wildlife viewing are abundant— huge deer, wild turkeys, and coyote are everywhere. A favorite event for horsemen at the park benefits St. Jude Children's Hospital in Memphis, Tennessee, and is one of the most well-attended equine-oriented fundraisers for the organization. Mule-driven wagon rides, horseback rides, dinner, and a live auction have enticed even the physicians at St. Jude to become annual participants.

✳ To Do

CANOE OUTFITTERS **Quapaw Canoe Company** (870-228-2266; www.island63.com), 411 Ohio Street, Helena–West Helena. Finally, there is an outfitter on the Mississippi River! The Quapaw Canoe Company opened in June 2008 and is the only outfitter on the lower Mississippi River. Helena is the only city directly on the river between Memphis and Vicksburg, making it a logical choice for the company. The Mighty Mississippi is not a solo gig for novice paddlers, however, and the owners caution that only those proficient in canoeing should attempt self-guided tours. Guided excursion options offered by Quapaw range from whole-day and half-day trips from Helena to multiday trips paddling the entire river. Fees include paddles, life jackets, and safety equipment. Quapaw Canoe is open Tuesday through Sunday 9–5 and by appointment.

GOLF **The Ridges at Village Creek** (870-238-6500; www.theridgesatvillagecreek .com), 4268 AR 284, Wynne. Open daily during spring and summer, excluding holidays, 6–7. Fall and winter play, weather permitting, is available Monday through Sunday 1–5. Even if you don't play golf, you will love this course. They could make a small fortune just renting carts to tourists interested in driving the cart paths for one of the best driving tours of Crowley's Ridge. Set on 600 acres next to Village Creek State Park, the striking green fairways cleared for play now allow for a clearer view under the lofty canopy of the Ridge's trademark hardwood forest. The 7,449-yard, par 72 course features 27 holes designed by international developer and world-class golf course architect Andy Dye. Day rates for 18 holes re $39.50 Monday through Friday, $49 weekends. Twilight rates begin at 2 and are $27.50 Monday through Friday, $32.50 weekends.

Sage Meadows (870-932-4420; www.sagemeadows.com), 4406 Clubhouse Drive, Jonesboro. This Tommy Bolt signature links-style course with zoysia fairways, bent grass greens, and Bermuda roughs features water on 9 of the 18 holes and 37 sand bunkers. Sage Meadows is one of only 13 courses that make up the prestigious Arkansas Golf Trail. The course plays at roughly 6,900 yards and is consistently ranked among the top semiprivate golf courses in the state. With a full driving range, double end tees, and a short game practice area, Sage Meadows has been featured in golf magazines and offers great tournament play. Holes of note include the 6th hole, with its tight tee shot between water on the left and trees on the right; the course's signature 9th hole, with its beautiful but treacherous water hazard from tee to green; and the 14th hole, which is considered one of the toughest on the course if not played properly. While tee times are preferred, walk-ups are allowed (but not easy). Proper golf attire is required, collared shirts and soft spikes only. Club facilities include a 5,000-plus-square-foot clubhouse with a fully stocked golf shop, grill and snack bar, and private lounge. Memberships for the private lounge are available to the general public for a nominal fee.

Forrest L. Wood Crowley's Ridge Nature Center (870-933-6787; www.crowleysridge .org), 600 East Lawson Road, Jonesboro. The center is open Tuesday through Saturday 8:30–4, Sunday 1–5. Indoor and outdoor exhibits walk you through the history and geology of this unique natural region in Arkansas. Outdoor skills workshops are held throughout the year. A calendar on the center's website will tell you what programs will be offered when you are in town. Walk into the main level of the center, where an exhibit hall and auditorium present the story of the Ridge's formation and its wildlife through several hands-on exhibits and a special 16-minute feature film with animation and special effects that will shake you where you sit. Surround sound, sure, but it is also a fascinating story with Mother Nature playing the lead. A two-story diorama extends from the lower level of the center upward to the main level. The display explores the plants, animals, and hydrology native to the Ridge's landscape.

✳ Wild Places

Arkansas's Game and Fish Commission is one of the largest land managers in the state, overseeing wildlife management areas, hunting and fishing permits, and the administration of outdoor safety programs. The agency's website, www.agfc.com, is an excellent resource, and it even includes safety education videos.

Earl Buss Bayou DeView (1-877-972-5438; www.agfc.com/en/zone-map/688/). This wildlife management area lies along the Bayou DeView River from AR 17 to just north of AR 214. The Weiner area is one of the principal rice-producing areas in the state and is considered by many to be one of the best duck-hunting areas in Arkansas. This management area is one of the few remaining blocks of bottomland hardwood timber left in western Poinsett County and still provides good quality waterfowl hunting. Lake Hogue is a 300-acre impoundment located on the east side of the bayou across from the south end of the Oliver tract. Access to the lake is off AR 49, about 2 miles south of Weiner. Crappie, bream, bass, and catfish provide good fishing year-round. Primitive camping areas are provided on each of the management area's three tracts. Except for graveled parking areas, there are no other improvements to camping facilities. Mosquitoes and biting flies are a nuisance in warm weather and insect repellent is essential. Venomous snakes, including cottonmouths, copperheads, and timber rattlers, are present. It is illegal to indiscriminately kill snakes, so they should be avoided and left alone when possible. The area can best be reached by county roads west out of Weiner on AR 49 or off AR 14 or AR 214.

St. Francis Wildlife Management Area (1-877-734-4581), AR 44, Marianna. This 20,946-acre forest, between the towns of Marianna and Helena–West Helena on the southern tip of Crowley's Ridge, is bounded on the east and south by the L'Anguille, St. Francis, and Mississippi Rivers, Wire Road on the west, and Jeffersonville Road on the north. It consists of upland hardwood forests located on the hilly Crowley's Ridge section, with approximately 2,500 acres of bottomland timber adjacent to the St. Francis and Mississippi Rivers. The St. Francis has two manmade lakes, Bear Creek Lake and Storm Creek Lake, established in 1938 and opened for fishing in 1940 and 1942, respectively. Both provide fishing and other water-based recreational opportunities, along with some of the most intimately situated campsites in the state. Bear Creek Lake is located on the north end of the forest near Marianna. Storm Creek Lake is located on the southern end, near Helena, making it a popular choice for campers attending the Arkansas Blues and Heritage Festival in the fall. The campsites at both Bear Creek and Storm Creek Lakes are semiprivate, meaning there are restrooms, tent pads, trailer areas, grills, picnic tables, and water sources, but no electricity. Both lakes have been stocked with bass, bream, crappie, and catfish, and Storm Creek with hybrid striped bass. Hiking trails have been established near the campgrounds on Bear Creek, where birdwatchers and wildlife photographers have ample opportunities to see and photograph wildlife, songbirds, and other nongame species. Beaver Pond on the east side along the St. Francis River has been stocked with alligators, and eagles have been sighted around the Bear Creek area.

A race of Indians known as the Mound Builders once inhabited the area. Their dead were buried in mounds, along with implements considered necessary for existence in another world. In 1961, archaeologists investigating a large mound near Helena found that these people were of a race much older than the American Indian. A French trading post was established above Helena in 1766; it later became Montgomery's Point, one of the most noted landings on the Mississippi River. The first white settlement was near the mouth of the St. Francis River, which has since been taken by the Mississippi River. It is said that the first white child born at this settlement was supposedly the first white child born in Arkansas. Two cemeteries with stones dating back to the early 1800s remind hikers and history buffs of the area's previous residents. This wildlife management area is accessible by AR 44 from Marianna and by AR 1 and AR 242 from Helena–West Helena.

St. Francis Sunken Lands (1-877-972-5438). This area can be reached off several state highways from south of Paragould to Marked Tree. Major access points are the Siphons Access off AR 63 near Marked Tree, Oak Donnick Access south of Trumann off AR 63 near Tulot, and Stephens Landing off AR 69 east of Trumann. The east side of the area may be reached by either of two county roads off AR 135 between Caraway and Rivervale. However, the best access to the interior of the area is by boat at ramps provided at Siphons Access, Oak Donnick Access, Stephens Landing, Mangrum Landing, Iron Bridge Access, and Lake City AR 18 bridge access. The Sunken Lands were the result of the New Madrid Earthquakes of 1811 and 1812. The lower end of the floodway contains St. Francis Lake, which is a large, open expanse of water. In reality, St. Francis Lake is a wide part of the St. Francis River. While the lake is fairly shallow due to accelerated silt deposits over the years, it still provides good catfish, bass, bream, and crappie fishing. Access to the lake may be obtained from either the Siphons Access or Oak Donnick Access. The area offers excellent opportunities for wildlife viewing and bird-watching. The Payneway Moist Soil Unit located on the west side of the river, just north of the St. Francis Lake control structure, hosts a variety of shorebirds, eagles, and several duck species. The area is flooded annually from October through February to provide wintering habitat for migrant birds and ducks. The area's designation as a

LAKE POINSETT STATE PARK

waterfowl rest area protects them from hunting, and as many as 50,000 ducks are commonly seen here. Bottomland hardwoods make up the primary species of timber types associated with the area and include white oak, red oak, hickory, locust, cottonwood, bald cypress, tupelo, elm, sycamore, and pecan.

For the L'Anguille and St. Francis Rivers, see "Exploring by River."

STATE PARKS ♂ ♿ **Crowley's Ridge State Park** (870-573-6751; www.arkansasstate parks.com/crowleysridge), 2092 AR 168 North, Paragould. Crowley's Ridge State Park in northeast Arkansas is a recreationally oriented park on 291 acres with a rich social and geological history. The park, situated on land that was homesteaded by nineteenth-century pioneer Benjamin F. Crowley, also preserves the structures built by young men in the Civilian Conservation Corps during the 1930s. Four CCC structures within the park—a bridge on the main park road, a bathhouse, the CCC comfort station, and the Group Lodge dining hall—are on the National Register of Historic Places. Because of the spring and tree-shaded grounds at Crowley's homestead, the site became a traditional summer campground, picnic site, and gathering place. Thus, it was the first choice of area residents when the state started accepting lands for public parks, and on July 21, 1933, it became the fourth of Arkansas's state parks. A massive stone-and-log CCC bathhouse/pavilion remains the focal point of the park, which also has a 31-acre fishing lake built in the mid-1960s. Four fully equipped cabins with kitchens, bunk cabins for group lodging, and 26 campsites offer visitors diverse lodging opportunities at the park. Picnic areas, a snack bar, hiking trails, and a 3.5-acre swimming lake round out the day-use facilities at the park. Crowley's Ridge State Park has 26 campsites: 18 offer electricity and water ($17 per night), and 8 tent sites are without hook-ups ($10). Cabin rates vary by occupancy and season; online booking is available on the park's website.

♂ ♿ **Lake Frierson State Park** (870-932-2615, www.arkansasstateparks.com/ lakefrierson), 7904 AR 141, Jonesboro. This park, located on the shore of 335-acre Lake Frierson, not only attracts visitors to the Natural State for year-round fishing but also draws the locals looking for fun and recreation. Bream, catfish, crappie, and bass satisfy those that want to wet their hook; fishing boats, kayaks, and pedal boats extend the fun from the shore onto the water. The park's resident gaggle of geese numbers about 40, and while they are not aggressive, they will waddle right up to you looking for food.

(Park staff keep it handy; ask in the visitor center.) An enclosed climate-controlled pavilion with outdoor grill on the lake's shore is an excellent spot for group gatherings in any season. The park's half-mile-long Dogwood Lane is a self-guided interpretive trail with a 0.2-mile spur that leads to the visitor center. Along this trail you should also watch for deer, squirrels, raccoons, opossums, snakes, box turtles, songbirds, and wildflowers. This park is active in the community and offers several neat interpretive programs from which to choose: Dutch oven cooking workshops, hand-led horseback rides for kids, and kayak dinner cruises are just a few of the unique activities available at this park. The evening kayak tour is followed by a Dutch oven meal on the shoreline and an interpretive astronomy program. Of course, by the time you get to the stargazing portion of the evening, flat on your back is a great place to be!

🎣 ♿ **Lake Poinsett State Park** (870-578-2064; www.arkansasstateparks.com/lakepoinsett), 5752 State Park Lane, Harrisburg. This recreational park is a special getaway for anglers looking for bass, bream, catfish, and crappie. Fishing enthusiasts find the shallow waters of 640-acre Lake Poinsett excellent for catching a large stringer of these species. The park offers 29 campsites, two picnic areas, a nature/hiking trail, a playground, and a pavilion, all spread out over 132 acres. Boat and kayak rentals are available for water play. Interpretative programs are available throughout the year, including guided-kayak tours and annual special events. The park attracts over 93,000 visitors annually. Of the 29 campsites available, four have 50-amp electric and water ($21), 22 have 30-amp electric and water ($17), and three have no hook-ups at all ($10).

🎣 ♿ 🚲 **Village Creek State Park** (870-238-9406; www.arkansasstateparks.com/villagecreek), 201 CR 754, Wynne. This beautiful park is 7,000 acres of outdoor fun in the heart of Crowley's Ridge. Much of Village Creek remains in its natural state, and frequently the white-tailed deer seem to outnumber the guests at the park. The park has two lakes (Lake Dunn and Lake Austell) for fishing and boating, with bait, boats, motors, kayaks, and pedal boats available late spring through Labor Day. The 33-acre Lake Dunn is about as close as an adult can get to fishing in a barrel without embarrassment; catfish in the 30-pound range have been hooked, along with lunker bass and pan-sized crappie. For over 20 years, Dunn has been delighting fishermen with a steady yield of big Florida-strain largemouth bass. Since 1987, dozens of over-8-pound bass have been caught in Lake Dunn. Lake Austell, at 85 acres, made headlines in 1989, when a 15-pound, 12-ounce largemouth bass was hooked by a lucky angler.

PRO TIP: Village Creek State Park is a great place for fall color. The last couple of weeks in October through the first week in November typically fall within peak viewing time. Generous green space between cabins and campsites turns yellow and gold, tangibly tinting the air with soft, warm light. On the Ridge, fall color isn't viewed from vistas but from within its forests, along its footpaths, and while boating its lakes and rivers.

The park has 10 fully equipped cabins with kitchens, flat-screen televisions, fireplaces, and screened-in porches. The park visitor center features an A/V theater, gift shop, and bicycle rentals in addition to year-round interpretive programs. Camping options at Village Creek include 24 with 50-amp electric, water, and sewer ($27 a day), 5 with 50-amp electric and water ($21), and 67 with 30-amp electric and water ($17) for RVs, tents, and horse campers.

🎣 ♿ **Mississippi River State Park** (870-238-2188; www.arkansasstateparks.com/mississippiriver), 2675 AR 44, Marianna. A special-use permit from the US Forest Service paved the way for Arkansas State Parks to develop state park facilities within the St. Francis National Forest near Marianna. With 20,946 acres available, Mississippi River State Park's development plan is scheduled to occur in three phases; the first project, the new Beech Point Campground at Bear Creek Lake, reopened under the state park management system in October 2015. The 625-acre lake lies within the north end of the St. Francis National Forest, and two national scenic byways—the Great River Road and the Crowley's Ridge Parkway—pass nearby. More than 15 miles of shoreline make for an abundance of good fishing for big bluegill and redear when the fish are in shallow water on the spawning beds. Look for beds of spawning fish on the gradually sloping banks, particularly near points, and also in the backs of the wider (and therefore shallower) coves. Abundant wildlife readily seen in the national forest includes white-tailed deer, squirrel, raccoon, rabbit, wild turkey, and a wide variety of other birds. Swimming and hiking are available at the lake, as are three campgrounds (41 individual campsites and 1 group site) that remain open year-round. No bathhouses are available, and the campgrounds rely on vault-style toilets. The only hook-ups available are for water at 17 campsites ($4).

❄ Lodging

BED & BREAKFAST INNS **Edwardian Inn** (870-338-9155; www.edwardianinn .com), 317 Biscoe Street, Helena. William Short built this Colonial Revival in 1904 as a family home for his wife and two daughters. Mr. John Crow's hospitality and the home's exquisite restoration and antique furnishings invite guests to immerse themselves in the South's relaxed pace and impeccable social graces. The earthy hues of quarter-sawn paneling used extensively throughout the house provide an elegant backdrop for its ornate antiques, luxurious drapery, and richly upholstered parlor. The huge porch that wraps around its sunny yellow exterior is sanctuary to spectators and storytellers on warm summer nights. One of the most unusual features of this property is the flooring—wood carpeting that was made of parquet from 1-inch wooden strips and mounted on canvas, then shipped from Germany on rolls. The Edwardian's nine rooms and three suites, each with separate bath, feature portraits of historically prominent southerners among their historical appointments. Modern conveniences, such as Wi-Fi, have been thoughtfully grandfathered into the home's modernization. Rates for the nine guest rooms start at $85; the three suites lease for $115 daily, with special packages available for extended stays. Smoking and pets are not allowed; obedient children are welcome. $–$$.

❄ Where to Eat

EATING OUT 🦐 **Bailee Mae's** (870-753-2809 or 870 338-2725; www.baileemaes .com), 209 Rightor Street, Helena. Open Monday through Friday 7–2, Saturday 8–1. Bailee Mae's is housed in the historic Lewis Supply Building in downtown Helena–West Helena. High ceilings and large windows fill the dining room with light. Exposed brick and duct work give the restored space an edgy, updated look. Owners opened Bailey Mae's to fill a void in town and provide locals and tourists with a specialty coffee shop in the morning that became a wine and craft beer bar in the evening. The menu is small, but the dishes are well prepared. Burgers and sandwiches, cactus chili, and exotic flatbreads provide a wide variety of flavors and appeal to the most discriminating palate. $–$$.

Granny Dee's Soul Food (870-817-0200), 426 Cherry Street, Helena–West Helena. Open seven days a week for breakfast and lunch; hours vary, but Granny will usually hang around until 2 p.m. or so on weekdays and 3 p.m. on the weekends. Granny Dee has the last remaining soul food restaurant in town. Sure, some folks bring out their grills for the blues festival, but Granny Dee is the only one you can count on like, well, your granny. Everything is fresh from the garden (or barn) and made from scratch by Granny Dee. Her maternal instincts kick in every half hour or so, and she emerges from her kitchen to mingle with diners and take pictures with tourists. Crispy, Southern-fried catfish and tangy BBQ ribs are staples on the lunch buffet, which includes a variety of salads and vegetable sides. Daily specials include pork chops, glazed ham, and chicken-fried steaks. Golden and flaky fruit cobbler tempts diners to loosen their belt buckles to sample the perfect rendition of this sweet Southern specialty. Menu items are all less than $10. $.

Pasquale's Original Tamales (870-338-1109; www.sucktheshuck.com), 1005 Highway 49, Helena–West Helena. These legendary packets of beef and spices are sold from a concession stand from 10:30–5 on Friday and Saturday. The rest of the week, you will have to order them from their website. If you are in Helena, you owe it to yourself to try them fresh. Pasquale St. Colombia migrated to the town from Italy in the late 1800s. He supported himself and his family by feeding the Hispanic migrant workers tending fields in the area. Pasquale was a friendly guy, and his ability to speak Italian enabled him to communicate with and befriend the workers. Soon they were sharing the techniques and recipes for their native dishes, and St. Colombia began to put his spin on the tamale, crafting a process that took three days to complete. In the 1940s, Pasquale built a commercial building and leased space to Maggie and Eugene Brown. Using Pasquale's recipe, the couple operated Elm Street Tamale Shop for 20 years. In the '60s, the Brown family died off and the business did, too. It would lay dormant for 30 years until Joe St. Colombia decided to retire from his career in beer distribution to revive the family business. Joe and his wife, Joyce, tinkered with the recipe a bit, perfecting the spice blend and settling on sirloin for the beef filling. The tamales are soaked for six hours in a broth so tasty customers commonly suck the cooking liquid from the shucks

that encase them. Thus the company's tagline: "So good you will suck the shuck." Pasquale's tamales have no preservatives and are flash-frozen following steaming to ensure their flavor holds for shipping. While they are best when eaten at the stand fresh from the pan, there is a reason thousands are shipped around the country every year. $–$$.

Red Goose Deli (870-236-6223), 117 Pruett Street, Paragould. Open daily for lunch and dinner. If you like a little frou-frou in your menu, the Red Goose Deli in downtown Paragould should suit your taste. It's not that the menu is so nouveau cuisine, it's more about the detail to the recipes. The sauces are just a little more complex, prepared by experienced hands, and feature fresh, locally grown ingredients. The house specialty sandwich, the Red Goose Royale, is a turkey and ham combination with a creamy parmesan spinach dressing and just a hint of jalapeño. The turkey and ham are folded side by side, a sophisticated twist. The homemade potato chips served on the side are crisp and perfectly seasoned. (Eat them while they are hot!) There is a daily special, and they are known for their hamburger steaks at night. Desserts are prepared fresh in-house every day and are well worth a doggie bag for half your sandwich if necessary. Soups, salads, and sandwiches are under $10. Dinner meals average $20 per person, including your non-alcoholic beverage. $.

DINING OUT **The Bistro Bar and Grill** (870-572-9707, www.cityofhelenawest helena.com/Bistro.html), 213 Plaza Street, Helena–West Helena. This little café in downtown Helena serves baskets with shrimp or chicken, mini cheeseburgers and sandwiches, as well as appetizers like nachos or chips with homemade salsa. They have a happy hour daily from 5–7p.m., and daily specials include porterhouse steaks, chicken and waffles, and catfish platters. $–$$

AWARD-WINNING CAJUN CRAWFISH IN THE DELTA

Cajun Express (870-457-2572), 5018 North AR 78, Wheatley. Cajun Express is the definition of destination dining. Located 4 miles north of the intersection of I-40 and AR 78, you could easily fly right by it if you didn't know where to look. But of course, now you will know. Robin and Randy Gehring are the chief cooks, bottle washers, and mudbug runners for the restaurant. Or at least from early spring to late June, when they harvest their own crawfish from the large agriculture pond behind their restaurant. And if you come through at the right time, or call ahead, you can hop on Randy's Inspector Gadget–like mudbug boat and go along for the ride. You will launch from the bank, so lean back when the boat enters the water, as your seat will get wet if water flows over the bow. If you are interested, one of them will find the time to show you their process from pond to pot. Everything that comes out of the kitchen has been prepared by Robin or Randy. "We decided when we started that we would succeed or fail by our own hands," Robin explains. That's the reason Cajun Express is only open two days a week: Friday and Saturday from 4:30–9:30 p.m. The menu is as you would expect from a restaurant with "Cajun" in the name, but prepare yourself for truly championship cooking. This Arkansas couple riled more than a few in Louisiana when they won the National Crawfish Boil down there in 2006. The decor is east Arkansas hunting lodge, with trophy fish and game mounted on the walls among photos of their neighbors and kids. Large, recycled tomato cans hold condiments and paper towels, and may get in the way when the waitress brings your food. It's hard to beat certified Angus beef, but you can put theirs up against the best of them. They refuse to reveal the spices they rub on the beef prior to cooking, but steak sauce would be a tragic waste in this case. Crawfish are served almost every way you can imagine—boiled, fried, in gumbo, and étouffée—and if you have never enjoyed a crawfish pie, this would be the time to try it. The tails are placed in a flaky torte shell with a cream base, covered with cheese, and baked until golden bubbly. Frog legs are lightly breaded, fried crisp on the outside, juicy on the inside, and without a drop of grease to spare. Robin recently added Gator Balls to the menu, and they are already a local favorite. Picture a cross between a hush puppy and a crab-cake and served with a Thai-inspired plum dipping sauce. The dessert menu changes daily, but if the pineapple cream cheese pie is available when you are there, get it to go. You won't have room to eat for a day or so, and it is not to be missed. $–$$$.

✳ Selective Shopping

Bubba's Blues Corner (870-338-3501) 105 Cherry Street, Helena. Open Monday through Friday 10–5, Saturday 10–2. When your shop is located on historic Cherry Street, just down the road from the studio where "Sunshine" Sonny Payne broadcast the longest-running blues radio program in the world, you meet a lot of blues musicians. You make a lot of friends, and you pick up unique memorabilia and hard-to-find music. Since opening in 1987, Bubba Sullivan's corner of the shop has grown in area and global recognition. Musicians and collectors from around the world have shared their music, their memorabilia, and their love of the genre and its history with Bubba and his customers. Look for great advice on music to buy and great gift ideas for the music lovers in your life.

✳ Special Events

May: **Loose Caboose Festival** (870-240-0544; www.loosecaboose.net), Paragould. Paragould's Loose Caboose Festival is the largest free music festival in the area, including bluegrass, rock, karaoke, and country, all leading up to Saturday night's featured entertainer. The festival also includes a 5K walk/run, large children's area, bike ride, fish fry, the state's

THE BIGGEST, THE BEST, THE BISCUIT

The King Biscuit Blue Festival (870-572-5223, kingbiscuitfestival.com), downtown Helena. Visit their website for dates, times, and lineup. There are those who note the passing of summer and arrival of fall by the changing color of the foliage as the nights grow cooler and shorter. However, blues lovers are more likely to see the fluffy, white tufts of cotton lining the two-lane backroads of Arkansas as signs that October has arrived, bringing with it a pilgrimage of musicians and fans to the town that first gave the genre national and international exposure. On November 21, 1941, *King Biscuit Time* aired its first broadcast, featuring Sonny Boy Williams and Robert Lockwood Jr. playing live in the KFFA studio in Helena. The 30-minute-long live program was named after its sponsor, King Biscuit Flour, which was distributed by the Interstate Grocer Company. KFFA was the only station in the country to broadcast music by African Americans, and it aired at 12:15 p.m. daily to coincide with Delta workers' lunch breaks. Jim O'Neal, blues historian and founding editor of *Living Blues* magazine, credits the program with linking the genre to the region. B. B. King, Robert Nighthawk, James Cotton, and Ike Turner have all credited the show with inspiring their careers. Helena became a stopping point for Delta blues artists traveling through the area on their way to the clubs in Chicago and Memphis. The program is now the nation's longest-running radio show, eclipsing mainstream standout *American Bandstand* and the legendary country program, *Grand Ole Opry*.

By the mid-1980s, Helena's once bustling economy was stagnant, as businesses closed and city leaders were at a loss as to how they could slow the exodus and shore up its financial resources. Small towns were encouraged to develop festivals to draw locals into town and attract visitors to support their remaining businesses with their tourism dollars. The Sonny Boy Blues Society saw an opportunity to solidify the town's musical heritage, and in 1986 the King Biscuit Blues Festival was born. The festival annually draws legendary performers like Dave Mason and Steve Cropper, Taj Mahal, and Bonnie Raitt to its headliner's stage, and it is also a proving ground for up-and-comers who set their own stage on Cherry Street.

largest Ferris wheel, and an incredible petting zoo.

June: **Annual Wynne Farm Fest** (870-238-4183), downtown Wynne. This family-friendly event features live entertainment, music, arts and crafts, children's games, food, a 5K walk/run, PBJ Happee Days Carnival, and more. Free admission.

September: ♂ ♿ **Annual Pumpkin Hollow Pumpkin Patch** (870-598-3568; www.pumpkinhollow.com), 610 CR 336, Piggott. Visitors are welcomed by colorful gourd-head scarecrows who invite you to sit with them for a photo opportunity. This is your chance to participate in corn mazes, hayrides, catfish feeding, pony rides (weekends), pig scrambles (weekends), farm animals, Li'l Kids Spookhouse, Fairytale Forest, kids' train ride, and more. Shop for pumpkins, mums, cornstalks, gourds, T-shirts, and souvenirs. Sample a slice of homegrown pumpkin pie or pumpkin roll.

OPPOSITE: ARKANSAS DEPARTMENT OF PARKS & TOURISM

THE WEST GULF COASTAL PLAIN

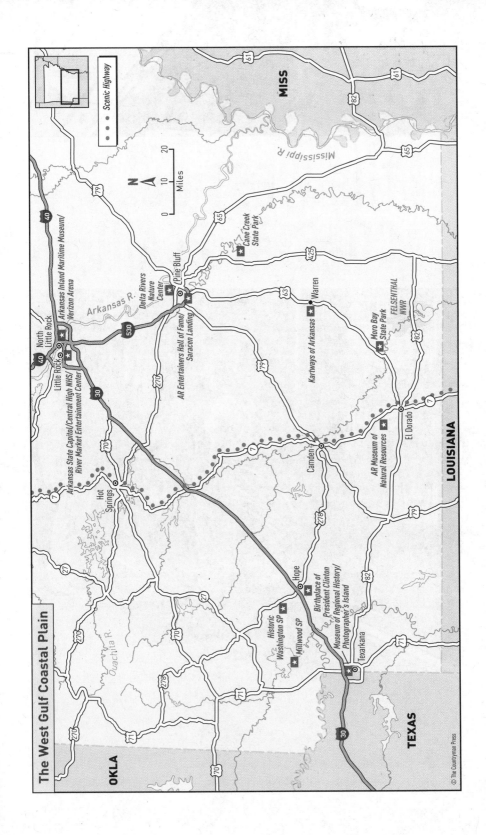

The West Gulf Coastal Plain

Scenic Highway

OKLA

Ouachita R.

270

27

8

70

70

278

70

771

30

TEXAS

71

82

Texarkana

Museum of Regional History/
Photographer's Island

Birthplace of
President Clinton

Hope

Millwood SP

Historic
Washington SP

67

70

278

82

79

LOUISIANA

El Dorado

7

AR Museum of
Natural Resources

FELSENTHAL
NWR

82

Moro Bay
State Park

Camden

278

Kartways of Arkansas

79

Warren

63

425

Cane Creek
State Park

65

Mississippi R.

65

82

61

61

MISS

Pine Bluff

AR Entertainers Hall of Fame/
Saracen Landing

Delta Rivers
Nature
Center

530

270

Arkansas R.

Arkansas Inland Maritime Museum/
Verizon Arena

North
Little Rock

40

Little Rock

Arkansas State Capitol/Central High NHS/
River Market Entertainment Center

30

40

70

7

Hot
Springs

7

79

N

Miles

0   10   20

© The Countryman Press

THE WEST GULF COASTAL PLAIN

The portion of the Coastal Plain Natural Division referred to as the West Gulf Coastal Plain (that part of the Gulf Coastal Plain west of the Mississippi River) extends from Oklahoma, Texas, and Louisiana, across southern Arkansas northward to the Ouachita Mountains, and reaches southern Little Rock (Pulaski County). Major Arkansas cities in this area include Magnolia (Columbia County), Camden (Ouachita County), Monticello (Drew County), El Dorado (Union County), and part of Pine Bluff (Jefferson County).

Geologically, the West Gulf Coastal Plain has been submerged by the Gulf of Mexico and its larger tributaries several times throughout Earth's history. Consequently, its loose, sandy soil, derived from the ocean bottom, is generally unsuitable for row-crop agriculture but makes a fertile field for the state's timber industry, earning its designation as "The Timberlands." Also found beneath the soil of this part of the state are healthy deposits of oil and brine, and the sparkling gems of North America's only public diamond mine. Sediment left by the larger rivers flowing through the region terraced the shelves along their banks with pockets of precious rich farmland, and blackland prairie appears sparingly in the region.

The gentle landscape of the region allowed its settlement to develop directly around its geological riches in El Dorado, near Arkansas's southern border with Louisiana, and in Murfreesboro near the diamond mine. A number of the state's political centers have historically been located in this region, most notably the Confederate Capitol at Washington (now a state park) and the current state Capitol in the Little Rock/North Little Rock metropolitan area. Between the two, the small town of Hope foretells national history at the birthplace of President William Jefferson Clinton. Texarkana, named for the two states that claim it, showcases the culture and heritage of both from its southwestern corner of the state.

The state's diamonds are scattered on the fields of Crater of Diamonds State Park, but there are gems scattered throughout the West Gulf Coastal Plain. This region is rich with nationally important historic sites, including the nation's 12th presidential archive and immaculately maintained Civil War battlefields. You will find upscale shopping and dining, and a cosmopolitan selection of entertainment options that range from symphonic strains on the banks of the Arkansas River to operatic arias on the gilded stage of the Perot Theatre. With a gentle terrain that welcomes all fitness levels, recreational facilities are abundant, providing a perfect setting for multigenerational family reunions.

This chapter separates the region into three sections: Little Rock/North Little Rock Metropolitan Area, Eastern Timberlands, and Western Timberlands.

AREA CODES The majority of the region, excluding the Little Rock–North Little Rock area, falls within the 870 area code. The capital city uses the 501 area code.

GUIDANCE The **Heart of Arkansas Travel Association** (501-370-3209; www .heartofarkansas.com) is a good resource for the Little Rock/North Little Rock

PRESIDENT BILL CLINTON'S BOYHOOD HOME IN HOPE   ARKANSAS DEPARTMENT OF PARKS & TOURISM

metropolitan area. There are two tourist associations representing the communities in the Eastern Timberlands area of the West Gulf Coastal Plain: **Land of Legends Travel** (870-536-8742; www.arlandoflegends.com) promotes attractions in the Pine Bluff area; **Arkansas' South** tourism association (870-814-9676; www.arkansassouth.com) represents the counties in southeastern Arkansas. **Arkansas's Great Southwest** (870-777-7500; www.agsw.org) is your source for information about the Western Timberlands. Information on attractions and events in all communities can be found by contacting the local chamber of commerce office. Addresses are listed for chambers that operate a visitor center or keep regular office hours. If no address is listed, start with the website, and if you need additional information, give them a call.

Bradley County Chamber of Commerce (870-226-5225; www.bradleychamber.com).

Camden Area Chamber of Commerce (870-836-6426).

El Dorado Chamber of Commerce (870-863-6113; www.GoElDorado.com), 111 West Main, El Dorado.

Greater Pine Bluff Chamber of Commerce (870-535-0110; www.pinebluffchamber .com).

Hope-Hempstead County Chamber of Commerce (870-777-3640; www.hope melonfest.com).

Arkansas at the Center (1-866-672-7682; www.arkansasatthecenter.com) is a partnership between the Little Rock and North Little Rock communities that markets their attractions jointly.

Little Rock Convention & Visitors Bureau (1-800-844-4781; www.littlerock.com).

North Little Rock Convention & Visitors Bureau (501-758-1424; www.northlittlerock .org).

Pine Bluff Convention & Visitors Bureau (870-536-2120; www.pinebluffcvb.org), 1 Convention Center Plaza, Pine Bluff.

Texarkana Chamber of Commerce (903-792-7191; www.texarkana.org).

GETTING THERE *By auto:* For most of this region, I-40 will provide the most direct east-west access. The exception would be the southern portion of the Coastal Plain, but you will find US 82 is a straight shot across the state's Louisiana border. AR 7 runs through the center of the state, providing a scenic drive from the Missouri or Louisiana border. If you are looking for a four-lane highway, I-425 enters Arkansas's southern border with Louisiana near Crossett and will take you most of the way to Little Rock.

By air: **Little Rock National Airport** (501-372-3439; www.clintonairport.com), 1 Airport Drive, Little Rock. Airlines that service the Little Rock Airport include Allegiant Air, American Airlines, Delta, Southwest, Frontier Airlines, United, and Via Airlines.

MEDICAL EMERGENCIES Three full-service hospitals in the Little Rock/North Little Rock area give you a few options for healthcare. The Baptist Health Group operates a number of clinics in addition to the hospital; if you aren't facing a medical emergency and clinic services will do, check their website for a location near you.

Baptist Health Medical Center–Little Rock (501-202-2000; www.baptisthealth .com) 9601 I-630, Exit 7, Little Rock.

St. Vincent Infirmary Medical Center (501-552-3000; www.chistvincent.com), 2 St. Vincent Circle, Little Rock.

University of Arkansas for Medical Sciences (501-686-8000; www.uams.edu), 4301 West Markham Street, Little Rock.

✳ Wandering Around

EXPLORING BY FOOT **Arkansas River Trail** (www.arkansasrivertrail.org) is an 88-mile loop along the Arkansas River through the central cities of the state including Little Rock, North Little Rock, Maumelle, and Conway. The flat terrain of the river's edge makes the trail an accessible recreational option for all ages and fitness levels. The entire project connects 38 parks, six museums, and 5,000 acres of federal, state and local parkland. There is also an urban route that is a 15.6 mile loop that starts at the Clinton Presidential bridge in Little Rock and crosses the river to downtown North Little Rock. The trail continues along the shoreline before crossing the river again at the Big Dam Bridge. There are three bike repair stations on the route, two information stations, and plenty of fully accessible restroom facilities. Bicycle rentals are provided by Rock Town River Outfitters with daily rental rates ranging from $54.50 for a comfort hybrid bike to $75.00 for a high performance street bike.

The Big Dam Bridge (501-340-6800; www.bigdambridge.com). The longest pedestrian/bicycle bridge in the world built specifically for pedestrians and bicyclists and the second longest in the United States, the over $9 million project connects 14 miles of trails on the Little Rock and North Little Rock sides of the Arkansas River. The bridge is 14 feet wide, rises nearly seven stories above the river, and connects with 7,000 acres of city, county, state, and federal park land.

Photographer's Island (903-792-7191; www.texarkana.org), 500 North Stateline Avenue, Texarkana. On the region's western border with the Lone Star State, Photographer's Island is a unique opportunity to shoot your selfie while standing in two separate states—Arkansas and Texas—at the same time. Texarkana's State Line Post Office and Federal Building is the only US post office that sits in two states. It is the second-most photographed courthouse in the country.

EXPLORING BY TROLLEY **River Rail Trolley** (501-375-6717; rrmetro.org/services/streetcar). Downtown areas of Little Rock and North Little Rock are now linked by replicas of vintage trolleys. The system comprises 3.4 miles of track and three operating streetcars. Attractions serviced include Verizon Arena, the State House Convention Center, the River Market, hotels, restaurants, the Historic Arkansas and Discovery Museums, Robinson Center Music Hall, and Riverfront Park and Amphitheater. An extension connects the route to the Clinton Presidential Center and Heifer International Global Headquarters.

EXPLORING BY WATER **Arkansas River** (501-324-5551; www.swl.usace.army.mil). Flowing between two of Arkansas's largest cities is one of the best fisheries in the state; the Arkansas River is loaded with game fish, including largemouth bass and catfish. The US Army Corps of Engineers manages numerous public use areas, including campgrounds, boat ramps, and fishing areas, along the length of the river through the state. **Maumelle Park**, the only public campground in Little Rock, is a Corps of Engineers facility on the river that features a fishing pier, playground, showers, flush toilets, 129 camping spaces with water and electricity, boat ramp, and day-use picnic area. Access to the park is 3 miles off AR 10 on Pinnacle Valley Road.

Ouachita River. Below Lake Ouachita, the river continues through the Ouachita Mountains, though two dams interrupt its flow near the resort town of Hot Springs to form **Lakes Hamilton** and **Catherine**. Below Lake Catherine, the stream travels south past Arkadelphia before leaving the Ouachita Mountain region and entering the West Gulf Coastal Plain, also known in Arkansas as the Timberlands region. Camden, a town known for its Civil War history, lies on the river's path. Before crossing the state's southern border, the stream passes near the towns of Smackover and El Dorado, key sites in southern Arkansas's oil history, and through the **Felsenthal National Wildlife Refuge** east of Crossett. Although limited in size and big-fish potential, short stretches of the Ouachita River provide excellent seasonal fishing for rainbow trout. Stocked rainbow trout are available in the tailwaters of dams in the Hot Springs area. Cold-water releases from **Blakely Mountain Dam** (Lake Ouachita) and **Carpenter Dam** (Lake Hamilton) provide good cool-season fishing for put-and-take rainbows for short stretches below each dam, from the bank or from a boat. Farther south, anglers seek bass, catfish, crappie, and bream in the Ouachita's waters. The Felsenthal refuge is one of southern Arkansas's most renowned fishing venues.

✳ Cities, Towns, and Villages

Little Rock and **North Little Rock** form a budding metropolis that spans both sides of the Arkansas River in the center of the state. With a combined daily population of over 500,000 people, these two cities offer a multitude of dining opportunities, unique shopping outlets, and a fast-paced entertainment scene offering live theater, music, and an excellent selection of nightclubs. Little Rock is the official state capital, and as you might imagine, a grand collection of museums showcases something for every interest—from art to history to aerospace. Be sure to visit the Little Rock River Market for tastes of exotic cuisines and produce harvested from nearby farms in season.

Extensive park systems in both cities provide the chance to play golf or tennis, fish for lunkers in the Arkansas River or on area lakes, hike leafy trails, talk to the animals in the parklike Little Rock Zoo, or picnic in beautiful natural settings.

EASTERN TIMBERLANDS

Camden (870-836-6426; www.growingcamden.com), 314 Adams Street Southwest, Camden. If you are a Civil War buff, you won't want to miss the rich history displayed in Camden. Start your tour at the restored 1913 train depot, which also serves as a community museum. Artifacts related to two famous Camden products, Camark pottery and Grapette soft drinks, as well as Civil War and railroad relics, are exhibited here.

When federal troops occupied Camden during the Red River Campaign of 1864, the McCollum-Chidester House served as their headquarters. Open for tours, the house still contains 1860s furnishings. Nearby, the site of the Battle of Poison Springs is preserved by Poison Spring State Park, one of three state parks commemorating the campaign. Other Civil War sites in Camden include Fort Sutherland and Oakland Cemetery.

Two major events held in the city are the spring Camden Daffodil Festival and autumn BPW Barn Sale. Other area attractions include White Oak Lake State Park; the Arkansas Museum of Natural Resources at Smackover, which recounts the story of South Arkansas's oil boom; and El Dorado's restored oil boom downtown.

El Dorado is best known as being the heart of the 1920s oil boom in south Arkansas, earning it the nickname Arkansas's Original Boomtown. While the city was founded in 1843, it remained isolated until the arrival of railroads allowed a prosperous lumber industry to evolve. El Dorado lived up to the promise of its name when oil was discovered a mile west of the city in 1921. The resulting gush of population and prosperity led to an architectural boom still seen in a self-guided walking tour of the city's restored downtown, now filled with beautifully renovated 1930s-style buildings. Many of the buildings are on the National Register, including the Rialto Theater, Arkansas's only working art deco theater, and several great restaurants. In 2004, the downtown area was declared a National Historic District.

The city is home to the South Arkansas Arts Center and South Arkansas Symphony. At the Arkansas Museum of Natural Resources, located in the small town of Smackover, visitors can learn more about the south Arkansas oil boom. Notable people from El Dorado include E. Fay Jones, architect and student of Frank Lloyd Wright, and Baseball Hall of Famer Lou Brock.

Pine Bluff. Thirteen colorful murals depicting the town's past brighten the walls of buildings in the downtown area and are the reason folks call Pine Bluff "The City of Murals." Just 45 minutes south of Little Rock, Pine Bluff is home to the Arkansas Entertainers Hall of Fame, which features exhibits chronicling careers of entertainers with Arkansas roots. You can also tour the only museum in the country devoted to musical band instruments at the Band Museum on Main Street. One of four of the state's nature centers is in Pine Bluff. The Delta Rivers Nature Center's exhibits and films reveal the history and importance of Arkansas's Delta streams and wetlands. Saracen Landing, a $4.2 million park facility in town, features a 10,080-square-foot pavilion and concrete fishing pier. It is home to the Pine Bluff Farmers' Market, plus a number of events every year. Visit the Dexter Harding House (870-536-8472), 110 North Pine Street, Pine Bluff; open Monday through Friday. Built in 1850, the restored home is now the city's and region's official tourist information center.

HOPE VISITOR CENTER

WESTERN TIMBERLANDS

Hope is President Bill Clinton's birthplace and the Watermelon Capital of the World. Start your tour at the Clinton Birthplace and Museum, browse the gift shop, and then drive by his childhood home. The Hope Visitor Center is housed just down the way in the old train depot. The depot offers a large collection of Clinton memorabilia and photographs from his early days in Hope, as well as his subsequent trips home during his later years.

Texarkana was founded in the early 1870s where two railroads met at the Arkansas-Texas border. As it sits on the border between the two states, it is technically two towns with one name. State Line Avenue marks the boundary between the two states and the two cities. The only US post office located in two states can be found at 500 State Line, where Photographer's Island is a popular spot for taking photos of people standing in two states simultaneously. Another unusual attraction is the Ace of Clubs House, built in the shape of a playing card club. Their slogan is "Life so large it takes two states."

Texarkana is also home to the Texarkana Regional Arts Center, which hosts touring exhibits and works by regional artists; the Perot Theater, where touring national and international acts perform in an ornate 1924 theater; the interactive Discovery Place Children's Museum; and the Texarkana Museum of Regional History.

✳ To See

MUSEUMS

LITTLE ROCK/NORTH LITTLE ROCK METROPOLITAN AREA

✎ 🐌 **Arkansas Inland Maritime Museum** (501-371-8320; aimmuseum.org), 100 Riverfront Road, North Little Rock. Call for hours of operation. This museum includes the

IMMERSE YOURSELF AT HISTORIC WASHINGTON STATE PARK

Historic Washington State Park (870-983-2684; www.historicwashingtonstatepark.com), US 278, Washington. Open daily 8–5; closed holidays. This park in west Arkansas interprets the town of Washington from 1824–75. This town was a major service center for area planters and merchants, and served as the Confederate capital of Arkansas from 1863–65. Start your tour at the park visitor center, the 1874 Hepmstead County Courthouse, for tour tickets and a map of the park; enjoy a leisurely stroll through beautifully restored buildings populated with park interpreters portraying Arkansas life in the era. Self-guided tours include the Confederate Capitol, Tavern Inn, re-created Blacksmith Shop (where the first Bowie knife is believed to have been made), Weapons Museum, and several residences. The nineteenth-century town includes a print museum, steam-powered cotton gin, and the Williams Tavern Restaurant. The restaurant is frequently named among the best restaurants in the state, with standard Southern fare like meatloaf and mashed potatoes, roast turkey and cornbread dressing, Southern-fried chicken, and catfish.

Washington's courthouse became the Confederate Capitol when Confederate Governor Harris Flanagin moved his state government after Little Rock was captured by Union forces in September 1863. Also the county seat of Hempstead, Washington thus became the cultural, political, and economic center of the area. The town was an important stopping point on the Southwest Trail, a major commercial route that connected St. Louis, Missouri, to Fulton, Arkansas, on the Red River. Historians believe that Davy Crockett, Sam Houston, and Jim Bowie all stopped here on the way to the Alamo to fight for Texas's independence. Bowie commissioned a local blacksmith, James Black, to make a knife while he was in town.

Historic Washington State Park includes 54 buildings on 101 acres. Many of the 30 historically significant buildings have been restored. Selected historic buildings are open for tours seven days a week. Among the many notable structures are the 1836 Hempstead County Courthouse; the Works Progress Administration (WPA) gymnasium; the Pioneer and Presbyterian Cemeteries, where many notable early Arkansans are buried; the Washington post office; American Bladesmith Society's Bill Moran School of Bladesmithing (the world's first college dedicated to teaching the art of making knives and swords by hand); and the Southwest Arkansas Regional Archives.

The park offers guided tours of historic homes and structures, museums, and interactive and living history programs. The park also hosts several special events annually, including the Five-Trails Rendezvous in February and the Jonquil Festival in March. In November, visitors converge on the park for Civil War Weekend, and in December the entire park is decorated in traditional nineteenth-century decorations for the Christmas and Candlelight celebration. Several tour options are available, based on the building open for any given day. The Washington Museum Experience, a guided tour of every facility open that day, is $8 for adults and $4 for kids 6–12. On select days and during special events, you can tour the park from the comfort of a horse-drawn carriage; call ahead for a list of dates when surrey rides are available. Group meeting facilities are also available in a couple of these historic structures. If your group is really cozy with one another, you might want to overnight in the 1914 Washington School, with its 48 bunk beds split into two rooms, using school lockers for storage. Modern amenities include DVD player and Internet access.

historic submarine USS *Razorback* (tours available), the World War II tugboat USS *Hoga,* and a 1939 towboat M/V *Patriot.* In addition to its historic vessels, the Arkansas Inland Maritime Museum (AIMM) also has a small research library and a number of permanent and rotating exhibits on submarines and naval history. After extensive renovation work, two barges were moved into place in January 2006 for additional interior work. The first barge, *Mary Munns*, serves as the ticket booth, waiting area, and gift shop for the museum. The second, *Savannah Lou*, holds the museum's interpretative exhibits, small theater, workshops, and library. The museum contains permanent exhibits on general submarine history, submarine training, and submarine operations such as firefighting and underwater escape, as well as the *Razorback's* operational history. An inactive torpedo is part of a memorial to the submarine *Snook*. Rotating exhibits interpret a variety of topics, such as Pearl Harbor and the many ships and submarines with names related to Arkansas. The library—a joint effort between AIMM and the United States Submarine Veterans, Inc. (USSVI)—includes more than 2,500 books, periodicals, videos, CDs, and DVDs on many topics, not just submarines. There are significant holdings on US naval history, general military history, the Vietnam War, and maritime piracy and pirate history. The library also has a large selection of fiction titles. Free.

✿ ♿ **Arkansas Museum of Discovery** (501-396-7050 or 1-800-880-6475; museumof discovery.org), 500 President Clinton Boulevard, Little Rock. Open Monday through Saturday 9–5, Sunday 1–5. This is a fun-filled indoor playground for kids and adults alike. Located in the heart of the River Market District, the museum has over 25,000 square feet of hands-on, interactive exhibits that focus on science, history, and technology. Surprisingly, this high-tech, state-of-the-art museum is also Little Rock's oldest museum and touts itself as a world of discovery for all ages. Permanent exhibits include one on Arkansas Indians, the *Health Imagination Station*, the *Passport to the World*, the *Discovery Express*, and the new *Room to Grow*, a special area for ages 6 and under. The museum rotates temporary exhibits regularly to ensure there is always something new to discover at the Discovery Museum.

✿ ♿ **Arkansas Sports Hall of Fame & Museum** (501-313-4158; www.arksportshall offame.com), Verizon Arena, North Little Rock. Open by appointment only. Memorabilia chronicling sports legends from the state is on display here. Exhibits highlight the three major sports—football, baseball, and basketball—plus golf, tennis, the Olympics, and more. The highly interactive exhibits are designed to appeal to youth. Fantasy sportscasting is available at the Alltel-Pat Summerall Broadcast Booth, which allows museum-goers to imagine what it is like to call the plays from the booth with a legendary sportscaster. Past inductees include such notables as Pat Summerall, Steve Atwater, and Cliff Harris (football); Brooks Robinson, George Kell, and Bill Dickey (baseball); Pat Day and Larry Snyder (horse racing); Mike Conley and Clyde Scott (track and field); Mark Martin (NASCAR); and Joe Kleine and Reece "Goose" Tatum (basketball). The $3.5 million showplace is located inside North Little Rock's Verizon Arena, bordered with displays and anchored by a 100-seat theater where a film about the history of sports in Arkansas is shown. Admission is $6 for adults (18–61); $4 for seniors (62 and over); $3 for military (with ID) and children (6–17); and free for ages 6 and under.

✿ ♿ **Arkansas State Capitol** (501-682-5080; www.sosweb.state.ar.us), Woodlane Street and Capitol Avenue, Little Rock. Free guided tours available Monday through Friday 7–5. The Capitol is also open for self-guided tours on weekends and holidays from 10–3. Call to schedule a tour. Its uncanny resemblance to the nation's Capitol has inspired filmmakers to fire missiles at its dome and lay motorcycle skid marks on its marble steps inside. During the 1980s, Arkansas's 5 percent rebate combined with the Capitol's familiar design to bring Hollywood to Arkansas, with both Brian Bosworth's theatrical release *The Brotherhood* and the made-for-TV movie *Under Siege*, starring Peter Strauss, filmed here. This stunning Neoclassical building in downtown Little Rock was completed in 1915 and is modeled after the US Capitol. It has two long wings extending from a center rotunda and a classical portico across the long facade.

OLD STATE HOUSE MARKS STATE AND NATIONAL HISTORY

Old State House Museum (501-324-9685; www.oldstatehouse.com), 300 West Markham Street, Little Rock. Open 361 days each year. Governor William Jefferson Clinton announced his run for US president on the front lawn of the State House and held victory-night watch parties there in 1992. The eyes of the world were trained on this building when the Clintons and the Gores stood between its great columns to accept the presidency and vice presidency of the United States. In 1997, the Old State House was designated a National Historic Landmark, the highest recognition a building can receive. It is the oldest standing state Capitol west of the Mississippi River. The structure was built to accommodate all branches of the new state's government. It served a multitude of uses before becoming, in 1951, a museum of Arkansas history. This museum portrays Arkansas's history from its first days of statehood to present. Built in 1836, the Old State House was the state's original Capitol until 1911 and served as the seat of both the Confederate and Union governments in Arkansas during the Civil War. It was also the site of the 1861 secession convention. Exhibits include first ladies' gowns, African American quilts, Civil War battle flags, and Arkansas art and pottery. The museum continues to host significant events.

The museum offers hourly tours and provides free on-site programming for visitors of all ages, including gallery talks and lectures, musical concerts, family programs, summer youth camps, hands-on activities for K–12 audiences, and living history. The museum's outreach program is extensive as well. ♿

The exterior is constructed of limestone from a quarry in Batesville, Arkansas, and the interior features Vermont, Alabama, and Colorado marble. The six solid bronze doors, purchased from Tiffany's of New York at a total cost of $10,000, are now estimated to be worth more than $250,000. A restoration of the front walk and gardens returned the area to its original design. Located on the grounds are several monuments: Vietnam Veterans; Arkansas Police Officer Killed in Action; Confederate Soldiers; Confederate Women; Confederate War Prisoners; and, most recently, the Little Rock Nine Memorial, a life-sized bronze statue immortalizing the nine black youths who made civil rights history at Central High in 1957.

The building contains nearly 287,000 square feet of space, which is no longer sufficient to hold the majority of state offices and departments. A complex of office buildings around the Capitol reflects the twentieth-century growth of Arkansas's bureaucracy.

🐾 ♿ **EMOBA—Ernie's Museum of Black Arkansans** (501-372-0018), 1208 Louisiana Street, Little Rock. Open February through September; call for hours of operation and exhibit schedule. Small admission fee. The Museum of Black Arkansans and Performing Arts has exhibits on prominent black Arkansans and the African American experience. EMOBA is also the site of one of the best haunted houses in town during the Halloween season. Guided tours are available. The gift shop sells souvenirs.

🐾 ♿ **Historic Arkansas Museum** (501-324-9351; www.historicarkansas.org), 200 East Third Street, Little Rock. Open Monday through Saturday 9–5; Sunday 1–5. Daily tours and seasonal special events. A historic site depicting Arkansas's frontier days, you can walk through five pre–Civil War houses that have been restored to antebellum appearances: the Hinderliter Grog Shop, the oldest standing building in Little Rock (circa 1827); the Brownlee House (circa 1848); the Woodruff Print Shop (circa 1824); the McVicar House (circa 1848); and the Plum Bayou Log House (circa 1830s). You will meet living residents throughout the compound during your tour. The center's museum features an outstanding collection of Arkansas-made decorative, mechanical, and fine art objects, plus a living history theater and educational areas. Free.

The compound has been honored by the National Trust for Historic Preservation as one of the most significant museum villages in the nation and has been called a little Williamsburg by travel writers. Recent additions include replicas of a smoke-house, slave quarters, a barn, and a privy, which combine with the authentic 1830s Plum Bayou Log House to re-create a pioneer homestead. Native Arkansas plants and period landscaping are also a part of the project. Improvements to other museum historic structures include the addition of a kitchen building and appropriate landscaping at the Brownlee House to better interpret a nineteenth-century yard.

♂ ♿ **MacArthur Museum of Arkansas Military History** (501-376-4602; www.ark militaryheritage.com), 503 East Ninth Street, Little Rock. Open Tuesday through Friday 9–4, Saturday 10–4, Sunday 1–4. The museum is located in the historic tower building of Little Rock's Old Arsenal, a National Historic Landmark and the birthplace of Gen. Douglas MacArthur (1880). The building now houses a museum of Arkansas's military heritage from territorial days to present. Exhibits feature artifacts, photographs, weapons, documents, uniforms, and other military items. The museum hosts special events throughout the year, so visit their website to see what's happening when you're there.

EASTERN TIMBERLANDS

♂ ♿ 🍴 **Arkansas Museum of Natural Resources** (870-725-2877; arkansasstateparks .com), 3853 Smackover Highway, Smackover. Open Monday through Saturday 8–5, Sunday 1–5; closed New Year's Day, Thanksgiving Day, Christmas Eve, and Christmas Day. This museum uses state-of-the-art exhibits inside and working oil field equipment outside to tell the story of the oil boom in south Arkansas. Ride the museum elevator down through a depiction of the formation of the oil strata into a re-creation of a 1920s Arkansas boomtown, complete with ruts in the street. In the 1920s, the country's attention focused on south Arkansas and the Smackover field, which was ranked first among the nation's oil fields. For a few months in 1925, the 40-square-mile field was the site of one of the wildest mineral booms in North America. Today, south Arkansas's oil fields produce petroleum throughout a 10-county area. Inside that area, Columbia and Union Counties also stretch over one of the largest brine (saltwater) reserves in the world. Bromine is derived from the brine, and local companies play an international role in the commercialization of bromine and its many applications. The museum features a 25,000-square-foot main exhibition/research building that includes a 10,500-square-foot exhibit hall, theater, exhibit work area, research center, and museum store/gift shop. Take a chance drilling and see if you will become an oil tycoon or go flat broke. Learn how 95 percent of the products we use daily are made of, or with, two of Arkansas's natural resources. Tour Oil Field Park adjacent to the main building, past full-sized operating examples of vintage derricks and equipment used from the 1920s to the modern era. The museum staff offers a wide variety of year-round educational and interpretive programs. Choose from guided tours of the museum and Oil Field Park, films, lectures, field trips, special demonstrations, and programs. Admission is free.

♂ **Arkansas Railroad Museum/Engine 819** (870-535-8819), 1700 Port Road, Pine Bluff. Open Monday through Saturday 9–3. Engine 819, Pine Bluff's legendary queen of steam, weighs 368 tons, measures 100 feet from front to back, and takes 150 gallons of water and 15 gallons of oil to run just 1 mile of track. Railroad buffs should not miss it! Volunteer craftsmen lovingly rebuilt Engine 819, the last 4-8-4 Northern-type steam locomotive built in Pine Bluff. Tours are available year-round. The museum also houses passenger cars, cabooses, and baggage cars—all restored to their original splendor—as well as many artifacts used back in the days of steam engines. Special tours can be arranged. Free admission.

RARE NILOAK POTTERY ON DISPLAY AT GANN MUSEUM IN BENTON

   ♭ **Gann Museum of Saline County** (501-778-5513), 218 South Market Street, Benton. Open Tuesday through Thursday 10–4 and by appointment. The museum is housed in the only known structure in the world made completely of bauxite. Originally the office of Dr. Dewell Gann Sr., the structure was built in 1893 by patients who couldn't afford to pay the doctor for his services. Today it houses a museum of Benton and Saline County, including a large collection of the rare Niloak pottery, which was produced in Benton from the 1920s to the 1930s. Admission is free, donations are accepted.

   ♭ **Grant County Museum & Heritage Village** (870-942-4496; www.grantcounty museumar.com), 521 Shackleford Road, Sheridan. Open Tuesday through Saturday 9–4. You will need to allow yourself a couple of hours to tour this facility's exhibits on the Union Army's failed Red River Campaign and the nearby Battle of Jenkins Ferry. The museum's collection of World War II artifacts includes 22 restored vehicles, which makes it the most extensive WWII vehicle collection in the country. It also has an extensive collection of Civil War artifacts; a restored Depression-era café; a collection of local history artifacts; and restored historic buildings. Free for county residents; nonresidents are $3 for adults, $1 for students.

   ♭ **Jacksonville Military History Museum** (501-241-1943; www.jaxmilitarymuseum .org), 100 Veterans Circle, Jacksonville. Open Monday through Friday 9–5, Saturday 10–5. The museum highlights the important contributions made by local men and women, civilians and military, from the Civil War era to present-day conflicts. Exhibits highlight the Battle of Reed's Bridge, a Civil War skirmish that took place in Jacksonville; the WWII-era Arkansas Ordnance Plant; the Vietnam War; and the 308th Titan II Missile Wing. Also featured is a collection of over 350 original WWII posters and the Mighty Mite Jeep from Vietnam, the smallest one ever produced.

WESTERN TIMBERLANDS

& **The Klipsch Museum of Audio History** (870-777-3540; www.klipsch.com/museum), 200 East Division Street, Hope. Open Monday through Friday 8–4, and by appointment at other times. A museum dedicated to the life and achievements of the late Paul W. Klipsch, a Hope resident and an audio engineer who manufactured his world-famous loudspeakers there. Contains replicas of his office, speakers, model railroad trains he built, photographs, and other memorabilia. The museum shares the restored Cairo-Fulton Railroad Depot (circa 1873) in downtown Hope with the Hope-Hempstead County Chamber of Commerce. Free.

& Texarkana Museum of Regional History (903-793-4831; www.texarkanamuseums .org), 219 North State Line Avenue, Texarkana. Open Tuesday through Saturday 10–4. This museum tells the story of the city located in two states. Housed in the town's oldest brick building, all-new galleries with exhibits tell of the region's history, including agriculture, early industry, civil rights, and World War II. Pottery made by members of the Caddo Nation and information about the early Spanish and French explorers are also on display. An interactive music exhibit tells of native son Scott Joplin, the Father of Ragtime Music; Huddie "Leadbelly" Ledbetter; and Conlon Nancarrow. This facility also includes the Wilbur Smith Research Library and Archives.

Turner Neal Museum of Natural History (870-460-1265; www.uamont.edu), University of Arkansas at Monticello. Hours vary based on the school's schedule; call for days and hours. A museum of natural history of South Arkansas with three collections of big game, it also houses the Pomeroy Planetarium, which seats 40. Free.

GALLERIES AND FINE ART

LITTLE ROCK/NORTH LITTLE ROCK METROPOLITAN AREA

& **Arkansas Arts Center** (501-372-4000; www.arkarts.com), MacArthur Park, Ninth Street and Commerce, Little Rock. Open Tuesday through Saturday 10–5. Located in Little Rock's historic MacArthur Park, the arts center is a first-class facility with an internationally recognized collection of drawings, with works dating from the Renaissance to the present. It is also the home of top-notch art exhibitions spread throughout seven galleries. Masterworks in the collection include paintings by Diego Rivera, Odilon Redon, and Francesco Bassano; sculpture by Henry Moore, Louise Nevelson, and Roy Lichtenstein; and prints by Rembrandt, Whistler, and Dürer. The second major area of collecting is contemporary objects in craft media, including teapots by contemporary artists, contemporary baskets, turned-wood objects, studio glass, ceramics, metalwork, and jewelry designed by artists. Among the highlights are works by Dale Chihuly, Albert Paley, Peter Voulkos, and Dorothy Gill Barnes. A casually elegant restaurant—Best Impressions—and a museum gift shop are on-site. A multimillion-dollar renovation in 2000 expanded the center to include the Arkansas Museum of Art (the galleries); the Museum School; State Services (traveling exhibitions); and the popular Children's Theatre. Check their website for the Children's Theatre's performance schedule; these plays showcase talented young locals on vibrant, creative stages. Admission to the museum and its galleries is free, excluding special exhibits.

EASTERN TIMBERLANDS

& **Arts & Science Center for Southeast Arkansas** (870-536-3375; www.artsscience center.org), 701 Main Street, Pine Bluff. Open Monday through Friday 10–4, Saturday and Sunday by appointment only. The center offers a diverse schedule of programs for the entire family. See exhibits of art in the galleries, from traditional paintings and sculpture to the innovative techniques of today. Turn your kids loose on one of the frequent interactive science exhibits or catch one of the several productions—perhaps a lighthearted musical or a drama. Fun, free, educational, and always changing! There's something for everyone at The Arts & Science Center for Southeast Arkansas. Admission is free.

WESTERN TIMBERLANDS

✐ ♿ **Texarkana Regional Arts Center** (903-792-8681; www.trahc.org), 321 West Fourth, Texarkana. Open Tuesday through Saturday 10–4. Housed in the former 1909 US Federal Courthouse, this fine arts center was renovated in 1992 at a cost of $1.6 million. The entire west end of the first floor was converted into museum-quality, high-security exhibit space. The former courtroom, now the Horace C. Cabe Grand Hall, has decorative paintings by the same artisans who worked on the Perot Theatre. All exhibits are art related now, and the center also offers lectures, classes, and concerts. With the only high-security galleries between Dallas and Little Rock, the Regional Arts Center is a frequent stop for visitors interested in seeing high-quality art exhibitions in the area. Admission to the galleries is free, excluding special events and exhibits.

CULTURAL SITES

LITTLE ROCK/NORTH LITTLE ROCK METROPOLITAN AREA

✐ ♿ ⚑ **Clinton Presidential Library and Museum** (501-374-4242; www.clintonpresidential center.org), 1200 East President Clinton Avenue, Little Rock. Open Monday through Saturday 9–5, Sunday 1–5. America's 12th presidential library is situated on the banks of the Arkansas River in the River Market District of downtown Little Rock. The $160 million structure contains 20,000 square feet of library and museum space and has earned great reviews from the over 3 million people who have visited. No matter how you feel about the former president or his administration, this museum will impress you.

As you walk into the first floor, you will see Clinton's presidential limousine at the foot of the stairs leading to the main library. The second floor is organized into three-sided policy kiosks and follows the major issues addressed during Clinton's two terms. From the impetus of legislation, through the debate and the signing, the kiosks incorporate video clips generously. Large panels in the center of the room mark Clinton's presidency chronologically, allowing you to look up your birthday, for example, and check out what was going on at the White House on that date. Upstairs, gifts of state are displayed around the perimeter of the floor, with highlights including a table set with the Clintons' presidential china, a Chihuli chandelier, and life-sized replicas of the couple in their inaugural attire.

The library, which is located in a 28-acre city park, contains the largest collection of presidential papers and artifacts in US history and an authentic replica of the Oval Office and the Cabinet Room. Forty Two, which gets its name from Clinton's place in the line of US presidents, is a full-service restaurant that offers an eclectic lunch menu Monday through Saturday, with a Sunday brunch. The University of Arkansas Clinton School of Public Service is also located on park grounds in the renovated 1899 Choctaw Train Station. Admission is $7 for adults (18–61); $5 for seniors, college students, and retired military; and $3 for kids.

Junction Bridge (501-374-3001; pulaskicounty.net/junction-bridge), 200 Ottenheimer Plaza, Little Rock. Open 24/7. Constructed in 1884 as the primary railroad bridge connecting the northern and southern railway lines, the structure has been renovated into a pedestrian and bicycle bridge joining downtown Little Rock and North Little Rock. It is believed to be the only converted lift-span bridge in the US. The lift span is locked in a raised position, allowing for uninterrupted barge traffic on the Arkansas River. Visitors may cross the entire 1,800 feet by riding elevators up to and down from the 360-foot lift span. Benches and other amenities are located along the way. Free.

✇ ♿ **Mosaic Templars Cultural Center** (501-683-3593; www.mosaictemplarscenter .com), Ninth Street and Broadway, Little Rock. Open Tuesday through Saturday 9–5. This building was badly burned shortly after the Department of Heritage gathered with local dignitaries to celebrate its pending renovation. Now beautifully reconstructed, the museum is dedicated to collecting, preserving, interpreting, and celebrating Arkansas's African American culture and community from 1870 to present. The Mosaic Templars of America organization was founded in Little Rock in 1882 as a fraternal organization by John E. Bush and Chester W. Keatts. It also informs and educates the public about black achievement, especially in business, politics, and the arts. The third-floor auditorium seats 400 and hosts performing arts productions, conferences, and public symposiums. Admission is free.

HISTORIC SITES

EASTERN TIMBERLANDS

Civil War Red River Campaign State Parks (501-682- 1191; www.arkansasstateparks .com). Three state parks, with outdoor exhibits and picnic sites, preserve battlefields of the Union Army's failed Red River campaign: Poison Spring (10 miles west of Camden on AR 76), Marks' Mill (AR 97 and AR 8, southeast of Fordyce), and Jenkins' Ferry (13 miles southeast of Sheridan on AR 46). Literature is available by phone or online.

WESTERN TIMBERLANDS

♿ **Clinton First Home Museum and Exhibit Center** (870-777-4455; www.clinton birthplace.org), 117 S. Hervey, Hope. Open Tuesday through Saturday 10–4. The first home of President Bill Clinton, this museum will let you tour the childhood home of the 42nd president. Listed on the National Register of Historic Places, the attention to detail is engaging—for example, playing cards are pinned to the curtains mimicking Virginia Kelley's tutoring of young Bill Clinton. Clinton lived here with his grandparents between 1946–50. The Virginia Clinton Kelley Memorial Rose Garden pays tribute to his mother. Free tour includes the home, photographic exhibits, and museum store.

LITTLE ROCK/NORTH LITTLE ROCK METROPOLITAN AREA

✇ ♿ **Little Rock Central High Museum and Visitor Center** (501-374-1957; www.nps.gov/ chsc), 2120 Daisy L. Gatson Bates Drive, Little Rock. Open daily 9–4:30, excluding holidays. It's pretty powerful to walk the sidewalk outside Central High School if you grew up with an awareness of the 1957 crisis at the school. The images of nine young black students against a mob of angry adults will escort you on your journey, if you did. If not, this museum has impressive exhibits to set the scene for your tour. The current center opened September 24, 2007, coinciding with the 50th anniversary of the 1957 desegregation crisis. It features 3,000 square feet of permanent exhibits covering the 1957 events that took place at Central High and its role in the greater civil rights movements in the US, audiovisual and interactive programs, and a bookstore. The former visitor center, a restored Mobil service station, is now used for special programs. Call ahead to reserve the ranger-led tour; it makes the trip. Free admission.

  🐾 ♿ **Little Rock Central High School National Historic Site** (501-374-1957; www.nps .gov/chsc), 2120 Daisy L. Gatson Bates Drive, Little Rock. Guided tours of the school are given by reservation only during the school year Monday, Wednesday, and Friday. A major US civil rights landmark, this National Historic Site is still a working school. Arkansas's first African American students—the Little Rock Nine—were admitted here in 1957 following a confrontation between Governor Orval Faubus, who used the state's National Guard to block desegregation, and President Eisenhower, who sent federal troops to enforce it. A commemorative garden (sculpture surrounded by a landscaped garden) is also on-site. Free.

  ♿ **Curran Hall Visitors Information Center** (501-371-0075; www.quapaw.com), 1206 South Main, Little Rock. Open Monday through Saturday 9–5, Sunday 1–5. The historic Walters-Curran-Bell House, or Curran Hall, was built in 1842 and is one of the oldest residential structures in Little Rock. The restored antebellum Greek Revival home serves as the city's visitors information center, the Mayor's reception hall, and headquarters of the Quapaw Quarter Association. The Historic Arkansas Gardens, a project of the Pulaski County Master Gardeners, features native and heritage plants common to the period and locale.

  🐾 ♿ **Little Rock Nine Memorial** (501-682-5080; www.sosweb.state.ar.us), Woodlane Street and Capitol Avenue, Little Rock. Nine life-sized bronze statues, located on the state Capitol grounds, pay homage to the nine Little Rock students—Melba Pattillo, Elizabeth Eckford, Ernest Green, Gloria Ray, Carlotta Walls, Terrence Roberts, Jefferson Thomas, Minnijean Brown, and Thelma Mothershed—who overcame major obstacles to integrate Little Rock Central High School (now a national historic site) in 1957.

  The Old Mill at T. R. Pugh Memorial Park (501-758-1424; www.northlittlerock.travel), McCain Boulevard and Lakeshore Drive, North Little Rock. Open 24/7. An authentic reproduction of an old water-powered gristmill, this striking structure appears in the opening scene of the classic 1933 film *Gone with the Wind* and is believed to be the only building remaining from the film. Also known as Pugh's Mill, it was built in 1933 by North Little Rock developer Justin Matthews, who had the structure designed to look as if it was built in the 1800s. The park is decorated with sculptures of toadstools, tree stumps, and a tree branch–entwined bridge that connects the mill to the rest of the park. Dionicio Rodriguez, a sculptor and artist from Mexico City, was responsible for all the details of each piece of concrete work made to represent wood, iron, or stone, as well as the design of the footbridges and rustic seats. In 1991, Rodriguez's work at the Old Mill was renovated by his grandson, Carlos Cortes. The Old Mill is listed on the National Register of Historic Places, and tour guides are available by appointment for groups. Admission is free.

  Over-the-Jumps Carousel (501-666-2406; www.littlerockzoo.com), 1 Jonesboro Drive, Little Rock. Zoo hours are 9–5 daily. The restored historic Spillman Engineering Over-the-Jumps Carousel (a.k.a. the Arkansas Carousel) is the focal point of the Little Rock Zoo's entry complex. Unlike most carousels where the horses move up and down, Over-the-Jumps features an undulating track, the only one remaining of the original four produced during the 1920s. The 40 prancing ponies have been meticulously restored, as have the four chariots. The turn-of-the-nineteenth-century architectural design center also has a gift shop. Zoo admission is $10 for adults, $8 for seniors and kids.

EASTERN TIMBERLANDS

Civil War Red River Campaign State Parks (501-682-1191; www.arkansasstateparks
.com). Three state parks, with outdoor exhibits and picnic sites, preserve battlefields of
the Union Army's failed Red River campaign: Poison Spring (10 miles west of Camden
on AR 76), Marks' Mill (AR 97 and AR 8 southeast of Fordyce), and Jenkins' Ferry (13
miles southeast of Sheridan on AR 46). Literature is available by phone or online.

WESTERN TIMBERLANDS

& **Clinton First Home Museum and Exhibit Center** (870-777-4455; www.clinton
birthplace.org), 117 South Hervey, Hope. Open Tuesday through Saturday 10–4. This
museum invites guests to tour the childhood home of the 42nd president. Listed on
the National Register of Historic Places, the attention to detail is engaging—for example, playing cards are pinned to the curtains, mimicking Virginia Kelley's tutoring of
young Bill Clinton. Clinton lived here with his grandparents from 1946 to 1950. The
Virginia Clinton Kelley Memorial Rose Garden pays tribute to his mother. Free tour
includes the home, photographic exhibits, and museum store.

URBAN OASES **H. U. Lee International Gate and Garden** (www.grandmasterhulee
.com/gate-and-garden), 101 East Markham Street, Little Rock. Open 24/7. A $1.4-million
project saluting the martial arts while serving as a symbol of friendship between South
Korea and America, this colorful and intricately carved tribute honors the founder of
the American Taekwondo Association (ATA). It was a gift to Arkansas by the family
of the late H. U. Lee, founder of the ATA, whose international headquarters is in Little
Rock. The 80-ton Douglas fir gate was handcrafted by South Korea artisans and leads
to a garden, a 9-foot tall fountain with reflective pool, a bust of Eternal Grand Master Lee, a 9-foot-tall wall of vision, and numerous statues and educational artifacts
explaining martial arts. Free admission.

   & **South Arkansas Arboretum State Park** (870-862-8131; www.arkansasstateparks
.com/southarkansasarboretum), Mount Holly Road and Timberlane, El Dorado. Open
daily 8–5, excluding holidays. This 13-acre site is lush with plants indigenous to Arkansas's West Gulf Coastal Plain, and walking trails wander lazily through flowering aza-
leas or camellias, depending on the season you visit. This little park is a great place to
stretch your legs or take a break, with a covered picnic area, 5 miles of walking trails,
and Arkansas native flora. Tour guides may be available with advance request. Free
admission.

ZOOS ✦ & **Crossland Zoo** (870-364-7732), 1141 Parkway Drive, Crossett. Open Monday through Saturday 9–6. One of only two zoos in Arkansas, you will find more than
75 different species of mammals, reptiles, and birds here. There is a nature trail, picnic
area, playground, and stock pond. Call for admission prices.

   ✦ & **Little Rock Zoo** (501-666-2406; www.littlerockzoo.com), 1 Jonesboro Drive,
War Memorial Park, Little Rock. Open daily 9–5. Over 750 mammals, birds, reptiles,
and amphibians call this nationally accredited facility home. The entry complex greets
visitors with the restored historic Spillman Engineering Over-the-Jumps Carousel, an
expanded gift shop, and the Lorikeet Landing interactive exhibit, where guests can
feed the birds a cup of nectar. The historic Works Projects Administration big cat
house has been converted to Café Africa, a full-service restaurant. Other zoo attri-
butes include special programs, a petting zoo, and miniature train rides. Admission to
the zoo is $10 for adults, $8 for seniors and children.

THE PERFECT PLAY FOR A RAINY, SUMMER DAY

Crater of Diamonds State Park (870-285-3113; www.craterofdiamondsstatepark.com), 209 State Park Road, Murfreesboro. You're on vacation and it's raining. Your spouse has cabin fever, and the kids passed that point hours ago. What will you do to recover precious family memories from these dreary depths? If you're on vacation in Arkansas, play in the mud! It's the only place on the North American continent where you can dig for diamonds for a small fee and keep what you find. Rainfall is the perfect precursor to your diamond expedition because the rain washes away the sediment for you, leaving the gems sparkling on the surface of the fields. And some of them are of decent size. Among the more notable finds: the 40.23-carat Uncle Sam—the largest diamond ever unearthed in the US; the 16.37-carat Amarillo Starlight; the 15.33-carat Star of Arkansas; and the 4.25-carat Kahn Canary diamond, found in 1977, which was worn by Hillary Clinton during the presidential inaugural balls and two gubernatorial inaugurations. The 3.03-carat Strawn-Wagner Diamond, found in 1990, was cut to a 1.09-carat gem graded D-flawless 0/0/0 (the highest grade a diamond can achieve) by the American Gem Society. The Diamond Discovery Center will introduce you to the art of diamond searching, provide equipment rentals (or you can borrow a pail and shovel from a child), and has an exhibit gallery so you can see a sample before you trample. Diamond Springs is a 14,700-square-foot, mining-themed aquatic playground that is fun for kids and adults. There are also camping and picnic sites, a hiking trail, a wildlife observation blind, and a gift shop.

GREAT FINDS FROM THE FAMOUS CRATER

Although thousands of people have dug and sifted through the volcanic kimberlite soil, there are still plenty of diamonds waiting to be discovered. Since the park opened in 1972, more than 19,000 diamonds have been found, many of which are of gemstone quality. Tom Stolarz, the park's superintendent, says about two diamonds are found by park visitors each day. "Most of them are about the size of a match head or smaller, and people usually keep them for souvenirs," he adds. If you are one of the lucky ones, you might find a big one. Even if you aren't lucky, you are sure to have a good time.

✳ To Do

GOLF ✧ **First Tee of Little Rock** (501-562-GOLF; www.thefirsttteear.org), 1 First Tee Way, Little Rock. First Tee of Little Rock offers those who would normally not have the opportunity to be introduced to golf a chance to learn the game. Open to the public and staffed with Professional Golfers' Association (PGA) professionals, the facility features a nine-hole, par 36, 3,400-yard course; a 16-acre driving range; a putting course; a short game area; and a nine-hole pitch and putt for both youth and adults. Founded by the Jack Stephens Youth Golf Academy, First Tee not only introduces young players to the game of golf, it also endeavors to nurture the soft skills inherent to the game—leadership, honesty, and integrity. Also located on the grounds is the Learning Center, a 7,000-square-foot multipurpose community center with a state-of-the-art golf library for member children, full-service golf shop, and three multiuse rooms with indoor hitting areas. This center is designed to accommodate non-golf corporate or association meetings or banquets.

Pippen Meadows Golf Course (870-835-2222), 1201 South Main. The nine-hole course features five par-four holes, two par-threes, and two par-fives. Owner is Hamburg native and former National Basketball Association (NBA) star Scottie Pippen.

Mystic Creek Golf Course (870-312-0723; www.mysticcreekgolf.com), 191 Club House Drive, El Dorado. This semi-private club opened in May 2013 in the rolling lands that surround El Dorado. The course sprawls through gentle slopes of towering pines with flashing bunkers and domed greens. Rates vary by time of day and day of the week, with nine holes ranging from $20–$40. Cart rental is included in your golf fees. If you don't have your clubs with you, you can rent them for $25 for 18 holes and $15 for nine. The club hosts special events and welcomes your call for assistance organizing your golfing outing or tournament. Since opening, both *Golf Digest* and *Golf Week* magazine have listed Mystic Creek among the highest ranked courses in the state. "In 2018, we were listed as number two," according to club manager David Cage. A clubhouse is slated to open in late summer of 2019 and will not only provide event facilities on site, but will also provide food, beverages, and a place to cool off between rounds.

GO-CART RACING ✍ **Kartways of Arkansas** (870-820-5595; www.kartways.com), 916 Bradley, AR 7 South, Warren. Go-cart racing on a combination 0.5-mile road course with a built-in 0.2-mile oval. Rentals of beginner- and professional-level go-carts; race-driving school; sanctioned local, regional, and national races; special events for corporations, parties, family reunions, and meetings; safety equipment included.

✳ Green Space

✍ **Heifer International Global Headquarters & Village** (1-800-422-0474; www.heifer .org), 1 World Avenue, Little Rock. Tours of the building are offered Monday through Friday 10–3. This four-story world headquarters building, semicircular and ecologically friendly in design, features recycled energy and rainwater made suitable for drinking. Interested in sustainable building products and green construction techniques? They have a tour for that. Heifer International is a nonprofit organization whose purpose is to alleviate hunger and poverty by teaching people to be self-sustaining. There are a variety of daily programs of varying length for kids K–12. There is a 90-minute scavenger hunt to spice up the exhibit tour for kids 12 and under. Those without a lot of time might want to opt for the 30-minute Exhibit Experience. A 3-acre urban farm not only services several central Arkansas food networks, but it also allows you to walk through the garden and learn how Heifer uses and teaches environmentally friendly gardening techniques. Meet alpaca, chickens, goats, and pigs and learn how Heifer International uses them to help families overcome hunger and poverty. There is no charge for building tours. Public events are held throughout the year, and most are free. Heifer Hour is held on the second Saturday morning of the month for families with kids ages K–5 to inspire children and their parents to join in the fight to end world hunger. "Creative Creatures" is a class that introduces toddlers to Heifer's work in the world. Annual events like Alpacalooza celebrate urban and rural farming with information booths, fun games and educational activities, and food trucks and local artisanal foods. Check the calendar on their website for dates and details about upcoming events.

✍ ♿ **Governor Mike Huckabee Delta Rivers Nature Center** (870-534-0011; www.delta rivers.com), Pine Bluff Regional Park, 1400 Black Dog Drive, Pine Bluff. Free. Open Tuesday through Saturday 8:30–4:30, Sunday 1–5; extended summer hours (Memorial Day through Labor Day), Friday and Saturday open until 7:30 p.m. Come and experience Arkansas's first nature center located in Pine Bluff Regional Park. The center has 130 acres for exploring nature trails, wildflower areas, and a chance to view some of the native wildlife. Indoors you will find exhibits featuring Delta wildlife and history, aquariums with Delta fish, and a gift shop with educational environment-related items.

An interesting mix of free programming includes feeding fish and alligators, and quilting. Free admission.

🌿 ♿ **Witt Stephens Jr. Central Arkansas Nature Center** (501-907-0636; www
.centralarkansasnaturecenter.com), 602 President Clinton Avenue, Little Rock. This
facility is on 3.4 acres in Little Rock's Riverfront Park overlooking the Arkansas River.
The river is the perfect setting for these exhibits highlighting the role of fish and
wildlife management and the many projects conducted throughout the history of the
Arkansas Game and Fish Commission. The location provides many watchable wildlife
opportunities within an urban area, including basking water turtles, butterflies, and
migrating pelicans. A portion of the Arkansas River Trail crosses the grounds, offering
more options for exploring the environment. Beds of native plants found throughout
the state are a major part of the landscaping, while the main building has an exhibit
hall, aquariums, gift shop, theater, and special educational programs. Little Rock's
Medical Mile passes the building, highlighted by decorative murals and sculptures;
the walk follows the river for about a mile before looping back to the River Market area.

SPECTATOR SPORTS 🌿 ♿ **Dickey-Stephens Park** (501-664-1555; www.travs.com),
400 West Broadway, North Little Rock. This state-of-the-art home of the Double-A
minor league Arkansas Travelers baseball team is located at the foot of the Broadway Bridge in North Little Rock. It was named Ballpark of the Year by ballpark.com
when it opened in 2006, making the cover of the national website's annual calendar.
The multimillion-dollar project, which favors the classic design found in major league
ballparks, has close and casual seating along with 24 luxury suites. Dickey-Stephens
seats 5,500 and has four concession areas in the general concourse and another in
right field behind the grass berm, where fans can sit on blankets to watch a game. A

DICKEY STEPHEN FIELD IN LITTLE ROCK   ARKANSAS DEPARTMENT OF PARKS & TOURISM

tradition from the Travelers' former home at Ray Winder field, the wooden "bleacher bum" section, is now behind the first-base line and consists of aluminum bleachers. It's located next to a draft-beer garden. The park is named for the Stephens family, who donated the land for the park, and Arkansas natives Bill Dickey, Baseball Hall of Fame catcher for the New York Yankees, and catcher George Skeeter Dickey, who played for the Travelers, Boston Red Sox, and Chicago White Sox. Single-game box seats are $12 for everybody. General admission and the bleacher bum section are $6 adults, $3 children, $5 for military with an ID.

THEME PARKS ✍ ♿ **Wild River Country** (501-753-8600; www.wildrivercountry .com), I-40 and Crystal Hill Road, North Little Rock. Hours vary; check the website for details. This water theme park features both dynamic and relaxing attractions like Cyclone, Vertigo, Pipeline, Vortex, Accelerator, Black Lightning, and White Lightning. Other attractions include the Lazy River, River Rapids, Wave Pool, Tidal Wave, and Lily Pad Walk. The Tad Pool has 11 entertaining children's areas. Tickets are $29.99 for adults, $20.99 for kids. PM Plunge (after 3 p.m.) tickets are $20.99, $15.99 Monday and Tuesday.

TOURS 🚌 **Little Rock Tours** (1-800-933-3836; www.littlerocktours.com), 3100 I-30, Little Rock. This company has been nationally recognized for its daily sight-seeing tours of Pulaski County. Former television journalists Cary and Gina Martin have crafted their excursions with the same nose for news that earned them acclaim while on the air. Buses have four DVD monitors with surround sound that show video and movie clips about the area. Highlights of the standard city tour include the Old State House, Little Rock Central High School National Historic Site, Quapaw Quarter historic district, State Capitol, the Old Mill, and a virtual tour of the Clinton Presidential Library and Center. Specialty, group, and school tours available; they specialize in convention groups, corporate parties, family reunions, and business outings. Prices vary based on the excursion; log on to the website or call for specific prices.

Texarkana Driving Tour-Texarkana Chamber of Commerce (903-792-7191; www .texarkana.org), 819 State Line Avenue, Texarkana. The Discover Texarkana Driving Tour is a self-guided audio tour of local attractions recorded on CD (CD only). Put your feet in the street where two states meet! Experience a truly unique Kodak moment as you strike a pose at the nation's only federal building built in two states: the State Line Post Office. Tune in to Scott Joplin's life while you check out the awesome interactive musical exhibit dedicated to the Father of Ragtime Music located inside the Museum of Regional History. This driving tour will take you to points of interest and provide informative and historical narrative for your journey.

✳ Wild Places

Felsenthal National Wildlife Refuge (870-364-3167; www.fws.gov/felsenthal), 5531 US 82 West, Crossett. The visitor center is open Monday through Friday; call for hours of operation. This is the world's largest green-tree reservoir, consisting of the 15,000-acre Felsenthal Pool that doubles to 36,000 acres during winter flooding. Geographically, the refuge is located in the Felsenthal Basin, an extensive natural depression laced with a vast complex of sloughs, bayous, and lakes. The region's two major rivers, the Saline and Ouachita, flow through the refuge. Popular outdoor activities at Felsenthal include fishing, hunting, and wildlife observation. Public use areas are at Crossett Harbor Recreational Park and Grand Marais. The visitor center exhibits include information about wildlife and Native Americans. Primitive camping is available at 11 sites within the refuge. Admission to the visitor center is free.

    & **Lorance Creek Natural Area** (501-324-9619; www.naturalheritage.org), Bingham Road off I-530 (Exit 9) in southern Pulaski County. Developed by the Arkansas Natural Heritage Commission, this natural area is primarily a deep swamp spreading along both sides of Lorance Creek. The entire Lorance Creek area is a mosaic of open water, bald cypress–water tupelo, beaver ponds, and sandy washes overlain with groves of swamp blackgum. All of these features are interconnected by a complex network of small streams and seeps, which support a rich aquatic flora. A handicapped-accessible trail and boardwalk will give you an opportunity to explore and learn more about this special area. The paved trail winds through a mixed pine and hardwood forest into a bald cypress–water tupelo swamp. Interpretive panels line the trail and boardwalk, illustrating the value and functions of wetlands, natural divisions of Arkansas, and plant and animal life of forested wetlands.

PARKS ♂ **Burns Park** (501-791-8537; www.northlittlerock.org), Exit 150 off I-40, North Little Rock. Funland Amusement Park open late March/early April through late October, Saturday 10–7 and Sunday 1–6. North Little Rock's Burns Park is one of the nation's larger municipal parks, covering 1,575 acres of one of the most diverse plots of land in the state. The park's features include family picnic areas, 15 pavilions, playgrounds, the Funland Amusement Park with children's rides, miniature golf, batting cages, a boat-launching ramp, disc golf, two boccie ball courts, hiking and walking trails, a BMX bike track, an RV park and camping area, and a softball, baseball, and soccer complex. Amusement park tickets are $10 for unlimited rides all day, $1 per single ride ticket.

   ♂ & **Cane Creek State Park** (870-628-4714; www.arkansasstateparks.com/cane creek), 50 State Park Road, Star City. To reach Cane Creek State Park from Star City, travel 5 miles east on AR 293. Located where the rolling terrain of the West Gulf Coastal Plain and the alluvial lands of east Arkansas's Mississippi Delta meet, this park offers you the opportunity to explore two of Arkansas's distinct natural settings in one visit. The 2.5-mile kayak trail is easy, and in 90 minutes you will paddle from the West Gulf Coastal Plain to the Delta and back. Your route will take you through both living and dead cypress forests and by spectacular beaver lodges. The water is blanketed with apple-colored lily pads and creamy ivory lilies. Hike or bike the park's 2,053 acres of woodlands in the Coastal Plain. Paddle or fish on 1,675-acre Cane Creek Lake, a timbered Delta lake. If you don't have a boat you can rent one with a motor ($27 for half-day, $49 per day) or without ($10 half-day, $15 per day). Park staff offer guided walking, biking, kayaking, and birding tours and other interpretive programs throughout the year.

   The campground at Cane Creek features 29 campsites (Class A, $27/day; Class B, $22/day), one Rent-An-RV ($85/day), and a modern bathhouse with hot showers. Cane Creek is one of the Arkansas State Parks system's three parks that offer a Rent-An-RV. This 30-foot RV is just like home, with heat and air-conditioning; beds for eight people; a fully equipped kitchen, including stove/oven, refrigerator, microwave, coffeemaker, pots, and dishes; satellite TV/VCR/DVD; and a built-in sound system with CD and radio. The unit also includes a slide-out area. Alongside the RV is an 11-foot-by-11-foot wooden deck with a table, chairs, and a cooking grill. The RV is permanently set up on a campsite featuring water, electric, and sewer hook-ups. You get all the convenience and amenities of an RV without the gas and hassle of setup. A $50 deposit is required per stay. Weekday rentals may be made for one day, but weekends require a two-day rental. Cane Creek State Park also features picnic sites, a screened pavilion, enclosed

KAYAKING AMONG THE CYPRESS AT CANE CREEK

climate-controlled pavilion, visitor center with exhibits and a gift shop, launch ramp, barrier-free fishing piers, hiking trail, kayak trail, bathhouse, restrooms, and a playground. Fishing boats, recreational solo and tandem kayaks, and bicycles (not mountain bikes) can be rented at the visitor center. Hiking, backpacking, mountain-biking trails, and a kayak trail offer outdoor adventure, including birding and other wildlife viewing opportunities. The 15.5-mile, multiuse trail goes through rolling terrain, along the lake, and across many bridges, including three spectacular suspension bridges. There is also a 2.5-mile multiuse trail for smaller adventures. The park's 2.5-mile kayak trail offers a relaxing outdoor aquatic adventure.

✎ & **Logoly State Park** (870-695-3561), McNeil. From US 79 at McNeil, go 1 mile on CR 47 (Logoly Road) to the park. Open daily; call for specific hours. At Arkansas's first environmental education state park, interpreters present workshops on ecological/environmental topics. The *Everyone has a Home* exhibit is a large, interactive exhibit where you open various doors to see what animals live in the various parts of a tree. Look for the queen in the living beehive exhibit. The park's natural resources provide a living laboratory for students and visitors, with trails bearing informative panels. Most of Logoly's 368 acres comprise a state natural area that includes unique plant species and mineral springs. Park facilities include six group tent sites (no hook-ups), a bathhouse with hot showers, standard pavilion (free to educational groups), picnic sites, playground, trails, and a visitor center with exhibits and an indoor classroom. Admission is free. Group camping is $3/person/day with a $9 site minimum.

✎ & **Moro Bay State Park** (870-463-8555), 6071 AR 600, Jersey. The park is located 29 miles southwest of Warren on US 63 or 23 miles northeast of El Dorado on US 63. Fishing is a popular activity at this park. Check with park staff about joining one of their many fishing workshops or tournaments. A couple of 0.25-mile trails are quick and easy for landlubbers. Park facilities include 12 cabins ($135/day), 23 Class AAA campsites ($34/day), picnic sites, a store, marina with boat rentals and gas pump, standard pavilion (screened), playground, trails, and the Moro Bay Ferry exhibit, featuring a historic tugboat and barge. Five rental cabins are fully equipped and feature a great room, kitchen, two bedrooms, and two bathrooms. These 1,100-square-foot cabins include an outside living area furnished with a picnic grill and table. One cabin is a barrier-free design to meet the needs of visitors with disabilities. They are located near the entrance to the park and all overlook the waters of Moro Bay. Call for updated rates on the cabins.

    ċ **Peabody Park**. Located behind the Little Rock Marriott in Riverfront Park, Markham Street, Little Rock. Designed from suggestions made by area children, this Little Rock playground includes outdoor and underground rooms, large native stones for climbing, and a large water-spray area in the middle of the park that has motion sensor–controlled waterspouts. The Ozark Pavilion located near the riverbank offers a view of the Arkansas River and the wetlands area containing indigenous plant species.

    ơ ċ **Pinnacle Mountain State Park** (501-868-5806; www.arkansasstateparks.com), 11901 Pinnacle Valley Road, Little Rock. The visitor center is open Monday through Saturday 9–5, Sunday noon–5. By the time you reach the top of this landmark, you won't believe you are only 15 minutes from half a million people. This west Little Rock oasis is a diverse day-use park that equally addresses recreation, environmental education, and conservation. Activities include interpretive/audiovisual programs, festivals, and exhibits depicting the natural resources of the area. Park facilities include

CANE CREEK'S KAYAK COURSE RUNS FROM THE WEST GULF COASTAL PLAIN TO THE DELTA

SARACEN LANDING IN PINE BLUFF

picnic sites, pavilions, launching ramps, and hiking trails. The Arkansas Arboretum includes a 0.6-mile barrier-free interpretive tail. The park's proximity to the Big and Little Maumelle Rivers provides a great chance to explore the habitat of the bottomlands. The park has canoe rentals and floats, barge tours, and paddleboats, if you don't have your own. Check the park calendar for programs and events that cater to Pinnacle Mountain's visitors, like technical rock climbing, fishing, hayrides, star parties, and numerous volunteer groups/activities. The visitor center overlooking the Arkansas River includes a meeting room and a gift shop.

Saracen Landing (870-536-0920; www.cityofpinebluff.com/parks), Martha Mitchell Expressway (US 65B), Pine Bluff. This $4.2 million park facility features a 10,080-square-foot pavilion and a concrete fishing pier, plus a fountain that sprays water 40 feet into the air. It is also the home of the Saracen Landing Farmers' Market. It's all located on the shores of 500-acre Lake Saracen in downtown Pine Bluff.

✥ ♿ **White Oak Lake State Park** (870-685-2748; www.arkansasstateparks.com/whiteoaklake), 563 AR 387, Bluff City. From I-30 at Prescott, travel 20 miles east on AR 24, then go 100 yards south on AR 299, then go 2 miles southeast on AR 387. Adjacent to Poison Spring State Forest, this park lies on the shore of White Oak Lake, 2,765 timber-filled acres for bass, crappie, catfish, and bream fishing. Rich in wildlife, the park offers regular sightings of great blue heron, egret, osprey, and green heron, and in winter, bald eagles. Park facilities include 45 campsites (41 Class B, and 4 tent sites); a store with supplies, bait, and gifts (open throughout the year); a marina with boat rentals; a launch ramp; a barrier-free fishing pier; a standard pavilion; along with picnic sites, hiking trails, almost 10 miles of mountain bike trails, and a playground. The visitor center includes exhibits and a park interpreter provides programs, guided hikes, nature talks, demonstrations, and evening presentations free of charge during summer months.

LAKES Lake Maumelle (501-372-5161 www.carkw.com/source/lake_maumelle.asp). Access to the lake is at Maumelle Park on AR 10 west of Little Rock off Pinnacle Valley Road. Like the state park, you will be amazed that you are only 15 minutes from one of Little Rock's fastest-growing developments at Chenal. This lake is Little Rock's main water supply (no swimming allowed), and it's also a popular boating and fishing lake. Sailing is a top sport here, with regattas held on a regular basis. Several marinas call the lake home, as does the Grande Maumelle Sailing Club. The lake, dammed in 1957, covers an area of 14 square miles and has a 70-mile shoreline. Bass is the main fishing lure here, with white, black, and hybrid striped being popular catches. Kentucky bass, crappie, bream, and catfish are also found in the lake.

Millwood Lake, located on AR 32, is 9 miles east of Ashdown in southwest Arkansas. This body of water was formed when the state's longest earthen dam (3.33 miles) was completed across the Little River. Every year, this lake is the site of numerous bass fishing tournaments and fishing derbies held by local and out-of-state organizations, which capitalize on the 29,000 acres of flooded timber that contribute to its renown with bass fishermen. The flooded timber provides exceptional cover for a wide variety of fish, including largemouth and spotted bass, crappie, white bass, striped bass, channel and flathead catfish, and bluegills. Boat lanes lead the way through the water, and there are 5,000 acres of open water near the dam. The lake and its surrounding environs are also rated one of Arkansas's best birding locations. The National Audubon Society named the area an Important Birding Area because of its massive and diverse migration population. Millwood Lake boasts more species on its checklist than any other location in the state. The US Army Corps of Engineers' project office near the Millwood Dam has wildlife displays and free brochures on subjects such as area birding and hunting. Located on the lake's southeast shore, **Millwood State Park** offers a full-service marina and boat dock, 117 campsites, and hiking and biking trails. Corps of Engineers' recreational areas on the lake offer 230 campsites, picnic areas, boat-launching ramps, and group picnic shelters available by reservation.

✳ Lodging

LITTLE ROCK–NORTH LITTLE ROCK, PINE BLUFF

BED & BREAKFAST INNS An Enchanting Evening Winery, Wedding Venue and Luxury Log Cabin (501-330-2182, www.anenchantingevening.com), 29300 Highway 300, Little Rock. This private and classic rustic lodge is set amid acres of scenic beauty, yet it is only a short 20-minute drive from Little Rock, making it a popular choice for weddings. Private rooms in the lodge provide space for the wedding party to get ready while guests gather in its main hall. The upper deck is a favorite for an outdoor ceremony, with guests seated to face the cliff's edge, and Pinnacle Mountain and Lake Maumelle providing a stunning backdrop for photos of the bride and groom. An infinity pool with outdoor bar and waterfall is an elegantly casual place for a reception under the stars. The property's understated elegance features granite counters and upscale finishings, and amenities include self-service chocolate fondue, a DVD lending library, and outdoor hot tub for two. Cabin rates are $195 for the first night, $145 for each subsequent night. A wine tasting room on the property is open Friday 5–8 p.m., Saturday 10–5, and Sunday noon–5. $–$$$.

The Elms Plantation (870-766-8337 or 501-454-7165; www.theelmsplantation .com), 400 West Elm Plantation Road, Pine Bluff. Tours Thursday 10–3; last tour begins at 2 p.m. Call ahead because the facility is closed at times for special events, weddings, and holidays. Huge old pecan and elm trees line the drive to this 1886 Altheimer plantation listed on the National Register of Historic Places. This plantation home is now a bed & breakfast and hosts special events such as retreats, weddings, receptions, and dinners. $–$$.

Empress of Little Rock Bed & Breakfast (1-877-374-7966; www.theempress .com), 2120 Louisiana Street, Little Rock. This AAA Four Diamond 1888 small luxury hotel/bed & breakfast is located in the Quapaw Quarter historic district. The multiple award-winning property features a majestic double stairwell, secret card room in the turret, feather-beds, candlelight gourmet breakfasts, fireplaces, spa/sauna/aromatherapy, and Jacuzzis. The eight distinctly decorated guest rooms, three suites, and three mini-suites have a private bath. Indoor and garden wedding packages available. $–$$.

Margland Inns Bed & Breakfast (870-536-7941; www.margland.net), 703 West Second Street, Pine Bluff. Winner of the 1985 Historical Preservation Award for Arkansas, Margland consists of four historic Southern homes circa 1879–1907 that have been turned into delightful bed & breakfast lodgings. Each of the four properties features elegant antiques and loft bedrooms, and some rooms also have Jacuzzis. The four properties share a light, sunny exercise room, a business center with fax and copy machines, a refreshing outdoor pool, quiet court-yard, and garden. Standard amenities include cable television, audio-visual services, and exhibit space, if needed. This property is an elegant and afford-able setting for family reunions, retreats,

and weddings. Group rates are available. Room rates range from $65/night to $110/night. $–$$.

Rosemont Bed & Breakfast (501-374-7456; www.rosemontoflittle rock .com), 515 West 15th Street, Little Rock. Rosemont is a beautifully restored nine-teenth-century farmhouse in the heart of the downtown historic district, within minutes of the River Market. Enjoy a restful, secluded garden, front porch, guest parlor, and dining room, all com-fortably decorated with antiques and vintage furnishings complemented by such twenty-first-century amenities as Wi-Fi, cable television, Jacuzzi tubs, and gas log fireplaces. The inn is listed on the National Register of Historic Places. Weekend rates for rooms are $99–150 single or double occupancy; Monday through Thursday rates are $89 single, $99 double occupancy. There is a $25 per night charge for additional guests. Whole-house bookings for the Rosemont require a two-night minimum stay at the rate of $750 per night. $$–$$$.

HISTORIC HOTELS ♿ **Capital Hotel** (1-800-766-7666; www.capitalhotel.com), West Markham and South Louisiana Streets, Little Rock. This totally restored historic landmark is a repeat AAA Four Diamond award winner; Ashley's restau-rant is also AAA Four Diamond. The Capital Bar is a great gathering place to unwind and to people-watch local mov-ers and shakers and visiting celebrities. This nineteenth-century hotel features an elaborate ornamental cast-iron facade, a restored lobby with mosaic tile floor, a grand marble staircase, and a stained-glass ceiling. The hotel is situ-ated near Arkansas's first state Capitol (now known as the Old State House) and has been part of the city's history since 1872. One of the most luxurious hotels in the state, it often served as an unofficial political headquarters, where decisions, as well as political careers, were made. In 1974, the hotel was listed on the National Register of Historic Places. One of the

Capital Hotel's most notable features is the prefabricated cast-iron facade, part of the original construction (though it has been enhanced). This architectural detail was built out of state—where is not known for sure—and shipped to Arkansas. The hotel has hosted many political and historic personages, including President Ulysses S. Grant. In fact, legend says that the Capital's unusually large elevator was built to allow Grant to take his horse to his hotel room.

Originally constructed as an office building in 1872, the Denckla Block was converted into a hotel in 1877 when The Metropolitan Hotel, the city's only luxury hotel, burned. Major John Adams and Colonel A. G. DeShon, the former manager of The Metropolitan, partnered to convince city officials and the building's agents of the city's need for upscale lodging. The new hotel got its name from a Little Rock matron, Mrs. Morehead Wright. When asked by Adams and DeShon to suggest a name, Wright noted that it was a "capital enterprise located in a capital building" in the "capital of the state," which she hoped would be a "capital success." As you might expect, as one of the city's most luxurious hotels, it is also one of the priciest. $$–$$$$.

 ♿ **Little Rock Marriott Hotel** (501-906-4000; www.marriott.com/hotels/travel/litpb-little-rock-marriott), 3 Statehouse Plaza, Little Rock. The ducks may be gone, but the luxury remains in this AAA Four Diamond hotel with 418 rooms ($119–$184 city view; $144–$214 river view), and two concierge floors. Club access can be purchased with your room package for an additional fee. In its upscale new concept restaurant, Heritage Grill Steak and Fin Restaurant, you will find American cuisine with a

ROSEMONT BED AND BREAKFAST IN LITTLE ROCK

creative twist. Beautiful banquettes line the exterior wall of The Lobby Bar, and they provide a cozy spot for people-watching and sharing a drink after dinner. All rooms are equipped with dual-line phone lines, irons and ironing boards, 24-hour room service, complimentary airport shuttle service, and cable television with premium channels. Express checkout services are available. $$–$$$.

REST OF THE WEST

RANCHES ☀ **Bar J Ranch** (870-748-2514; www.barjranch.biz), 7938 Calion Highway, El Dorado. Pets accepted. This is a working ranch with lodge and stables, trail riding, black Angus cattle, horses, fishing, camping, and a shooting range. Summer camp is offered, as are trail, pony, and hayrides, birthday parties, and weenie roasts. The bunkhouse has a private bath, in-room refrigerator, and microwave; campfire, and continental breakfast. The Ranch House Lodge has private room or bunkhouse style, and includes continental breakfast, use of large common room with fireplace, full bath, wraparound porch with rocking chairs, as well as use of two horses for a guided trail ride. A hot country-style breakfast will be prepared for you for at an additional charge. Contact the ranch for large group rates. Campsites ($10/night) are available that include riding packages, as are RV hook-ups ($30/night) if you want to bring your own camper. Horse lodging and boarding ($15/night) are provided if you want to bring your own horse. Two cabins, each sleeping two adults and two children, are available for couples and families. Dreaming of a horseback wedding? They can help you plan a memorable one. Lodging rates range from $99 per night for a cabin for four to $299.99 per night for Robber's Roost which sleeps 10. $–$$$.

INNS **Union Square Guest Quarters** (870-864-9700; www.usgq.net), 234 East Main, El Dorado. Union Square Guest Quarters has a variety of lodging options for your El Dorado stay. Two executive suites are located downtown, and an executive apartment is located at the Myrtelles House. In addition, a beautifully restored and furnished 1925 oil-boom mansion with four bedrooms is available and can be used for weddings, receptions, and family gatherings. The guest quarters consist of 32 suites, and 17 luxury suites with sitting areas, large dressing rooms, and private baths equipped with the finest modern amenities. Four full suites are in a restored circa 1875 home. A number of the luxury suites overlook Corinne Court. Free high-speed wireless Internet and cable television are in all rooms. Room rate includes continental breakfast and use of nearby fitness center, which has indoor and outdoor pools. This wide selection of lodging options is available for an equally wide range of prices. Suites range from $139–$169 per night, with luxury suites topping out at $279. $–$$$$.

✳ Where to Eat

EATING OUT **Brave New Restaurant** (501-663-2677; www.bravenewrestaurant.com), 2300 Cottondale Lane, Little Rock. Open Monday through Saturday 11–10. Situated discreetly on the banks of the Arkansas River, Brave New Restaurant's deck is an ideal setting for lunch or dinner during the mild days of spring and fall in the Natural State. You will also find that the breeze coming off the river will keep you cool enough to enjoy lunch on the deck during most of the summer. Peter Brave has made quite a name for himself using locally grown, organic produce and basing his ever-changing menu around whatever is in season at the time. Brave's mussels in garlic butter appetizer is considered among the best in the state; a fresh fruit and Brie plate is a great accompaniment to your end-of-day glass of wine. Brave also has a way with veal; it will be on the menu and is well worth a try. Meals average $30 per person or less. A banquet room and catering services are available. $$–$$$.

Café Africa (501-666-2406; www .littlerockzoo.com), 1 Jonesboro Drive, Little Rock. Open 9–2 during winter months and 9–4:30 March through October. Café Africa is housed in a renovated historic lion house at the Little Rock Zoo. Built in 1933, this Works Progress Administration all-stone building features a stone fireplace, multilevel dining, and a wide variety of menu items to appeal to kids and adults alike: sandwiches, burgers, chicken fingers, tater tots, and fries; specialty menu items include a daily hot plate special and panini sandwiches. Café Africa is also available for private party rental. Prices average $10–12 per person, including drink. $.

& ⛾ **Flying Fish** (501-375-3474; www .flyingfishinthe.net), 511 President Clinton Avenue, Little Rock. Open daily 11–9. The Flying Fish is a fun place to eat. The clever decor includes outboard motors, singing bass, and flying fish. You just have to see them to appreciate them. The food is always great, and their catfish rivals the best in the state. This is not your typical catfish place, however; with oysters, salmon, and tilapia on the menu, it seems more like a seafood restaurant. Plan to spend $15 for lunch and $25 per person for dinner. $–$$.

The Mammoth Orange Café (870-397-2347 or 870-397-2572), 103 North AR 365, Redfield. You won't need your GPS to find this restaurant, located halfway between Little Rock and Pine Bluff. It is a giant orange that was inspired by a similar restaurant in Fresno, California, circa the 1950s. The menu includes hamburgers, hot dogs, salads, and daily specials. Very affordable diner fare at $10–12 per person. $–$$.

Whole Hog Café (501-753-9227; www .wholehogcafe.com), 5107 Warden Road, North Little Rock. Open daily 11–6. The Whole Hog Café competes in the Memphis-in-May and the Kansas City Barbeque Society Barbeque Championship Circuits as the Southern Gentlemen's Culinary Society. Menu items are mostly variations with pork, beef, or chicken on a plate, in a sandwich, or spread over a potato or a salad. Ribs are also popular, and the potato salad is unique. Basically, Whole Hog knows how to cook the potato. Choose one, or many, of seven levels of BBQ sauce ranging from #1 (mild) to #9 (volcano). Listed in Fodor's Travel America Guide: Don't Miss in Arkansas. The restaurant has also been featured on the Food Network's *Rachael Ray's Tasty Travels*. Ribs are $17/slab, with sides à la carte. Plates and sandwiches range from $7–10 with drink. $–$$.

DINING OUT & ⛾ **Cajun's Wharf** (501-375-5351; www.cajunswharf.com), 2400 Cantrell Road, Little Rock. Restaurant hours are Monday through Thursday 5–10, Friday and Saturday 5–11. Cajun's bar is open Monday through Saturday from 4:30 p.m. to close. Cajun's Wharf is one of Arkansas's best-known restaurants at one of Little Rock's premier locations, overlooking the Arkansas River. The rustic exterior is abandoned once you are inside. A sleek, modern design prevails in the main dining room, featuring a bank of glass to the riverside, and large aquariums in the center of the room provide romantic and soothing ambient lighting. The Cajun-style menu features oysters, shrimp, crab legs, several fish dishes, and steaks. Three courses for dinner, with wine, will average $60 per person, depending on the wine you select from the restaurant's extensive cellar. You can also make a mighty fine meal from Cajun's appetizer menu. The crabcake sandwich ($6) is one of the best versions in town and is plenty to eat. The bar is urban upscale, with lots of frosted glass and cobalt pendant track lighting. The bar offers live music Thursday through Saturday most weeks, featuring very talented local and regional acts. The large deck upstairs is partially covered and has ceiling fans to stir the breeze on hot summer evenings. This is one of the best places to watch the sunset in central Arkansas. Happy hour is often accompanied by a solo guitarist, and the food, drink, and location combine for the perfect place to unwind and watch the river traffic float by. $$–$$$.

& ₸ **Loca Luna Bold American Bistro** (501-663-4666; www.localuna.com), 3519 Old Cantrell Road, Little Rock. Open for lunch Monday through Friday 11–2. Dinner is served Sunday through Thursday 5:30–9, Friday and Saturday 5:30–10. Sunday brunch runs 10–2. Loca Luna is one of Arkansas's most celebrated restaurants. In addition to scores of local dining awards and glowing four-star reviews, Loca Luna has been nationally recognized in *Southern Living*, *Gourmet*, *USA Today*, *Food Arts*, *New York Times*, *Atlanta Journal-Constitution*, and many others. *Bon Appetit* called Loca Luna one of America's best neighborhood restaurants. Attire is up to you; owner Mark Abernathy recommends "whatever you feel good in." Abernathy calls Loca Luna's cuisine "nouveau schizophrenic" because it's all over the map, and this truly is one of those places where there is something for everyone. At dinner the focus is on grilled meats, fresh seafood, creative pastas, and wood-fired, brick-oven pizzas. It's international cuisine with a Southern twist. The lunches are legendary. In addition to outstanding soups, salads, and sandwiches, Loca Luna offers award-winning Best Plate Lunches with traditional Southern roots. Items like pot roast, chicken-fried steaks, chicken and dumplings are on the menu, all with a huge assortment of homestyle vegetables like greens and real mashed potatoes with pork thyme cream gravy. Great appetizers and homemade desserts round out the offerings. Prices are moderate, with lunches around $7–8 and dinners between $12–18. $–$$.

✳ Entertainment

LITTLE ROCK/NORTH LITTLE ROCK METROPOLITAN AREA

& **Arkansas Symphony Orchestra** (501-666-1761; www.arkansassymphony.org), Robinson Center Music Hall, West Markham and Broadway, Little Rock. The Arkansas Symphony performs more than 30 concerts annually at Little Rock's Robinson Center Music Hall and at numerous special events. A variety of performers and music types are featured in the Masterworks Series, the Pops Series, and the Chamber Music Series. The Symphony Youth Orchestras provide opportunities for young musicians of Arkansas. Nationally known guest artists who have performed with the orchestra include Itzhak Perlman, Van Cliburn, Marilyn Horne, Bernadette Peters, Doc Severinsen, Michael Bolton, and Olivia Newton-John. The website maintains a schedule of performances and ticket prices.

& **Ballet Arkansas** (501-223-5150; www.balletarkansas.org), Robinson Center Music Hall, West Markham and Broadway, Little Rock. Call or visit the website for a schedule of performances. Ballet Arkansas was founded in 1978 as a nonprofit organization, and it traces its roots back to the Little Rock Civic Ballet. Throughout the years, Ballet Arkansas has seen many accomplishments, such as Cynthia Gregory performing with the ballet, bringing Mikhail Baryshnikov to Little Rock, and receiving the Stream Award from the Southwestern Regional Ballet Association Festival. Performances include the annual *Nutcracker* each holiday season.

& ₸ **River Market**, President Clinton Boulevard, Little Rock, is a carefully crafted and diverse medley of owner-operated shops, stalls, and/or day tables filled with a huge variety of vendors and flavors for your dining pleasure. Located in the heart of Little Rock's River Market

District, the River Market is an exciting public food market that will entice your senses with its relaxing entertainment and rich cultural experiences. The farmers' market is held here through the growing season. Open May through October, Tuesday and Saturday 7–3.

Major elements of the River Market District include the Central Arkansas Main Public Library, the Arkansas Museum of Discovery, several restaurants/bars, specialty retail stores, residential living, Julius Breckling Riverfront Park, and the River Market. The River Market's Ottenheimer Market Hall houses nearly a dozen permanent merchants who offer market specialties year-round. There is a wide selection of fantastic food from all over the globe, whether you're looking for something terrific to take home for dinner or just stopping by for lunch. Among the growing list of specialties, you'll find hand-crafted artisan breads and pastries; homemade pies and cakes; meats and poultry—pork, beef, chicken, and turkey—smoked, barbecued, glazed, and deli cuts; locally roasted gourmet coffees and specialty espresso drinks; authentic Mexican, Japanese, Middle Eastern, and Central European cuisine and groceries; fruit smoothies; and gourmet chocolates, jellies, preserves, sauces, spices, and seasonings. If you've got a picky palate, the Ottenheimer Market Hall is the place to be!

 & ♿ **Verizon Arena** (501-340-5660 or 501-975-9000; www.alltelarena.com), One Verizon Arena Way, North Little Rock. A state-of-the-art, multipurpose facility, the arena is situated on the Arkansas River in North Little Rock. It seats 18,000 for basketball and is home to the Arkansas Twisters Arena II football team. It has hosted such special events as the Ringling Bros. and Barnum & Bailey Circus, Champions on Ice figure skating exhibition, Southeastern Conference regional men's and women's NCAA basketball tournaments, and concerts by such major entertainers as Journey

and Def Leppard, Shania Twain, Kevin Hart, Pink, Fleetwood Mac, and Miranda Lambert.

WESTERN TIMBERLANDS

♿ **Perot Theatre** (903-792-4992; www.trahc.org/perot.shtml), 221 Main Street, Texarkana. Built in 1924 and originally known as the Saenger Theatre, this fully restored Italian Renaissance theater has hosted such performers as Douglas Fairbanks, Will Rogers, and Annie Oakley; it now hosts top national/international stars and Broadway touring productions. Ticket prices vary; the website posts details on performances.

MICROBREWERIES ♿ ♿ **Diamond Bear Brewing Company** (501-708-BREW; www.diamondbear.com), 323-C Cross Street, Little Rock. Beer produced in the old, time-honored traditional methods of European brewers, using only two-row malted barley, hops, yeast, and great Arkansas water. Being brewed locally gives the beer a great advantage in freshness, capturing some of the world's most famous styles of beer without the use of adjuncts or preservatives. Free tours of the brewery are conducted every Friday at 5 p.m. and Saturday and Sunday at 4 p.m., and include a walk-through of the facility and samples of the product. Root beer is available for those who are under the legal drinking age of 21 in the state. Private tours and meeting facilities are available upon request for larger groups. A gift shop sells Diamond Bear souvenirs and the beer. All of Diamond Bear's draft beers have been brewed on-site from the beginning, and as of the fall of 2006, their bottled beers have also been brewed locally. The bottled beer was previously brewed and bottled in Minnesota, but after purchasing a bottling line from a company in Wisconsin, the brewery is able to produce all of its products here. This also allows the brewery more flexibility in the varieties it can offer. The water used in the beer production comes from Lake Winnetoka outside Hot Springs. The brewery specializes in craft beers, which are beers that contain no adjuncts, chemicals, or additives. Eight types of beer are brewed annually at Diamond Bear; including a non-alcoholic beer and one seasonally produced. Diamond Bear has won numerous national and international awards for its world-class brews, including Gold Medals at the prestigious Great American Beer Festival and World Beer Cup. The Arkansas Ale House located inside the brewery serves "beer-centric" sandwiches, soups, and stews as well as daily and weekly specials. It is open Tuesday through Sunday 11 a.m.–9 p.m., and the bar stays open Friday and Saturday night until 10 p.m.

THEATER ♿ ♆ **Arkansas Repertory Theatre** (501-378-0445; www.therep.org), 601 Main Street, Little Rock. The Rep, as it is affectionately called, has a national reputation as one of the finest repertory theaters in the country. Contemporary comedies, cutting-edge dramas, musical theater, and literary classics are presented by the company. Since its creation in 1976, The Rep has produced more than 230 shows, including 30 world premieres. Located in downtown Little Rock, the company mounts productions in its 354-seat MainStage Theater, a venue for The Rep's more stylistically traditional work. The company's Second Stage, a 100-seat black box space, reflects The Rep's interest in the works of emerging playwrights and offers newer and lesser-known works in a more developmental context. Ticket prices vary according to show. Details are posted on the website.

Wildwood Park (501-821-7275; www.wildwoodpark.org), 20919 Denny Road, Little Rock. The facility's hours are dependent upon the event. Wildwood is located on 105 acres of virgin forestland in west Little Rock. This acclaimed performing arts park grew out of the Arkansas Opera Theatre and now serves as home for the company. Seven spectacular gardens and an 8-acre lake provide a beautiful background for outdoor musical performances. The renowned Wildwood Music Festival is held each June and highlights the performing and visual arts, plus up-and-coming young artists. Past guest performers include Peter Duchin, Crystal Gayle, Judy Collins, the Glenn Miller Orchestra, Riders in the Sky, and the Preservation Hall Jazz Band. Ticket prices are based on the event and range from $10 for the Harvest! Festival each fall to $75 for the Wine & Food FEASTival, one of its best-attended events.

EASTERN TIMBERLANDS

South Arkansas Arts Center Theatre (870-862-5474; www.saac-arts.org), 110 East Fifth Street, El Dorado. Open Monday through Friday 9–5. The South Arkansas Arts Center (SAAC) provides monthly gallery exhibits featuring local, regional, and nationally acclaimed artists; a season of community theater productions annually; and classes for children and adults in visual arts, photography, ballet, music, and drama on-site as well as Artists-in-Education in area schools. SAAC's 22,500-square-foot facility houses three art galleries, a ballet studio, a 206-seat theater, a scene and costume shop, a photography studio, educational classroom space, and an open studio for artists offered free of charge to anyone in the community.

✳ Selective Shopping

LITTLE ROCK/NORTH LITTLE ROCK METROPOLITAN AREA

Bernice Garden Farmers' Market (501-617-2511) 1401 S. Main Street, Little Rock. Open every Sunday from mid-April until mid-October. Sustainably raised and grow produce, cheese, nuts, salsa and soap are among the wide array of products available in this charming garden market in the hip SOMA district. Frequently a popular area for live music and food trucks. Open 10 a.m.–2 p.m.

EASTERN TIMBERLANDS

James Hayes Art Glass Co. (870-543-9792; www.hayesartglass.com), 2900 Ridgway Road, Pine Bluff. James Hayes is a Pine Bluff native and professional glass blower. Tour his shop and see the treasure trove of extraordinary glass works in an astounding array of brilliant colors and remarkable shapes. Some of Mr. Hayes' honors include an invitation from the White House to design a Christmas tree ornament, designing gifts for the 2003 Lieutenant Governors Conference, and the design of the 2001 Governor's Arts Awards. He also provides demonstrations for scheduled tours.

El Dorado Downtown (1-888-921-BOOM; www.mainstreeteldorado.com), El Dorado. Boutiques and shops on this historic square feature a wide variety of wares. Stretch your legs and combine a walking tour of these architecturally significant buildings, many financed by the South Arkansas oil boom and the timber industry.

WESTERN TIMBERLANDS

Sweet Things Vintage Antique Mall (870-773-1006; www.sweetthingsvintage.com), 620 East Seventh Street, Texarkana. Open Monday through Saturday 9–5. Come here for vintage jewelry, elegant glassware, and a variety of collectibles, including furniture, decorative items, and linens.

✳ Special Events

March: ✒ **Camden Daffodil Festival** (870-836-9243; www.camdendaffodilfestival.com), 3064 Roseman Road, Camden.

One of most beautiful festivals in the state! Includes tours of four daffodil gardens, a cemetery walk with live reenactments, historic home tours with reenactors, a downtown festival with over 100 vendors, arts and crafts, a quilt show, children's activities, and Civil War reenactors with cannons blasting over the banks of the Ouachita River. Also an antique car show, live entertainment, and a grand finale of the Championship Steak Cook-Off on Saturday evening. Admission: garden tours $20 adults, $8 children; home tours $7 each house; Oakland Cemetery Walk $7 adults, $3 children.

May: ✒ **Annual Riverfest** (501-255-3378; www.riverfestarkansas.com), Little Rock and North Little Rock. The banks of the Arkansas River in Little Rock and North Little Rock come alive every May for an annual celebration of music, dance, and art. For more than a quarter of a century, tens of thousands of people have joined for a weekend of food and fun for the family. Special areas for children include face painting and crafts; special performances by local dance troupes and magicians; and a river fun area that has games with prizes. Every type of food vendor you can imagine is here, plus headline musical acts in every genre. Arkansas performers are also spotlighted on special stages. The trolley runs constantly, making it more convenient to tote your blanket or lawn chair from stage to stage and to enjoy acts like Bonnie Raitt, the Dave Matthews Band, and back-in-the-day bands like Jethro Tull. Check the website for a schedule of performances. An annual fireworks display caps off the event and is accompanied by the Arkansas Symphony. Tickets are sold in advance while supplies last (multiday $50–60; single-day $25–30). Children 4 and under admitted free with an adult. Children 5–12 years of age $10 per day.

September: ✒ **Annual Camden BPW Barn Sale** (870-231-6244; www.bpwbarnsale.org), Oakland Farms,

Oakland at Monticello Street, Camden. No gate admission; $4 per car for parking in reserved area. The massive old oak trees provide plenty of shade as you stroll beside the historic barn while listening to an old-fashioned gristmill grind cornmeal throughout the day. Watch a potter or woodcarving artist at work or purchase a newly made treasure from one of the 160 crafters. All crafts are original and handmade. Expect to find handcrafted wooden pieces, ceramics, paintings, floral arrangements, handmade clothing, jewelry, stained glass, and much more. This is South Arkansas's largest arts and crafts festival, and it includes an antique and classic car show, 5K run, pancake breakfast, and spaghetti dinner, plus many other activities around town.

THE OUACHITA
MOUNTAINS

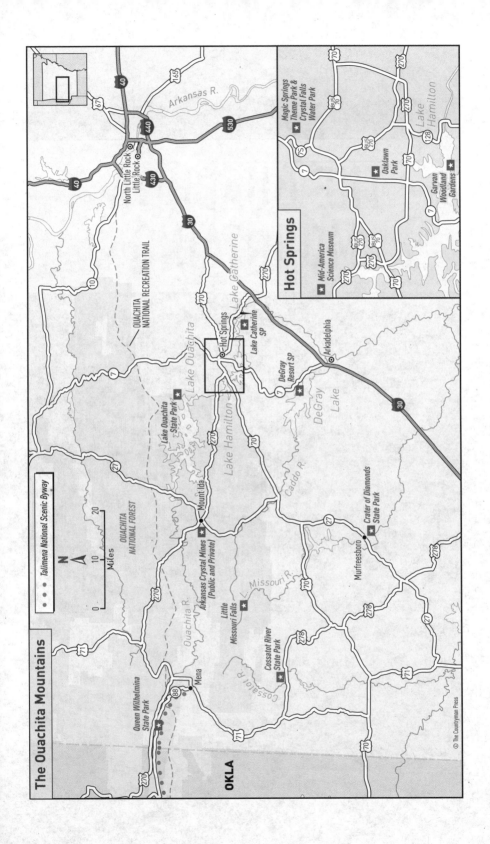

The Ouachita Mountains

Talimena National Scenic Byway

N

Miles
0   10   20

OUACHITA NATIONAL FOREST

OKLA

Queen Wilhelmina State Park

Mena

88

Little Missouri Falls

Arkansas Crystal Mines (Public and Private)

Mount Ida

Cossatot River State Park

Cossatot R.

Ouachita R.

L. Missouri R.

Murfreesboro

Crater of Diamonds State Park

Caddo R.

DeGray Lake

Lake Ouachita State Park

Lake Ouachita

OUACHITA NATIONAL RECREATION TRAIL

Lake Hamilton

Hot Springs

Lake Catherine

Lake Catherine SP

DeGray Resort SP

Arkadelphia

Arkansas R.

North Little Rock
Little Rock

Hot Springs

Magic Springs Theme Park & Crystal Falls Water Park

Lake Hamilton

Oaklawn Park

Garvan Woodland Gardens

Mid-America Science Museum

© The Countryman Press

THE OUACHITA MOUNTAINS

The South's oldest national forest stretches from near the center of Arkansas to southeast Oklahoma; the pristine Ouachita National Forest was created December 18, 1907, by President Theodore Roosevelt. The rugged Ouachita Mountains were first explored in 1541 by Hernando de Soto's party of Spaniards. French explorers followed, flavoring the region with names like Fourche la Favre River. The range takes its name from the French spelling of the Native American word Washita, which means "good hunting grounds." Constituting more than 1.8 million acres, the mountain scenery, tall pines, and many species and varieties of vegetation form a unique attraction for forest visitors.

The Ouachitas are prized for their outdoor adventures, but the forest also is valued for the timber and other forest products it provides for the nation. The forest's ecosystem management policy guarantees that the land is healthy now and encourages careful use of the forest for the future. The Ouachita Mountains are generally characterized as folded ridges and valleys composed of Paleozoic rocks. They are unusual in North America in that the ridges are generally aligned east to west, unlike the Rocky Mountains or Appalachian Mountains, where the ridges usually run north to south. The most striking result of this orientation is that there is an extensive south-facing slope on each ridge that is exposed to the heat and light of the sun, as well as a north-facing slope that is protected from direct solar radiation and is consequently cooler and moister.

The dry south-facing slopes are often covered with pine forests or woodlands, or even drier oak woodlands, while the moister north-facing slopes are covered with diverse hardwood forests. This results in distinct east-to-west bands of vegetation that can be seen from an airplane or by satellite. The bands usually shift repeatedly from pine forest to hardwoods and back, moving from north to south. This is particularly apparent in the winter, when the green color of evergreen pines contrasts dramatically with the brown of the leafless deciduous hardwoods.

Alternating layers of sandstone and shale are the dominant rocks underlying the Ouachitas. They are usually tilted, with erosion-resistant layers of sandstone forming the crest and one slope of a ridge. Rocks of other types are less extensive than in the Ozark Mountains, where limestone and dolomite underlie large areas.

The largest city in the Ouachita Mountains is Hot Springs, and the region extends eastward into Pulaski County and the western part of Little Rock. Much of the Ouachita Mountains are still forested, and a substantial portion is within the boundaries of the Ouachita National Forest, which covers almost half the total area.

Congress established Hot Springs Reservation on April 20, 1832, to protect hot springs flowing from the southwestern slope of Hot Springs Mountain. Known for its 47 thermal springs, this national park was the nation's first, predating Yellowstone by 40 years. Within it you will find more than 30 miles of hiking trails through the glorious Ouachita Mountains. The park is popular for its scenic drives and overlooks, hot water cascade, and picnic areas and campsites.

The city of Hot Springs has a colorful past as a favored destination for some of the nation's most notorious bad actors. Al Capone and Lucky Luciano were regularly seen in the lobby of the historic Arlington Hotel. Lovingly preserved through the years, it is easy to understand why its popularity spans decades. Huge, glorious murals decorate the walls behind the massive mahogany bar on one side and the dance floor on the other. The elevated dining platform in the lobby's center is the perfect vantage point for people watching, both inside and outside the hotel.

The Arlington is situated at the end of Bathhouse Row, a boulevard of unique and historic buildings once filled with thousands of bathers who sought their soothing waters. Two of them remain as operating bathhouses, while others have been repurposed. The Hot Springs National Park Visitor Center now occupies one of them, the Museum of Contemporary Art occupies another. Regal, centuries-old magnolias provide picturesque shelter for your stroll down Bathhouse Row.

Five crystal clear lakes, known as the Diamond Lakes, lure tourists who love water and beautiful scenery. The largest, Lake Ouachita, offers a wilderness experience combined with the amenities of full-service resorts. Luxury houseboat rentals are available at DeGray Lake and Lake Ouachita. And at many locations, you can enjoy a round of golf after you've finished a morning fishing excursion. Rock hounds will also find themselves right at home in Mount Ida, where you can search for crystals prized around the world at one of many private mines in the area.

Streams such as the Cossatot River and Little Missouri River run from north to south and cross the ridges in their paths. At each crossing, they created a steep rapids

AERIAL VIEW OF THE ARLINGTON HOTEL IN HOT SPRINGS   ARKANSAS DEPARTMENT OF PARKS & TOURISM

or waterfall and emptied the valleys of their sediments. As a result, these streams have a much different character than those of the Ozarks, making them very challenging for white-water canoes and kayaks. The Cossatot, in particular, is hugely popular with paddlers throughout the country.

AREA CODES The western edge of this region falls under the 479 area code. Mount Ida and the Lake Ouachita area are covered by the 870 area code. Hot Springs through central Arkansas uses the 501 area code.

GUIDANCE The Ouachita Mountains fall within the purview of a couple of the state's regional tourism associations.

The Western Arkansas Mountain (479-783-6118; www.westarkansastourism.com) region includes the Mena area.

Diamond Lakes Travel Association (501-321-1700; www.diamondlakes.dina.org) posts very helpful information on the five major lakes, their lodging, and their attractions on its website.

Arkadelphia Chamber of Commerce (870-246-5542; www.arkadelphia.org) lists events, lodging, and dining options on their website for Arkadelphia and Bismarck, near DeGray Lake.

Conway Area Chamber of Commerce (1-866-7Conway; www.Conway Arkansas .org), 900 Oak Street, Conway. As the only town in the state that is home to three colleges, as well as one of the state's most popular festivals, Toad Suck Daze, this community brings in great lecturers, theatrical performances, and concerts.

Hot Springs Convention & Visitors Bureau (1-800-SPA CITY; www.hot springs.org), 134 Convention Boulevard, Hot Springs. With offices strategically located within the Hot Springs Convention Center, you can be sure that if it's a happening in Hot Springs, you can hear about it here.

Hot Springs Visitor Center (1-800-SPA-CITY), 629 Central Avenue, Hot Springs. This visitor center is not only a great source for literature on the entire Diamond Lakes region, but its staff will gladly give you directions, discount coupons for area attractions, and literature about upcoming festivals and events.

Mena Polk County Area Chamber of Commerce (479-394-2912; www.menapolk chamber.com). Cabins and small lodges are prominent throughout the Ouachitas, and this chamber is your connection to the rich and the rustic around Rich Mountain.

Mount Ida Area Chamber of Commerce (870-867-2723, www.mtidachamber.com), Mount Ida. If you find yourself strangely drawn to Mount Ida, you might be tuning in to the rich quartz crystal deposits that have made this small town world famous. The history of quartz mining in the Ouachitas, mining tips, and public and private mines are listed on their website.

GETTING THERE *By auto:* If you are traveling from the east or west, the Ouachitas are easily accessed via I-30, which basically constitutes the southern border of the entire region. AR 7 runs from the Louisiana state line near El Dorado to Diamond City, near the Missouri state line, and is preferred pavement for a more leisurely and scenic excursion. Along the state's western border, US 71 connects with Oklahoma at Fort Smith and Texas in Texarkana.

By air: **The Little Rock National Airport** (501-372-3439; www.clintonairport.com), 1 Airport Drive, Little Rock. Air travelers will find that the Little Rock airport, which is located at the eastern edge of the region, is the closest major terminal. Allegiant Air, American Airlines, Delta, Frontier Airlines, Southwest, United, and Via Airlines service the facility.

MEDICAL EMERGENCIES **National Park Medical Center** (501-321-1000; www
.nationalparkmedical.com), 1910 Malvern Avenue, Hot Springs. Centrally located
within the region, this 166-bed, full-service hospital can handle any medical emergency.

✳ Wandering Around

EXPLORING BY CAR **Scenic 7 Byway.** One of the state's most popular routes with
motorcycle riders is the 60 miles of AR 7 that pass through the Ozark and Ouachita
National Forests and have been designated by the US Forest Service as part of the
National Forest Scenic Byways system. But you don't need to be on a Harley to appreciate this drive, which takes you from the gentle folds of the Ouachitas to the rugged
peaks of the Ozarks.

There are numerous recreation areas providing opportunities to camp, hike, mountain bike, canoe, and ride horses along or within a few miles of the highway. Discover
many natural attractions here, such as the **Alum Cove Natural Bridge**, a 130-foot arch
that is all that remains of a large sandstone cave. Follow the path of the first settlers
to the **Mystic Caverns** and learn the legend of the spider monkey while you take in the
cave coral and other formations along the cavern walls. Finally, hike up to the top of
Pedestal Rocks for one of the more spectacular views in Arkansas.

Talimena Scenic Byway. One breathtaking panorama follows another as this
National Forest Scenic Byway winds along forested mountaintops between Mena,
Arkansas, and Talihina, Oklahoma. Cresting the highest points between the Appa-
lachians and the Rockies, this byway showcases the four distinctive seasons of the
Ouachita National Forest at their best. Information stations are located at each end of
the drive.

EXPLORING BY FOOT **Lake Ouachita Vista Trail** (www.lakeouachitavistatrail.org).
Open year-round, Lake Ouachita Vista Trail is a series of unsurfaced hiking and
mountain-biking trails and loops winding along the banks of the largest lake in Arkansas. Hikers and bikers can choose from several routes and levels of difficulty ranging in length from 1.25 miles to 6.2 miles. Waterfalls and breathtaking views of **Lake
Ouachita** are also seen at several points along the way as the trail winds through the
hardwood and pine forest. Bald eagles soar through the winter skies over **Eagle Vista**;
strategically placed benches invite hikers and bikers to take a break and enjoy brilliant
wildflower displays in spring and summer. Along the trail, pits left by quartz and silver
speculators, an old cattle dip, and the remains of a moonshiner's still are evidence of
the area's colorful history.

Ouachita National Recreation Trail (501-321-5201). Open year-round. An abundance
of spurs and access points make the Ouachita Trail an obvious choice for day trips,
weekend excursions, and extended backpacking trips. The trail's western terminus is
at Oklahoma's Talimena State Park, and it spans 225 miles across the entire western
half of central Arkansas before reaching **Pinnacle State Park**, 15 miles from Little Rock.
Unique in the country, the mountains in the **Ouachita National Forest** run east to west,
with moist, northern slopes covered with hardwoods and southern slopes blanketed
with pines. Two state parks—Pinnacle and **Queen Wilhelmina**—and three national recreation areas—**Big Brushy, Iron Springs, and Lake Sylvia**—offer facilities and campsites
for extended stays. This is an extremely diverse trail with numerous side trails to recreation areas and scenic overlooks. Elevations range from 600 to 2,600 feet.

    Ⴊ **Hot Springs Gallery Walk** (501-624-0550 or 501-624-0489; www.hotsprings.org),
Downtown Central Avenue, Hot Springs. Downtown galleries are open late with music

and refreshments. The artists are available to chat with visitors on the first Friday of each month. Enjoy some of the finest contemporary art in America as you stroll through beautiful downtown Hot Springs.

EXPLORING BY RIVER The **Caddo River**, flowing out of the Ouachita Mountains in west-central Arkansas, is described by those that know it as among the best family outing–type streams in the state. It begins in southwestern Montgomery County and flows for 40 miles near or through the communities of Black Springs, Norman, Caddo Gap, Glenwood, and Amity before entering the backwaters of **DeGray Lake**. Probably the most popular Caddo River float trip is the 6-mile journey from **Caddo Gap** to **Glenwood**. One highlight is a swinging footbridge over the river at the put-in (the low-water bridge west of the Caddo Gap community). Rock gardens are common along this stretch and can cause consternation when the water is low. The actual gap for the Caddo occurs about 1.5 miles into the float trip (just above the AR 240 bridge). At this point, the river passes through a narrow opening between the ridges, and so do AR 8 and the railroad— all three are bunched closely together. The gap is also the site of a geological oddity: some hot springs bubble up into the streambed here. For those wishing to experience these thermal waters, here are some rough directions: go upstream 200–300 yards from the old low-water bridge; the springs will be on the west bank and are usually at or below the river's surface; barefoot waders will have no trouble recognizing the spot. The Caddo's South Fork enters from the west 2.5 miles later. Small rapids, long gravel bars, and an occasional willow thicket characterize the stream as it approaches Glenwood. Like most of Arkansas's canoeing streams, the Caddo usually gets too low in the summer and early fall for good float trips. The best months for successful float trips are March through June. The Caddo River is an easy stream to access. There are numerous access points, and the shuttle routes are almost always along paved roads. Traditional put-in and take-out points include the bridge immediately west of Norman; the low-water bridge west of Caddo Gap; the old low-water bridge on AR 182 north of Amity; and the AR 84 bridge northeast of Amity. The Caddo is one of the most underrated and overlooked cold-water fishing streams in Arkansas. That's unfortunate, for this small river offers excellent fishing in a peaceful setting that's ideal for a weekend family getaway. This is one of the few cold-water streams where white bass are an important species. These scrappy fighters migrate upstream from DeGray Lake during their spring spawning runs and are taken by boaters and bank fishermen alike using live minnows, jigs, spinners,

CONTEMPORARY ART ON DISPLAY IN RENOVATED OZARK BATHHOUSE

and minnow-replica crankbaits. Also, the Caddo can be floated below DeGray Lake to its confluence with the Ouachita River. This short stretch is one of the most convenient in the state, crossed by I-30, US 67, and AR 7.

Cossatot River (870-387-3141; www.waterdata.usgs.gov/nwis/uv?07340300). One man's impassible raging river is another's opportunity for world-class white-water rafting. The National Park Service describes this river as "probably the most challenging white-water float in the state," but the US Army Corps of Engineers makes no buts about it, calling it "the most difficult white-water stream in the state." Early Native Americans called it Cossatot, "skull crusher." Located south of Mena, the Cossatot forms Cossatot Falls, a rugged and rocky canyon that challenges the most experienced canoeists and kayakers with its Class IV and V rapids. When the water is high, the paddlers are here. This National Wild and Scenic River is a watershed basin with flow levels dependent on rainfall. After significant precipitation, the river level rises, allowing experienced paddlers the opportunity to test their skills in challenging Class IV and V whitewater. At the river's **Cossatot Falls** area, a rocky canyon with distinct ledges, the river drops 33 feet in elevation within 0.3 of a mile. Late winter to early spring is peak white-water paddling season here. Class III to V whitewater is for experts only. Floatable river levels are usually limited to late fall, winter, and spring. For river stage information (in feet) from the AR 246 access, call or visit the US Geological Survey website for real-time Cossatot River data.

Ouachita River. The Ouachita River originates in the Ouachita Mountains of west-central Arkansas near the Arkansas and Oklahoma border and flows 600 river miles before joining the Black and Red Rivers in north-central Louisiana. It is a river of diverse beauty that begins as a small mountain stream at Eagleton and flows eastward approximately 120 miles. It winds through lush mountain valleys, steadily building as it flows on its 600-mile course amid banks of moss-covered oaks to the swampy bottoms of Louisiana. The Ouachita is noted for its great fishing, especially bass, bream, and white perch. Wildlife is prolific along the banks of the river. The Ouachita is a vital artery for those living in mid-central Arkansas and is the source of three large manmade lakes in that region—**Lake Ouachita, Lake Hamilton,** and **Lake Catherine**—all of which are used for recreational purposes. The Ouachita turns south after it leaves Lake Catherine on its course toward Arkansas's southern border. The river then flows approximately 250 miles through sparsely populated areas, intermittently dotted by the cities of Arkadelphia (Clark County), Camden (Ouachita County), and El Dorado (Union County), then continues into Louisiana for another 200 miles to its juncture with the Black River. The Ouachita played a great role in the establishment of these towns, for it was the river that provided access to these areas for buyers from as far away as New Orleans who were purchasing cotton, a basic product that supported many Southern communities in the late 1800s and early 1900s.

✳ Towns and Villages

Arkadelphia (870-246-5542; www.arkadelphia.org) is located in Clark County along I-30, about 65 miles from Little Rock, 40 miles from Crater of Diamonds State Park, and 25 miles from Hot Springs. Founded as Blakelytown in the early 1800s, this town changed its name in 1838, but it wasn't until after the Civil War that Arkadelphia found its direction for the future. In 1873, the Cairo and Fulton Railroad, following the Military Road (Southwest Trail), joined Arkadelphia and Little Rock for the first time. The city's history as both a farm market and trading center is due to reliable transportation and water outlets from its prime locale near the Ouachita River.

Spring of 1997 brought a rebirth to the town following a devastating tornado that leveled 4 blocks of downtown and damaged a surrounding 40-block area. The city continues to revitalize after the tragedy, largely because of planning by the Arkadelphia 2025 Commission, formed in response to President Bill Clinton's urging to use the tragedy as inspiration to shift gears and focus on the town's goals and dreams for its future. Promoting a vibrant downtown was high on the list and has led to a restored courthouse and new downtown post office, police station, and town hall. By 2013, Arkadelphia was reporting on gains just one year after joining the nationwide Mainstreet USA program to inspire growth in the heart of small town America.

Arkadelphia has an enduring commitment to education and is home to two universities: Henderson State and Ouachita Baptist. The town's recreation opportunities are plentiful, with local spots such as Feaster Park, a 78-acre site with picnic areas, pavilion, outdoor basketball courts, softball fields, and the Arkadelphia Aquatic Park and Recreation Center. A new 80-acre Youth Sports Complex features soccer, softball, and baseball facilities and a fishing pond. Feaster Trail is another recreational asset—a paved and lighted trail that spans the length of the city, popular with walkers, joggers, bikers, and in-line skaters.

Conway (1-866-7CONWAY; www.conwayarkansas.org), 900 Oak Street. Approximately 30 miles northwest of Little Rock along I-40 is one of the fastest-growing communities in the state. As the home to not one but three colleges—the University of Central Arkansas, Hendrix, and Central Baptist—there's always something going on in this town of 50,000, whether it's a theatrical production, an art exhibit, a concert, or a lecture by a renowned speaker. There are two schools of thought as to why the name Conway was selected. One is it was named for the steam locomotive that pulled the first train into the station. The other is that it was named for the Conway family, prominent Arkansas residents since territorial days.

Hendrix College, a nationally ranked private institution, was established in 1890. Three years later, in 1893, Central College for Girls (now Central Baptist) was established, and Conway, Arkansas, was on its way to becoming an educational center. The University of Central Arkansas followed in 1907, then called the Arkansas Normal School.

Locks and dams on the Arkansas River in Little Rock and Conway have created pools—such as those at Toad Suck Park in Conway—that comprise approximately 19,000 acres of water. This area is particularly popular with anglers and boaters. Cadron Settlement Park, a US Army Corps of Engineers property on the river, preserves a spot where the Cherokee Indians stopped along the Trail of Tears. Lake Conway, the largest manmade game-and-fish-commission lake in the United States, at 6,700 acres, provides excellent fishing, while Beaverfork Lake is popular for water recreation. Shopping and antiquing prospects abound, as do opportunities for both fine and casual dining.

Hot Springs (1-800-SPA-CITY; www.hotsprings.org) has long been and remains Arkansas's top tourist destination, and for good reason. Hot Springs National Park, with its famed Bathhouse Row; the area's thermal baths; and live and simulcast thoroughbred racing at Oaklawn Park have made the town a favorite as an adult playground for more than 100 years. Magic Springs/Crystal Falls Theme and Water Park and the 210-acre Garvan Woodland Gardens are twentieth-century additions that have earned national acclaim and broadened its appeal to families. Wander a charming downtown of eclectic architecture housing a renowned arts community, magic and music shows, amphibian city tours, and the family favorite—Josephine Tussaud's Wax Museum.

Outdoor activities in the Hot Springs area include golf, horseback riding, and mining for quartz crystals, as well as fishing and water sports that center around Lakes

THE ROAD TO THE TRIPLE CROWN RUNS THROUGH OAKLAWN IN SPRING   ARKANSAS DEPARTMENT OF PARKS & TOURISM

Hamilton, Catherine, Ouachita, and DeGray. Those activities combine with private lakeside resorts, rental houseboats, and other accommodations, including those at three state parks nearby, to create numerous vacation options. Additional recreational opportunities are afforded in the nearby Ouachita National Forest.

Visit the sites related to President Bill Clinton—his boyhood homes, high school, and favorite hamburger hangout. Self-guided driving tour brochures are available at the visitor center on Bathhouse Row.

Mena (479-394-2912; www.menapolkchamber.com) was founded in 1896 as a railroad town at the eastern foot of Arkansas's second highest peak, Rich Mountain (2,681 feet). It is the eastern gateway to the Talimena Scenic Drive, a 54-mile byway that travels the crests of Rich and Winding Stair Mountains between Mena and Talihina, Oklahoma. The drive passes through Queen Wilhelmina State Park, 13 miles northwest of Mena, which offers visitors a 38-room lodge, a restaurant, campsites, and hiking trails. The byway and park provide impressive vistas of the Ouachita Mountains.

The Mena Depot Center, located in a restored 1920 railroad depot, greets the town's visitors with tourism information, art and local history exhibits, and railroad memorabilia. In Janssen Park stands an 1851 log cabin still on its original site. Located east of Mena in the Pine Ridge community, the Lum & Abner Jot 'Em Down Store & Museum houses memorabilia related to the popular 1940s radio comedy team of Lum and Abner. The late Norris Goff of Mena portrayed Abner.

Outdoor recreational opportunities abound in the area and range from fishing on Lake Wilhelmina and area streams to challenging whitewater in the Cossatot River State Park/Natural Area, or more peaceful float trips on the Ouachita River, hiking on the Ouachita National Recreation Trail, and riding on the Wolf Pen Gap ATV Trail.

Shady Lake Recreation Area is one of the Ouachita National Forest's more popular hot spots and offers an easy half-mile hike complemented with interpretive panels explaining the formation of the forest and weather's impact upon it.

Mount Ida (870-867-2723; www.mtidachamber.com). Rock shops line the highways in and around Mount Ida, but that is to be expected in a town that proclaims itself the Quartz Crystal Capital of the World. Private quartz mines, usually associated with rock shops, allow visitors to dig their own crystals for a fee.

Though renowned for the quality and quantity of the quartz crystal deposits found in the surrounding Ouachita Mountains, Mount Ida is also celebrated because of an abundance of nearby outdoor recreational opportunities. To the east, the 40,100-acre Lake Ouachita offers such activities as fishing, camping, swimming, houseboating, sailing, waterskiing, scuba diving, powerboating, and viewing of wintering bald eagles. The lake is home to private resorts and marinas where visitors can find a variety of accommodations, meeting facilities, and restaurants. US Army Corps of Engineers' recreation areas on the lake provide campgrounds, swimming beaches, and boat launch ramps. Striped bass topping 50 pounds, largemouth bass, catfish, crappie, and bream are among the game fish anglers haul from the lake. Fishing guides are available. Floating and stream fishing are available near Mount Ida on the upper Ouachita and Caddo Rivers. Cabins are available near both streams.

The Ouachita National Forest provides numerous recreational amenities close to Mount Ida, including campgrounds, day-use and scenic areas such as Little Missouri Falls, hiking and backpacking trails, and many miles of backcountry roads for touring. Among the campgrounds, the Albert Pike Recreation Area, located along the Little Missouri River near the southwest corner of Montgomery County, is the most popular.

✳ To See

MUSEUMS **Faulkner County Museum** (501-329-5918; www.faulknerhistory.com/museum) 805 Locust Street, Conway. Open Monday through Thursday 9–4. This museum preserves the history of Conway and Faulkner County, focusing on the range of environmental conditions and how inhabitants, from prehistoric to the present, adapted to changes. Housed in the historic 1869 County Jail on Faulkner County Courthouse grounds, the exhibits include artifacts, equipment, household items, clothing, historic and modern crafts, and photographs. These materials are arranged in a series of educational, attractive, and self-explanatory exhibits that are combined on the unifying theme of everyday life in the past. Free admission.

Heritage House Museum of Montgomery County (870-867-4422; www.hhmmc .org), 819 Luzerne Street, Mount Ida. Open weekends 1–4, Monday through Wednesday and Friday 9–4; closed Thursday. Dedicated to preserving the history of Montgomery County from 1800 to 1975, the Heritage House preserves words, deeds, and activities that made up the daily lives of county residents, with special emphasis on the effects and contributions of the timber industry, quartz crystal, and Lake Ouachita. Free.

Gangster Museum of America (501-545-0700; www.tgmoa.com), 113 Central Avenue, Hot Springs. Open Sunday through Thursday 10–6; Friday and Saturday 10–9. This museum reveals a slice of Hot Springs' history that until now has been mostly the stuff of legend. The Gangster Museum of America concentrates on the 1920s–'40s era of Hot Springs. The museum highlights the stories of many notorious gangsters such as Lucky Luciano, Al Capone, Bugs Moran, and Frank Costello, who were known to vacation in the Spa City. Tour guides share stories and video footage of interviews with those who were there. You can take your picture with a life-sized replica of Al himself.

Memorabilia includes slot machines and gaming tables from the era. General admission tickets are $9; seniors $8; kids (6–12) $4; under 6 years of age are free.

Josephine Tussaud Wax Museum (501-623-5836), 250 Central Avenue, Hot Springs. Open 9–6 daily. Over 100 wax figures depict 38 scenes, including the Stairway of the Stars (famous movie stars of the past and present), the World of Horrors (medieval tortures that are historically accurate), the Hall of Battles (momentous scenes in the building of America), the World of Religion (Da Vinci's *Last Supper*, the *Pieta*, and the *Crucifixion*), the World of the Mighty (famous personages from the past), World of Make Believe (*Alice in Wonderland*, *Snow White*, and more), the Royal Grand Hall (British and French royalty with US presidents), and the Crown Jewels of England (authentic reproductions). Admission for adults is $10; kids are $7.

Lum & Abner Jot 'Em Down Store & Museum (870-326-4442; www.lum-abner.com), AR 88, Pine Ridge. Call for operating hours. Lum & Abner radio and movie memorabilia, museum, and an old-time, small-town atmosphere are provided in two general stores, built in the early 1900s, that are listed on the National Register of Historic Places. Free admission.

Mid-America Science Museum (1501-767-4561; www.midamericamuseum.org), 500 Mid-America Boulevard, US 270 West, Hot Springs. Open Monday through Saturday 10–6, Sunday 1–6 p.m. in summer; Tuesday through Sunday 9–5, Sunday 1–5 p.m. Labor Day through Memorial Day. With over 100 hands-on exhibits focusing on energy, matter, life, and perception, Mid-America is perfect for any age group. The museum is home to the most powerful conical Tesla coil on earth. Demonstrations are held regularly during museum hours. The presentation includes a demonstration of the Tesla coil and a talk on the many inventions of Nikola Tesla (the Father of Electricity) and the importance of Tesla to our way of life. Tesla invented the AC electric generator, AC motor, radio, turbine, and over 250 other life-changing and enriching inventions, including the Tesla coil, which can raise normal household current to millions of volts of electricity. Mid-America is also home to the state's first permanent outdoor dinosaur display. Roam among 18 lifelike creatures on the museum's 21 scenic acres. The Oaklawn Foundation's Digital Dome Theater displays the heavens in 180 degrees. The Bob Wheeler Science Skywalk is a unique award-winning architectural exhibit extends 180-feet from the museum, allowing you to take in the museum grounds from above. A music bench, fog bridge, and rope bowl net suspended 40-feet in the air provide opportunity for both scientific investigation and distraction for your fear of heights. Admission to exhibits is $10 per adult, $8 for seniors, kids, and military. Tesla and digital dome theater shows are $3 per person.

CULTURAL SITES **Bathhouse Row** (501-624-3383; www.nps.gov/hosp/index.htm), 1 Central Avenue, Scenic AR 7, Hot Springs. Named a National Historic Landmark in 1987, Bathhouse Row consists of eight bathhouses built between 1911 and 1923. The Fordyce serves as a visitor center/museum, the Buckstaff and the Quapaw are the only working bathhouses on the Row.

Buckstaff Bathhouse (501-623-2308; www.buckstaffbaths.com), 509 Central Avenue, Scenic AR 7, Hot Springs. Open March through November, Monday through Saturday 8–11:45 a.m. and 1:30–3 p.m., Sunday 8–11:45 a.m.; December through February, Monday through Friday 8–11:45 a.m. and 1:30–3 p.m., Saturday 8–11:45 a.m., closed Sunday. Enjoy traditional thermal mineral baths and Swedish massages at this bathhouse on historic Bathhouse Row. The Buckstaff, named for controlling shareholders George and Milo Buckstaff, replaced the former Rammelsberg Bathhouse. Designed by Frank W. Gibb and Company, the present bathhouse cost $125,000 to build and contains 27,000 square feet on three main floors. Because it has been in continuous

THE BIRTHPLACE OF THE SPA IN AMERICA

Hot Springs National Park is the logical place to start your Arkansas spa experience because the thermal waters here have been rejuvenating travelers since the days of de Soto and his explorers. Hot Springs spas run the gamut, from the Arlington Hotel, historic Buckstaff Bathhouse, and Quapaw Baths and Spa on Bathhouse Row to the modern facilities at the Embassy Suites and The Austin.

Quapaw Baths and Spa now occupies the historic 1922 Spanish Colonial Revival Quapaw Bathhouse and features a large central dome covered with colored mosaic tiles, capped with a copper cupola. It has large-capacity public hot water pools with fountains and whirlpools, and a semiprivate tub area. A day spa with massage and beauty treatments will relax you and doll you up for Spa City's exciting nightlife.

Turtle Cove Spa at Mountain Harbor Resort (870-867-1220; www.turtlecovespa.com), 994 Mountain Harbor Road, Mount Ida. Just west of Hot Springs on the edge of Lake Ouachita in Mount Ida, Turtle Cove Spa at Mountain Harbor Resort is a full-service facility that has been selected as #7 in the Top 100 Spas of 2017 and the top spa in Arkansas by spasofamerica.com. From the shores of one of the cleanest lakes in the country, Turtle Cove Spa is the state's leader in wellness retreats and offers a number of signature treatments that pamper guests who come here from throughout the country. As the leading Arkansas provider of holistic spa services, Turtle Cove offers a variety of treatments like Crystal Energy Balance Massage Therapy using locally mined Arkansas quartz crystals. Additional cutting-edge treatments provided include sound therapy, chakra balancing, and raindrop massage therapy. Turtle Cove Spa's custom massage, couples massage, Ouachita Hot Stone, prenatal, deep tissue, and other bodywork treatments will soothe your body and your mind. Thermal M, an exclusive steam capsule, and Vichy Shower, to which aromatherapy, scalp massage, and mini-facial can be added, will clear your pores and your thoughts. Special spa packages for men, women, and couples are available, as are gift certificates.

operation since it opened on February 1, 1912, it is one of the best preserved of all of the bathhouses on Bathhouse Row, but it has also undergone many changes over the years. Originally, it had a large hydrotherapeutic department, which only the Fordyce and the Imperial also had. The Buckstaff Bathhouse still offers a traditional-style treatment with its staff of highly trained and dedicated personnel. Offering you the privacy of individual tubs, the bathhouse has an all-men's department on the first floor, and the second floor is dedicated to ladies. To bathe at the Buckstaff, you need only present yourself during the admission times (no reservations or appointments accepted). All supplies and linens are provided to cover yourself Roman-style between your bathing stations (bathing suits optional). Some age and health restrictions may apply; call the bathhouse for specific details.

The Buckstaff offers traditional thermal mineral baths and Swedish-style massages. Services include a 20-minute tub bath at a maximum temperature of 100 degrees; hot packs for a maximum of 20 minutes; sitz bath for 10 minutes; vapor cabinet (steam cabinet) for a maximum of 2 minutes with the heads-in cabinet or 5 minutes in the heads-out cabinet; finishing it off with a 2-minute maximum rinse in the needle shower, all for the low, low price of $33. Each tub is equipped with its own whirlpool. You may then top the whole experience off with a full-body Swedish-style massage ($71 for the total package). Allow approximately 90 minutes for the entire process, longer during peak periods. Beauty packages include the Moisturizing Paraffin Treatment ($12) for hands, which helps remove dry skin and leaves your hands soft and moisturized. Manicures and pedicures are also available, but appointmentss are required.

& **Quapaw Baths and Spa** (501-624-5679; www.quapawbaths.com), 210 Central Avenue, Hot Springs. The Quapaw, which reopened as a bathhouse in 2008, offers guests a unique way to experience the acclaimed thermal mineral water in four large-capacity soaking pools, as well as their private bathing area. Skylights over the public bathing pools give it an airy, outdoorsy feel. The public baths, called Quapaw Thermal Waters are $20 for the day, and allow you to experience the therapeutic hot spring mineral water in the uniquely peaceful setting of shared pools. This water has been carbon-dated at 4,000 years old and is high in silica, calcium, magnesium, free carbon dioxide, bicarbonate, and sulfate. A private bath ($40 per person, $55 per couple) includes the service of a bath attendant to draw your bath, schedule additional services, or provide additional linens or towels. A day spa offers massage and beauty treatments.

Mountain Valley Water Visitor Center (1-800-643-1501; www.mountainvalleyspring .com), 150 Central Avenue, Scenic AR 7, Hot Springs. Open Monday through Friday 9–5, Saturday 10–4, Sunday noon–4. Among the best-known structures in the historic Hot Springs downtown district, the Mountain Valley Water building is a fine example of the Classical Revival style. Constructed in 1910, this two-story building was originally home to the DeSoto Mineral Springs. In fact, the building was built over a spring that can still be seen today at the rear of its first level. In 1921, a third level was added to accommodate a Japanese-styled ballroom, where bands such as The Southerneers played the waltz and foxtrot to large crowds. Located half a block from the Arlington Hotel, you can sample the water and learn the history of Mountain Valley Water, which is shipped worldwide. Tours of the historic spring site and bottling facility are held each Tuesday (except for holidays) at 9 a.m. and 10 p.m. Free admission.

Hot Springs National Park (501-624-2701; www.nps.gov/hosp), 101 Reserve Avenue, Hot Springs. Congress established Hot Springs Reservation on April 20, 1832, to protect hot springs flowing from the southwestern slope of Hot Springs Mountain. Known for its 47 thermal springs, this national park was the nation's first, predating Yellowstone by 40 years. The hot spring water at Hot Springs National Park becomes heated at a depth of approximately 1 mile before beginning its journey back to the surface through a fault. Thermal-features tours are offered in summer. The *African Americans and the Hot Springs Baths* exhibit in the Fordyce Bathhouse is a popular permanent display at the visitor center. All campsites have full hook-ups (including 30- and 50-amp electrical connections, water, and sewer connections at each site) and are $30 per night ($15 for seniors). Each campsite at Gulpha Gorge Campground also has a picnic table, pedestal grill, and water nearby. While there are no showers, there are modern restrooms.

Hot Springs National Park Visitor Center and Historic Museum (501-624-2701; www.nps.gov/hosp), 369 Central Avenue, Hot Springs. Open daily 9–5. The restored Fordyce Bathhouse now serves as visitor center for Hot Springs National Park and a museum for the thermal bathing industry. From the lobby's marble and stained-glass transoms, to the marble partitions of the bath halls, to the stained-glass ceiling in the Men's Bath Hall, you can see why the Fordyce Bathhouse was considered to be the best. A bookstore, orientation film, and self-guided tour will help you if you want to wander. Guided tours are available with advance notice.

Hot Springs Mountain Tower (501-623-6035; hotspringstower.com), 401 Hot Springs Mountain Drive, Hot Springs. Hours vary by season. This 216-foot superstructure affords a breathtaking panoramic view of beautiful Hot Springs, the Ouachita Mountains, and the surrounding Diamond Lakes area. Admission is $8 for adults, $7 for seniors, $4.50 for children ages 5–11, and free for children under 5.

National Park Aquarium (501-624-3474; www.nationalparkaquarium.org), 209 Central Avenue, Hot Springs. Open year-round with seasonal hours. Call for exact times. At this aquarium, Arkansas reptiles, fish, and many saltwater species are displayed in their natural habitats. Admission: adults $6.25, seniors $5, children 4–12 and under $4.50, children 3 and under are free.

The Winery of Hot Springs (501-623-9463; www.hotspringswinery.com), 1503 Central Avenue, Hot Springs. Hours vary by season. Take a free tour in a branch of the Arkansas Historic Wine Museum and follow it with an official tasting. A gift shop has bottles available for sale following your tasting.

URBAN OASIS **Garvan Woodland Gardens** (1-800-366-4664; www.garvangardens .org), 550 Arkridge Road, Hot Springs. Open daily 9–6. Located about 15 minutes from Hot Springs National Park, Garvan Woodland Gardens covers 210 acres of a forested peninsula jutting into Lake Hamilton. Check the website before you go to find out what's blooming during your visit. Garvan also constantly holds events that are open to the public, from art shows to teas. The gardens showcase floral landscapes, free-flowing streams, and waterfalls, as well as architectural structures in a natural woodland setting. The woodland habitat is home to hundreds of natural and exotic plant and animal species; the Anthony Chapel is popular for weddings. You wouldn't normally think of a garden as a scenic spot during winter months, but Garvan Woodland Gardens is an exception. More than 1.7 million holiday lights illuminate the gardens from 5–9 p.m. daily during the Holiday Lights season, transforming the woodland landscape into a winter wonderland of delight. The display is one of Arkansas's most impressive holiday events. An outdoor café serves sandwiches, hot dogs, soups, and salads. Hours vary with the season; call the office at 501-262-9300 to check current opening times. The Holiday Lights season begins mid-November, when they open from noon–9 p.m. through the end of the year. Admission prices to the gardens are $15 for adults, $5 for kids age 4–12. Tickets to Holiday Lights are $15 for adults and $5 for kids 4–12.

✳ To Do

GOLF **Glenwood Country Club** (870-356-4422; www.glenwoodcountryclub.com), 584 US 70 East, Glenwood. Hours vary based on season; phone the pro shop for current hours. One of the top 10 courses in the state, this secluded, scenic course is set on the rolling terrain of the Ouachita Mountains. Glenwood offers 18 holes of superb par-72 play across a mature and graceful layout. Call for rates and tee times.

    Hot Springs Country Club (501-624-2661; www.hotspringscc.com), 101 Country Club Drive, Hot Springs. Call the pro shop for tee times and current greens fees. If you want to hit the links in the Ouachitas, you'll find 36 undulating holes set amid natural hot springs and fresh cool lakes. Hot Springs has two championship 18-hole courses: the Arlington, refurbished by Ben Crenshaw and Bill Coore, originally designed by William Diddel; and the Park, designed by Willie Park Jr. Collared shirts are required and no cutoffs are allowed. The Arlington Course was built on hilly terrain, and water hazards come into play on three holes. It is heavily wooded and considered the more difficult course. The Park Course is not as rolling, but there are still water hazards coming into play on two holes. It is considered to be about five shots easier than the Arlington Course. *Golf Digest* rated the Arlington Course as the third Best Public Course in the state for 1996 and the Majestic Course as seventh Best Public Course in the state for 1996. *Golf Digest* also rated the Arlington Course as the ninth Best in State course for 1997–98. William Diddel redesigned the Majestic Course in 1932, and Smiley Bell redesigned both of the 18-hole courses in 1949. You may play nine holes if you wish, but you still have to pay the 18-hole greens fee. Open daily year-round. Greens fees are $97 plus tax and include your cart and range balls. This course is included the state's Natural State Golf Trail, 15 courses that meet the standards set forth by the state that John Daly calls home. For information on other courses on the trail, posts, detailed descriptions, golf packages, and tourism information, log on to the website.

GUIDE SERVICES **A-1 Guide Services** (501-767-6488; www.a-1guideservices.com) Standpipe Road, Hot Springs. One of Lake Hamilton's first professional guides, A-1 specializes in black and hybrid bass fishing on Lake Hamilton, Lake Ouachita, Lake DeGray, and Lake Greeson. Open daily. Call for pricing.

    Action Fishing Trips with Jerry Blake (501-844-9028; www.actionfishingtrips .com), 127 Ranchero Place, Pearcy. Year-round guide service. Call for pricing.

    Captain Ron's Striper Guide Service (501-991-3208; www.oneeyedstriperfishing .com), 514 North Crystal Springs Road, Royal. Capt. Ron Waymack guides customers right into the heart of big striper country and has helped hundreds of people catch the fish of a lifetime. Fishing trips are taken on any of the Hot Springs lakes—Hamilton, Ouachita, or Catherine. Hours and prices vary by season.

    Family Fishing Trips Guide Service with Darryl Morris (501-844-5418; www .familyfishingtrips.com), 4192 US 70 West, Kirby. Darryl Morris will serve as your guide and take you to Lake Greeson for crappie or striper fishing. Morris offers a money-back guarantee—if you don't catch your dinner, your next trip will be free. Rates and hours are seasonal; phone for a quote.

    Trophy Striper Fishing with John T. Hall (501-767-1468; www.fishing4stripers.com), 120 Waggoner, Hot Springs. Fishing guide services start at $400 (rates may vary based on fuel prices) and include 4–5 hours of fishing, bait and tackle, drinks, and snacks. Your guide will even clean and package your catch if you want to take it with you.

THEME PARKS **Magic Springs/Crystal Falls Theme and Water Park** (501-624-0100; www.magicsprings.com), 1701 US 70 East, Hot Springs. Call for seasonal hours of operation and ticket prices. This theme park, named as one of the three most family-friendly parks in the nation by *Better Homes and Gardens* magazine, offers over 75 attractions and two parks for the price of one. This park improves consistently, but one of the park favorites is still the X-Coaster, the first of its kind in the United States and only the second in the world. Built at a cost of $4 million, the coaster is the highest upside-down inversion in the world, at 150 feet. Cool off at Crystal Falls in the Crystal Lagoon, seven brightly colored slides (three are body-only slides, four are tube slides) plus a play pool; there is also High Sierra Slide Tower, Crystal Falls Wave Pool, Kodiak Canyon Lazy River, and Bear Cub Bend for smaller children. A summer concert series brings nationally known acts to the park over a dozen times per season.

TOURS *Belle of Hot Springs* **Riverboat** (501-525-4438; www.belleriverboat.com), 5200 Central Avenue, Hot Springs. Open Monday through Saturday 9–6, Sunday 11–6. Sit back and relax aboard this 250-passenger riverboat and enjoy the captain's narration as he shares secrets from Hot Springs' history. This entertaining tour includes million-dollar mansions, natural islands, quaint resorts, panoramic views of the Ouachita Mountains, and colorful anecdotes mixed amid well-researched historical information. Sight-seeing cruises, without meals, are $25 per adult, $15 per child (ages 3–12). Choose from a two hour dinner cruise for $61 plus tax per person, or simply enjoy the views without the meal for $25. Menu items include a barbecue plate, catfish, or smoked chicken. A weekend special is available during summer months that will give you 90 minutes of sightseeing from the boat for $25. The Belle has random booze cruises scheduled throughout the year. Call ahead for details.

Hot Springs Carriage Company (501-321-4779) Hot Springs National Park, Hot Springs. Open Tuesday through Saturday 6 p.m.–close. Horse-drawn carriage tours are available throughout the downtown and national park areas. Call for rates.

National Park Duck Tours (501-321-2911; www.rideaduck.com), 418 Central Avenue, Hot Springs. You have seen them before, the large boats driving down the road that resemble a fish, or in this case, a duck, out of water. These tours are 75 minutes and roam through Hot Springs National Park and Lake Hamilton aboard these World War II amphibious vehicles that will take you right into Lake Hamilton. Seasonal rates apply; call for details.

✳ Wild Places

Arkansas Alligator Farm & Petting Zoo (1-800-750-7891; www.alligatorfarmzoo .com), 847 Whittington Avenue, Hot Springs. Open May 1 through October 20, 9:30–5 daily. The alligator farm, the oldest attraction in Hot Springs, was founded in 1902 by H. L. Campbell and sold to Danny S. Older between 1902 and 1929. It was known as the Hot Springs Gator Farm, with over 1,500 Mississippian alligators and a small museum. You'll definitely want to come for lunch, at least on Thursday, Saturday, or Sunday, when you can watch over 3,000 alligators vie for prime real estate during the farm's feeding show. Note to self: don't bring chicken; it's the house specialty. Mountain lions, llamas, turtles, and a merman are on display, and a petting zoo allows kids to have a hands-on experience without risking life or limb. A small museum acquaints visitors with the farm and its residents; the gift shop's inventory includes handmade crafts and souvenirs. Admission is $9 for adults, kids are $7.

THE STAKES ARE GROWING AT OAKLAWN PARK

Horse Racing and Electronic Gaming Oaklawn Park (1-800-OAK-LAWN; www.oaklawn .com), 2705 Central Avenue, Scenic AR 7, Hot Springs. Oaklawn celebrated its centennial year in 2004 with increases in both attendance and in money wagered. In 2005, Oaklawn Park and the Cella family were awarded an Eclipse Award of Merit, the most prestigious award in racing, by the National Thoroughbred Racing Association, in association with the *Daily Racing Form* and the National Turf Writers Association. The award was given in recognition of increases in attendance and wagering at the track over the previous five years running. Oaklawn is the first racetrack in the country to receive an Eclipse Award. The live thoroughbred racing season begins in late January and is capped off in mid-April with the Racing Festival of the South. The largest horse racing operation outside New York and California, the track also features simulcast racing from Triple Crown Races, Breeders' Cup, Louisiana Downs, and Saratoga.

According to Oaklawn Park history, the first Arkansas Derby ran in 1936 with a purse of $5,000. The derby is the most prestigious race regularly held at Oaklawn Park and is considered a preliminary for contenders at the highest levels of national thoroughbred horse racing. Several participants in the Arkansas Derby, such as Smarty Jones and Count Fleet, have gone on to compete in and win some or all of the races that make up the Triple Crown.

In 2000, the addition of electronic gaming required the conversion of areas previously dedicated to live racing on the lower level at the south end of the facility. This self-contained electronic-gaming arena, complete with its own restaurant, proved enormously popular and was expanded again in 2009 from 500 terminals to 900.

Across the street from the track, a local landmark has also been the beneficiary of the popularity of Oaklawn's gaming salon. The Winners Circle (501-624-2531; www.bestwesternhs .com, 2520 Central Avenue) became a Best Western and was treated to a $4 million facelift. According to Jim Shamburger, the hotel's owner, the complete renovation involved every one of its rooms. New pillow-top mattresses, 32-inch LCD televisions, and granite counters replaced the old fixtures. Microwaves, refrigerators, and free high-speed wireless Internet were among the modern conveniences added.

Throughout Oaklawn Park's history, the facilities have been regularly improved and expanded to serve greater numbers of patrons and accommodate changes in the business. Expansions and additions during the latter half of the twentieth century increased the size of the facility and improved available amenities. In 1992, the largest handcrafted artwork at any thoroughbred racetrack in the country was completed on the front facade of Oaklawn. The mural, which measures 240 feet by 14 feet, represents a race from post parade to finish and can be seen along the upper edge of the building over the main, or southernmost, entrance.

PARKS **DeGray Lake Resort State Park & Lodge** (1-800-737-8355 or 501-865-2851; www.degray.com), 2027 State Park Entrance Road, Bismarck. DeGray is the first resort in the Arkansas State Parks system, situated on this 13,800-acre lake at the foothills of the Ouachita Mountains. The 96-room lodge, located on its own island in DeGray Lake, is a wilderness retreat for outdoor enthusiasts. Each of its rooms comes with a view and offers color cable TV, Internet access, mini refrigerators, coffeemakers, hair dryers, iron/ironing boards, and room service. A heated swimming pool, indoor hot tub, and fitness room are situated with views of the picturesque shoreline and lake. The park offers horseback riding, Jet Ski rentals, a visitor center, full-service marina, golf, tennis, campsites, pavilion, nature programs, hiking trails, gift shop, and restrooms. Room rates are based on season, ranging from an $80 weekend rate in winter to $95 in summer. Weekday rates average about $5 less per night. Bicycles rent for $3/hour or

$10 a day to let you take full advantage of the park grounds and lakeside location. Hit the links for $19 per 18 holes during the week, or $25 a weekend, making it some of the most affordable golf you will ever play. Guided horseback riding, for those over the age of 6, is $20 per person. All types of watercraft rent at the marina, from a 27-foot party barge ($230/day) to a water bike ($6/hour). Ask about the interpreter-led scenic barge tours of DeGray Lake; they are a tranquil way to end the day. They are $8.50 for adults, $4.50 for kids 6–12. The little guys ride for free.

& **Lake Catherine State Park** (501-844-4176; www.arkansasstateparks.com), 1200 Catherine Park Road, Hot Springs. To reach Lake Catherine State Park, take Exit 97 off I-30 near Malvern and go 12 miles north on AR 171. The everlasting grace of the Civilian Conservation Corps' handiwork is on display at the park just outside Hot Springs. Nestled in the natural beauty of the Ouachita Mountains on 1,940-acre Lake Catherine, the park features CCC/rustic-style facilities constructed of native stone and wood by the CCC in the 1930s. Situated along the lake's shore, the park's 18 cabins feature fully equipped kitchens, and most have wood-burning fireplaces.

The park's fully accessible Polly Crews Cabin was designed to serve the needs of visitors with disabilities. The structure includes its own private and fully accessible fishing pier and boat dock. The 1,160-square-foot cabin design was inspired by the rustic architectural designs of five other cabins in the park. An accessible parking space and path provide barrier-free access. The two-bedroom cabin includes a bathroom offering both a spa tub and a roll-in shower. Just outside the cabin's screened porch is a large flagstone patio overlooking the lake, with a picnic table and pedestal grill.

DeGray has 113 campsites and three Rent-A-Yurt sites that have lake and woodland views. Yurts are $55 a day for the large round, high-walled tent with electricity, wood floors, screened windows, and locking doors. They come equipped with cots, lantern, stove, and ice chest—you just supply the linens, food, and fun. Additional vehicle parking is scattered throughout the camping areas. The campgrounds include two barrier-free campsites located adjacent to the two bathhouses. Both bathhouses now offer barrier-free access for visitors with disabilities.

The park's marina, open in summer only, sells bait and fuel. Rental boats are available throughout the year. Gifts, groceries, snacks, and ice are available for sale daily at the visitor center that overlooks the swimming area and nature center (open during the summer only). Campsites have electrical and water connections, renting for $22 per day.

Lake Ouachita State Park (501-767-9366; www.arkansasstateparks.com), 5451 Mountain Pine Road, Mountain Pine. Lake Ouachita State Park sits on the shoreline of beautiful Lake Ouachita, known for its scenic natural beauty and the clarity of its waters. Named one of the cleanest lakes in America, 40,000-acre Lake Ouachita is a water sports mecca for swimming, skiing, scuba diving, boating, and fishing. The lake is the state's largest man-made lake, and angling for bream, crappie, catfish, stripers, and largemouth bass can be enjoyed in open waters or quiet coves along the lake's 975 miles of shoreline. Located just a short drive from the spa city of Hot Springs on the lake's eastern

COZY CABIN ON THE WATER AT LAKE OUACHITA

THE WORLD'S FINEST QUARTZ CRYSTALS

The ancient Ouachita Mountain area of Arkansas was considered a mystical location by Native American tribes. The hot and cold springs in the Valley of the Vapors (now the city of Hot Springs) was considered a place of peace, even for warring tribes. Shamans traveled to power points, or vortexes, in the mountains where the earth's energy was said to be the strongest, and the beautiful Arkansas quartz of the Ouachitas was believed to have sacred and spiritual significance.

You will find quartz crystal from Mount Ida displayed among the best in the world and priced accordingly. Fortunately, for a fraction of the cost of some of these pure sparkling clusters, you can have the joy of discovering them for yourself.

You will be surprised how easy it is to mine for crystals. The mines are not underground. In fact they are open pits, frequently accented by large bulldozers, where you can usually get by with a screwdriver and some gloves. There are seeded mines, where the operators add coins, geodes, and other gems and minerals, or you can go for the real rock-hound experience and hit a pit, or some tailings, on your own. Regardless of the area where you dig, it is best to wear old clothes and shoes because you will get dirty. Although most crystal mines allow people to dig for crystals year-round, the best time of year to mine is during the spring and fall when temperatures are cool. The World Championship Quartz Crystal Dig at Mount Ida, held the second weekend in October, lets you try your hand at digging crystals for cash.

Arrowhead Crystal Mine (501-538-9627 or 870-326-4380; www.arrowheadcrystals.com), Mount Ida. Open various days, weather dependent, year-round. You probably want to call before you go; if they don't have plans to open the mine, you can probably talk them into it if your group is large enough. From Mount Ida, just drive 3.5 miles south on AR 27 (when you see the large mobile phone tower on the left coming from Mount Ida, you are getting really close). Take a left onto Owley Road and travel 3 miles (you will pass a cemetery, a one-lane bridge, and the entrance to the Wegner Ranch). Look for the handwritten sign for Arrowhead Crystal mine. At the base of the sign you will see a placard that says OPEN or CLOSED. As such, calling in advance is always recommended.

There are several mines in the Mount Ida area set up for you to pay a fee, dig all day, and keep everything you find. They all have dramatically different types of packages, from pay by the day to pay by the group. Since most of them are open pits, you will find their hours are weather dependent and also based around regional and national gemology shows, because they are scheduled during the hottest time of the year. You won't find anyone who will guarantee anything about what you will find, but one thing I found to be undeniable is a parking lot that captures your attention. I have spent several hours at the Arrowhead Crystal Mine on a couple of occasions, and there are so many crystals on the surface of the parking lot, I have yet to see anyone turn away. Speaking for myself and the dozen or so people I mined with on both occasions, we all went home with impressive hauls of clusters and points that were very clear and unblemished, certainly worth more than the $20 we paid for the day. Arrowhead is a favorite with the diehard rock hounds who know it for its reputation in the World Championship Quartz Crystal Dig that is held in Mount Ida every year.

The mine is open year-round, but like all of the mines, weather will often force them to close. Arrowhead in particular is off the beaten path; in fact, I wouldn't recommend the drive in a low-rider. What makes Arrowhead unique is the willingness on the part of the operator to educate the people who come through the mine. Brian Levering spends countless hours of his time explaining the formation of the crystals, how to find and clean the crystals, and showing off his own collection of minerals, which is amazing in itself. To look for crystals in the mine for the day runs $20 per adult (the price is the same whether you actually dig or just look around, picking up loose crystals). Kids 16 and under are $10.

Most of the mines offer options allowing you to sort through tailings, or piles of dirt and rock that have basically been mined for you by an earth-mover. This is a great option if you really want to haul out some big rocks, or if you have a group. At Arrowhead, for an additional $100, they will excavate one pocket for you, and they rate the quality of your yield as varying from great to fantastic. Packages go up from there, basically with more pockets for more money. But when you consider the retail value of some of these rocks (in many cases they can easily go for a few hundred dollars apiece), that is not too much to pay, particularly for a group. You're guaranteed to come away with some really nice crystals worth many times what you paid. One or more people can do this dig!

Brewer Crystal Mining (870-867-4033), 192 Diamond Mist Road, Mount Ida. Open various hours, year-round. Call for an appointment and price; both are dependent on the time of year and size of your group.

Starfire Mines (870-867-2431), 5403 US 270 East, Mount Ida. Call for an appointment to dig. Retail store is open seasonally, but generally Monday through Saturday 10–5. Starfire offers public mining options on a weather-dependent basis. The retail store offers Arkansas quartz, plus a number of other gemstones and minerals for sale—retail or wholesale. Call for quotes.

The Crystal Seen Trading Company (870-867-4072; www.digyourowncrystals.com), 2572 US 270 East, Mount Ida. Crystal Seen has a 10-acre rock-hounding mine where you can actually mine for Arkansas Quartz, plus geodes and foreign coins that are seeded in the mine, or in a small tailing area guaranteed to yield a harvest. The cost is $20 per day per adult, with kids 7–11 half price. Kids 6 and under are free. A gift shop on-site sells various items made with gems and minerals.

Sweet Surrender Crystal Mine (870-867-0104; www.sweetsurrenderscrystals.com). Take highway 27 north from Mount Ida through Washita. Half a mile north of Washita, you will see the Sweet Surrender sign on Horseshoe Bend Road. Turn right and go a little over a half a mile. When you see the first mailbox on the right, you will see a sign that says CRYSTAL MINE ENTRANCE. Turn right and go to the top of the hill until you see the picnic tables. Sweet Surrender, like all of these outdoor dig-your-own mining operations, will vary their hours due to the time of year and the weather. They will close for rain or when it gets too hot to dig. Generally, the mine is open from 9:30–4. After a brief chat about safety while digging, you will be free to dig until your buckets are full or you want to take a break at one of picnic tables. A $20 fee buys you the day at the mine and the right to keep everything you find. Crystals are also available for sale if you don't find what you are looking for, or if you would rather shop than dig.

Wegner Quartz Crystal Mines (870-867-2309; www.wegnercrystalmines.com), 82 Wegner Ranch Road, Mount Ida. Open Monday through Friday 8–4 and most holidays. During peak season (spring and fall), you may find them open seven days a week, but all miners must arrive prior to 2 p.m. Wegner offers tours of their mine in addition to a couple of mining options. The Gemstone Sluice area is a 100-foot-long trough that is covered, so you have shelter against sun or rain. It is situated by a point and waterfall. A $14 fee admits two people. Additional gemstone pails are available for $9.50 each. This area is open to the public without reservations. Wegner guarantees their tailing piles, which are also open to the public with no reservation. Adults are $10.50, and both seniors and kids 10 and under are $6.60. Wegner also has a large showroom with huge crystals and amethyst displays and a gift shop for retail sales.

shore, Lake Ouachita State Park is your gateway to this popular water sports lake. Fully equipped cabins include seven that overlook the lake and one that offers a woodland view. Park campgrounds feature 103 campsites (40 Class AAA, 25 Class B, 24 Class D, and 12 hike-in tent sites). Other park facilities include picnic areas, hiking trails, a swimming area, and a marina with boat rentals, bait, and supplies. The park's visitor center includes exhibits and a store. Cabin rentals range from $215 per day for six adults in a three-bedroom with spa tub and fireplace, to $112 per day for four adults in a two-bedroom without the fancy amenities. You can also get a two-bedroom cabin with a spa tub for $125 per day. Campsite rates vary from Class AAA, which includes 50-amp electrical, water, and sewer for $27 per day, to a simple site with no hook-ups for $10 per day. The marina rents watercraft and toys. You can rent a fishing boat with motor for $70 per day or a 30-foot party barge for $325 daily. Kayaks and pedal boats are $25 per day. Lake Ouachita's interpreters conduct guided kayak tours of the lake that are very popular. Lasting 90 minutes, they are $10 for adults and $5 for kids 6–12.

✳ Lodging

HOT SPRINGS AND CENTRAL ARKANSAS

BED & BREAKFAST INNS **1884 Wildwood Bed & Breakfast Inn** (501-624-4267; www.wildwood1884.com), 808 Park Avenue, Hot Springs. Marvel at this restored 1884 Victorian Queen Anne mansion, listed on the National Register of Historic Places and recipient of the Arkansas Preservation Association Restoration Award, with its original stained glass and woodwork. Rates for the individually appointed rooms in the mansion range from $139–199 per night. Packages are available that include spa services at local bathhouses and spas, or bundled with flowers, champagne, and chocolate for a romantic getaway. You also get use of the refrigerator, microwave, and ice machine. A large TV room with cable, DVD, free Wi-Fi, and surround sound are also available to guests within the mansion. Cottage suites include two-person whirlpool tubs, separate showers, an outside porch area, private fridge, toaster, microwave, coffeemaker, continental breakfast items, drinks, and homemade goodies. Cottage suites also get turndown service that includes a rose, rose petals on your bed, and chocolate mints on your pillow. $$–$$$.

Bartee Meadow Bed & Breakfast (1-877-962-9100; www.barteemeadow.com), 129 Bartee Trail, Hot Springs. Bartee Meadow is located on 13 acres of wooded hilltop just 10 minutes from downtown Hot Springs. It's a rustic, contemporary home with two lodging options available: the two-bedroom Woodlands Suite and the romantic Starlight Cottage. Both have private decks with outdoor hot tubs for two and wood-burning chimenea fireplaces. The grounds also feature a lighted tennis court, a terrace with swing and firepit, a lighted deck around a pond with two fountains, and a hammock. A stay runs $149 a night and includes afternoon snacks, bedtime cookies, and a hearty country breakfast. Children are welcome in the Woodlands Suite. You can opt for a one-hour personal session with a Hot Springs licensed massage therapist ($75 an hour) in the privacy of your suite or cottage—or, in nice weather, on your walled deck or patio. Packages are available for most holidays and occasions, small weddings, receptions, honeymoons, and vow renewals. $$–$$$.

Butler Manor Bed & Breakfast (1-888-520-5705), 123 Butler Lane, Hot Springs. This 9,000-square-foot stone manor has five luxurious guest rooms, and while all are uniquely decorated, each has a king-sized bed, a flat-screen TV and DVD player, and a private bath.

Amenities include a lakeside Jacuzzi; game room with a pool table, big-screen TV, and Nintendo Wii; and a book and movie library. Add a tray of champagne, strawberries, and cheese for your arrival, and a lakeside private candlelit dinner to enhance your stay ($100). Outside, a boardwalk, stone fishing pier, boathouse, swimming area, and outdoor grill will help you enjoy the outdoors. Concierge services, free high-speed Internet, and the award-winning ablution: a day spa and salon are enhanced services you won't find everywhere. Room rates range from $175 to $375 a night. $$–$$$.

   ♿ **Captain Henderson House Bed & Breakfast** (1-866-478-4661; www.hsu .edu/community/ hendersonhouse), 349 North 10th Street, Arkadelphia. This Victorian-era home has seven guest rooms, two of which are suites. All are equipped with clock radios with alarm, cable TV, VCR, telephone, wireless Internet access, individual climate control, and private baths. Additional amenities include irons and ironing boards, hairdryers, and guest robes. Captain

Henderson House offers a flexible breakfast schedule and check-in/check-out times. Rooms are $80/night. $–$$.

INNS AND LODGES ★ **Lookout Point Lakeside Inn** (1-866-525-6155; www .lookoutpointinn.com), 104 Lookout Circle, Hot Springs. The inn is 1.5 miles south of the Hot Springs Mall just off Scenic AR 7 Byway. This nationally recognized inn is located on beautiful Lake Hamilton in the highly desirable 7 South area of Hot Springs. Just minutes from thoroughbred racing, art galleries, sizzling nightlife, and eclectic cuisine, this serene inn will make you feel like you are, nonetheless, on an island of your own. Proprietors Ray and Kristie Rosset built the arts and crafts–style bed & breakfast in 2003, relocating to Hot Springs from Dallas, Texas. It was selected by *National Geographic Traveler* magazine for its top 150 hotels list and chosen one of America's Greenest Hotels 2008 by *Forbes Traveler*. The inn's foyer is one of the most inviting you will ever enter. The stairway splits at the open-air

CAPTAIN HENDERSON HOUSE BED AND BREAKFAST IN ARKADELPHIA   ARKANSAS DEPARTMENT OF PARKS & TOURISM

landing; on your right, a sweeping stair-case to the lower level common areas. A cozy den with fireplace, a colorful sun-room, and a large dining room highlight the quality of workmanship and the mod-ern construction with the detail of his-toric architecture. The open hallway left of the foyer leads to guest rooms that are uniquely decorated, but all feature lake views, private baths, whirlpool tubs, fire-places, free Wi-Fi, writing tables, and television. Amenities include hearty breakfasts and afternoon refreshments. A two-bedroom, 1,500-square-foot lake-front condo, Lakeview Terrace, is also available and perfect for families. The inn specializes in intimate weddings, held in the gorgeous gardens lakeside. Limited accommodations are available for well-behaved dogs, subject to prior approval. Room rates range from $189 for queen suites to $339 for king suites and $459 a night for Lakeview Terrace. $$–$$$.

🐾 **Iron Mountain Lodge & Marina** (1-800-243-3396; www.iron-mountain .com), Iron Mountain Marina Drive, Arkadelphia. This lodge offers cottages on DeGray Lake that include televi-sion, DVD, hot tub, full kitchen, and wood-burning fireplaces. The lodge is pet friendly and has a full-service marina, scuba air station, ski boat, party barge rentals, and a conference room. You can rent a two-bedroom, two-bath cottage for $255 a night during the week and $310 on weekends. Three-bedroom, three-bath units are $370 a night on weekdays and $493 nightly on weekends. Call for sea-son discounts during winter. $$–$$$.

Self Creek Lodge and Marina (1-866-454-7353; www.selfcreek.com), 4192 US 70 West, Kirby. This 50-year-old family-owned resort and marina on Lake Greeson offers log cottages, a full-service marina, and a ships store. The log-sided cottages include both two- and three-bedroom floor plans with fully equipped kitchens, washers and dryers, stone fireplaces, decks with hot tubs, and a panoramic view of Lake Greeson. Self Creek's marina has pontoon and ski boat rentals and offers houseboat, party barge, and runabout slips. Three-bedroom cottages rent for $310 a day; two-bedroom units are $225. Season dis-counts and packages are available; check their website for details. $$–$$$.

HOUSEBOAT RENTALS **DeGray Lake Houseboat and Jet Ski Rentals** (870-246-8800; www.anchorsawayhouseboats .com), 140 Iron Mountain Marina Drive, Arkadelphia. This is the only houseboat rental company operating on Lake DeGray. The amenities onboard these houseboats exceed a lot of homes. Each sleeps 14, with six private bedrooms and a large living area with queen-sized sleeper sofa. A recliner chair provides additional sleeping space. All boats have

LOOKOUT POINT LAKESIDE INN IN HOT SPRINGS

two full baths with showers. A swim platform, water slide, and four- to eight-person hot tub will help ensure you get your feet wet. The website uses detailed graphics to guide you through a complicated calendar and explain their rate structure. Their off-peak season is April 8 through the weekend prior to Memorial Day andweekend after Labor Day through September 20; their peak season is Memorial Day through Labor Day weekends. Just to give you a ballpark, weekly rates range from $3,250 off-season to $5,200 at peak season. $$$.

Almost Home Houseboat Rentals (1-877-256-6785; www.almosthome houseboats.com), 190 Shore View Loop, Hot Springs. Select from custom-designed, 75-foot, six-bedroom houseboats with hot tub, satellite television, fully equipped kitchen, cooking and eating utensils, icemaker, 25-foot covered party top, and waterslide. Their peak season is from May 25 through mid-August; rates during this period are $3,600 for weekends and $6,500 a week. $$$.

RESORTS **The Arlington Resort Hotel & Spa** (1-800-643-1502; www.arlington hotel.com), 239 Central Avenue, Hot Springs. The colorful history of the three eras of The Arlington is not architectural beauty and uniqueness alone. Always the center of activity in Hot Springs, The Arlington has hosted hundreds of grand balls and social events since 1875. Politicians, dignitaries, actors, gangsters, and entertainment and sports legends bathed in its bathhouse, danced to its music, and enjoyed its splendor and charm. The Arlington has survived a devastating fire, economic downturns, changing social attitudes, and much more. Originally opened in 1875, its original wooden structure was three stories high and boasted 120 guest rooms, which was the largest in the state at the time. The original building was razed in 1893, and replaced with a 300-room Spanish Renaissance structure which was referred to as "the most elegant and complete hotel in America" in Charles Cutter's 1892 Guide Book. The new Arlington's spacious veranda with arcades ran the full length of the hotel. This building was destroyed by fire on April 5, 1923.

Many famous guests sought out the luxury of The Arlington Hotel including US presidents Franklin Roosevelt, Harry Truman, George H. W. Bush, and native son Bill Clinton. The great Babe Ruth, is just one of the famous athletes who have relaxed and enjoyed the thermal baths at The Arlington. Tony Bennett, Barbra Streisand, and Yoko Ono are just a few of the celebrities to seek out the healing, thermal waters of the city's hot springs at The Arlington. Al Capone, whose favorite room was 442, would book the entire fourth floor for his staff and bodyguards. From the vantage point of his window, Capone could monitor the activities at the Southern Club, which is now the wax museum.

Room rates are both seasonal and based on occupancy. Standard rooms at The Arlington consist of a king or two double beds and a shower for $125–158 a night. Deluxe rooms at The Arlington are the largest regular rooms and feature a king or two double beds, a tub and shower, and run $99–129 a night. The Historic Room rate includes a king or queen bed and shower. Rates range from $105–138. Junior suites ($198–205) are large rooms with a king or two double beds, tub and shower, refrigerator, and a sitting area at one end. Parlor suites are available with one bedroom ($295) or two bedrooms ($395) and have a large living room and refrigerator. The historic rooms in the hotel, where Capone ($350), Reagan ($305), and Clinton ($350) slept, are surprisingly affordable. Located in the downtown historic district, The Arlington offers a bathhouse, two pools, a hot tub, lounge and bar, food services, weekend entertainment, salon, exercise room, shops, and three restaurants— Lobby Café, Venetian Dining Room providing breakfast and dinner, and the

Fountain Room grill, open for dinner only Thursday through Saturday (coat required). A Starbucks is also available in the lobby. $$$–$$$$.

MENA AND WESTERN ARKANSAS

BED & BREAKFAST INNS **The Carriage House Inn** (479-243-0957; www.the carriagehouseinn.net), 701 12th Street, Mena. This is a National Register of Historic Places mansion featuring a 1,000-square-foot private guest house with a separate bedroom, living area, dining area, and kitchenette with refrigerator and microwave. Conveniently located within walking distance of downtown and a city park, amenities include complimentary coffee, tea, snack basket, and freshly baked cookies; TV, DVD, and wireless Internet; and bicycles for wandering around town or visiting Janssen Park. Baby equipment (high chair, pack-n-play, hiking backpack, strollers) can be provided for a nominal fee. Rates range from $90–120 a night. $–$$$.

INNS AND LODGES ♿ **Backwoods Lodge** (870-818-0892; www.backwoods lodgemena.com), 560 CR 78, Mena. Located in the Ouachita Mountains adjacent to the Ouachita National Forest, this lodge is perfect for hunting and ATV riding. In season, guided hunts for deer, bear, or turkey are available. Hunts catering to the disabled and special baited-bear hunts are also provided. Escape to this four-bedroom, four-bath lodge and submerge in the six-person hot tub on the 675-square-foot deck. It's idea for weddings, honeymoons, family reunions, corporate meetings/retreats, and B&B vacations. Backwoods offers sleeping for eight adults with king-sized beds that can change out to two singles, a complete kitchen with cook, daily housekeeping, in-room satellite TV, central heat and air, and ceiling fans. The entire lodge rents for $250 a night during the week and $290 a night weekends. $$–$$$.

Cornerstone Mountain Retreat (479-216-2495; www.cornerstone mountainretreat.com), 255 CR 30, Hatfield. Cornerstone is located 1 mile off US 71, 7 miles south of Mena. An 18,000-square-foot, fully equipped, three-story lodge invites you to its three bedrooms, two baths, full kitchen, dining area, full utility room, upper deck, lower deck, front porch, big hot tub, gas grill, and TV and DVD player with library of movies. The lodge rents for $200 a night for two, with an additional $10 charge for each additional person. $$–$$$.

Cossatot River's Sugar Creek Lodge (1-866-394-7747; www.cossatotriver.com), 140 Edgewater Lane, Mena. Sugar Creek has a variety of lodging options from which you can choose. The Mountain Lodge is three bedrooms with a king in the master, a king in the second bedroom, and a full and twin in the third. It also includes a sleeper sofa, kitchen, washer/dryer, central air, fireplace in the living area and master bedroom, shower, two toilets, and a jetted tub in the master bedroom. Price is $160 minimum up to six people, then additional charges will apply. Eagle Lodge is a two-bedroom unit with a king in both the master and the second bedroom, and a day bed in the living area, kitchen, central air, fireplace in living area and master bedroom, bathtub, shower, jetted tub in master, two toilets, and a washer/dryer. The lodge rents for $140 a night for up to four people, then additional charges apply. A general store, soda fountain, restaurant, and chapel complete the property's amenities. $–$$.

RESORTS **Highway 27 Fishing Village** (870-867-2211; www.highway27fishing village.homestead.com), 214 Fishing Village Road, Story. Every unit has a lake view and is fully furnished, with air conditioning, heat, and in-room TV. There is convenient waterfront access from cabins and waterfront electrical hook-ups. Amenities include a marina with boat rentals, gas, oil, tackle, and fishing licenses available, as well as a biking and hiking trail and swimming area. Breakfast, lunch, and dinner are available in the restaurant. Rates range from $69–85 a might with a two-night minimum on the weekend. $.

Mountain Harbor Resort (1-800-832-2276; www.mountainharborresort.com), 994 Mountain Harbor Road, Mount Ida. Motel lodging includes lake-view rooms ($125 weekday/$175 weekends) with two queen beds or one king bed. All have sleeper sofa, coffeemaker, small personal-sized refrigerator, microwave, DVD, and a patio overlooking the lake. The poolside cabanas ($165 weekdays/$210 weekends) offer one large room with the sleeping area separated from the living room by the kitchen and bath. Each has two queen beds and a queen sleeper sofa, plus fully equipped kitchen—and opens out onto the pool. The luxurious Lodge Cottages offer a choice between a lake view ($315 weekdays/$399 weekends) and woodland view ($299 weekdays/$375 weekends). The two-bedroom, two-bath cottages all have native stone fireplaces with gas logs, hot tubs, and charcoal grills on the deck, as well as fully equipped kitchens. One king-sized bed is in the master and two queen-sized beds are in the guest bedroom. No sleeper sofa. All lodging includes in-room coffee, hot cocoa, and popcorn, as well as daily room service. All the guest rooms are nonsmoking and pet friendly. A waterfront restaurant offers a complete menu, including a terrific breakfast buffet with amazingly crispy bacon. The full-service marina has boat storage, ski boats, party barges, water toys, houseboat rentals, the Ocean Extreme Dive Center, and guide services. Swimming, tennis, horseback riding, and hiking are all available on the property. Turtle Cove Spa, a nationally recognized spa, is also on-site. $$–$$$.

Wolfpen ATV Campground & Cabins (479-394-0404; www.wolfpenatv.com), 559 CR 61, Mena. Wolfpen ATV Campground near Mena has more cabins than any campground in the area, from A-frame primitive cabins with electric and air conditioning to fully furnished cabins with kitchens and satellite TVs. The property includes a laundry room, two pavilions, and 11 camper cabins. Cabin prices range from $38.50–71.50 per day. There is a $10.80 housekeeping charge. Fully equipped, two-bedroom cottages rent for $105 nightly and have complete kitchens, satellite TV, and DVD players. $–$$.

HOUSEBOAT RENTALS **DreamChaser Houseboat Rentals** (1-877-867-3480; www.bigboats.net), 60 Marina Drive, Mountain Harbor Resort, Mount Ida. DreamChaser offers luxury houseboat rentals on Lake Ouachita, with water slides on all boats and no boat older than a 1999 model. The four-, five- and six-bedroom boats sleep up to 14 people and have full bathrooms and kitchens. Hot tubs are available on most models, and WaveRunner rentals are also available. There are a number of factors in play when determining houseboat rental rates, and details are posted on DreamChaser's website. Peak season (June 1 through August 9) rates range from $2,495–$2,695 for three-day weekends and from $4,295–$6,495 a week. Off season rates run about 40 to 50 percent less than peak season, depending on the boat your choose. Definitely check the website because even the dates defining peak season are spread throughout the calendar. $$$.

Lake Escape Houseboats (501-760-2659; www.lakeescapehouseboats.com), 720 Caribbean Cove, Royal. Lake Escape offers houseboats with four to six private bedrooms on Lake Ouachita. Hot tubs and slides are available, and amenities include front decks with patio furniture and gas grill, fully equipped kitchens, televisions, DVDs, and stereos. Sea-Doo rentals are also available. Seasonal rates apply; peak season rates are $2,499 per weekend and $4,499 by the week. $$$.

✳ Where to Eat

EATING OUT **Allen's Barbeque** (870-403-0331), 3100 Hollywood Road, Arkadelphia. Open daily 11–6. Most southerners have a favorite BBQ joint. They are usually joints, too, lacking fancy decor or extensive menus. Most smoke their meat and have a secret family recipe they use for their sauce. So anytime someone claims to have a line on the best BBQ place, well, frequently, them's fightin' words. Allen's Barbeque has the best BBQ in the state. Their meats are smoked to perfection, their sauce is tangy but not too tangy, and the prices are screaming great. You can feed four people for about $20 for lunch, $30 for dinner. One of the best things on the menu is the smothered baked potato. It is a combination of smoked beef and pork spread over a huge, flaky potato, covered with smoky baked beans and cheese. They are hard to finish at one sitting and only $4.50. Everything is good, from the sandwiches to dinner plates, which include your choice of smoked meat, potato salad, baked beans, and coleslaw for $7.50. Allen's makes their flaky fried pies daily. The decor, well, there really isn't any. Allen's serves from a trailer surrounding by a deck with a few picnic tables for seating. $.

Cajun Boilers (501-767-5695; www .cajunboilers.com), 2806 Albert Pike, Hot Springs. Open Monday through Saturday 11–2 and 4–10 (9 p.m. in winter). Located on Lake Hamilton, Cajun Boilers has been serving seafood on the water here for more than 30 years. The menu includes burgers and sandwiches, salads and pasta, steak and chicken, plus the house specialties—oysters and crawfish. Everything on the menu deserves recommendation, and on mild days the deck overlooking the lake is a serene setting for lunch or dinner. The desserts are homemade and change daily. Your meal will run you about $35 per person for dinner, including an appetizer and dessert. $$–$$$.

The Cheese Corner (501-624-3040; www.thecheesecorner.com), 303 Broadway Street, Hot Springs. Open 8–4 Monday through Friday; serving lunch from 10–2:30. This delicatessen has the finest and widest selection of imported cheeses and specialty items in town. Gift baskets from around the world, cheese and party trays, and meats cut fresh daily highlight their menu. Moderately priced menu, with an average ticket of $10. $–$$.

McClard's Bar-B-Q (501-624-9586; www.mcclards.com), 505 Albert Pike Road, Hot Springs. Open Tuesday through Saturday 11–8. McClard's is a legendary family-owned restaurant that has achieved national recognition not only for its food but also for the prominent political figures who make it a point to visit whenever they are in Arkansas, like former president Bill Clinton. Their meat is pit-smoked daily on the premises. They have bottles of their sauce available for sale at the register. The sauce, coleslaw, beans, and hot tamales are made with old family recipes. In addition to their barbecued meats and ribs, McClard's is well known for their hot tamales. One of their signature dishes is the hot tamale spread—layers of tamales, shredded smoked pork, beans, onions, and cheese—for under $10 for a huge portion that easily feeds two. McClard's was featured in *Southern Living* and *Gourmet* magazines and on *The Best Of* television show on the Food Network. Everything on the menu is said to be made from scratch. The list of the restaurant's commendations includes most of the major travel outlets in the country. It was named one of Travelocity's Local Secrets, Big Finds; one of the Travel Channel's Top Ten BBQ Restaurants; included in the book *The French Fry Companion* for its fries; cited in *Gourmet* magazine; and endorsed by *Runner's World* magazine as a great place to eat after running a 10K race. $–$$.

Rod's Pizza Cellar (501-321-2313; www .rodspizzacellar.com), 3350 Central Avenue, Hot Springs. Open 11–9 Tuesday through Thursday, 11–10 Friday and Saturday, 11–9 Sunday. Since 1975, Rod's Pizza Cellar has served up the freshest pizza, pasta, salads, and sandwiches in Hot Springs. Made-from-scratch doughs and sauces plus freshly sliced cheese are the common denominators in a menu that includes interesting combinations in signature dishes, including its famed Godfather pizza. Rod's features a lunch buffet for less than $10 per person. A large Godfather is less than $30. $.

Queen's Restaurant (1-800-264-2477), 1309 US 71 North, Mena. Open throughout the year, the restaurant at the Queen Wilhelmina State Park Lodge opens at 7 a.m., serving breakfast until 10 and lunch 11–4. Dinner is served from 5–9. Absorb the quaint and cozy atmosphere as you make your way to Queen's Restaurant with full-window views from atop Rich Mountain. Locals and travelers alike enjoy American, Mexican, and good old Southern dishes either from the menu or as part of a buffet. For those with a serious sweet tooth, don't miss the homemade dessert bar offered with the buffet. Banquets and groups welcome. $–$$.

DINING OUT **The Avenue** (501-625-3850; www.theavenuehs.com), 340 Central Avenue, Hot Springs. The Avenue is open Monday through Tuesday from 4–8 p.m.; Wednesday through Thursday from 4–9 p.m., and weekends from 4–11 p.m. There is an outstanding Sunday brunch offered from 9 a.m.–2 p.m. This chef-driven restaurant made an immediate mark on the Hot Springs culinary scene due to the prestigious reputation of its chef, Casey Copeland. An alumnus of Austin Culinary Academy Le Cordon Bleu, Copeland's Arkansas resume includes many of central Arkansas's finest restaurants, including 42 Bar and Table at the Clinton Library. An extensive small plate menu features flavors from around the globe for very affordable prices. Duck confit tacos ($12), Korean fred wings ($9), and Thai Manila clasm ($13) are just a few of the options from

which you can choose. Entrées range from The Avenue Burger, ground with ribeye and tri-tip, for $14 to smoked ribeye medallions for $32. $$–$$$.

✳ Entertainment

Capone's Ohio Club (502-627-0702; www.caponesohioclub.com), 336 Central Avenue, Suite A, Hot Springs. Open Monday through Saturday 11 a.m.–1 a.m. Named after the infamous Chicago gangster who took up part-time residence just down the street at The Arlington Hotel. The club is known for its live music.

Conway Symphony Orchestra (1-866-810-0012; www.conwaysymphony.org), 201 Donaghey Avenue, Reynolds Performance Hall, Conway. Approximately 75 professional musicians perform classical, pops, and family concerts each year. Founded in 1985, the Conway Symphony provides enjoyable performances for all ages. Led by Maestro Israel Getzov, the repertoire ranges from traditional to modern, with several internationally renowned guest artists sharing the stage. Reynolds Performance Hall is a state-of-the-art performance facility that seats 1,200 and accommodates full orchestras and large theatrical productions. It is also used for guest speakers, lectures, and large conference and teleconference meetings.

Little Bitty City (501-525-7529; www.littlebittycity.com), 4332 Central Avenue, Hot Springs. Open Monday through Saturday 10–5. This indoor, creative playground for kids provides a safe, fun-filled environment for youngsters to dream and explore through self-directed play. Admission is $7 per child.

The Lobby Bar at The Arlington Hotel (501-623-7771; www.arlingtonhotel.com), 239 Central Avenue, Hot Springs. Open Monday through Thursday 11 a.m.–2:30 a.m.; Friday and Saturday 11 a.m.–1 a.m.; Sunday noon–10. This is a great place for a drink, a cup of coffee, or just people watching. Willie Davis and Co., a jazz

LIVE MUSIC AT BIG CHILL IN HOT SPRINGS

Montgomery County Front Porch Stage (870-867-2723; www.mtida chamber.com), Montgomery County Courthouse Lawn, Mount Ida. May through October, Saturday night 7–9. Free performances include bluegrass, gospel, country, and other music.

Pocket Theatre (501-623-8585; www .pockettheatre.com), 170 Ravine Street, Hot Springs. This community theater performs classical, comedy, mystery, and drama; it's a nonprofit group that stages four productions each year in a 200-seat theater.

The Poet's Loft (501-627-4224; www .thepoetsloft.com), 514-B Central Avenue, Hot Springs. Open Tuesday through Saturday 10–5 and late on Wednesday, Friday, and Saturday. This coffeehouse and performance venue boasts the most beautiful beer garden in the downtown area and is the home of the world's oldest continuously running open-mic poetry reading.

combo, is a weekend fixture, performing most Thursdays and every Friday and Saturday evening.

Maxwell Blade Theatre of Magic (501-623-6200; www.maxwellblade.com), 817 Central Avenue, Hot Springs. Hours vary by season. This show will take you on a magical journey, celebrating magicians from the past 100 years in a unique, intimate, 100-seat Victorian theater. This Las Vegas–style production of magic and illusions features Maxwell Blade; the show is suitable for all ages. Call for show times and ticket prices.

Historic Malco Theatre (501-623-7751), 817 Central Avenue, Hot Springs. This art deco–style building is home to live magic performances year-round, special documentary film screenings, and the Hot Springs Documentary Film Festival in October. Special variety and family shows are held throughout the year.

✳ Selective Shopping

Alison Parsons Gallery (501-655-0604; www.alisonparsons.com), 1017 Lakeshore Drive, Hot Springs. Open by appointment. Sisters Alison Parsons and Lori Arnold project vivaciousness into their art, creating unforgettable glass art jewelry and original paintings, prints, and note cards.

American Art Gallery (502-624-0550; www.americanartgalleryand gifts.com), 724 Central Avenue, Hot Springs. Open Monday through Saturday 10–5:30. This 4,000-square-foot gallery exhibits fine art by local, regional, and national artists. The upstairs gallery showcases the work of Thomas Kinkade.

Artists Workshop Gallery (501-623-6401; www.artistsworkshopgallery.com), 810 Central Avenue, Hot Springs. Open Monday through Saturday 10–4 and 11–5 Memorial Day through Labor Day. The Artists Workshop Gallery is an art cooperative of local and regional artists.

It carries affordable, original art, prints, and note cards. The gallery is staffed by the artists, who often can be seen painting.

The Battlefield, A Civil War Bookshoppe (501-844-1846; www.parkhotelhotsprings.com), 211 Fountain Street, Hot Springs. Open Monday through Thursday 9–8 and weekends 9–9. At The Battlefield you can browse among more than 2,000 current, limited-edition, rare, and collectible books on the American Civil War, as well as an assortment of relics and artifacts from the 1860s.

Dryden Pottery (501-623-4201; www.drydenpottery.com), 341 Whittington Avenue, Hot Springs. Visit the largest pottery showroom in the state for an inventory featuring pottery that is world famous for its vibrant colors. The secret may be in the clay itself, which contains coveted Mount Ida crystals. Pottery-making demonstrations feature three generations at work. The family's 60 years of experience are evident in one-of-a-kind decorative items, dinnerware, ovenware, and the world's largest wheel-thrown vase.

Fox Pass Pottery (501-623-9906; www.foxpasspottery.com), 379 Fox Pass Cutoff, Hot Springs. Open Tuesday through Saturday 10–5. The showroom and studio of Fox Pass Pottery offer a large selection of wood-fired and gas-fired stoneware, featuring both functional and sculptural pieces, including kitchenware, vases, and teapots.

Downtown Hot Springs (501-318-2787), Central Avenue, Scenic AR 7, Hot Springs. Stroll the downtown area and browse galleries along historic Bathhouse Row. The first Friday of each month, galleries stay open late, offering music, refreshments, and a chance to chat with the artists.

Pickles Gap Village (501-327-8049; www.picklesgap.com), 315 US 65 North, Conway. This quaint little Ozark shopping village gets its unique name from the legend of a German immigrant who overturned his load of pickles while crossing the creek. It features The Pickle Barrel Fudge Factory, Something's Brewing coffee shop, General Store, Native American Store, Mack's Knife Shop and Bull Pen, and Precious Memories Antiques. The home office of the Arkansas Cherokee Nation also is located on-site. Kiddie Land has rides and a petting zoo where kids can feed the animals.

The Villa Gifts & Apparel (501-318-4438), 111 Central Avenue, Hot Springs. Open Monday through Saturday 10–5:30, Sunday 11–3. (Hours vary January through March.) Recognized twice by *Southern Living* as one of the top 50 shops in the United States for gifts and apparel. Two upscale boutiques offer unique gifts, luxury linens, and fashion lines such as Betsey Johnson, Free People, and Hobo.

✳ Special Events

May: **Toad Suck Daze** (501-327-7788; toadsuck.org). Conway's annual early May festival, is one of the largest and most popular in the state. It derives its attention-getting title from the legend of Toad Suck, one of the state's most colorful. According to local folklore, long ago, when steamboats plied the Arkansas River and the water wasn't the correct depth, the captains and their crew docked where the Toad Suck Lock and

POTTERY THROWING DEMONSTRATION AT DRYDEN POTTERY

Dam now spans the river to wait until the water level rose. While waiting, they occupied themselves at the local tavern, to the displeasure of the locals who lived nearby. The residents described the sailors this way: "They suck on the bottle 'til they swell up like toads." Hence, the name Toad Suck. The tavern is long gone, but the legend lives on at Toad Suck Daze.

October: **Hot Springs Documentary Film Festival** (501-321-4747; www.hsdfi .org), 817 Central Avenue, Hot Springs. This noncompetitive documentary film festival offers expanded opportunities for you to challenge your worldview and experience new perspectives. Over 1,000 documentary films are submitted, and 100 are selected for the festival. Filmmakers from all over the world come and participate in Q&As with the audience. There are numerous workshops, musical events, and festivities that culminate in the black-tie Filmmaker Gala at the historic Arlington Hotel.

THE ARKANSAS
RIVER VALLEY

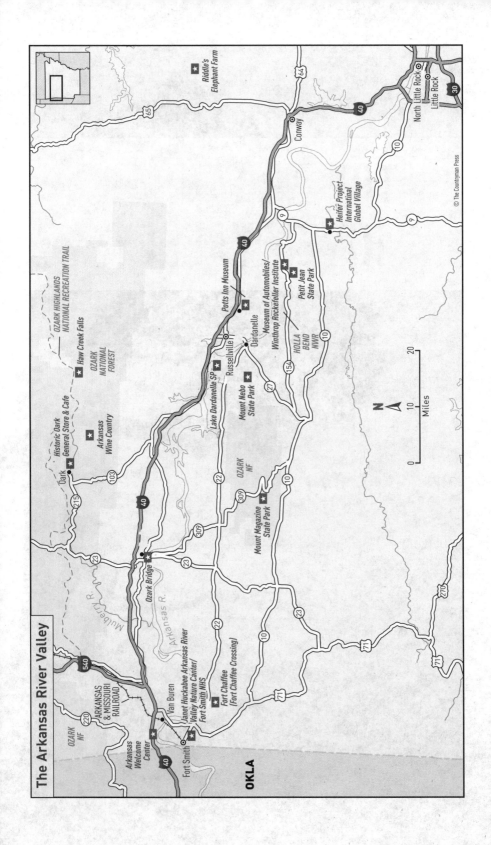

The Arkansas River Valley

Riddle's Elephant Farm

Little Rock
North Little Rock

Conway

Heifer Project International Global Village

Potts Inn Museum

Dardanelle

Museum of Automobiles/
Winthrop Rockefeller Institute

Petit Jean State Park

HOLLA BEND NWR

Russellville

Lake Dardanelle SP

Mount Nebo State Park

OZARK HIGHLANDS NATIONAL RECREATION TRAIL

Haw Creek Falls

OZARK NATIONAL FOREST

Historic Oark General Store & Cafe

Arkansas Wine Country

Oark

OZARK NF

Mount Magazine State Park

Ozark Bridge

Mulberry R.

Arkansas R.

ARKANSAS & MISSOURI RAILROAD

OZARK NF

Arkansas Welcome Center

Van Buren

Janet Huckabee Arkansas River Valley Nature Center/
Fort Smith NHS

Fort Chaffee (Fort Chaffee Crossing)

Fort Smith

OKLA

N

Miles
0   10   20

© The Countryman Press

THE ARKANSAS RIVER VALLEY

Running between the Ozarks and Ouachitas natural regions is the Arkansas River Valley. This area has the best of both ranges: flat-topped mountains like those found in the Ozarks, and folding ridges like in the Ouachitas. But it also has the great Arkansas River flowing through its center, providing those who settled in the River Valley with the scenic beauty of the mountainous regions and soils as rich as the Delta. The tallest mountain in the state, Mount Magazine, can be found in this region, as well as Mount Nebo and Petit Jean Mountain. All three mountains are home to beautiful state parks with lodging for cozy overnights gazing at stars from their peaks.

The wide bottomlands with fertile soil that are found along the river produce many different crops. Pines and hardwoods, prairie grasses, bottomland forests, and swamps mark the landscape. In the 1700s and early 1800s, bison and elk were frequently seen as the area's large and small game migrated the corridor. Today, migrating birds still follow the Arkansas River through the valley.

The Caddo and warlike Osage inhabited the area before European settlement. Henri de Tonti, a French explorer, visited the valley in the early 1700s. Fort Smith was the state's Wild West town. Founded as a military outpost to quell intertribal conflict, it bordered the Indian Territory until 1907, when Oklahoma became a state. In 1849, it became a major departure point for gold seekers headed to California, as did nearby Van Buren. By the late 1850s, the Butterfield Stage Line ran through the Arkansas River Valley before heading to California. Judge Isaac C. Parker, known as the "Hanging Judge," sentenced 160 men to death from his bench in Fort Smith from 1875 until 1896.

Fort Smith, Pottsville, Paris, Booneville, Atkins, Ozark, Clarksville, Van Buren, Russellville, Morrilton, and Dardanelle are the largest communities found in the River Valley.

One of the area's most important events occurred during the 1960s, when the US Army Corps of Engineers completed the McClellan-Kerr Arkansas River Navigation System that made the Arkansas River navigable to Tulsa, Oklahoma. Anglers find the series of locks and dams enhance fishing opportunities in the pools formed along the river's shores, which are maintained and stocked by the Arkansas Game Commission.

River, rail, and highway travel have helped to populate this area and contributed to its growth. Today, it possesses beautiful mountains and scenic waterways and is considered by some to be one of the most attractive places to live in the state. An excursion train offers a scenic overview from a historic carriage while dining on local cuisine.

AREA CODES The western half of the River Valley falls under the 479 area. The eastern half uses 501.

GUIDANCE **Western Arkansas's Mountain Frontier** (479-783-6118; www.westarkansastourism.com) is one of two regional tourism associations in this area. It provides information on Fort Smith, Arkansas Wine Country, and various festivals in the region; their website is updated regularly.

Arkansas River Valley Tri-Peaks (1-800-564-6508; www.arvtripeaks.com) is the other tourism association for this region. As their name implies, this group's emphasis is on the River Valley's three prominent mountains—Mount Magazine, Mount Nebo, and Petit Jean Mountain—and the area surrounding them.

Clarksville/Johnson County Chamber of Commerce (479-754-2340; www.clarksville archamber.com).

Dardanelle Chamber of Commerce (479-229-3328; www.dardanellechamber.com), 2011 AR 22 West, Dardanelle.

Fort Smith Convention & Visitors Bureau (479-783-8888; www.fortsmith.org), #2 North B Street, Fort Smith.

Ozark Area Chamber of Commerce (1-800-951-2525; www.ozarkarkansas.com), 300 West Commercial Street, Ozark.

Van Buren Advertising & Promotion Board (1-800-332-5889; www.vanburen.org), 813 Main Street, Van Buren.

GETTING THERE *By auto:* The larger communities in the River Valley are connected by I-40, which runs east-west from the Oklahoma border at Fort Smith through the center of the region to Little Rock. Additional scenic routes connect the northern destinations along the interstate with the parks, mountains, and Wine Country farther south. Along the western boundary, US 71 from Missouri runs through Fort Smith to Rich Mountain in the Ouachitas. Fruit stands and old-time country stores make US 65 a fun and tasty drive in the east. Finally, Scenic AR 7 never fails to impress, and the River Valley's portion is no exception, passing Mount Magazine, Mount Nebo, and Petit Jean Mountain.

By air: There are three options for air travel to the River Valley, the first being the **Fort Smith Regional Airport** (479-452-7000; www.fortsmithairport.com), 6700 McKennon Boulevard, Fort Smith, serviced by American Airlines and Delta. A little over an hour away is the relatively new (in airport years—it was completed in 1998) **Northwest Arkansas Regional Airport** (479-205-1000; www.flyxna.com), 1 Airport Boulevard, Bentonville. Airlines offering flights to XNA include Allegiant Air, American Airlines, Delta, and United. Expanded flight options are available at the **Little Rock National Airport** (501-372-3439; www.clintonairport.com), 1 Airport Drive, Little Rock. Allegiant Air, American Airlines, Delta, Frontier Airlines, Southwest, United, and Via Air offer service to the capital city.

MEDICAL EMERGENCIES **St. Edward Mercy Medical Center** (501-484-6000; www.stedwardmercy.com), 7301 Rogers Avenue, Fort Smith.

THE BOSTON MOUNTAINS

✳ Wandering Around

EXPLORING BY FOOT The **Ozark Highlands National Recreation Trail** (479-754-2864; www.ozarkhighlandstrail.com) has been rated as one of the most scenic in the nation. From its western terminus at Lake Fort Smith State Park, it travels east across the entire Ozark National Forest before turning north toward its eastern destination, the Buffalo River. In between the two lie 209 miles of the most remote areas in the Ozark National Forest. Noted for its mountainous terrain, scenic bluffs, lush upland hardwood forests, unique rock outcroppings and clear, mountain streams, the OHT is a favorite with both casual hikers and serious backpackers.

EXPLORING BY RIVER Locks and dams along the **Arkansas River** have helped to create some of the best fishing in the country. The Arkansas Game & Fish Commission stocks pools formed by these dams with sport fish such as bass, crappie, catfish, and bream, making the river a popular location for major fishing tournaments such as the Arkansas Big Bass Classic. One of the most popular is the Big Bass Bonanza, which spans 300 miles of eligible fishing from Fort Smith to Dumas—the entire length of the river within the state's borders.

The US Army Corps of Engineers manages 37 public access points from Oklahoma to Little Rock, providing easy river entrance for recreational boaters and fishermen.

One of the more productive early season bass hot spots is the shallow, backwater areas adjacent to the Arkansas River. You can find these backwaters almost anywhere along the river from Fort Smith to Arkansas Post. However, the lower ends of the 12 navigational pools generally contain more backwater areas than the upper ends of those pools because the water level is higher relative to the riverbank in the lower ends. Saugers and whites up to 3 pounds are a common catch on the Arkansas River during winter. Fishing tailwaters is the way to load a stringer, with those below Ozark, Dardanelle, and Murray dams among the best. Be on the water at night or just before dawn and dusk for best success.

Stripers are caught along the entire 320-mile length of the Arkansas River in Arkansas, from the river's mouth in Desha County to Fort Smith on the Arkansas/Oklahoma border. In spring, they migrate upriver into the tailwaters below river dams. Slack-water periods, when few or no gates are open, are great times for fishing with medium-weight tackle and live minnows. Spring fishermen also congregate below the Ozark-Jetta Taylor Lock and Dam (L&D) on the lake's upstream end, and below Dardanelle L&D, which impounds the lake.

In addition to making the wide tree-lined river more enjoyable, the navigation system also created two lakes that are recreation havens for outdoors enthusiasts. Ozark Lake covers 10,600 acres and extends 36 miles along the Arkansas River. The shoreline of the lake varies from steep bluffs and tree-lined banks to open farmlands and level fields. Ten parks, three of which are day-use only, provide 157 campsites along the lakeshore. **Lake Dardanelle**, home to Lake Dardanelle State Park, is one of the most popular lakes in Arkansas for fishing tournaments because of large populations of catfish, white and largemouth bass, bream, and crappie. Dardanelle stretches some 50 miles through the Arkansas River Valley and has over 34,000 acres of boating and fishing waters.

The approximately 55-mile **Mulberry River** is definitely one of the state's wildest rivers during spring. From its beginnings deep in the Ozarks to its confluence with the Arkansas River, the Mulberry flows over stone ledges, shoots through willow thickets, and whips around sharp turns. These wild characteristics are what give the stream its

Class II/III rating and high marks from the floating public. In drier times, it's a good place to swim, wade, skip rocks, and fish. Visitors to the Mulberry can expect prime Ozark Mountain scenery—narrow canyons, tree-lined bluffs, and dense woods. A good assortment of wildlife is found in the immediate area, including one of the state's largest concentrations of black bears. The stream itself is clear and cool. In 1985, the General Assembly declared the Mulberry to be a Scenic River of the State of Arkansas, and in 1992 it was named a National Wild and Scenic River.

The Mulberry River is a great stream for fishing in spring and early summer. The river is an excellent choice when angling for smallmouth, largemouth, and spotted bass, and green and longear sunfish. If you are up for some hiking up or down a slippery streambed, the potholes can be fished in drier months.

The Mulberry flows in a west-southwesterly course. Access points are fairly common, particularly where the stream is within the Ozark National Forest. Primary points of access include Wolfpen ATV Campground (off AR 215), AR 23, AR 103, AR 215, Campbell Cemetery (off Forest Road [FR] 1512), FR 1501, FR 1504, and US 64. And while the Mulberry is located in some of the state's wildest country, the stream is amazingly convenient; the AR 23 crossing is less than a dozen miles north of I-40. Outfitters are located on and near the river, and supplies and overnight accommodations or camping can be found easily.

EXPLORING BY TRAIN **Arkansas & Missouri Railroad** (1-800-687-8600; www.am railroad.com/excursions), 813 Main Street, Van Buren. Open April through mid-November on Wednesday, Friday, and Saturday, and January through March on Saturday. Train departs at 8 a.m. from Springdale for the Springdale to Van Buren excursion. Train departs from Van Buren at 11 a.m. for the Van Buren to Winslow route. Ticket prices range from first class at $95 to coach seats for $55 for the day trip, which includes a three-hour layover in downtown Van Buren. The three-hour excursion rates range from $40 for coach to $84 for seating with a table. Hop aboard these beautifully restored turn-of-the-century passenger cars for a scenic excursion through the Boston Mountains and into the historic Arkansas River Basin. Each excursion train is staffed with knowledgeable passenger conductors to provide a nostalgic touch and historical commentary—a treat for the beginning and seasoned rail traveler alike. Travel over 125-foot high trestles and through the 1,700-foot 1882 Winslow tunnel. Two trips are available on this historic train: round-trip from Van Buren to Winslow; and from Springdale to Van Buren.

✳ Towns and Villages

Clarksville, Johnson County. More than 250 geocaches are hidden in Johnson County, making it a hot spot for geocachers in Arkansas. The sport, a high-tech scavenger hunt utilizing global positioning systems (GPS), is a popular activity throughout the Natural State. With the entire northern half of the county composed of the Ozark National Forest, all forms of outdoor activity are abundant here. Also home to the Walton Fine Arts Center and the University of the Ozarks.

Dardanelle. America's anglers appreciate the fishing and the tournament weigh-in facilities at Lake Dardanelle State Park. National tournaments are held at the facility, which also features interpretive programs, kayak rentals, and a visitor center with sweeping views of the 34,300-acre reservoir on the Arkansas River. Updated event and tournament information is posted online.

Fort Smith (479-783-8888; www.fortsmith.org). The 2019 opening of the US Marshals Museum will be the culmination of one of the state's most sought-after attractions since the Clinton library. The museum will share the stories of the oldest law enforcement agency in the country and is a great addition for a town that treasures its local history. Miss Laura's Visitor Center, charged with greeting travelers and distributing literature on the many attractions in town, is also the only former brothel listed on the National Register of Historic Places. On the banks of the Arkansas River, Fort Smith celebrates its Wild West history at museums like the National Historic Site, through preservation of numerous historic homes, and through annual festivals such as its Old Fort Days Rodeo, held each spring. The city is also creating new traditions that embrace the artistic vision you will find throughout the Northwest Corridor of the state. The Unexpected brings urban and contemporary artists from around the world to Fort Smith, where they create lasting public imagery on the historic downtown. Families enjoy the retro amusement park downtown and the area's ability to please the entire family with additions like the nature center and shopping district. There are over 62 miles of hiking and biking trails maintained by the city's Parks and Recreation Department and connecting its downtown with attractions on the river. Fishing opportunities abound with the Arkansas River Navigation System, which has created scores of quiet inlets and bayous filled with many kinds of native Arkansas fish. The Fort Smith area also has a reputation as a bird sanctuary. Other outdoor recreational opportunities such as hiking and canoeing can be found nearby at Devil's Den State Park and the Mulberry River. Located on the Arkansas-Oklahoma border and near the junction of I-40 and I-540, Fort Smith is 5 miles from Van Buren, 47 miles from Arkansas Wine Country, and 63 miles from Fayetteville.

MEET MISS LAURA AT FORT SMITH VISITOR CENTER   ARKANSAS DEPARTMENT OF PARKS & TOURISM

Ozark. This small community's location. where the foothills of the Ozarks meet the Arkansas River, brings outdoor enthusiasts from all over the country for white-water canoeing and rafting, mountain biking, and hiking. Ozark Lake, the Mulberry River, and the Ozark National Forest are but a few miles from town, making Ozark a great place to replenish and refuel. Murals adorn its quaint town square surrounded by antiques and gift shops. A visitor information center has details on over 200 camp-sites, area waterways, lodging, and dining.

Russellville is one of the largest communities on Lake Dardanelle, considered one of the best bass fisheries in the Southwest. Russellville hosts numerous tournaments each year, including the GoPro Bassmasters Elite in 2017. The Arkansas River Visitor Center chronicles the development of the river. Also popular with birders, Russellville's Bona Dea Trails and Sanctuary provides 186 acres of wetlands and wooded lowlands that shelter 200 species of birds. Mount Nebo State Park is just 10 miles southwest of the town, with cabins built by the CCC in the 1940s and breathtaking views of the Arkansas River that haven't changed since the cabins were built.

Van Buren (1-800-332-5889; www.vanburen.org) is 5 miles from Fort Smith, 42 miles from Mount Magazine State Park, and 80 miles from Russellville. Six blocks of art galleries, antiques shops, restaurants, and historical attractions are clustered con-veniently along a lovingly restored Main Street. You're just a phone call away from a helpful visitor guide and true appreciation for the rich history of this charming town. Steamboats and stages, Civil War soldiers and Native American warriors have all left their mark on Van Buren. A restored depot, built in 1901, serves as Van Buren's cham-ber of commerce office and includes an exhibit honoring native son Bob Burns, a radio and motion picture star of the 1930s and '40s. Entertainment options are abundant with excursion train rides, theater productions at the King Opera House, and special annual events. Surrounding parks and recreation areas, including Lee Creek, afford many opportunities for fishing, boating, hiking, and golfing.

FORT SMITH REGIONAL ART MUSEUM ARKANSAS DEPARTMENT OF PARKS & TOURISM

SPECTACULAR STREET ART AND FESTIVAL CREATE GLOBAL SPLASH FOR FORT SMITH

The Unexpected (www.unexpectedfs.com) Houston, Texas; Perth, Australia; Montreal, Quebec; and the small but mighty town of Fort Smith, Arkansas, were featured in a 2016 piece published in *Afar* magazine's online edition titled, "Eight Surprising Cities with Amazing Street Art." In 2015, 64.6 Downtown, a nonprofit community development group, was formed to develop a sense of place for Fort Smith. The idea was to bring in urban artists from all over the world to display their talents on the town, culminating in a weeklong street festival as the artists completed their work. It was a good idea with sound reasoning: thousands and thousands of people were traveling I-40 from Little Rock to I-540 near Fort Smith to get to Bentonville and the Crystal Bridges Museum. The Unexpected launched the same year with 10 artists and countless volunteers.

By 2016, *Afar* magazine would include Fort Smith's public art project with cities 10 times its size, saying, "If someone were to drop a street art festival where you'd least expect it, Arkansas might be the spot. So, The Unexpected is an appropriate name for the big contemporary and public art project, now in its second year, that takes over downtown Fort Smith, brightening the city with epic works of art."

There are now 30 murals around the historic downtown area, and the number grows annually. Old buildings and warehouses, grain silos, and storefronts have been revitalized with spectacular, vibrant imagery. There are paintings in every style imaginable: fantasy and whimsy, abstracts in bright primary colors, realistic portraits that convey every detail. *American Heroes*, a series of six-story pieces that cover the exterior of silos, features locals from Fort Smith representing the town's diverse culture. Visit the website for information on the annual festival, maps so you can take a walking tour of the finished pieces, and information on their latest mobile app so you can use your smartphone as your tour guide. Festival dates are usually announced in late summer (for example, October 22–28; 2018 dates announced end of August 2018), so check back if dates are not listed on the website earlier in the year.

✳ To See

GALLERIES AND FINE ART **Fort Smith Art Center** (479-782-1156; www.ftsartcenter .com), 423 North Sixth Street, Fort Smith. Open Thursday through Saturday, 9:30–4:30. Housed in the Vaughn-Schaap House, a Victorian Second Empire structure, the center presents changing exhibits and permanent collections. A quarter-century older than first thought, this gracious home was built about 1857 by Ethelbert Bright and had several owners before the turn of the twentieth century. During the Civil War, soldiers were billeted here. It was owned for almost 60 years by the John Schaap family until it became the home of the Fort Smith Art Center in 1959. It later was the first house restored to its original elegance when the Belle Grove historic district was created. Galleries of fine paintings, sculptures, and permanent and changing exhibits make it worth a visit. A gift shop on the premises sells original works by local artists and artisans. Free.

MUSEUMS **Altus Heritage House Museum** (479-468-4684), 106 North Franklin, Altus. Call for hours of operation. Originally the German-American State Bank circa the 1800s, it features early coal-mining equipment and local history. This building is listed on the National Register of Historic Places.

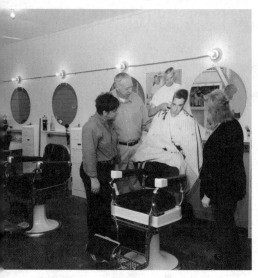

FORT CHAFFEE BARBERSHOP MUSEUM ARKANSAS DEPARTMENT OF PARKS & TOURISM

Fort Chaffee Crossing, Fort Chaffee. Built in 1941, this 72,000-acre military base was the training site for thousands of troops heading overseas during World War II. In 1958, Elvis Presley was inducted into the US Army and began basic training here. It has served as an annual reserve training center and was the Ellis Island point of entrance for Vietnamese, Laotian, and Cuban refugees coming to the United States. In 2005, Fort Chaffee temporarily housed thousands of evacuees from Hurricane Katrina. It was also a location used in the movies *Biloxi Blues*, *The Tuskegee Airmen*, and *A Soldier's Story*. Several memorial plaques honor World War II units formed here. The area of the camp that includes the barrack facilities is now part of the 7,000 acres being developed for commercial, residential, and industrial purposes known as Chaffee Crossing.

Enchanted Doll Museum (479-478-0225), 7201 Terry Street, Fort Smith. A 1,500-square-foot museum of about 5,000 dolls, it contains a life-sized Ken and Barbie,

FORT SMITH AIR MUSEUM ARKANSAS DEPARTMENT OF PARKS & TOURISM

antique dolls such as Madame Alexander, Effanbee, Kewpie, Betsy Wetsy, Cabbage Patch Kids, Annie, and Gerber brands. Displays feature *Gone with the Wind* and Shirley Temple. Doll furniture is also exhibited. Open by appointment only.

Fort Chaffee Barbershop Museum (479-769-0402; www.chaffeecrossing.com), 7313 Terry Street, Fort Smith. Open Monday, Wednesday, and Friday 9–4. One of the most famous barbershops ever—this is where Elvis Presley received his much-publicized GI haircut in 1957 when he entered the Army. The facility contains a replicated barbershop restored with items authentic to the period, from bathroom fixtures to the barber pole. The barbershop takes up the front portion of the building and includes a life-sized

FORT SMITH HISTORY MUSEUM   ARKANSAS DEPARTMENT OF PARKS & TOURISM

cutout of Presley in his uniform in the barber chair. The back portion of the building contains some Elvis memorabilia, such as the script from the *King Creole* movie he finished filming the day before he was inducted and original photos. Free.

Fort Smith Air Museum (479-785-1839; fortsmithairmuseum.com), 6700 McKennon Boulevard, Fort Smith. Open 7 days a week, 365 days a year. The Fort Smith Air Museum is dedicated to preserving the history of the development of aviation in Western Arkansas and Eastern Oklahoma. Visitors can view a wide variety of displays honoring the pioneer and military aviators from the area and chronicling the history of airline service to Fort Smith. Special exhibits feature the 188th Air National Guard, the Fort Smith Civil Air Patrol, and the growth of corporate and general aviation in the Fort Smith area. Visitors can enjoy a self-guided tour of the museum. Free.

Fort Smith Museum of History (479-783-7841; www.fortsmithmuseum.org), 320 Rogers Avenue, Fort Smith. Open Tuesday through Saturday 10–5; Sunday 1–5 June through August only; closed Monday. Adjacent to the historic site is the Fort Smith Museum of History, a three-story building containing numerous exhibits, displays, and artifacts that tell the story of Fort Smith's colorful history: from the first fort in 1817, through the westward expansion, the Civil War, and Fort Chaffee, to the emergence of a modern city. One of the highlights is an old-fashioned drug store and a working soda fountain. Artifacts depict the history and culture of the Fort Smith area from Native Americans to present, military activity, and notable personalities. Revolving exhibits and a gift shop, too.

Fort Smith Trolley Museum (479-783-0205; www.fstm.org), 100 South Fourth Street, Fort Smith. Museum open Saturday 10–5. Take a ride from Garrison Avenue to the National Cemetery on a 1926 Birney electric streetcar that is listed on the National Register. Railroad and transportation memorabilia is also on display. During the 1920s and '30s, streetcars were popular in most cities. The Fort Smith Trolley Museum features a working, fully restored 1926 electric streetcar that makes regular half-mile runs between the Fort Smith National Cemetery and a west-end stop at the Varsity Sports Grill on Garrison Avenue (Main Street). Tickets can be purchased at the Fort Smith Museum of History. Inside the trolley museum—a stop on the route—is a fascinating collection of old railroad passenger cars, engines, old Fort Smith buses, and other transportation artifacts. Trolley rides are $2 per adult, $1 per child. Trolley runs

TAKE THE TROLLEY IN DOWNTOWN FORT SMITH   ARKANSAS DEPARTMENT OF PARKS & TOURISM

summer (May 1 through October 31): Monday through Saturday 10–5, Sunday 1–5; winter (November 1 through April 30): Saturday 10–5, Sunday 1–5.

Museum of Automobiles (501-727-5427; www.museumofautos.com), 8 Jones Lane, Petit Jean Mountain, Morrilton. Open daily 10–5. The Museum of Automobiles was founded in 1964 by the late Arkansas governor Winthrop Rockefeller. It housed his collection of antique and classic automobiles until 1975, when the collection was sold and the building and grounds donated to the Arkansas Department of Parks and Tourism. A nonprofit group reopened the museum in 1976 with cars on loan from collectors around the country. During the following years, the display was enlarged and upgraded, including a permanent collection of 30 automobiles donated by supporters in Arkansas and surrounding states. An antique gun collection and automobile-related memorabilia are also displayed. Exhibits are updated on a regular basis from an inventory of over 50 cars dated from 1904–67. The museum plays host to two car shows/swap meets annually. Museum admissions are $7 for adults, $3.50 for students ages 6–17, $6.50 for seniors. No charge for children under 6 with their parents.

Potts Inn Museum (479-968-1877), 25 East Ash Street, Pottsville. Open Wednesday through Sunday 10–5. One of the best-preserved stagecoach stations on the Butterfield Overland Mail Route, this restored antebellum home, built circa 1850, has period furnishings. Five log structures are located on the grounds and contain hat and clothing collections from 1870 on, antique farm equipment, and historic photos. The large gazebo on the grounds is popular for weddings. Free.

Rockefeller Legacy Gallery (1-866-972-7778; http://rockefellerinstitute.org /exhibits), 1 Rockefeller Drive, Morrilton. The decision of Winthrop Rockefeller, fourth son of John D. Rockefeller, to settle in Arkansas changed the state forever. This history is on display in a permanent exhibit titled *Winthrop Rockefeller: A Sphere of Power and Influence Dropped into a River of Need*. The exhibit spans approximately 3,000 square feet and uses the rich visual image of a water drop causing concentric waves. Over 300 restored and enlarged photographs are incorporated into 180 murals and inter-pretative panels to tell the story of the man, his heritage, the mountain, his influence, and his legacy. Located in the Legacy Gallery right off the Rockefeller Institute's main lobby, the exhibit is free and open to the public. Special tours can be arranged for students or groups.

CULTURAL SITES **Arkansas River Visitor Center** (479-968-5008; www.arkansas .com/attractions-culture/arkansas-river-visitor-center), 1598 Lock and Dam Road, Russellville. Open Monday through Friday 8–4, Saturday and Sunday 10–4. This facility was designed to acquaint visitors with the Arkansas River and its man-made transformation into a safe, useful, and productive waterway. *Renaissance of a River* interpretive exhibits chronicle the development of the river. Managed by the US Army Corps of Engineers. Free.

Miss Laura's Visitor Center (1-800-637-1477; www.fortsmith.org), 2 North B Street, Fort Smith. Open Monday through Saturday 9–4, Sunday 1–4:30. This visitor center (a.k.a. Miss Laura's Social Club) is located in historic downtown Fort Smith in a restored former bordello, the first bordello to be listed on the National Register of Historic Places. Make this your first stop and take a tour of this Victorian mansion, which has been restored to its original ambiance. Perched on the banks of the mighty Arkansas River, Fort Smith's frontier history is preserved in several sites around the town. Of the seven houses on "The Row" in 1900, Miss Laura's is the only survivor and has served as Fort Smith's official visitor center since 1992. Museum, gift shop, tours, local information.

Cadron Settlement Park (501-329-2986), AR 319. Open 24/7. One of the most historic spots on the Arkansas River, this settlement on the north side of Conway was an important French trading post in the late 1700s. The 1.3-mile Tollantusky Trail is in the park and will take about 45 minutes to hike. The trail is named for Tollantusky, a distinguished chief of the Arkansas Cherokees who came to Arkansas from Tennessee in 1809. Facilities include the Blockhouse restoration, the Cherokee Trail of Tears, a boat-launching ramp, hiking trails, restrooms, picnic areas, a pavilion, handicapped trails and parking areas, a historical mural of this pioneer settlement, markers, and interpretive signs. Free.

Ozark Bridge (1-800-951-2525; www.ozarkarkansas.com), AR 23 and Commercial Street, Ozark. Spanning the Arkansas River as Scenic AR 23, this structure is listed as one of the 16 most beautiful long spans in the United States by the American Institute of Steel Construction. A lighting project showcases the structure at night.

Subiaco Abbey (479-934-4411), 405 North Subiaco Avenue, Subiaco. Open year-round; call for hours and tour information. This complex includes impressive circa 1891 sandstone buildings and Romanesque-style Abbey Church. A self-guided walking tour brochure of the parklike grounds and architecture is available at Coury House; guided and group tours are available with advance notice.

HISTORIC SITES **Fort Smith National Historic Site** (479-783-3961; www.nps.gov /fosm), Third and Rogers, Fort Smith. Open daily 9–5; closed Christmas Day and New Year's Day. Perhaps the most prominent stop in this town is the Fort Smith National

Historic Site, which includes the remains of the original 1817 fort on the Arkansas River. One of the highlights is the two-story barracks from the second fort, which in the early 1870s became the federal courthouse for the Western District of Arkansas. Inside is the restored courtroom of the famed "Hangin' Judge" Isaac C. Parker and the dingy frontier jail aptly named "Hell on the Border." The site, which underwent a $7 million renovation in the late '90s, also contains the remains of two frontier garrisons, a reproduction of the 1886 gallows, and the 1846 commissary. A strategic point for both sides during the Civil War, this site was seized by rebel troops on April 23, 1863, and then recaptured by federal forces two years later. Admission is $5, free for ages 16 and under.

Fort Smith Trolley Museum (479-783-0205; www.fstm.org), 100 South Fourth Street, Fort Smith. Take a ride from Garrison Avenue to the National Cemetery on a 1926 Birney electric streetcar that is listed on the National Register. Railroad and transportation memorabilia is also displayed.

Fort Smith National Cemetery (479-783-5345; www.fortsmith.org/fort-smith-national -cemetery/), 522 South Sixth Street, Fort Smith. When the first Fort Smith was laid out in 1817, land was set aside for a military cemetery. Granted national status in 1867, the 21-acre US National Cemetery contains almost 10,000 graves—among them those belonging to Judge Isaac Parker and Darby's Rangers founder William O. Darby. The colorful Avenue of Flags is displayed each year on patriotic holidays. This is the oldest national cemetery in the country.

✳ To Do

WALKING TOURS **Belle Grove historic district**, Van Buren. Beautifully restored homes and buildings line the streets of the 22-block Belle Grove historic district and reflect an architectural span of 150 years, including Romanesque Revival, Queen Anne, Eastlake Victorian Renaissance, Gothic Revival, Craftsman, Prairie, Federal, and Neoclassical architecture. Structures in Belle Grove include the homes of noted figures such as William Henry Clayton, the prosecuting attorney for Judge Parker's court; Southern Jewish author Thyra Samptor Winslow; Fort Smith forefather John Rogers; Gen. William O. Darby, founder of Darby's Rangers (which evolved into the modern Army Rangers); the widow of Bvt. Brig. Gen. Benjamin Bonneville, former commander of Fort Smith and famed Oregon Trail explorer; and other leading citizens of early Fort Smith. The district was added to the National Register of Historic Places in the 1970s. Brochures for self-guided walking tours are available at Miss Laura's Visitor Center.

WINE COUNTRY **Arkansas Historic Wine Museum** (1-800-419-2691; www.cowie winecellars.com), 101 North Carbon City Road, Paris. Open daily, hours vary, so call ahead. This is the only wine museum in the nation dedicated to the wine history of a state. Within the museum you will see commercial and home wine-making equipment; most of these items are from wineries that are no longer active. They enable you to see the process as it existed many years ago and follow this art step-by-step from the grape to the bottle. Free admission.

Chateau aux Arc Vineyards & Winery (1-800-558-WINE; www.chateauauxarc.com), 8045 Champagne Drive, Altus. Open Monday through Saturday 10–5, Sunday noon–5. Located in Arkansas's Wine Country, this winery is the world's largest planter of Cynthiana grapes, the largest US Chardonnay vineyard outside California, and the largest Zinfandel planter in Arkansas. Featuring scenic views of the vineyard and landscaped grounds, the tasting room is a great place to try out new vintages of Chateau aux Arc

CARRIAGE RIDE THROUGH THE HISTORIC DISTRICT

wines while enjoying one of the most breathtaking views in the Arkansas River Valley. The tasting room is also a gift shop offering a large selection of gourmet food and wine-related items. Tours are free, and there is a small charge for tastings.

Cowie Wine Cellars (1-800-419-2691; www.cowiewinecellars.com), 101 North Carbon City Road, Paris. Open daily, varying hours, so phone for details. Cowie offers free tours of the winery that include a complimentary wine tasting with cheese. The tour will give you a chance to observe their wine-making operation and the Gallery of Barrels, which features oil paintings on the barrel heads. Free.

Mount Bethel Winery (479-468-2444; www.mountbethel.com), 5014 Mount Bethel Drive, Altus. Open Monday through Saturday 8:30–6, Sunday noon–5. This historic cellar offers its over 100-year-old tradition of wine making, bottling, and tasting, plus tours. Mount Bethel has several traditional grape wine varieties, as well as several specialty wines made from Arkansas-grown fruits such as blueberries and strawberries. A gift shop is on-site to purchase bottles for home.

Post Familie Vineyards & Winery (1-800-275-8423; www.postfamilie.com), 1700 Saint Mary's Mountain Road, Altus. Open Sunday noon–5, Monday through Saturday 9:30–6. Tours by request 11–3. Since 1880, five generations of Posts have cultivated and harvested their grapes to make Post Familie wines. The founder of their wine heritage and Altus viticulture was Jacob Post, a German who arrived in America in 1872. He sold the first Altus wines from his cellar to passengers on the Iron Mountain Railroad when the train stopped by his farm for fuel and water. Post offers tours that include wine and juice tastings. The grape-related gift shop sells their wines and wine-related items.

Wiederkehr Wine Cellars and Wiederkehr Village (1-800-622-9463; www .wiederkehrwines.com), 3324 Swiss Family Drive, Wiederkehr Village. Open daily, excluding major holidays. Tours of the winery and cellars are held every 45 minutes from 9–4:30 daily. The oldest and largest winery in mid-America, Wiederkehr Wine Cellars has been located on the southern slopes of the Ozark Mountains since 1880. Tour the historic cellars made of native stone and mortar, where the award-winning Wiederkehr wines are aged. The family's Swiss-German heritage is portrayed in the structure and decor you will find at this winery, and don't be surprised if you run into Dennis Wiederkehr, fifth generation of the family, in full costume, guiding tours. The Weinkeller Restaurant is open daily: Monday through Saturday, lunch 11–3 and dinner 5–9; Sunday 11–9. The restaurant serves excellent Swiss and other European specialties in charming, candlelit surroundings. The original wine cellar, hand-dug by Johann Andreas Wiederkehr in 1880, was converted to house the Weinkeller in 1967. The restaurant is now listed on the National Register of Historic Places and for years has been voted "most romantic" and "best ethnic" by Arkansas diners. The Vintage 1880 Wine Shoppe is open Monday through Thursday 8:30–6, Friday and Saturday 8:30–7, Sunday noon–6. Browse through the award-winning wines, a wide selection of gourmet food items, wine accessories, and exquisite gifts from around the world.

✳ Green Space

Heifer Ranch Lodging, Retreat & Conference Center (501-889-5124; www.heifer.org/ranch), 55 Heifer Road, Perryville. Visitor center hours are Monday through Saturday 9–5. In the Ouachita Mountains, one hour west of Little Rock on AR 9/10, Heifer Ranch offers an opportunity for you to get fully involved in Heifer International's global mission. Heifer Learning Center at the ranch is one opportunity to learn about Heifer's educational efforts. Programs include tours, Global Village immersion experiences, and service-learning events. Experiential, hands-on, interactive, and fun, Heifer Ranch is also a working example of the sustainable agriculture the organization supports around the world. The ranch has three modern lodges for groups (accommodating up to 78 people total), a dining hall with meals served cafeteria-style, and two meeting rooms. Each can accommodate up to 50 people and includes a dry erase board, flipcharts, television with DVD/VCR players, high-speed Internet, and wireless access and audiovisual equipment (upon request). A guest business center includes computers and a printer/copier. A large outdoor firepit serves as a relaxed nighttime gathering area. Package rates are available that include lodging, meals (breakfast, lunch, dinner, and two snack services), meeting space, and a hayride tour of the campus. Educational offerings such as challenge course activities are available for additional fees. Call for rates and details about special programs.

Janet Huckabee Arkansas River Valley Nature Center (479-452-3993; www.river valleynaturecenter.com), 8300 Wells Lake Road, Barling. Open Tuesday through Saturday 8:30–4:30, Sunday 1–5. Opened in August 2006, the Janet Huckabee Arkansas River Valley Nature Center sits on 170 acres of land in Fort Smith that were previously part of Fort Chaffee. Exhibits play a large part in the nature center. You will find representations of the Ouachita and Ozark Mountains, a life-sized oak tree exhibit crawling with game and nongame animal displays, and a 1,200-gallon aquarium with native Arkansas fish. In addition to the interactive displays and exhibits, the center houses a classroom for educational programs such as hunter and boating safety courses, and a multipurpose room for community events. In addition to the spacious building surrounded by hickory and oak trees, the grounds are home to a series of trails and Wells Lake, a popular fishing destination. The rear deck overlooking Wells Lake is an excellent place to take in the view and enjoy a quiet moment outdoors. The trails around the

ARKANSAS RIVER VALLEY NATURE CENTER   ARKANSAS DEPARTMENT OF PARKS & TOURISM

lake feature exhibit signs that highlight the lake, grounds, and animals that call the area home. The $5 million center, the third in a series of four nature centers operated by the Arkansas Game and Fish Commission, includes a gift shop, classroom, aquarium, and catering kitchen for special events. Free.

✳ Wild Places

Holla Bend National Wildlife Refuge (479-229-4300; www.fws.gov/HollaBend), 10448 Holla Bend Road, Dardanelle. A birdwatcher's paradise, this refuge is home at different times of the year to Canada geese and several species of ducks, bald eagles, and other wildlife. The refuge is situated on a bend of the Arkansas River that was cut off when the US Army Corps of Engineers straightened the river in 1954 for flood control. Refuge lands include over 7,000 acres of agricultural fields, bottomland forest, and open water. The area was established to provide essential habitat for migratory birds in the Mississippi Valley Flyway. During these spring and fall migrations, as many as 14 species of ducks and 4 kinds of geese will stop by the refuge for a short visit. During the winter, it is not uncommon for the refuge to host up to 100,000 ducks and geese at once. Bald eagles are also common from December through February. Spring brings thousands of neotropical migratory songbirds that use the refuge as a rest area on their journey from Central and South America. Many species of vireos, warblers, buntings, and orioles inhabit the woodlands during this time. Most only stay for a short time to rest, but others use the refuge as a nesting area. Herons, egrets, and other wading birds feed in shallow pools, and alligators can be seen in the refuge lakes and ponds.

PARKS **Lake Dardanelle State Park** (479-967-5516; www.arkansasstateparks.com/lakedardanelle), 100 State Park Drive, Russellville. Lake Dardanelle, a 34,300-acre reservoir in Russellville, provides some of the best bass fishing in Arkansas. Its proximity to the Arkansas River has brought national attention and major bass fishing tournaments to the area. Park facilities occupy two sites on the shores of the sprawling reservoir; one is at Russellville, and the other is in nearby Dardanelle. Both the main park in Russellville and the Dardanelle location offer camping (74 sites: Russellville—16 Class AAA, 14 Class AA, and 26 Class B; Dardanelle—18 Class B), bike and kayak rentals, launch ramps, standard pavilions, picnic sites, restrooms, and bathhouses with hot showers. The Russellville site also features a striking 10,527-square-foot visitor center on the lakeshore overlooking Lake Dardanelle. Engaging interpretive exhibits and state-of-the-art touch screen kiosks share information on the park, the area's water resources, and its history. One exhibit that never fails to fascinate visitors features four aquariums that hold fish found in the lake, the Arkansas River, and its tributaries—Piney Creek and the Illinois Bayou—which all pool together in the lake behind the visitor center. It is an elegant living demonstration of the food chain that dominates the aquatic species found in the river, from the first tank that houses scampering baby crawfish and glittering flashes of tiny bass, to the final tank populated by the elders of the waterway, which dwarf the former many times over. Most fascinating for anglers—park interpreters believe that as large as these big boys are, the largest ones are still in the lake. Also featured at the site in Russellville is a 1,861-square-foot

HIKING AT MOUNT MAGAZINE   ARKANSAS DEPARTMENT OF PARKS & TOURISM

SUNSET FROM MOUNT NEBO

fishing tournament weigh-in pavilion. This is a world-class facility and the first in the nation to serve as a staging area for tournaments. Campsite pricing ranges from $27/day for Class AAA sites that include 50-amp electrical, water, and sewer to $17/day for Class B sites with 30-amp electrical and water. Kayak rentals are $14 for a half day and $20 for a full day. Interpretive staff conduct guided kayak tours on Lake Dardanelle for $12 per adult and $6 for kids 6–12.

✳ Lodging

BED & BREAKFASTS **Beland Manor Bed & Breakfast** (1-800-334-5052; www.fortsmith.net), 1320 South Albert Pike Avenue, Fort Smith. All guests of this charming B&B are treated to a homemade full breakfast. A great room with movie library and books will let you enjoy a quiet evening on the property, complete with complimentary snacks and soft drinks. Four of the inn's guest rooms are equipped with in-room spa tubs. All rooms have private baths with showers, 400- to 600-thread-count sheets, wireless Internet, cable TVs with DVD players, and luxurious robes. In-room candlelight breakfasts are also available. Room rates range from $109/night to $185/night. Children 8 and over are welcome, pets are not. $$.

The Winery Bed & Breakfast (479-963-3990; www.cowiewinecellars.com/thebed.htm), 101 North Carbon City Road, Paris. Choose from the quiet Cynthiana Suite, which features a cathedral ceiling, fireplace, antique bed, stained-glass window, and a double-whirlpool bath. Or enjoy the secluded Robert's Port Suite with a private inner court, king-sized bed, double-whirlpool bath, and kitchenette. Accommodations are for one or two adults. A masseuse is available

ARKANSAS'S ROCKEFELLER REMEMBERED ON PETIT JEAN MOUNTAIN

Winthrop Rockefeller Institute (1-866-972-7778 or 501-727-5436; rockefellerinstitute.org), 1 Rockefeller Drive, Morrilton. In 1953, Winthrop Rockefeller decided his future was in Arkansas, and in doing so changed the prospects for the state. From his new home on Petit Jean Mountain, his view of the landscape stretched for miles, and his vision for the state's potential had no boundaries. His influence on the state is seen in its arts, education, civil rights, agriculture, and almost every socially relevant area of community you can imagine. Rockefeller's perpetual support of the state's prosperity is seen atop his beloved mountain in the legacy that is the Winthrop Rockefeller Institute. On the surface or in a brochure, it is a superior group lodging facility with 60 guest rooms, 12 suites, and 8 fully furnished houses, some with fireplaces, all with refrigerators, coffeemakers, satellite TV, irons, and hair dryers. There is Internet service in the conference center and some guest rooms. The amenities are endless and the facilities are exquisite. But this institute is much more than a lodge or conference facility. It embodies the spirit of the man as if he were still there, tending cattle every day.

The institute actively develops programs in the social areas Rockefeller pursued passionately during life. While the program offerings vary dramatically based on their focus, they fall within one of the following areas: agriculture, arts and humanities, civic engagement, economic development, and health. This makes for a wide range of opportunities for you to take advantage of the institute's warm invitation to the public to attend lectures, workshops, and special events of national importance. The institute ensures that Rockefeller's vision for Arkansas's potential will forever be within its reach.

The institute is rapidly developing a national reputation as a highly productive oasis for growing teams and the people on the team. A sense of tranquility permeates the grounds of the lodge, its entry marked by a massive stone water feature that curves along the contour of the building. The outdoor deck of the River Rock Grill also overlooks the architect's homage to the Arkansas River. A fitness center with men's and women's dry saunas, bicycle rentals, paddleboats and fishing, jogging/walking trails, and indoor tennis courts all remind you that this is no ordinary place. Conference and lodging facilities are available for meetings and gatherings. The staff at the institute is very flexible and will accommodate day groups and overnight groups. The conference facilities are state of the art, featuring over 17,000 square feet of meeting space, 16 meeting and breakout rooms, professional on-site meeting managers, an in-house executive chef, projection and presentation equipment, T1 high-speed Internet and network capabilities, a full-service business center, and audiovisual equipment.

with prior request. Room rates are $90 for the Cynthiana Suite and $120 for the Robert's Port Suite. Daily continental breakfast is included in the rate. $$.

CABINS **Nebo State Park** (479-229-3655), 16728 West AR 155, Dardanelle. Set 1,350 feet above the Arkansas River Valley, Mount Nebo State Park has been popular for its sweeping views of the valley since it was first chosen as a park site in 1933. The Civilian Conservation Corps used native stone and logs from the mountain to construct many of the park's bridges, trails, rustic cabins, and pavilions. The park has 14 miles of trails that encircle Mount Nebo, passing historic springs, Fern Lake, and rockwork done by the CCC in the early 1930s. The park offers 34 campsites (24 Class B, 10 hike-in tent sites), no dump station, and 14 fully equipped cabins with kitchens. Mount Nebo State Park is one of two state parks offering launch sites for hang gliding enthusiasts. (For more information about outdoor sports and extreme adventure opportunities in Arkansas's state parks, go to www.adventurestate

Lodging choices vary dramatically, but all are uniquely Rockefeller. Think rustiche, rustic elements with a very elegant, high-end presentation. The President's Lodge features 30 deluxe guest rooms that include a king bed or two queen beds, glass walk-in shower with natural slate floors, microwave, and a 32-inch HD flat panel television. Suites are equipped with two 32-inch HD flat panel televisions and a living area, and some also have jetted tubs. The Meadows, The Grove, and The Orchard are smaller, freestanding options for smaller groups. The Pines consists of 6 two- and three-bedroom houses fully furnished with all the amenities of home, including full-sized refrigerators, microwaves, washers and dryers, stoves, dishwashers, as well as wood-burning fireplaces (firewood included) in the three-bedroom units. Rates are seasonal and also depend on whether your date coincides with one of the many special events hosted at the institute. Call for more information. $$–$$$.

THE SILOS STILL STAND AT THE WINTHROP ROCKEFELLER INSTITUTE

parks.com.) Park facilities include a pool, tennis courts, picnic areas, playgrounds, extra-large enclosed and standard open pavilions, and a ball field. The visitor center offers exhibits, a store, and bicycle rentals. Interpretive programs tell about the mountain's history and natural resources. Mount Nebo has several options for lodging, both modern and rustic. The rustic cabins constructed by the CCC come with fireplaces, both with ($104–114) and without ($94) spa tubs. A modern three-bedroom with spa tub and fireplace ranges between $169–199 daily

and sleeps six adults. In between the two, you can rent a two-bedroom A-frame with fireplace for $134 a day. Class B campsites that include 30-amp electrical and water are $17/day. $–$$.

LODGES AND RESORTS **Camp Ouachita** (501-889-5176; www .campouachita.com), 618 AR 324 South, Perryville. This historic camp, built between 1936 and 1941, is listed on the National Register of Historic Places. It is the only surviving Works Progress Administration and/or Civilian

Conservation Corps–constructed Girl Scout facility in the United States. It overlooks Lake Sylvia, has been restored, and can host conferences, family reunions, and other groups. Call for rates and dates. $–$$.

Mount Magazine State Park (1-877-665-6343; www.mountmagazinestatepark .com), 16878 AR 309 South, Paris. The Lodge at Mount Magazine debuted with great fanfare in May 2006. The $33 million lodge represents the single greatest capital investment by the Arkansas State Parks system to date. Its setting on the peak of the 2,753-foot mountain, the highest in the state, provides commanding views of the valley below. The luxurious 60-room lodge welcomes guests into a grand lobby reminiscent of Missouri's Big Cedar Lodge. An indoor swimming pool and adjacent exercise center offer year-round fitness opportunities. Fine dining, a stunning view, and a constantly changing menu at Skycrest Restaurant draw people from throughout the state for special occasions. The conference center, meeting rooms, and gift shop have also helped the lodge gain a name with business groups. All lodging facilities have views of the Petit Jean River Valley and Blue Mountain Lake below; the 13 full-service cabins with fireplaces, a bathroom for each bedroom, and wraparound covered porches with outdoor hot tubs offer a more secluded environment. The park's visitor center has interactive exhibits that tell the story of the lodge and the mountain. Campsites, all with water, electric, and sewer hook-ups, can be reserved at the visitor center or online. A bathhouse with hot showers is nearby. Rates for this resort are seasonal; lodge rooms range from $89 to $209. Cabins have one, two, or three bedrooms and range from $179 to $384. Campsites are $24/day.

Rugged, isolated, and rich in natural resources, including rare and endangered species, Mount Magazine has long lured explorers, adventurers, scientists, and naturalists who take advantage of this outdoor laboratory for nature study. Today, park interpreters present a wide variety of nature programs for the education and enjoyment of visitors and school groups that visit the park. One of the park's most popular programs revolves around the 90 species of butterflies that summer on the mountain. Through the years, the mountain has been a place to enjoy outdoor recreational pursuits like sightseeing, hiking, picnicking, camping, horseback riding, birding, and wildlife watching, activities still enjoyed by today's park visitors. The more adventuresome can also enjoy the challenges of backpacking, rock climbing, rappelling, hang gliding, biking, mountain biking, and ATV trail adventure. The high-tech sport of geocaching can be enjoyed here, too. $$$.

Petit Jean State Park (1-800-264-2462; www.petitjeanstatepark.com), 1069 Petit Jean Mountain Road, Morrilton. The natural beauty and archaeological significance of this rugged mountain was the inspiration for Arkansas's state park system. *Camping Life* magazine picked Petit Jean State Park first on their list of the nation's Top 10 State Parks. The flagship of the state parks system, built in the 1930s by the Civilian Conservation Corps, is a mountaintop retreat with both cabin lodging and rooms in Mather Lodge. The home cooking in the lodge restaurant overlooking spectacular Cedar Falls brings people up this mountain from miles away. Swimming pools, boating and fishing on Lake Bailey, hiking trails, and a visitor center with interpretive exhibits round out the park's facilities. The lodge has 24 rooms; the park has 127 campsites and 33 fully equipped cabins, including a honeymoon cabin with hot tub. Mather Lodge's restaurant serves traditional Southern fare, offering both buffet and off-the-menu service. Order the lemon pie . . . it is a distinctly citrus-flavored chiffon in a crumbly graham cracker crust. The 20 miles of hiking trails will help you burn off the calories. $.

THE ARKANSAS RIVER AT DAYBREAK FROM PETIT JEAN MOUNTAIN'S OVERLOOK

White Rock Mountain Cabins & Group Lodge (479-369-4128; www.white rockmountain.com), FR 1505, Mulberry. Three CCC-style housekeeping cabins and a 20-person group lodge provide gorgeous views from White Rock Mountain. Featuring full kitchens, fireplaces, and grills, the cabins rent for $70 a night. $.

✳ Where to Eat

EATING OUT **Feltner's Whatta-Burger** (479-968-1410; www.whatta-burger.com), 1410 North Arkansas Avenue, Russellville. Open daily 11–8. This dairy bar has become a legend in Arkansas, featuring custom-made hamburgers, french fries, malts, milkshakes, and hand-dipped cones. Burgers with all the trimmings will run you about $10 apiece.

Historic Oark General Store & Café (479-292-3351; www.oarkgeneralstore .com), 117 CR 5241, Oark. Open Monday through Friday 7–6, Saturday 7–8, Sunday 8–5. This is the oldest continuously operating store in Arkansas, established in 1890. The building has the original floors, walls, and ceiling. The café features home cooking, including smokehouse-style steaks, ribs, catfish, frog legs, and homemade fried chicken. Located in the tiny Arkansas River Valley town of Oark, the moderately priced menu will feed two for $40.

Neumeier's Rib Room & Beer Garden (479-494-RIBS), 424 Garrison Avenue, Fort Smith. They cook up Memphis-style dry ribs that some say compare favorably to any in the Bluff City. Ribs and all the trimmings will set you back about $25 per person.

Pho Vietnam (479-782-3227), 2214 Rogers Avenue, Fort Smith. A former Asian grocery store, Pho Vietnam opened as a restaurant about five years ago on busy Rogers Avenue. Diners seeking to learn about Vietnamese food might want to make this pleasant spot their first stop. Any of the dozen sandwiches are delicious. Entrées average $10 per person.

SAMPLING THE GRAPES AT WEIDERKEHR VILLAGE ARKANSAS DEPARTMENT OF PARKS & TOURISM

Taliano's (479-758-2292), 201 North 14th Street, Fort Smith. Its location in this restored Victorian home makes Taliano's feel like home, at least if you are Italian. Well-prepared Italian specialties served here include standard classics, plus a few with a twist. A meal for two runs $60 with three courses. Fort Smith is not a dry county, so if you enjoy a glass of wine with your meal, Taliano's will be happy to serve you.

DINING OUT **Doe's Eat Place** (479-784-9111; www.doesfortsmith.com), 422 North Third Street, Fort Smith. Doe's opened January 12, 2004, in the heart of Fort Smith's entertainment district. Open Monday through Thursday 5–9, Friday and Saturday 5–10; closed Sunday. Voted Best Steak by *Entertainment Fort Smith* in 2005 and 2006. Located inside the Knoble Brewery, the three-story stone structure was built in 1848 by German immigrant Joseph Knoble. The historic building contains an original underground cellar where the beer was stored. The building has a colorful history that parallels much of Fort Smith's past. A connecting outdoor beer garden that made Knoble's a popular nineteenth-century gathering place is still intact. A full bar is available at Doe's. It is non-smoking inside, but smoking is allowed on the patio. The average meal price is about $30 per person.

Weinkeller Restaurant (1-800-622-9463; www.wiederkehrwines.com), 3324 Swiss Family Drive, Wiederkehr Village. Open Monday through Saturday 11–3 and 5–9, Sunday 11–9. Closed on these major holidays: New Year's Day, Easter Sunday, Thanksgiving Day, Christmas Eve (open for lunch only), and Christmas Day. The Weinkeller serves award-winning dishes featuring Swiss and other European cuisine. The restaurant is known for its Swiss onion soup; the menu includes Swiss cheese fondue, Italian pasta dishes, Matterhorn schnitzel, chicken, lobster, fish, and steaks. Desserts include

Swiss apple strudel, Black Forest cherry cake, caramel custard, ice cream, and cheesecake. Housed in the original 1880 wine cellar at Wiederkehr Wine Cellars & Vineyards, the restaurant is open every day (except major holidays) for dining and wine sales. Reservations are recommended. The wide and varied menu fits all budgets, but for three courses expect to spend $20 per person for lunch, $35 for dinner.

✳ Entertainment

Fort Smith River Park (479-784-1006; www.fsark.com), 121 Clayton Expressway, Fort Smith. This is an excellent venue for entertainment in Fort Smith. The complex includes the River Park Events Building, amphitheater, Don Reynolds Stage, and grounds. The events building has a capacity of 170 with a concession area; the amphitheater has seating for 1,200; and the Don Reynolds stage is 35 by 40 feet. The chamber maintains a schedule of events for the park that includes ticket pricing on their website.

Performing Arts Center (479-452-7575; www.fortsmithsymphony.org), 55 South Seventh Street, Fort Smith. Formed in 1923, the Fort Smith Symphony is not only the oldest in Arkansas, but it is also made up of musicians from several surrounding states. The symphony schedules six public performances annually, attracting classical music lovers from Arkansas, Oklahoma, and Missouri. Season and single ticket orders can be made by phone or mail. Tickets may also be purchased at the Fort Smith Symphony office located in Suite 617, Central Mall in Fort Smith. Open Monday through Friday 8:30–4:30; closed noon–1 for lunch. Single concert ticket prices are based on seating but generally range from $30 per adult in the conductor's section to $13 general seating for students. Online ticket sales are currently unavailable.

FAMILY ENTERTAINMENT **The Park at West End** (1-800-371-1477), 15 North Second Street at Garrison Avenue, Fort Smith. Open weekdays 11–9 or "whatever the market demands." A restored original late-1930s Ferris wheel from the Eli Bridge Company, built and displayed at the 1935 San Diego World's Fair, centers this old-fashioned amusement park. The park also includes a hand-painted carousel from Italy, a 1957 Pullman dining car that has been converted into the Nickel & Dime Diner, a 1963 British Leyland double-decker bus that has been turned into a concession stand, and a penny arcade of retro games.

Starlight Cinema (501-977-2142; www.uaccm.edu), 1537 University Boulevard, Morrilton. A free outdoor movie night sponsored by the University of Arkansas Community College at Morrilton is offered to the community each month (from May through October) on campus. The free event, typically held on the first Thursday or Friday of each month, features both pre–home release and classic films for the public.

THEATER **Rialto Community Arts Center** (501-477-9955; www.rialtoartscenter.com), 213 East Broadway, Morrilton. This restored historic 1911 movie theater offers performances of country-western, big band, gospel, bluegrass, and western swing music, as well as live poetry readings. It was originally named Vail's, after Guy O. Vail, who opened it in 1911. This was the first motion picture theater in Morrilton. Call for showtimes and ticket prices.

✳ Selective Shopping

American Bonsai Nursery (479-474-9225; www.american-bonsai.com), 5141 Industrial Park Road, Van Buren. Open Monday through Saturday 9–5. Browse finished bonsai that are styled and grown at the nursery, or find the supplies to create your own at the only bonsai nursery in Arkansas. Hundreds of trees are on-site in preparation to become bonsai.

Millyn's (479-229-4144), 124 South Front Street, Dardanelle. Open Monday through Friday 10–5. For 29 years this has been the largest gift shop between Little Rock and Fort Smith. Millyn's inventory includes a large selection of tabletop merchandise, a full range of gifts and home accessories, and collectibles such as Department 56, Hummels, and Waterford crystal.

Riverside Furniture Factory Outlet (479-452-6700; www.riverside-furniture .com), 6801 Phoenix Avenue, Fort Smith. This is an outlet store for Arkansas-owned and operated Riverside Furniture Corporation, a century-old company with manufacturing facilities and corporate offices in Fort Smith. Riverside manufactures and imports bedroom furniture, dinettes, home office furniture, entertainment centers, wall units, and occasional furniture.

THE OZARK MOUNTAINS

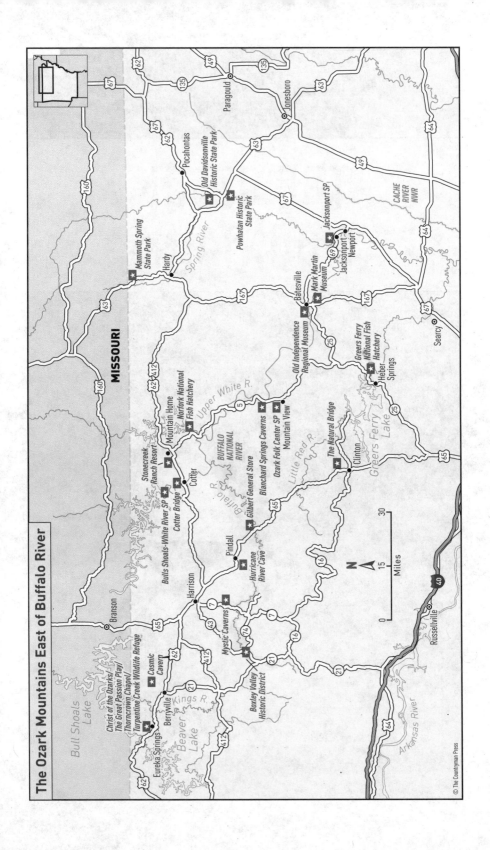

The Ozark Mountains East of Buffalo River

THE OZARK MOUNTAINS

Covering the northwestern and north-central part of Arkansas, the Ozarks are known for their rugged topography. Rivers have carved deep valleys into the high, flat plateaus here. A common rock known as limestone has formed brilliant caves like those found at Blanchard Springs near Mountain View. The Paleozoic rock is broken by valleys cut by the state's best-known fishing rivers, including the White, Buffalo, King's, Mulberry, Norfork, and Little Red. Lakes like Beaver, Norfork, and Bull Shoals are hugely popular recreational sites.

The magnetism of the Ozark Mountain range has drawn travelers to its beautiful bluffs since Native Americans first climbed these hills. But within the Ozark Plateau there are really three dramatically different worlds with their own topography, geology, history, and culture: the Springfield, the Salem, and the Boston Plateaus. Distinct geology defines each of the three and, in addition to shaping their landscape, was pivotal in defining the lives of the people who settled here.

The craggy cliffs of the Boston Plateau, more commonly known as the Boston Mountains, were notoriously difficult for those brave enough to venture to travel here, so modern man is the first to have easy access to its dazzling beauty. The Bostons skirt both the Springfield and Salem Plateaus, and you are most likely to experience them while passing through them to get to the other two. There are some treasures to be found along the way, so don't be in a hurry. It is a good idea to double, or triple, the time you allot for your journey to allow you to take advantage of the many shops and overlooks along the winding roads. The businesses and people you will find clinging to the precipitous cliffs of the Boston Mountains are like bonsai, beautifully crafted by their environment.

With its extensive, fairly level areas, the Springfield Plateau was much easier to develop for transportation, agriculture, and urban centers than the Boston Mountains. Because it combines the scenery and quality of life of the Ozark Mountains with relatively level topography that can be readily developed, the Springfield Plateau has become a growth center of significance not only in Arkansas but regionally and nationally as well. That growth has occurred in spite of previous barriers to transportation, now addressed by an interstate highway and a regional airport.

Like the Springfield Plateau, the Salem Plateau, at an elevation of about 1,500 feet, often forms extensive plains, as at Berryville. Several distinct areas of hills have been cut into the plateau by rivers, most prominently along the White River and its tributaries. Other extensive hills have been cut by the Spring and Strawberry Rivers. The Salem Plateau is often underlain by dolomite or dolostone, similar to limestone. Although dolostone is not dissolved by water as readily as limestone, caves are present, as well as large springs such as the one at Mammoth Spring near the eastern border of this area.

As different as each of the plateaus may be from the others, they share a dependence on Arkansas's pure waters and their ability to draw travelers their way. The rivers that carve their way through the northern half of the state have drawn millions of people through the years, looking for the thrill of rushing whitewater, the comfort of healing mineral waters, or the challenge of a river teeming with trout. Damming of the rivers created lakes which became major recreational attractions in their areas. When damming compromised the native fish that inhabited the streams, hatcheries were built to

TROUT FISHING ON THE UPPER WHITE RIVER

support populations of trout. Today, White River trout fishing is world famous. Flippin, Cotter, Mountain Home, and, to some extent, Calico Rock have benefited from recreational use of the White River. Hardy and Mammoth Spring have become thriving communities, in large part based on tourism associated with the Spring River and the Mammoth Spring at its source.

The forests of the Ozarks are mostly upland hardwood; oak and hickory trees are numerous. The density of the forest combines with the cooler climes to produce glorious displays of color in fall that are named with New England's as the nation's most beautiful. The once formidable roads are now prized as pleasure drives by motorists with four wheels and two. Handmade quilts, dulcimers, furniture, and pottery, once accessible only to the adventurer, are now sold all over the country. As technology advances and the world seems to grow smaller, the remote expanse and seclusion of the Ozarks are now selling points.

Just a little over a century ago, the railroad broke the isolation of the Ozark region. Today, major industries like Tyson and Walmart have made the Ozarks their home. Emigration to the northwestern corner of the state is very high, and the region is one of the most popular vacation areas in the state. Time has marched on in the Ozarks, as it has all over the world. But this is one place where a commitment to the environment ensures that its beauty will not be trampled by the parade of progress.

AREA CODES Most of the northwestern corner of the state uses the 479 area code. Destinations from about Berryville eastward are located in the 870 area code.

The Springfield Plateau and Western Boston Mountains

GUIDANCE The unspoiled beauty of the Ozark Mountains has inspired visitors to blaze trails through its remote wilderness since the nineteenth century. It comes as no surprise that northwest Arkansas's tourism bureaus are experts in guiding travelers through the Boston Mountains to the progressive communities on the Springfield Plateau. The **Northwest Arkansas Tourism Association** (479-855-1336; www.nwatourism .org) publishes a regional brochure with details on events and destinations in the Northwest Corridor. The scenic, winding roads of the Ozarks have inspired a number of motorcycle rallies to the delight of riders throughout the country. The **Fayetteville Convention & Visitors Bureau** (1-800-766-4626; www.experiencefayetteville.com) maps out the details for Bikes, Blues, and BBQ, the largest nonprofit rally in America. If you're wondering why the chicken crossed US 71, it was to get to Springdale (**Springdale Chamber of Commerce**; 1-800-972-7261; www.springdale.com), best known as home to Tyson Foods and J. B. Hunt. The addition of Arvest Ballpark, Ballpark.com's Best New Ballpark of 2008, now lures more than chickens to venture across the highway for minor league baseball, concerts, and events.

It's hard to imagine a corporation having a greater impact on a region than Walmart has had on northwest Arkansas. In fact, you could say that Walmart put **Bentonville** (479-273-2841; www.bentonvilleUSA.com) on the map. By 1998, the volume of corporate travel to their global headquarters necessitated a new regional airport to accommodate the traffic. Nothing succeeds like success, and nationally recognized retailers soon followed to set up shop in the neighboring communities of **Rogers** and **Lowell** (479-636-1240; www.rogerslowell.com). Today, nearly 20 years after the opening of the Northwest Arkansas Regional Airport (XNA), there are as many people traveling to

WALNUT STREET NATIONAL HISTORICAL DISTRICT   ARKANSAS DEPARTMENT OF PARKS & TOURISM

THE SCOTT FAMILY AMAZEUM IN BENTONVILLE

the Northwest Corridor for an art experience as there are going to watch the Razorbacks play. The 2011 opening of the Crystal Bridges Museum of American Art transformed the town, once again, and its impact is visible throughout the region. The town has gained respect nationally largely due to the surprisingly high level of quality and diversity in its hospitality product. It doesn't just have an upscale, boutique hotel. Bentonville has a 21C Museum Hotel, a remarkably unique property that considers itself "an art museum with sleeping rooms." Looking for a fun place for your kids to play and learn and, oh by the way, they range in age from 2 to 15? One word. Amazeum. If Willy Wonka's candy factory were an educational experience, it would be Amazeum.

GETTING THERE *By auto:* If you are coming from the north, US 71 enters Arkansas at Bentonville before turning into I-540, which extends north and south through the length of the Northwest Corridor.

By air: The airport in Bentonville, **Arkansas Regional Airport** (479-205-1000; www .flyxna.com), 1 Airport Boulevard, Bentonville. Airlines offering flights to XNA include Allegiant Air, American Airlines, Delta, and United. Expanded flight options are available at the **Little Rock National Airport** (501-372-3439; www.clintonairport.com), 1 Airport Drive, Little Rock. Allegiant Air, American Airlines, Delta, Frontier Airlines, Southwest, United, and Via Air offer service to the capital city.

MEDICAL EMERGENCIES **Northwest Medical Center of Benton County** (479-553-1000; www.northwesthealth.com), 3000 Medical Center Parkway, in Bentonville, and the **Northwest Medical Center of Washington County** (479-751-5711; www .northwesthealth.com/nmew.cfm), 609 West Maple Avenue in Springdale, are both managed by the Northwest Health Group. At the southern end of the corridor, over 200 physicians represent 37 areas of specialty at the **Washington Regional Medical**

Center (479-713-1000; www.wregional.com), 3215 N. Northhills Boulevard in Fayette-ville. Washington Regional Medical Center is the newest high-tech medical center in Fayetteville, located near the intersection of I-540 and US 71. The facility provides 233 beds and contains state-of-the-art equipment and technologies.

✻ Wandering Around

EXPLORING BY CAR **National Scenic Byway AR 7**, Harrison (www.byways.org). One of the most scenic drives in the country, AR 7 runs from the Louisiana border to Mis-souri, passing through both the Ouachita and Ozark Mountains. You will cross into the Boston Mountains at Russellville (you can also jump on Scenic 7 from I-40 here, if it better suits your itinerary or schedule). You can make the drive from Russellville to Missouri in three hours or three days. There are numerous resorts and attractions along the route, as well as scenic overlooks. It is particularly popular with motorcy-clists, with a number of resorts that cater specifically to two-wheelers. You will cross the Buffalo River at Jasper, offering at least one chance to wet your feet in the waters of the nation's first federally protected river. Downtown Jasper is something of a sur-prise; native rock facades on a number of the businesses on the downtown square add to its unique character and relationship to the river. Wildlife management areas flank

GORGEOUS VIEWS ALONG I-49 TO FAYETTEVILLE

AR 7 for the majority of its Ozark section, offering ample wildlife-watching opportunities, and you will definitely want to keep an out eye for deer.

The Boston Mountains Scenic Loop, Scenic US 71/I-540. This scenic loop offers breathtaking vistas of the hills and valleys of the Arkansas Ozarks and makes a great half-day excursion. Take I-540 in Fayetteville to US 71, then south to I-40. Go west on I-40 to I-540 North for a 40-minute drive back to Fayetteville. The US 71 part of your drive winds through the Boston Mountains and was one of the primary connections to the northwestern corner of the state before the interstate highway was built. Small towns like Mountainburg, Winslow, and West Fork enjoyed steady traffic from travelers who were actually headed to Fayetteville but were inspired to stop regularly along the way to take in the scenery. When I-540 opened, the majority of traffic past the small burgs chose it over US 71, not just because it is the quicker route, but because it offers a terrific vantage point from above the mountains. Antiques and craft shops and cafés are still scattered sporadically along US 71, stocked with a combination of handmade crafts by native artisans and hand-me-down treasures from family ancestors. Three state parks are within 20 minutes of I-540, including Devil's Den State Park, which is situated among the crevices of the Boston Mountains, and you can get a completely different perspective of them from here. The restaurant at Devil's Den is open for breakfast and lunch (call for hours, seasonal times vary) with daily specials, burgers, and sandwiches. The I-540 section of the drive is 37 miles and will give you a chance for a real overview of this area, as bridges and overpasses leap over the valleys below. Kids love to honk the horn in the lengthy Bobby Hopper Tunnel that cuts through the Boston Mountains near Winslow.

Pig Trail Scenic Drive. Recognized as the most scenic route in the northwest corner of the state, the actual Pig Trail is only 19 miles of AR 23, from the south boundary of the Ozark National Forest to its intersection with AR 16 at Brashears. From Fayetteville, you will start by heading southeast on AR 16 as it snakes its way parallel with the upper White River, before turning south at Brashears on AR 23. The heavy canopy envelops the road in places, and leaf peepers are drawn to its tunnels of scarlet and umber in the fall. This drive takes you by the Ozark Highlands Trail and across the Mulberry River. On the byway you will find lodging and outfitters, including public facilities at Turner Bend. Nearby White Rock Mountain Recreation Area also offers cabins and campgrounds, and makes for a panoramic picnic area from its setting 2,260 feet up. This is all a relatively short drive, so you can turn around at its end in Ozark for the return trip. Or you might want to take I-40 west to Alma, and take I-540 north back to the Northwest Corridor for a snappy, yet spectacular, drive over the mountains.

EXPLORING BY FOOT **All Seasons Trail** (1-800-766-4626; www.fayettevilletourism .com), 15 West Mountain, Fayetteville. This is a 90-minute self-guided driving tour through historic neighborhoods; a brochure is available at the chamber of commerce office. Handicapped accessible.

Buffalo National River Civil War Heritage Trail (870-741-5443; www.nps.gov/buff). The Buffalo National River is a 95,000-acre national park that preserves unique natural and cultural features of the Arkansas Ozarks. During the Civil War, the rugged terrain became a battleground for aggressive independent Confederate units and the Union forces holding northwest Arkansas. Skirmish sites, saltpeter caves, and Civil War–era farms are interpreted within the most scenic and recognizable wilderness area in Arkansas. Exhibits are on display at the Tyler Bend Visitor Center on US 65 at Silver Hill.

Historic Van Winkle Trail, Hobbs State Park. Just a couple of miles west of the Hobbs Visitor Center is the Historic Van Winkle Trail, a level-ground walk through the remnants of a historical plantation that was once a thriving sawmill, gristmill, black-smith shop, and antebellum garden. This nineteenth-century former commercial hub is accessed through a walking tunnel underneath AR 12. You will stroll on the same road used by Yankee and Confederate soldiers during the Civil War, when the Van Winkle mill ground the corn to feed both sides.

Ozark Highlands National Recreation Trail (479-964-7200; www.fs.fed.us/oonf/Ozark). This 178-mile trail winds along mountaintops and bluffs, past waterfalls and over streams, while passing through some of the most remote and scenic country in the Ozark National Forest and near the Buffalo National River. The trail is used for day hikes as well as weekend and extended backpacking trips. The national forest contains campgrounds, picnic areas, cabins, wilderness areas such as East Fork, Hurricane Creek, Leatherwood, and Richland Creek, and many additional hiking trails.

EXPLORING BY RIVER The three distinct and heavily eroded plateaus that charac-terize the Ozark Mountain landscape also belie the age of this grand old range. The Paleozoic rock is broken by valleys cut by small streams that are also headwaters of the state's best-known fishing rivers, including the White, Buffalo, Kings, Mulberry, and Little Red. The White River meanders in every direction for 720 miles, from its head-waters near Fayetteville and up through southern Missouri to its reentry in Arkansas and on down to the Mississippi. In its entire journey, the river's flow is interrupted by at least eight dams, six in Arkansas and two more in Missouri.

The headwaters of the White are similar to the beginning stretches of other Ozark streams—fast and furious in the wet months, and comparatively calm the rest of the year. Here you'll find a series of pools and shoals with overhanging trees, tight turns, and gravel bottoms amid bluffs, forests, and quiet pastures. As its journey continues, the White feeds dammed lakes, and its tailwaters then become rewarding cold waters for trout fishing below Beaver Dam and Bull Shoals Dam. Scenery is popular here too, with picturesque bluffs and thin layers of fog suspended delicately above the stream each morning around sunrise. Here, water level is determined less by rainwater and more by power generation at dams. There are numerous access points to the river pro-vided by state and federal agencies and private resort owners.

The upper White River's assortment of bass (smallmouth, largemouth, rock, and Kentucky), catfish (channel, blue, and flathead), and sunfish should satisfy nearly any angler. Spinnerbaits, crawfish imitators, and skirted jigs (with pork tails) are recom-mended, along with minnows, crawfish, and other natural baits. Below Bull Shoals Dam, the White River takes on an entirely different character. Here it is internation-ally known for premier trout fishing. The Game and Fish Commission stocks hundreds of thousands of rainbows in the White annually, and more than 90 percent of them are caught each year by anglers who come here from all corners of the globe. Stream-running walleye are also found in the upper White. Guides and outfitters are as plenti-ful as the fish and much easier to catch. In fact, guides along the shores of these rivers know not only where to find them but their preferred menu for the day.

✳ Towns and Villages

Bentonville. More than 2,000 hotel rooms and 100 restaurants are testament to the economic impact Sam Walton made on his corner of the universe. Now widely recog-nized as one of the fastest-growing cities in America, Bentonville has proven enor-mously successful at converting business travelers into full-time residents as the company's vendors took up residence there. Literally millions of Americans refer to

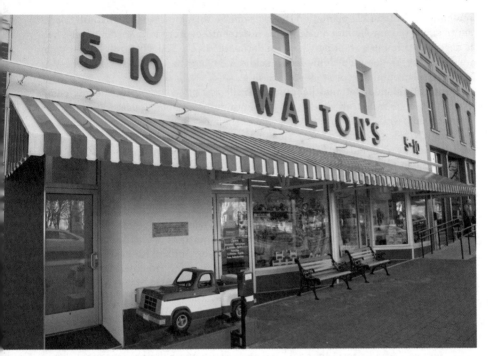

SAM WALTON'S FIRST FIVE & DIME IN BENTONVILLE

their local Walmart as Wally World, and they look forward to their weekly visits to the store with the anticipation of a 12-year-old planning a trip to Six Flags. The Walmart Visitor Center, located in the original variety store on Main Street, gives you a peek behind the curtain and a look at Sam Walton's journey from Main Street merchant to national retail giant.

Bentonville transformed again when Helen Walton, Sam Walton's daughter, realized her vision for the town as a national center for the arts. The Crystal Bridges Museum of American Art is her brainchild, and she apparently learned well at the foot of her father. Among the important American art treasures that grace the walls of this stunning facility: *George Washington* by Gilbert Stuart and *Kindred Spirits* by Asher Durand. Visitation to the town has grown dramatically every year, and local businesses have elevated their products, their services, and their thinking to take a more artistic approach to their work. Actress Geena Davis was so enamored with the town, she founded an annual film festival focused on the contribution of women in film. Each edition of the Bentonville Film Festival (BFF) introduces new people from around the world to this little slice of elegance in the Ozarks, and the town continues to grow deliberately, thoughtfully, and artistically.

Fayetteville. High-octane, urban experiences await you in the heart of Fayetteville. This is definitely not your typical sleepy little college town. As the epicenter of entertainment in northwest Arkansas, the downtown is alive with a nightlife unparalleled in the region. Aside from the unique shops, excellent restaurants, and lively bars, the area also hosts a number of annual festivals and events, including Bikes, Blues, and BBQ (www.bikesbluesandbbq.org) and the Fayetteville Arts Festival (www.fayettevilledowntown.org/faf). Fayetteville's mark on American history is preserved at countless historic sites, most notably the first home of a newly married future president, William J. Clinton. The town is also home to the University of Arkansas, the Walton Arts Center, and the Fayetteville Public Library.

Rogers. In 1881, C. W. Rogers, vice president and general manager of the Frisco Railroad, had the foresight to strike a deal that sent the Frisco Line right through this area. Local business prospered through trade and train passenger service, and in appreciation residents named their city after him. A century later, the city's roots in the railroad industry are displayed at Frisco Park, and merchants trade their wares in its historic downtown area, one of only 19 Main Street communities in Arkansas. Throughout the Northwest Corridor, each community seems to have its own niche in making this part of the state both progressive and historic. In Rogers you will find great shopping and dining, with more national brands and larger hotels. This same timeless charm is also found in the newer, more cosmopolitan shopping venues in Rogers. Pleasant Crossing, with more than 1 million square feet of lifestyle center shopping, incorporates a pedestrian-friendly main street design complete with water features, landscaping, and public spaces.

Springdale is a major industrial center with a population that almost doubled between 1980 and 2000 and is still on the increase; as of 2017, it was estimated at just over 72,000. In 2003, *Forbes* magazine rated it third best in the nation for business and career opportunities. People have lived here for about 12,000 years. Early settlers came and stayed because of abundant natural resources, just as later European settlers did. The community's continued appreciation for those resources was reiterated when a majority of voters dubbed Springdale's new minor league baseball team the Northwest Arkansas Naturals.

CRYSTAL BRIDGES MUSEUM OF AMERICAN ART HOUSES AN INTERNATIONALLY ACCLAIMED COLLECTION OF PAINTINGS AND SCULPTURES   ARKANSAS DEPARTMENT OF PARKS & TOURISM

WALTON'S VISION IS REALIZED AT CRYSTAL BRIDGES

Crystal Bridges Museum of American Art (479-418-5700; www.crystalbridges.org), 600 Museum Way, Bentonville. Open Monday 11–6, Wednesday through Friday 11–9, and Saturday and Sunday 10–6.

When Helen Walton finally went from the ranks of the knowledgeable private collectors to a public philanthropist building a significant collection of American art for public display, she attracted national attention. There were those who were outraged she would take national treasures like George Washington's official portrait to a small unknown town in the Ozarks. There were more who questioned the wisdom of the investment and the museum's ability to draw viewers to the collection. Today, years after its opening in 2011, Walton's dream is now a reality, and the result is an art experience that is unmatched because of its unique, rural setting in small-town Middle America. Most important art museums are located in downtown areas in cities with hundreds of thousands, even millions

CHILDREN HAVE A GALLERY DEVOTED TO CREATING THEIR OWN WORKS OF ART

of people. But until you have experienced art in a scenic and relaxed environment, you can't imagine the difference it makes to have the art removed from the frenetic energy of a busy downtown district. Everything about the museum encourages you to savor each of its pieces in harmony with the natural setting of its verdant grounds. There are walkways throughout the 100-acre campus with benches, a picnic table, and sculptures installed along the way.

Crystal Bridges takes its name from the unique glass-and-wood building design, created for the natural setting by world-renowned architect Moshe Safdie. The museum's campus is within walking distance of downtown Bentonville. The complex includes 100,000 square feet of gallery space; library, meeting, and office space; a Great Hall; areas for outdoor concerts and public events; as well as sculpture gardens and walking trails. Crystal Bridges houses an impressive permanent collection of masterworks from American artists along with galleries dedicated to Native American and regional art. The growing inventory is composed of paintings and sculptures by American artists from the colonial period through the modern era. Temporary exhibits rotate regularly; check the museum's website for a current schedule of events.

The design reflects an appreciation for the natural beauty of the Ozarks and an awareness of its importance to the visitor's total experience. Architects specifically approached the Crystal Bridges site with a goal of enhancing and protecting the natural beauty of the site, employing cutting-edge conservation technologies to maximize sustainability. Plant life is integrated into the architecture, creating a constant dialogue between the building and the landscape.

In 2013, Crystal Bridges purchased the Bachman-Wilson House, an example of Frank Lloyd Wright's classic Usonian architecture. *Usonian* is a term Wright used to describe a distinctly American style of residential architecture he developed during the Great Depression to be within the reach of the average middle-class American family. Helen Walton's collection has grown to reflect the country's artistic expression in every form it can be found.

Even the food. The restaurant at the museum, 11, specializes in modern American comfort food with an emphasis on traditions of the High South—the Ozarks. Their goal is to continue the narrative of a great story of American spirit inspired by the art, natural beauty, and connection to history that surrounds it.

GEORGE WASHINGTON'S PORTRAIT

Walmart sponsors admission to Crystal Bridges, so there is no charge to view the museum's permanent collections; however, there is frequently a charge for special exhibits.

INSTALLATIONS LINE PATHWAYS ON THE MUSEUM'S GROUNDS

✳ To See

ARTS CENTERS AND GALLERIES **Arts Center of the Ozarks** (479-751-5441; www
.artscenteroftheozarks.org), 214 South Main Street, Springdale. Ticket prices vary and
are available for purchase online. This 425-seat theater offers live performances of dramas and musicals. Classes are offered in visual arts. Check the website for information
on gallery showings and special events.

MUSEUMS **Clinton House Museum** (479-444-0066; www.clintonhousemuseum.com),
930 California Drive, Fayetteville. Open Monday through Saturday 8:30–4:30. Newly-
weds Bill and Hillary Clinton called this 1930s English-style bungalow home during
their years in Fayetteville. As the story goes, Hillary turned down the first proposal,
so the future president sweetened the deal with a $3,000 downpayment on the $17,000
house. She said yes, and the rest is history that you can explore in the couple's first
home. The museum features photographic and memorabilia displays, and videos
replay campaign commercials and political debates from Clinton's first campaigns in
Arkansas. A gift shop sells Clinton-related souvenirs. Admission is $5 per person.

    Daisy Airgun Museum (479-986-6873; daisymuseum.com), 202 West Walnut, Rog-
ers. Open Monday through Saturday 9–5; closed major holidays. Located in Rogers'
historic downtown is Daisy Manufacturing Company, Inc., the world's oldest and largest manufacturer of air guns, ammo, and accessories. Introduced in 1939, the Daisy
Red Ryder has sold over 9 million units, easily making it the most famous BB gun ever
built. In March of 2000, Daisy relocated its extensive collection of antique Daisy air
guns and advertising memorabilia from its corporate offices into its current location, a
building that dates back to 1896 and is best known to local residents as the old Rexall
Drug Store and Soda Fountain. Gun and history enthusiasts come to see the collection of antique air guns dating to the 1600s. In 2016, private equity firm Bruckmann,
Rosser, Sherrill & Co. in New York acquired the historic BB gun manufacturer. BRS also
owns Gamo Outdoor, a global manufacturer of airguns, accessories, and archery products. Daisy collectors come to walk through the company's timeline and view old pack-
aging and advertising. Baby boomers come to see an example of the first Daisy made
and reminisce about the one they had as
a kid. Shoppers come for the complete
line of current Daisy products and unique
collectibles, which are exclusively available through the Daisy Airgun Museum.
Admission is $2 per person.

DAISY AIRGUN MUSEUM

    Headquarters House Museum (479-
521-2970; www.washcohistoricalsociety
.org), 118 East Dickson Street, Fayetteville. Call or check their website for current operating hours and special event
information. This Greek Revival–style
home was built by Judge Jonas Tebbetts
in 1853 and miraculously survived the
Civil War. The Battle of Fayetteville was
fought on its front lawn, and a doorway
bears the scar of a Minié ball, preserved
in testament to the battle that earned the
intersection of College and Dickson the

HEADQUARTERS HOUSE MUSEUM IN FAYETTEVILLE

title Bloody Corner. This home served as headquarters for both Union and Confederate forces during the Civil War. Located in the historic district of Fayetteville, the museum offers daily house tours, walking tours of the gardens and grounds, and educational programs to teach local children about the history of Fayetteville. The site hosts the annual Heritage School during summer months to promote awareness of past traditions and manners. It also provides numerous luncheons and receptions each year for visitors and guests. Group tours and living history presentations are available by appointment. Free.

Museum of Native American Artifacts (479-273-2456; www.museumofnativeameri canartifacts.org), 202 Southwest O Street (AR 72), Bentonville. Open Monday through Saturday 9–5. This museum features artifacts from the private collection of founder David Bogle, along with 47 items from the former University of Arkansas Museum. Among the pieces on display are nine rare pots in the shapes of a head or body. The 5,000-square-foot space west of downtown provides individual audio wands that lead visitors on self-guided tours. Free.

Rogers Historical Museum (479-621-1154; www.rogersarkansas.com/museum), 322 South Second, Rogers. Open Tuesday through Saturday 10–4; closed major holidays. The caboose is open the same hours from May 1 through October 31. The history of Rogers is told through thought-provoking exhibits crafted to immerse visitors in the bygone days of its origin. The Attic captures the imagination and attention of kids, while adults take guided tours of the historic 1895 Hawkins House. Museum staff will also lead guided tours of Rogers' historic downtown area. Call before you travel. Free.

Shiloh Museum of Ozark History (479-750-8165; www.shilohmuseum.org), 118 West Johnson Avenue, Springdale. The museum takes its name from the pioneer community of Shiloh, which became Springdale in the 1870s. In 1881, a five-year-old Nebraska boy named Guy Howard found an arrowhead in the family garden, sparking an interest in Native American lore that would last a lifetime. The Howard family moved from Nebraska to Springdale by covered wagon in the 1890s, and Guy Howard

MUSEUM OF NATIVE AMERICAN ARTIFACTS IN BENTONVILLE

soon discovered that the Ozarks were full of American Indian artifacts. His collection grew and grew. By the 1920s, local people were flocking to the Howard home to see Guy Howard's museum. In 1966, Springdale purchased the huge collection, which contained some 10,000 prehistoric and historic artifacts and 260 books and pamphlets on anthropology and archaeology. The Shiloh Museum officially opened on September 7, 1968, with exhibits featuring artifacts from Howard's collection, medical instruments used by local physicians, and a research library. In the 1980s, four historical buildings (an 1850s log cabin, an 1870s general store, an 1870s country doctor's office, and a 1930s outhouse) were moved onto the museum campus, complementing an 1870s home already on the property. Free admission.

University of Arkansas Sports Museums (479-575-2000; www.uark.edu), University of Arkansas Campus, Fayetteville. Both museums are open during regular business hours. The Tommy Boyer Hall of Champions Museum in Bud Walton Arena and the Jerry Jones/Jim Lindsey Hall of Champions in the Frank Broyles Athletic Center display a century of Arkansas sports memories. Razorback heroes and hallmarks are remembered in photographic and video exhibits. Free admission.

CULTURAL SITES **Fayetteville Visitor Center** (479-521-5776; www.experience fayetteville.com), 21 South Block Avenue, Fayetteville. Open Monday through Friday 8–5. The visitor center is a great resource for literature for all of northwest Arkansas. A brochure display contains Fayetteville information on one side, and regional and statewide information on the other. Fayetteville publications include the overall visitor guide as well as specifics on historic walking tours, trails, museums, antiques, shopping, and historical sites. City and parking maps are also on hand. The entire back wall of the center is a map of the city, with a magnified view of the downtown area and a small overview of the region. Icons symbolize trails, hotels, and attractions. A seating area, book of menus to Fayetteville restaurants, and wireless Internet access are other amenities. Retail items such as shirts and coffee mugs contain the Fayetteville or Arkansas Razorbacks logo. Also for sale are locally made food products, books from the University of Arkansas Press, snacks, and drinks.

Walmart Visitor Center (479-273-1329; www.walmartstores.com/AboutUs/287 .aspx), 105 North Main Street, Bentonville. Open 9–5 Tuesday through Saturday. Located in Sam Walton's original Bentonville variety store, the Walmart Visitor Center takes you from the company's birth on Main Street to the world leader it is today. The center was created as an educational and informative facility for those interested in this American retailing success story. Admission is free.

Walton Arts Center (479-443-5600; www.waltonartscenter.org), 495 West Dickson Street, Fayetteville. The Walton Arts Center is the state's largest performing arts center, drawing over 140,000 visitors annually. A regional showplace and the centerpiece of a vibrant arts community, the center hosts more than 350 public events annually and provides a wealth of arts programs you would normally find in major metropolitan areas. The 1,201-seat Baum Walker Hall attracts touring Broadway shows, and the 220-seat Starr Theatre is a versatile black box–type performance space that accommodates arts events, parties, and receptions. Bradberry Amphitheater is a 2,000-square-foot outdoor space in a gardenlike setting, a choice location for elegant events and weddings. The Nadine Baum Studios and Just Off Center administration building allow more versatility, with paintings, pottery, quilts, and other artwork displayed throughout. A detailed calendar is posted on their website; tickets are available for purchase by calling the box office or ordering online.

War Eagle Mill/War Eagle Bridge (479-789-5343), on War Eagle Road, off Scenic AR 12, Rogers. War Eagle Mill is open daily 8:30–5, February through November. Closed Monday, Tuesday, and Wednesday during the winter. This working water-powered gristmill offers group tours demonstrating how the mill operates and the process of

SHOP FOR OLD-FASHIONED CANDY AND TOYS AT THE WALMART VISITOR CENTER IN BENTONVILLE

ELEGANCE IN THE OZARKS

Bentonville's first claim to fame was the great merchant for the masses, the late Sam Walton, founder of Walmart stores. The company may have grown into an empire, but Sam Walton always retained his image as a small businessman, albeit an extremely savvy small businessman. Walton nurtured this image, driving an older pickup and shrugging off the external, material trappings of wealth. Bentonville also embraced the image, preserving the "five-and-dime" storefront and ice cream parlor of the original Walmart on its main square.

As the business grew, sales executives and business owners flocked to the small town with the hope of placing their products on the successful retailer's shelves. Today, the vendors and company executives own homes in Bentonville, having relocated to the Ozarks from around the world. Restaurants and shops reflect their broadened palates and tastes; diners find exotic flavors, and shops stock goods from every continent except Antarctica. Local farmers and ranchers learned how to satisfy the taste of discriminating chefs with top quality produce abundant enough to stock booths at the weekly farmers' market.

LIME-GREEN PENGUINS WELCOME GUESTS TO 21C MUSEUM HOTEL IN BENTONVILLE   ARKANSAS DEPARTMENT OF PARKS & TOURISM

When Walton died, his daughter Helen invested millions of dollars in acquiring the remarkable collection of American treasures displayed at the Crystal Bridges Museum of American Art in Bentonville. Just as her father's vision for mass retailing transformed his variety store and the town around it, Helen Walton's passion for Bentonville's place in the world of American art has elevated the town once again. Artisans abound in Bentonville. Local businesses were already on the leading edge of products and palates, but Crystal Bridges inspired the community to grow to another level. Imagine Aspen in the Ozarks, complete with its own nationally ranked film festival founded by Geena Davis.

Bentonville includes one of the most artistically driven boutique hotels in the country, 21C Museum Hotel. Founders Steve Wilson and Laura Lee Brown launched their concept of an "art museum with sleeping rooms" in their hometown of Louisville, Kentucky, as an investment in

grinding. A gift shop stocks organic products, including salsas, flours, meals, cereals, whole grain mixes, jams, jellies, preserves, salad dressings, bread mixes, and soup starters. Each fall, the Ozark hills come alive with the sights, sounds, and aromas of the War Eagle Mill Antique & Craft Shows in October, easily the largest craft shows in Arkansas. Free admission.

downtown revitalization. Combining provocative contemporary art with reimagined historic space delivered a curated lodging product and rave reviews. A conversation with Helen Walton brought the third 21C Museum Hotel to charming downtown Bentonville. This time, however, the hotel is a juxtaposition to the historic square, in a newly built and site-specific modern brick and glass building.

Bentonville's 21C continues the brand's commitment to engaging the public with art. Exhibits are free and open 24/7, and if you take advantage of the sleeping rooms available above the gallery, you will find yourself drawn to the collections at all times of the day. From kinetic pieces that move when you do to digital media films to view, you should take your time exploring at 21C. Hotel guests are encouraged to interact not only with the art but also the mascot, any one of more than 200 three-foot-tall, lime-green plastic penguins scattered about the hotel. Dining alone? Not for long, because you will no doubt find one of these guys at the table with you at The Hive, the official restaurant for the hotel. The Hive offers its own signature dining experience under the guidance of executive chef and James Beard finalist Matt McClure.

There is an air of elegance now that permeates the town, spilling over into its shops, parks, and people. In the decade since Crystal Bridges opened its doors, artistic expression has reached Level 10 in Bentonville. And it's going up.

PENGUINS PERCH FROM THEIR VANTAGE POINT OVERLOOKING DINERS AT THE HIVE   ARKANSAS DEPARTMENT OF PARKS & TOURISM

HISTORIC SITES **Fayetteville Confederate Cemetery** (479-521-1710), Junction Rock and Willow Streets, Fayetteville. The cemetery was founded in 1872 by the Southern Memorial Association of Washington County, which paid to have the remains of Confederate casualties at Pea Ridge and Prairie Grove, as well as from less-storied combats, removed and reinterred in what remains a picturesque and moving site.

WAR EAGLE MILL

Pea Ridge National Military Park (www.nps.gov/peri), US 62, Pea Ridge. Pea Ridge National Military Park is the site of one of the largest Civil War battles west of the Mississippi River and is prized among Civil War enthusiasts as one of the nation's best preserved. It marks the successful culmination of the Union's effort to secure control of the Missouri and Mississippi Rivers and protect the arsenal at St. Louis, which eased supply lines for General Grant's Vicksburg campaign. The park spans over 4,300 acres and includes a 7-mile self-guided tour with 10 stops featuring wayside exhibits, a 9-mile horse trail, and a 7-mile hiking trail. If you are not up for the entire 7 miles, there are shorter loops accessible from tour stop #7. The park also has a visitor center, museum, and bookstore, and a 30-minute film of the Battle of Pea Ridge. Pea Ridge and Prairie Grove Battlefield State Park host annual battle reenactments the first weekend of December, swapping every year as host site. It is the largest battle reenactment in the state, drawing history buffs, schools, and families who not only get to witness the battle but can visit the battle camps to see great demonstrations of the life of the Civil War soldier. Pea Ridge hosts the event on the odd-numbered years.

Prairie Grove Battlefield State Park (479-846-2990) US 62, Prairie Grove. The museum is open daily 8–5. The picnic area and restrooms are open daily from 8 a.m. to one hour after sunset. Museum tours are $3 for adults, $2 for kids 6–12, and $10 for families. You can add a guided tour of the historic buildings for an additional $2 per adult, $1 per child, and $5 for families. The Battle of Prairie Grove was the last time two armies of almost equal strength faced each other for control of northwest Arkansas. The battle proved decisive in establishing Union control over the region. When the cannon smoke cleared on December 7, 1862, both sides had suffered massive casualties. It is believed to be the bloodiest day in Arkansas history. Recognized as one of the most intact Civil War battlefields, the site has a 5-mile driving tour that brings the battlefield to life. Arkansas's largest battle reenactment is held here the first weekend in December on even-numbered years.

URBAN OASES **Botanical Garden of the Ozarks** (479-750-2620; www.bgozarks.org), 4703 North Crossover Road, Fayetteville. The Botanical Garden of the Ozarks sprawls luxuriously across the 86 acres it occupies adjacent to Lake Fayetteville. Themes portrayed in the nine 2,000-square-foot gardens include a children's garden, Japanese garden, four seasons garden, herb and vegetable garden, rock and water garden, native Ozark species garden, rose and perennial garden, and a sensory garden. The children's garden is enchanting. The closer you look, the more you see. Fairies and dragons peep beneath ground cover, and a concrete walkway leads to a bird's-eye view of the grounds. The Carl A. Totemeier Horticulture Center and outdoor plaza are popular venues for weddings and special events. Unlike most public gardens, the Botanical Garden of the Ozarks was cultivated by a volunteer-led, grassroots effort, and the Center's calendar of events is filled with creative events that are open to the public. From June through August, the garden opens every Tuesday evening from 5–8 p.m. for Terrific Tuesday Nights, a family friendly event featuring concerts and educational programs and demonstrations. Art in the Garden, Chefs in the Garden, and the Firefly Fling are just a few of the annually scheduled events posted on the garden's website. Adults (13 and older) are $7; kids 5–12 are $4; children younger than 5 are free. The gardens also offer free admission Saturday mornings from 9–noon.

Compton Gardens (479-254-3870; www.comptongardens.org), 312 North Main Street, Bentonville. Hours: dawn through dusk daily. In 2002, the Peel House Foundation was given the 6.5-acre garden and home of Dr. Neil Compton, physician, author, photographer, naturalist, and savior of the Buffalo River. The garden has been developed into a native woodland garden, which is quickly becoming a regional destination. This beautiful and peaceful environment contains an extensive native and woodland plant collection. The garden is dedicated to the advancement and appreciation of gardening, horticulture, and conservation within an aesthetic landscape. The Compton home site has been remodeled to incorporate a conference center on its upper level. The lower level is home to the Northwest Arkansas Genealogical Society, the Benton County Historical Society, and the Benton County Cemetery Preservation Group. Admission is free for self-guided tours.

THE BOTANICAL GARDENS OF THE OZARKS

✳ To Do

Arkansas & Missouri Railroad (1-800-687-8600; arkansasmissouri-rr.com), 306 East Emma, Springdale. Travel through the Boston Mountains in vintage rail cars, on trestles over 125 feet high, and through the 1882 Winslow tunnel. Three excursions are offered, including one from Springdale to Van Buren with a layover for shopping and lunch. (See River Valley listing for more details.)

    Scott Family Amazeum (479-696-9280; www.amazeum.org), 1009 Museum Way, Bentonville. Open Monday and Wednesday through Saturday 10–5, Sunday 1–5; closed Tuesday. This 45,000-square-foot playground emphasizes interactive art and science exhibits, including a climbable canopy structure, a "tinkering studio" for young inventors, and an acre of outdoor space. Exhibits include a market sponsored by Walmart, a pioneer-style cabin and farm, a water play room, a weather and nature section, and an art lab. There is a special Hershey's Chocolate Lab, the only one outside of the company's headquarters in Pennsylvania. The Nickelodeon Lab allows kids to play around with filmmaking and musical composition. The experiences are designed to foster imaginative play, prompt social interaction, and have the flexibility to provide new and evolving challenges as visitors grow and return to the gallery on repeat visits. Throughout the experiences, Nickelodeon characters provide encouragement and participate in the fun via graphics, digital representations, and as the subjects of the activities. Admission is $9.50 for everybody over 2 years of age.

SPAS **Belladerm** (479-521-BELL; www.belladermfay.com), 577 East Millsap Road, Fayetteville. Open Monday through Thursday 10–6, Friday 10–5, Saturday by appointment only. Warm brick walls give Belladerm an edgy industrial feel, but the grand crystal chandelier reminds you that you are in an elegant salon. It is a fitting environment

NETTING PROTECTS KIDS EXPLORING THE CANOPY AT AMAZEUM

AMAZEUM'S OUTDOOR PLAY AREA ARKANSAS DEPARTMENT OF PARKS & TOURISM

for the cutting edge beauty treatments from which you can choose. Belladerm's signature facial is 75 minutes of steam, exfoliation, massage, hydrating/soothing masque, extractions, AHA peel, and/or partial Dermasound. Oxygen infusion therapy, Dermatude, HydraFacials, a variety of peels, and several other non-invasive alternatives to face lifts are also available.

Glo Limited (479-571-4456; www.glolimited.com), 577 East Millsap Road, Fayetteville. Open Monday through Friday 10–5, Saturday 10–4. This elegant salon's menu includes facials, massages, manicures, pedicures, microdermabrasion, and micro peel. Facials last about an hour and are customized for each customer featuring NaturaBisse products. Hand and arm massage are also part of the treatment. You can get waxed, scrubbed, and wrapped. Botox and Juvederm injections are also available. Facials range from $70–$175, and massages range from $70–$175, dependent upon the length of the session. This is a great place to pick up high-end makeup, and the Glo Girls are happy to share samples when they are available.

SWEET SCIENCE IS SERVED IN THE HERSHEY LAB
ARKANSAS DEPARTMENT OF PARKS & TOURISM

SPECTATOR SPORTS Northwest Arkansas Naturals (479-927-4900; www.nwa naturals.com), I-540, Springdale. Based in Springdale, the team is a member of the Texas League and serves as the Double-A affiliate of the Kansas City Royals. The Naturals season consists of 140

CARNALL HALL IN FAYETTEVILLE

games—70 home games and 70 road games—and is five months long, beginning in early April and finishing Labor Day weekend. Typical game times are 7 p.m. Monday through Saturday, 4 p.m. Sunday. Special event game times will occur at various points throughout the season. The stadium is centrally located off I-540 at the southwest corner of 56th and Watkins.

University of Arkansas (479-575-2000; www.uark.edu). This scenic campus includes a number of historically significant structures, including the two towers of Old Main (completed in 1875), the Chi Omega Greg Theatre (built in 1930), and Edward Durrell Stone's Fine Arts Center (1950). Just west of Old Main is the Fulbright Peace Fountain, designed by E. Fay Jones and commemorating the work of J. William Fulbright to promote international understanding. A nearby statue of Fulbright was dedicated by former president Bill Clinton. The Inn at Carnall Hall, a former women's dormitory, is now a unique lodging option on campus. Other university sites include the University of Arkansas Sports Museums, Anne Kittrell Gallery, Fine Arts Center Gallery, Mullins Library, and Senior Walk.

✳ Wild Places

Hobbs State Park–Conservation Area (479-789-2380; www.arkansasstateparks.com), 20201 East AR 12, Rogers. Arkansas's largest state park in land area sits on 11,744 acres on the southern shore of 28,320-acre Beaver Lake. Starting in the 1840s and continuing throughout his life, Peter Van Winkle, a successful Fayetteville wagon maker, acquired vast amounts of land in northwest Arkansas. The current property that makes up Hobbs State Park Conservation Area was part of Van Winkle's holdings and is rich with archaeological artifacts relating to Van Winkle's home and sawmill, which was the first steam-driven sawmill in Arkansas. The park is a natural area with little development. It currently offers hiking trails, an all-weather public shooting range, regulated seasonal hunting, undeveloped access to the lake, and interpretive programs. A multiuse trail with access to the Van Winkle Historical Site was opened in 2005. The area features remnants of the sawmill and an antebellum garden. Arkansas Archeological Survey digs have unearthed evidence of Van Winkle's estate—slave quarters, a blacksmith shop, a slave graveyard, a mill site, the Van Winkle house site, and nineteenth-century dump sites. The park has four hiking trails, including a 0.25-mile barrier-free historical trail and a 16-mile multiuse trail. The story of this natural area is told through creative interpretive programming and exhibits displayed in the park visitor center.

PARKS **Lake Fort Smith State Park** (479-369-2469; www.arkansasstateparks.com/lakefortsmith), US 71, Mountainburg. Located on the western side of 1,400-acre Lake Fort Smith, this state park reopened in May 2008 in a completely new location due to the expansion of Lake Fort Smith and Lake Shepherd Springs into one reservoir to serve Fort Smith. The park evokes the WPA-style of its previous incarnation and features all new facilities, including campsites (20 Class AAA and 10 Class B), a group lodge with kitchenette that can accommodate up to 32 people (16 in each wing), picnic sites, pavilion, a 2,660-square-foot swimming pool with adjacent wading pool and splash pad, marina with boat rentals, double-lane boat launch ramp, hiking trails, a playground, and an 8,000-square-foot visitor center with exhibits, a meeting/classroom, and an outdoor patio featuring a native stone wood-burning fireplace and a view toward the lake. The exhibit gallery tells the story of how, through time, good water made this valley a place of hope, faith, and sacrifice. The gallery includes a log cabin, covered wagon, re-created Shepherd Spring, and a diorama of the lake. A 16-minute video further connects the water resources of this valley with man's presence here. Interpretive programs are offered in the park throughout the year by the park staff. Campsites range from $27 a day for the Class AAA sites to $17 for Class B. Call the park for group rates.

LAKES Ask a local in Fayetteville, Rogers, or Springdale what they do for fun, and four out of five will recommend **Beaver Lake** (479-636-1210; www.beaver lake.com). The 28,370-acre reservoir with 487 miles of shoreline, completed in 1966, was one of the first Corps of Engineers reservoirs in the country to supply the municipal and industrial water supply needs for a community. The lake's clear waters and idyllic setting encouraged the corps to further invest in recreational facilities that capitalize on its natural beauty. Paved access roads wind through 12 developed parks. Over 650 individual campsites are sprawled over 2,008 acres in the Ozark Highlands. Campers can enjoy such conveniences as electricity and fire rings. Drinking water, showers, and restrooms are nearby. Other facilities—picnic sites, swimming beaches, hiking trails, boat-launching ramps, sanitary dump stations, group picnic shelters, and amphitheaters—are also available in the parks. Marinas and outfitters are plentiful. Cabins, resorts, and other lodging ring the lake, and campgrounds are also available in good number.

Lake Atalanta (479-621-1117), Rogers. Two parks are located here. The city park on the lake has 17 acres with two handicapped-accessible restrooms, a large stage area, 27 picnic tables, a 2-mile walking trail with 18 exercise stations, large reflection pond with fountain, pavilion, miniature golf course, and a 100-year-old cabin available for small groups. The complex includes Lake Atalanta Bait Shop, with paddleboats, canoes, and fishing boat rentals available. Built in 1936, it is the second oldest park in Rogers.

SUNNING AT BEAVER LAKE ARKANSAS DEPARTMENT OF PARKS & TOURISM

Other amenities include an Olympic-sized swimming pool with water slide and concessions. A 4,000-square-foot banquet facility can be rented for groups. There is also an 8,000-square-foot special event building that seats 680 people, with tables, chairs, and kitchen available. Below the Lake Atalanta Dam is a park that was completed in 1987. Full of beautiful mature trees, it contains 12 picnic tables, a playground, and is also connected to the 2-mile walking trail.

✳ Lodging

21C Museum Hotel (1-855-535-0273; www .21cmuseumhotels.com/bentonville) 200 Northeast A Street, Bentonville. *Travel + Leisure* magazine ranked 21C in the top 15 city hotels in the nation in the 2017 edition of its World's Best Awards. If you love art, unique lodging, and great dining, this is a must-see-stay-do for the northwest corner of the state. The hotel features more than 12,000 square feet of exhibit space showcasing modern American artists in various mediums. Staff are briefed on the collections when they rotate every six months, and you will meet more than a few employees with art degrees who moved to Bentonville just to work at this hotel because they love art. The guest rooms and suites are spacious, with high ceilings, large windows, and a decidedly residential feel, providing a comfortable respite from the thought-provoking art and activity that fills the museum galleries. Outfitted with custom-designed furniture, comfortable beds, plush robes, and MALIN+GOETZ bath amenities, the rooms will make you feel refreshed, restored, and ready to explore. Room rates vary greatly and are based on availability, but you can expect to pay between $300 a night for a deluxe king up to $600 a night for a luxury suite. James Beard finalist Matt McClure's restaurant, The Hive, provides the culinary artistry for the hotel. McClure elevates all the things grown local to a level you would never expect in a town with a population of 50,000. $$–$$$.

Aloft (479-268-6799; www.aloftrogers.com), 1103 South 52nd Street, Rogers. Aloft is just a few minutes from the global headquarters of Walmart, J. B. Hunt, and Tyson Foods, enhancing its popularity with corporate travelers. Easy access to Pinnacle Hills Promenade Shopping Center, golf courses, plus countless dining choices also attracts a healthy number of leisure travelers in addition to providing recreational and entertainment activities for business travelers. The hotel's lobby bar is a cozy place for an after-dinner drink, and a 24/7 pantry stocks sweet, savory, and healthy snacks for your midnight cravings. Complimentary wireless is available hotelwide. Ultra-comfortable beds and oversized showers are standard in all rooms, as well as their nifty plug-and-play connectivity center for charging your electronics and linking to the 42-inch plasma TV. Room rates range from $109 per day for a standard room to $219 for the Aloft upgrade featuring the hotel's signature Performance platform bed. $$–$$$.

Inn at Carnall Hall (1-800-295-9118; www.innatcarnallhall.com), 465 North Arkansas Avenue, Fayetteville. This completely restored 1906 building is now a first-class inn offering a unique lodging experience on the University of Arkansas campus. Carnall Hall is the U of A's second-oldest building and its first women's dormitory. Of course, its previous residents didn't enjoy the numerous amenities available for guests today. The inn has 50 guest rooms, 6 with hot tubs.

Guests are pampered with nightly baked biscotti on their pillows, plush Egyptian cotton linens, high-speed Internet access, and valet parking. You will find almost as many locals as guests in the richly appointed, 50-seat lounge downstairs. Alumni rallied around the building's conversion to public lodging and support the lounge and adjacent restaurant, Ella's at Carnall Hall, through regular patronage. They will be more

21C MUSEUM HOTEL LOBBY

THE RENOVATED DORMITORY AT CARNALL HALL IS A
NOSTALGIC LODGING OPTION IN FAYETTEVILLE

LODGES AND CABINS Rocky Branch Resort (479-925-1688; www.rocky branchresorts.com), 20510 Park Road, Rogers. Rocky Branch Resort on Beaver Lake has a few different options for you to consider based on your lodging needs: the 14-room lodge; a cabin with fireplace and Jacuzzi; the Lake House; and the Treetop House. The freestanding units each sleep eight, and all have access to the resort's swimming pool. An air-conditioned cabin sleeps people comfortably in two bedrooms with a king bed in each and a single sleeper sofa in the lounge. There is a huge fireplace in the living room, a Jacuzzi tub in the bathroom, a fully stocked kitchen, and a satellite TV with a DVD and stereo. The main lodge has 14 spacious and well-maintained rooms, all but 2 with kitchenettes. All rooms are furnished with a table and four chairs and have one king-, two queen-, or two full-sized beds. All rooms have combination tub/shower units. Outside each room are picnic tables, patio furniture, benches, and charcoal grills. The kitchenette units include a refrigerator, stove top, microwave, coffeepot, crock pot, and all the pots, pans, dishes, glassware, and flatware that you will need to make it seem like a home away from home.

The three-bedroom Lake House is huge and will very comfortably accommodate eight people. Just 50 yards from Beaver Lake's shoreline, this unit is perfect for a weeklong stay. You will feel like you are home with the cozy living room with fireplace, family room, 36-inch satellite TV with DVD player, fully equipped kitchen, two bathrooms, and a sun porch for relaxing at the water's edge.

The spacious and airy Treetop House is perched on top of the hill overlooking the resort. The beautifully appointed property will comfortably accommodate up to eight people with three bedrooms, two baths, and two fireplaces, making it a great getaway for large families or multiple couples. Two large living areas, a 54-inch satellite TV with surround

than happy to share stories of their good old college days on campus and share some insider insights into the many special events happening around town. Fayetteville is known for the excellence of its culinary products, with literally dozens of outstanding restaurants for every cuisine imaginable. But you need look no further than Ella's for a superior fine-dining experience. The menu leans toward nouveau cuisine, and menu items change regularly based on the season. A continental buffet breakfast served daily features bagels, fruit, yogurt, pastries, cereal, and gourmet coffees. A full menu is also available and highly recommended. If you like pancakes, Ella's rank with the best in the state. Smothered in fresh strawberries and dusted with powdered sugar, they will make you want to wake up early. $$–$$$.

sound and a DVD player provide all of the comforts of home. High-season rates for lodge rooms are $98 for rooms and $119 for suites nightly, the cabin rents for $229 per night, the Lake House is $399 per night, and the Treetop House rent for $359 per night. Off-season rates average $20 less per night for each property. $$–$$$.

BOUTIQUE INN **Pratt Place Inn & Barn** (479-966-4441; www.prattplaceinn.com), 2231 West Markham Road, Fayetteville. Pratt Place Inn on Sassafras Hill is a unique retreat in an urban milieu, which the third generation of the Pratt family is preserving. Just a few blocks west of the University of Arkansas campus, this elegant property tucks you away in peaceful solitude that is only disturbed when 80,000 fans are calling The Hogs. The seven-room inn is located on the hilltop property that Cassius and Margaret Pratt purchased in 1900. The house, built

in 1895, was at the time the only house west of the university. The residence and its surroundings became known as Pratt Place, a name that is reborn with the restoration and expansion of the original house into one of America's premier inns. Nearby is the English cottage Evangeline Pratt and her husband Julian Waterman built in 1929. In addition, there is a classical gambrel-roof barn in the adjacent pasture. These houses and barn are situated on 140 acres, now in the heart of Fayetteville between the university and I-540.

No expense was spared during the restoration, with each of the seven rooms richly appointed with antiques collected by its current owners during their world travels. All, however, have pillow-top king-sized beds, museum-quality French armoires, Ch'ing Dynasty wedding chests as TV cabinets, Persian rugs on hardwood floors, fireplaces, marble bathrooms with walk-in showers and double

PRATT PLACE INN IN FAYETTEVILLE

whirlpool tubs, and separate water closets. Five have private verandas overlooking the inn's manicured grounds, woods, and the four Haflinger horses grazing in the pasture.

The Catalpa is the queen's room of the mansion; its bathroom features a solid marble hand-carved replica of Cleopatra's bathtub with two matching marble basins. This sumptuous bathroom also has a large walk-in shower. The room, with its bright periwinkle walls and king-sized canopy bed, has a large private veranda overlooking Sassafras Hills' woods and pasture. Guests awaken to fresh fruit, scones, juice, and coffee, either in-room or in the dining room. The scones are perfection with a slightly crispy exterior and fluffy, sweet center. In the evenings, complimentary refreshments are served in the lounge or on the large wraparound porch. The inn has a private dining room, in-house spa, 49-seat conference room, and a media center. It sits on 140 acres atop Sassafras Hill and has 2 miles of private walking trails in the woods. Pratt Place Barn holds up to 350 and is used for weddings, parties, dances, and tailgating. Room rates range from $269 a night for the Catalpa to $199. A quaint, but well appointed two-bedroom cottage is also on the property, renting out for $495 nightly. Well-behaved children are welcome, pets are not. $$$.

RESORTS AND LODGES **Devil's Den State Park** (479-761-3325; www.arkansas stateparks.com), 11333 West AR 74, West Fork. This park's rustic wood and stone structures date back to the 1930s, constructed by the Civilian Conservation Corps, FDR's answer to the country's need to employ an idle workforce and provide much-needed conservation and development of the country's natural resources. An impressive rock dam spans Lee Creek near the park's restaurant, where a life-sized statue of a CCC worker pays homage to the enduring

THE BARN AT PRATT PLACE INN IS A POPULAR WEDDING VENUE

TRY THE PANCAKES AT DEVIL'S DEN STATE PARK'S RESTAURANT

legacy left by this hard-working group of men. Every day, park interpreters organize a pickup game of softball with park visitors, a tradition that began with the CCC men who built Devil's Den State Park. The turnout for the daily tribute is surprisingly heavy, and players range from elementary school–aged children to their grandparents. Fishing, canoeing, kayaking, and pedal boating are popular activities on Lake Devil, an 8-acre lake adjacent to the park's restaurant and swimming pool. Hiking, backpacking, and mountain bike trails wind through the crevices and caves that frequently inspire park visitors to linger in their cool spaces. Park interpreters lead guided hikes along the park's many trails, including the 15-mile Butterfield Hiking Trail. Seventeen cabins with kitchens and fireplaces, a group camp, standard pavilion, swimming pool, playground, and park store all bear the signature style of the CCC. The park also offers 143 campsites, including 42 located in the Horse Camp that have

HIKING AT DEVIL'S DEN STATE PARK

access to the horse trails as well as water and electrical connections. Cabin rental rates range from $100 per day for a studio with fireplace to $180 per day for a three-bedroom, two-bath cabin that has a fireplace and spa tub. Campsite rentals vary from $27/day for deluxe Class AAA sites with 50-amp electrical, water, and sewer to hike-ins (tent only) at $10/day. $–$$.

OUTFITTERS, CAMPING, RVS, AND CAMPGROUNDS **Hideway Campground and RV Park** (1-800-209-0081; www.beaverlakehideaway.com), 8369 Campground Circle, Rogers. This hideaway is tucked away on 66 acres along the shores of Beaver Lake, providing beautiful scenic views and easy access to the lake. The family-owned site offers its own amenities, including laundry facilities, a horseshoe pit, ping pong table, swimming pool, playground, convenience store, gift shop, tent sites, boat slips, cottages, and cabins. Daily rates are $20 for tent sites and $24–$26 for RV sites. The cottages rent for $35 a night and include a double bed, sleeper sofa, and microwave, but you will need to bring your own bedding. Poolside cabins include a queen bed, kitchenette, all utensils, and bedding, and are $60 nightly. A lakeside cabin with two full beds, full kitchen, outdoor grill, all utensils, and linens is $70 per night. $.

✳ Where to Eat

EATING OUT **Emelia's Kitchen** (479-527-9800), 309 West Dickson Street, Fayetteville. When Kevork and Sara Ouyoumjian opened Emelia's Kitchen on Dickson Street more than a decade ago, they had a clear vision of the flavors and feel they hoped to deliver to their diners. The menu is inspired by the traditional Armenian recipes of Kevork's mother, Emelia Ouyoumjian, and updated with a Mediterranean flair. The menu includes kebabs made of lamb, shrimp, steak, chicken, and veggies ranging in price from $13–$18 per portion. Specialty items like chicken piccata, roasted pork loin, and citrus salmon range in price from $15 to $19 a plate. On Wednesdays and Sundays, Emelia's offers a "Date Night Special," that includes an appetizer, side salads, entrées, dessert, and a bottle of wine for $55 per couple. Brunch is served Friday, Saturday, and Sunday with spins on traditional brunch fare such as Lobster Eggs Benedict and specialty cocktails. $$–$$$.

The Farmers Table (479-966-4125; www.thefarmerstablecafe.com) 1079 School Avenue, Fayetteville. The Farmer's Table serves breakfast and lunch Tuesday through Sunday from 7 a.m.–3 p.m.; dinner is served Friday and Saturday nights from 5–9 p.m. Locally sourced ingredients are spotlighted here, and each menu item names the specific farm, dairy, mill, or bakery providing the fresh products featured. You'll find standard breakfast items like egg sandwiches, omelets, pancakes, and hash elevated by the quality of the produce, meats, cheese, and grains. Sweet potato pancakes, topped with candied pecans and cinnamon butter are a local favorite. Sandwiches and burgers comprise a significant portion of the lunch and dinner menus. A few specialty dishes emerge on the dinner menu, including orange beef, summer pappardelle, eggplant steak, and fried chicken. This is a great spot for vegetarians with substantial and creative choices beyond salads and grilled veggies. In addition to the eggplant steak and summer pappardelle, the swiss kraut banzo features a garbanzo patty and the mushroom mash gets its heartiness from vegan sausage. $–$$.

Herman's Ribhouse (479-442-9671), 2901 North College, Fayetteville. This local icon is legendary for . . . wait for it . . . their ribs. Herman's has been a Fayetteville favorite for decades, its smoky scents tantalizing drivers as they pass the faded, whitewashed brick building.

The ribs are fall-off-the-bone tender, served with your choice of baked beans, potato salad, or creamy coleslaw. In addition to the ribs that made them famous, menu items include standard American fare; Herman's hamburgers are a popular second choice. Herman's is packed on weekends, so prepare for a wait if dining in prime time. $–$$.

Oven and Tap Restaurant and Bar (501-658-7724; www.ovenandtap.com), 215 Main Street, Bentonville. Bright and airy, this is the place your craft beer lover will remember. Named for the custom-built wood stove and tap wall that is the heart and inspiration for the restaurant, Oven and Tap's menu is both rustic and contemporary. In addition to an inventive selection of wood-fired pizzas, the restaurant makes every item from scratch with locally sourced ingredients whenever they are available. Imagine homemade lasagna kissed with smokiness from that big wood stove. Almost anything you can cook in an oven they can cook in a wood stove, delivering a signature spin on classic dishes. Sixteen craft beers are poured from the tap wall, and house-made cocktails round out the libations available. Oven and Tap's large deck is a great place to capitalize on the mild climate of northwest Arkansas, people watch, and enjoy fresh, homemade dishes that are a little bit Southern and a little bit Italian. $$.

The Hive (479-286-6575; www.21c museumhotels.com/bentonville/category /the-hive), 200 Northeast A Street, Bentonville. This chef-driven restaurant in the 21C Museum Hotel marries perfectly with the hotel's brand. Chef Matt McClure's approach to his menus reflects a respect for the farmers and ranchers in the region with an emphasis on the state's culinary identity. Bone up on your lingo before you go because his food is so delicious you will be searching for words to describe it. McClure transforms ingredients into works of art. How does he coax so much flavor from a tomato for his gazpacho? Have you ever had a crispy pig tail? Imagine succulent pork ribs encased in a crispy light skin. McClure could probably make shoe leather tasty. He was a finalist

OVEN AND TAP IN BENTONVILLE

CHEF MATT MCCLURE OF THE HIVE

or semifinalist for James Beard's Best Chef in the South in 2014, 2015, 2016, 2017, and 2018. *Food and Wine* magazine named him The People's Best Chef in the Midwest in 2015. In 2014, *Southern Living* magazine named The Hive's bar to its Top 100 Bars in the nation list; featured cocktails vary with the season and the

harvest. Watch the master work in the open kitchen or take in the hotel's art displayed throughout. A piece titled "Buzz-Kill" is designed to engage viewers with hidden surprises only uncovered when the three-dimensional piece is explored. Reservations are recommended. $$$.

Tusk & Trotter American Brasserie (479-268-4494; www.tuskandtrotter .com), 110 Southeast A Street, Bentonville. Open Monday 4–9:30, Tuesday through Thursday 11–9:30, Friday 11–11, Saturday 10–11, Sunday 10–9. Housed in Sam Walton's former office and warehouse just off the town square, Tusk & Trotter retained the best features of the old building: exposed trusses, acid-stained concrete floors, Sam's original warehouse door. Because it's one of the few downtown restaurants open on Sunday afternoons, many tourists find it simply because it is open. Most leave planning to come back because there is more on the menu they want to try. Regulars advise to visit at least four times a year because the menu changes with the seasons—duck in the winter and lamb

NOSE-TO-TAIL DINING AT TUSK & TROTTER IN BENTONVILLE

in the spring. Brunch is also a favorite, and it isn't just about the bacon. Pommes Frites, Duck Ham Benedict, Figgy French Toast, Lemon Souffle Pancakes, and Crispy Pig Ear Salad share space harmoniously on the spring menu. There is a surprise and flavor for every diner at Tusk and Trotter. And, just as the name implies, from nose to tail, the chefs use local products in a sustainable manner. $$–$$$.

DINING OUT **Bordino's** (479 527 6795;bordinos.com), 310 West Dickson Street, Fayetteville. Bordino's serves upscale Italian fare in an elegant, modern environment. Open Tuesday through Friday for lunch from 11:30 a.m.–2 p.m.; for brunch on Saturday and Sunday from 10 a.m.–2 p.m.; and for dinner Monday through Thursday from 5–10 p.m., and Saturday from 5–11 p.m. Craft drinks and an innovative small plate menu make Bordino's a local favorite. Highlights includes unctuous meatballs made with beef tenderloin and the charcuterie with its array of pate, cheese, sausage, and spicy condiments, while the vegan crabcakes and crispy Cajun-inspired calamari are worthy of a second visit if you skip them the first time. Pasta dishes, except the lasagnas, are available with gluten free options. The seafood risotto is rich with seafood and topped with a luscious bourbon mascarpone crema. Smoked duck breast, beef tenderloin, salmon, and pork Porterhouse highlight the proteins featured in specialty dishes composed with locally sourced ingredients whenever possible. $$–$$$.

Ella's Restaurant (479-582-1400; www.innatlhall.com), Maple and Arkansas Avenues, Fayetteville. This world-class restaurant is located in the historic Inn at Carnall Hall, a former women's dormitory that is now an upscale boutique hotel on the University of Arkansas campus. Heirloom vegetables are prominent throughout the menu; the heirloom tomato salad with fresh basil and buffalo mozzarella is a local favorite. The menu favors northern Italian cuisine, with homemade pastas and wood-fired pizzas topped generously with fresh herbs and fine cheeses. Seared fresh tuna and aged Angus beef are among the American entrées perfectly prepared in the kitchen at Ella's. A number of excellent desserts are offered, with sorbet flavors changing daily. The restaurant also serves breakfast, with a choice between a continental buffet of pastries, fruit, cereal, and gourmet coffees and a full menu of omelets, egg and meat combos, waffles, and melt-in-your-mouth pancakes dressed with fresh strawberries and powdered sugar. Dinner for two with wine, appetizer, and dessert will run you about $150. Breakfast, off the menu, averages about $15 per person. $$–$$$.

Pesto Café (479-582-3330; www.pestocafe.com), 1830 North College, Fayetteville. Open Monday through Thursday 11–10, Friday and Saturday 11–11. Fayetteville's first choice for gourmet Italian is Pesto Café, known for the rich, flavorful sauces that adorn their homemade pastas and pizza. Pesto and blended farm cheeses are favored ingredients on a number of the house's specialty pizzas, which vary in price from $9.95 for the Pesto (an herb-based thin crust topped with pepperoni, fresh tomatoes, blended farm cheeses, fresh herbs, and pine nuts) to $11.95 for Le Chicken Coupe (pesto, bell peppers, grilled chicken, artichoke hearts, purple onions, squash, zucchini, carrots, sun-dried tomatoes, and farm cheeses). Naturally, classic Italian dishes like the lasagna will pass the taste test of all of The Family, with handmade pasta and homemade tomato sauce. On the more exotic side of the menu, Seafood Vera Cruz (with fresh shrimp and scallops seared with shallots, bell peppers, white wine, cilantro pesto, and capers, served over angel hair pasta in a cream sauce) highlights the café's gourmet designation. The lasagna is served with angel hair pasta and is a bargain at $13.95. Even the specialty dishes, like the Seafood Vera Cruz, only top out at $23. The portions here are large and the desserts are excellent, so you might want to think doggie bag, or share your meal just to try the tiramisu or pear Frangelico (a pear sautéed in Frangelico, cinnamon, and nutmeg, served over vanilla ice cream). Both are under $5. Pesto features live music on Mondays, Thursdays, and Saturdays. $$.

Theo's Bar & Dining Room (479-527-0086; www.theosfayetteville.com), 318 North Campbell Avenue, Fayetteville. Theo's opened in 2005 and rapidly popped on the radar of Fayetteville foodies for its first-rate service, inviting atmosphere, but most significantly its sophisticated and elegant menu that is impeccably prepared by Executive Chef Brian Aaron. Theo's is named after owner Scott E. Bowman's father and grandfather, and Bowman's passion for the restaurant is evident in every detail of its decor, design, and delivery.

Gleaming black leather banquettes line the dark-paneled walls of the inviting 66-seat dining room, which is decorated with contemporary art. But Fayetteville's mild weather makes the large patio irresistible seven months of the year. Restaurant aside, Theo's is a destination for its cocktails alone. Famous for its martinis, the cocktail menu is as extensive as most restaurants' dinner menus. Dozens of flavors of martinis, mojitos four ways, and specialty infusions live up to Theo's philosophy of the drink, and the last sip is as good as the first. Appetizers are equally creative. For example, the quesadillas feature duck, jack cheese, crème fraîche, and tamarind BBQ sauce ($8). Pastas are made fresh in-house daily and range in price from $14–18 (try the lobster ravioli). In addition to their Italian dishes, the American Kitchen Classics menu includes bone-in double-cut veal chop ($29), seared rare filet of ahi tuna ($29),

DECK DINING AND PEOPLE WATCHING AT THEO'S ON DICKSON STREET

and molasses-marinated pork tenderloin ($24). The latter is served with a creamy cornbread pudding, haricots verts, and a bourbon reduction, and will make you want to kiss the cook. $$–$$$.

✳ Entertainment

DRIVE-IN THEATER **112 Drive-In** (479-442-4542), 3352 AR 112, Fayetteville. The cooler climes of the Ozark Mountains are perfect for an old-time American favorite—the drive-in. The 112 Drive-In shows recently released, full-length movies for a $12-per-car admission. Open Friday, Saturday, and Sunday. Call for showtimes, as they have a tendency to run toward oh-dark-thirty.

NIGHTLIFE **Dickson Street Entertainment District** (479-571-3337; www.downtowndickson.com), Fayetteville. This colorful, eclectic area located near the University of Arkansas campus is filled with bistros, nightclubs, and galleries, and is home to the impressive Walton Arts Center. You'll find a couple of local landmarks here, as well as two microbreweries.

Brewski's Restaurant & Draft Emporium (479-973-6969), 408 West Dickson Street, Fayetteville. This microbrewery, one of two in Fayetteville, has an excellent selection of house brews, plus a full bar. Brewski's menu features all-American favorites in the Dickson Street entertainment district.

Hog Haus Brewing Company (479-521-2739; www.ozarkbrew.com), 430 West Dickson Street, Fayetteville. Hog Haus Brewing Company has a complete bar, with domestic and imported beer on tap as well. Haus house specialties include Haus-made ales, an array of traditional and eclectic appetizers, soups, salads, sandwiches, pizzas, steak, fish, and more. Hog Haus is located directly across the street from the Walton Art Center, toward the university's end of Dickson Street. The second-floor balcony

tables are perfect for enjoying Fayetteville's mild climate and people-watching on Dickson Street.

SPORTS **Arvest Ballpark** (479-927-4900; www.nwanaturals.com), 3000 South 56th Street (off I-540 at the southwest corner of 56th and Watkins), Springdale. Home field for the Northwest Arkansas Naturals, a minor league baseball team based in Springdale. This beautiful park, named one of the country's best new ballparks in 2008 by Ballpark.com, also hosts concerts and special events throughout the year. Built with natural stone mined in local quarries, the stadium is a refreshing departure from traditional red brick facilities and is particularly appropriate for a team known as The Naturals. Iron and glass enhance the open feel of the stadium, capitalizing on the scenic setting on which the park was built. Native plants are thoughtfully placed on the grounds, and lighted canopies finish the stadium providing a unique ambience for evening events and games. Performance schedule and ticket information is available on their website.

THEATER **Arkansas Public Theatre** (479-631-8988; www.arkansaspublictheatre.org), 116 South Second Street, Rogers. Call for showtimes. The Victory Theater, listed on the National Register, was designed by architect A. O. Clark and opened as the first motion picture theater in northwest Arkansas in 1927. The historic building is now the site for theater, concerts, and children's shows. Performance and ticket information is available online. At the theater's inception, founders Charley Marshall and John Cooper sought to enrich the relatively new town of Rogers, Arkansas, with a site that would bring entertainment and news to the town from many miles away. They invested $75,000, and with Clarke's vision established a showplace not only for entertainment, but more importantly a place that people would be drawn to for decades. There is an inherent difficulty in trying to make a place. But with Rogers being relatively new as a town, the theater essentially acted as a common fairground for the development of the town's sense of community.

✳ Selective Shopping

Artist Point Gift Shop & Museum (479-369-2226), 19924 US 71 Scenic Byway, Mountainburg. Open 9–5 daily. This scenic byway was the first major artery to traverse the Boston Mountains, linking the communities on the Springfield Plateau with the Arkansas River Valley. It's hard to imagine the obstacles they encountered when they tackled this rugged terrain to build this road, but their efforts have been appreciated by the millions of awestruck travelers who have driven it since. With every mile you travel, yet another breathtaking view awaits. Most drivers start looking for a place to pull over and snap a photo shortly after they exit I-40 at Alma. Just about the time you are ready to park on the winding road's gravel shoulder, you will reach Artist Point. Its observation deck overlooks a stunning view of the Boston Mountains with Lake Shepherd Springs and White Rock Mountain in the distance. Telescopes are available for a closer look. This family-owned business is run by the second and third generations. The gift shop has a variety of unique items, including handmade dolls, Indian artifacts, homemade jams and jellies, and other small treasures, all of which are produced by local craftsmen. Artist Point also has hiking trail access.

Dickson Street Bookshop (479-442-8182), 325 West Dickson Street, Fayetteville. Open Monday through Saturday 10–6. Antiquarians lose themselves for hours on end in this city landmark. Sure, every college has its used bookstore, shuffling the owners of collegiate texts. At the Dickson Street Bookshop, you will find 100,000 used and out-of-print books. It's an excellent spot for hunters of antique and rare volumes.

Fayetteville Farmers' Market, Downtown Square, Fayetteville. Open April through November, Tuesday, Thursday, and Saturday 7–1. The Fayetteville's Farmers' Market is one of the most popular and successful venues for localvores in Arkansas. It's hard to say whether it is the charm of its downtown setting, or the quality and variety of freshly grown produce and handmade crafts that set it apart. Without a doubt, it's a winning combination for the thousands of people lucky enough to stock their pantries amid its festive atmosphere. Saturday shoppers are frequently serenaded by talented musicians as they browse through everything from hand-thrown pottery to potted herbs and houseplants.

House of Webster (1-800-369-4641; www.houseofwebster.com), 1013 North Second Street, Rogers. Open daily 10–6. The House of Webster has successfully promoted the Ozark palate since its 1934 inception. Webster's huge selection of Ozark food products includes jams, jellies, and preserves made from tame and rare wild fruits, War Eagle meats, and Hickory Creek cheese and candy. Homestyle pickles, relishes, and salsa are all packed in one-pint Mason fruit jars, labeled in longhand with gold-lacquered lids, just like your grandma did. Or maybe Martha Stewart's grandmother. Cleverly titled packages, like The County Fair, bear colorful descriptions in true Ozark Mountain fashion—"made from wild and native fruit that is gathered by rugged mountaineers from the dwindling patches along the ravines, creek banks, ledges, and ridges . . . from deep in the wilderness." The House of Webster also stocks canister sets and early American replica appliances.

Mount Sequoyah Gift Center (479-251-7754; www.mountsequoyah.org), 150 Northwest Skyline Drive, Fayetteville. Call ahead to confirm hours of operation. This gift center is located on the grounds

FAYETTEVILLE'S FARMERS' MARKET ON THE DOWNTOWN SQUARE

of Mount Sequoyah Conference Center in the heart of Fayetteville. Mount Sequoyah specializes in Fair Trade gifts from around the world. Featured merchants include Ten Thousand Villages, A Greater Gift, and World of Good. Set amid 30 acres of wilderness hiking trails, grassy lawns, and acres of flowers overlooking historic downtown and Dickson Street.

Ozark Folkways Heritage Center (479-634-3791; www.ozarkfolkways .org), 22733 North US 71 Scenic Loop, Winslow. Open daily 9–5. Ozark Folkways is a unique learning center complete with a school of sculpture. The extensive gift shop features the work of about 145 native craftspeople, with art, pottery, heritage crafts, baskets, quilts, china paintings, dolls, jams, jellies, and woodwork. Have a free cup of coffee and learn about area culture, or learn a new craft such as wood carving or quilting.

Pinnacle Hills Promenade (479-936-2160; www.pinnaclehillspromenade .com), I-540, Rogers. Open Monday through Saturday 10–9, Sunday noon–6. White House/Black Market, Coach, Anne Taylor LOFT, Fossil, Build-A-Bear Workshop, and Hollister are just a few of the recognizable retailers you will find at this upscale center along I-540. While you stroll among elegant shops and lush landscaping, dine at one of many premium restaurants such as P. F. Chang's China Bistro, Houlihan's, Mimi's Café, or Longhorn Steakhouse. A 12-screen theater entertains the browsers, while serious shoppers explore a unique collection of shops and restaurants.

Riverside Furniture Factory Outlet (479-621-6400; www.riverside-furniture .com), 100 North Dixieland Road, Suite C-1, Rogers. Call for hours. Rogers is blessed with this outlet store for Arkansas-owned and -operated Riverside Furniture Corporation, a century-old company with manufacturing facilities and corporate offices in Fort Smith. Riverside manufactures and imports bedroom furniture, dinettes, home office furniture, entertainment centers, wall units, and occasional furniture.

Terra Studios (1-800-255-8995; www .terrastudios.com), 12103 Hazel Valley Road, AR 16 in Durham. Open daily 10–5. This unique art park's claim to fame is a little glass bird crafted from molten glass, first introduced by Leo Ward in 1982. Since their introduction, over 9 million bluebirds have been sold. Each is individually crafted by artisans at Terra Studios and signed and dated. But the grounds of this amazing facility will engage you whether or not you consider yourself artistic. Composed of several areas, each is made unique by the individual artists who helped create it. Take the Mural Garden, for example, where the murals are glazed stoneware tiles. The pavilion is ferrocement with stained glass inserts and a fountain in the middle. Glass bluebird demonstrations (call for schedule) will let you see the artists in action.

✳ Special Events

June: **66th Annual Rodeo of the Ozarks** (479-927-0464; rodeooftheozarks.org), Parsons Stadium, Springdale. The Rodeo of the Ozarks has been recognized twice by the Professional Rodeo Cowboys Association (PRCA) as one of the top five rodeos in the country. Nearly 500 contestants, all professional athletes, compete in seven PRCA- and Women's Professional Rodeo Association sanctioned events—tie-down roping, steer wrestling, barrel racing, bareback riding, saddle bronc riding, team roping, and the ever-popular bull riding.

August: **Annual Tontitown Grape Festival** (479-361-2615; www.tontitown grapefestival.com), St. Joseph Festival Grounds, Tontitown. Tontitown Grape Festival is a celebration of family, fun, and tradition. There is no other festival like this anywhere in the country, and this one has loyal attendees who come from all over Arkansas every year for the spaghetti dinner and the grape stomp. There is something for everyone—free shows from nationally recognized performers each night, a huge carnival, internationally famous homemade Italian spaghetti dinners, arts and crafts fair, and grape ice cream! Spaghetti dinner tickets are $10 for adults and $5 for children. Armband prices are $20 for all ages and all rides. Armbands are only $15 Saturday from noon–4.

September: **Bikes, Blues, & BBQ Motorcycle Rally** (479-527-9993; www .bikesbluesandbbq.org), Dickson Street and The Randal Tyson Track Center, Fayetteville. The largest nonprofit, family-friendly motorcycle rally in the country for people seeking to enjoy the best in motorcycle riding, blues music, and BBQ while helping those in need. The rally has donated over $2 million to local charities since 2000. During the day, all main stage entertainment is free. In addition, for a reasonable price, some of the biggest headliners in the country perform at the Arkansas Music Pavilion (AMP) on Thursday and Friday nights. Past acts have included Molly Hatchett and the Marshall Tucker Band. Admission to the rally is free. Admission to the Beer Garden is $1. Saturday night concert fees are listed on the website.

November: **Lights of the Ozarks** (1-800-766-4626; www.experiencefayette ville .com), Downtown Square, Fayetteville. Lights of the Ozarks illuminates Fayetteville's historic town square in early November. The entire downtown square is transformed into a winter wonderland, with over 400,000 lights, street vendors, carriage rides, local coffee, food, miniature horses, and timeless holiday family fun.

The Salem Plateau and Eastern Boston Mountains

The Salem Plateau's beauty spans the state's northern border with Missouri. For years, it was cut off from modernization by the Boston Mountains, capturing each community in its own moment in time. If there were ever a part of the world where each community inspires its own snow globe, this part of Arkansas is it. Every bank in the road reveals the Ozarks in their glory, and you will wonder that it is even possible that there are so many different panoramas to behold in one place. From endearing Eureka Springs to laid-back Mountain Home, it's possible to fill albums with photographs you shoot in one day.

AREA CODES Within this area, you will find all three of Arkansas's area codes represented. Eureka Springs falls under the 479 area code; Harrison, just 30 minutes down the road, uses the 870 area code. The Heber Springs area is reached with the 501 area code.

GUIDANCE The Ozark Mountains have been one of the most popular recreational areas in the state for years, and you will find the abundance of chambers of commerce and visitor bureaus (not to mention local residents) are knowledgeable about their area and eager to enhance your stay.

Northwest Arkansas Tourism Association (479-855-1336; www.northwestarkansas .org) will provide you with an excellent overview of the events and attractions in the northwestern section (Eureka Springs area) of this region.

Ozark Mountain Region (1-800-544-6867; www.ozarkmountainregion.com) masterfully markets destinations in the central Ozarks, from the Buffalo River area to just east of Mountain View. You will find maps, driving tours, and blogs reporting everything from festival schedules to preferred baits.

Greers Ferry Lake and Little Red River Tourist Association (www.visitgreersferry lake.org) covers the lake and river, and the lodges, cabins, and attractions around both.

Ozark Gateway Tourist Council (1-800-264-0316; www.ozarkgateway.com) represents eight counties in the eastern third of the range, starting near Mountain View and extending to its foothills in the north Arkansas Delta.

Greater Eureka Springs Chamber of Commerce (479-253-8737; www.eureka springschamber.com) is conveniently located "up top," above the historic downtown area, for tram tours, local maps, and information on whatever festival is scheduled during your stay (they seem to average one per week). Their well-maintained website is also a great resource for dining, area attractions, and the dozens (hundreds?) of bed & breakfast inns and cabins in the area.

Harrison Convention & Visitors Bureau (1-888-283-2163; www.harrisonarkansas .org) is your best resource the Buffalo River area's lodging, dining, and event information.

Mountain Home Area Chamber of Commerce (870-425-5111; enjoymountainhome .com) provides information on the area's two lakes, three rivers, mountain scenery, and local attractions.

MEDICAL EMERGENCIES **North Arkansas Regional Medical Center** (870-414-4000; www.narmc.com), 620 North Main, Harrison, is a 174-bed, fully certified medical facility providing a wide range of hospital services.

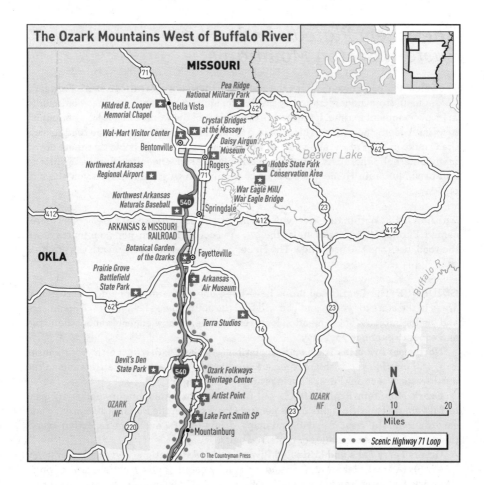

The Ozark Mountains West of Buffalo River

MISSOURI

Mildred B. Cooper Memorial Chapel
Pea Ridge National Military Park
Bella Vista
Wal-Mart Visitor Center
Crystal Bridges at the Massey
Bentonville
Daisy Airgun Museum
Northwest Arkansas Regional Airport
Rogers
Hobbs State Park Conservation Area
Beaver Lake
War Eagle Mill/ War Eagle Bridge
Northwest Arkansas Naturals Baseball
Springdale
ARKANSAS & MISSOURI RAILROAD
Botanical Garden of the Ozarks
Fayetteville
Prairie Grove Battlefield State Park
Arkansas Air Museum
Terra Studios
Devil's Den State Park
Ozark Folkways Heritage Center
Artist Point
OZARK NF
OZARK NF
Lake Fort Smith SP
Mountainburg

OKLA

N

0   10   20
Miles

● ● ● Scenic Highway 71 Loop

© The Countryman Press

Baxter Regional Medical Center (870-508-1000; www.baxterregional.org), 624 Hospital Drive in Mountain Home, is rated one of the top medical facilities in the state and offers a complete menu of health-care services.

✳ Wandering Around

EXPLORING BY CAR The majority of the Ozark National Forest's 1.2 million acres is located in northern Arkansas, and no turn is a wrong turn for adventurous explorers looking for spectacular views seen by only a handful of people every year. The **Sylamore Scenic Byway** (870-269-3228; www.fhwa.dot.gov/byways) allows you to experience the rugged beauty of the Ozarks from the comfort of your car. The 26.5-mile route serves as the primary link between the quaint and aptly named town of Calico Rock to the north, and one of the forest's most unique treasures—the town of Mountain View—to the south. The first 16.5 miles of the byway follow AR 5 from the patchwork bluffs of **Calico Rock** to the banks of the **White River** in Allison, where it merges with AR 16 for 6.7 miles. The final 3 miles along Forest Service Road 1110 terminate at **Blanchard Springs Caverns**, named "one of the most extraordinary finds of the century" by *Life* magazine. The Sylamore Byway's lengthy stretches along limestone bluffs, rushing waters, and tranquil pools entice you to stop frequently and savor every minute (or hour?) of the all-too-brief drive. Both Calico Rock and Mountain View have charming shopping opportunities, and camping is readily available at **Blanchard Springs**, **Gunner Pool**, and **Barkshed Recreational Areas**. This drive is particularly stunning in the fall, when the white oak–hickory forest saturates the landscape in brilliant hues of scarlet, ochre, and amber. If you are an art lover, the annual **Off the Beaten Path Studio Tour** held in September spotlights the brilliance of the season on the byway as well as the many talented artisans that reside alongside it.

EXPLORING BY FOOT **Eureka Springs Historic Downtown Walking Tours** (479-244-5074), Eureka Springs. Guided tours of this storied Victorian village are offered Thursday through Saturday, leaving from Basin Spring Park at 11 a.m., noon, and 1 p.m. The tour is free and takes about a half hour. Wear comfy walking shoes. No reservations required; just show up!

 Black Bass Lake, Eureka Springs. This way-cool trail takes a half hour to walk, is within five minutes of downtown, and even though you're in the city limits you'd swear you were in the deep woods. Maps and more information are available at the Eureka Springs Visitor Center.

 Pigeon Roost Trail, Eureka Springs. East of Hobbs State Park Conservation Area (HSPCA) Visitor Center is the trailhead for the Pigeon Roost Trail, a figure-eight formation of two 4-mile loops. Hikers can choose either loop or the entire 8-mile walk. This moderately strenuous trail has breathtaking overlooks of Beaver Lake, campsites with fire rings, and uncommonly bountiful wildlife.

EUREKA SPRINGS' ENTIRE DOWNTOWN IS ON THE NATIONAL HISTORIC REGISTER

Hidden Diversity Trail, Eureka Springs. This trail is actually four loops—Little Clifty Creek Loop is 9 miles; War Eagle Loop, 5 miles; Bashore Ridge Loop, 3 miles; and Dutton Hollow Loop, 3 miles. Together, with an added 1 mile of connecting trail, Hidden Diversity offers 21 miles of manicured, mostly level trails for hiking, biking, and horseback riding. There are designated watering holes for horses, and some trails are wheelchair accessible. Hidden Diversity Trail is designed for day use and is not open for camping. Most of the trail is within half a mile of a highway, so should you feel lost, you're not. Stay put, bring a whistle, and you will be found and turned around in short order.

Shaddox Hollow Trail, Eureka Springs. On AR 303, 1 mile north of AR 12, is the Shaddox Hollow Trail. This trail is only 1.5 miles long, winding along a ridge before dropping down to the actual hollow. Because the trail has its moments of dramatic descent, remember that it will have the same exhilarating slope coming back up the ridge.

EXPLORING BY RIVER High in the mountains of Madison County lie the beginnings of the **Kings River**. From this steep country the stream twists its way northward to the **White River** and finally flows into southern Missouri's **Table Rock Lake**, a distance of approximately 90 miles. In its upper reaches, the Kings cuts a narrow gorge through sandstone, shale, and limestone. Downstream the surrounding countryside is not quite so precipitous, but the water is the same—clear and cool. The Kings' most attractive features are the flora and fauna found along its rocky banks and bluffs. The headwaters area at **Kings River Falls Natural Area** is favored by hikers, while the rest of the river offers excellent floating and fishing. Deep pools, overhanging trees, occasional rapids, and several large bluffs adorn your journey, and you will find some fine gravel bars in the lower stretch of the river for breaks and picnicking. The state's fondness for this special stream was formalized in 1971 when the Arkansas General Assembly passed legislation protecting the portion of the river in Madison County, noting that it "possesses unique scenic, recreational, and other characteristics in a natural, unpolluted and wild state."

Little Red River emerges from the Greers Ferry Dam, providing the icy cold waters that are essential for a thriving trout population. Trout were introduced to the Little Red in 1966, some three years after the completion of the lake project. Rainbows, browns, and cutthroats are caught for some 35 river miles below the dam near Heber Springs. The world record for a brown trout is 40 pounds, 4 ounces, caught by Howard "Rip" Collins on this river in 1992. Brown trout weighing 5 to 8 pounds are common, and a 20- to 30-pounder is always possible. Mid-October through November is when brown trout begin their spawning run, making this an excellent time for fishing the Red. This popular Ozark Mountain tailwater trout stream is beautiful in its own special way, running clear and cold, skirted by scenic hardwood hillsides alive with wildlife—otters, raccoons, deer, ducks, songbirds, and eagles.

The North Fork (of the White) River originates in Missouri, crossing into Arkansas as an arm of Norfork Lake. It flows only a scant 5 miles below the Lake Norfork Dam before merging with the main White River at Norfork, and yet its fame for world-class trout fishing rivals any river in the state, with numerous 10-pound-plus brown trout landed from its depths. When the water is low, wade fishing, particularly fly-fishing, is popular; when the generators raise the river's depth, anglers float its length in canoes and johnboats. The river is a natural laboratory for the advancement of trout fishing: the nutrient-rich water supports an abundant and healthy population of the fish, and several access points, both public and private, encourage anglers to take advantage of its thriving population. Quarry Park, just below Norfork Dam, has both a concrete boat-launching ramp and public access for bank fishing and wading. Bank fishing at the mouth of Dry Run Creek, which enters the tailwater in Quarry Park, is popular. Fishing in Dry Run Creek is all catch-and-release with tackle restrictions, and only open to kids 16 years of age and younger and the disabled. River Ridge Access features a handicapped-accessible fishing pier and walk-in access. Four species of trout—brook, rainbow, cutthroat, and brown—are caught in the river. A world-record German brown trout weighed in at nearly 39 pounds in 1988, claiming the top spot on the list of record-breaking trophies landed within the river's 5 short miles. This catch still ranks number two worldwide. The current state record brook trout was a chunky 5-pounder from these tailwaters. The mainstay of the North Fork is rainbows from 11 to 14 inches long, just as it is on all the state's other trout waters. Fishing resorts on the North Fork provide excellent lodging, equipment rentals, boat rentals, and professional guide services.

The Spring River flows in a southeastern direction through nearly 75 miles of northeastern Arkansas before it empties into the Black River near Black Rock. Its headwater is at **Mammoth Spring**, adjacent to the Arkansas-Missouri state line, which expels more than 9 million gallons of water each hour through a vent located 80 feet below the surface of Spring Lake. The depth of the vent not only camouflages the impact of the spring as it feeds the lake, the consistent discharge at the lake's bottom keeps the river above a minimum depth year-round. The Spring River is joined several miles downstream by the South Fork, which flows eastward from its origin near Salem. As it is not fed by Mammoth Spring, the South Fork carries a less consistent volume of water and sometimes is not suitable for canoeing during late summer and early fall; however, its extensive gravel bars provide good sites for camping and picnicking. The upper portion of the Spring River is especially popular for swimming and canoe trips. Fishing also draws many visitors to the river. In addition to fish native to the area, the cool water temperature allows the stocking of trout throughout the year. Fly-fishing for rainbow, brown, and cutthroat trout has become a popular sport. Two fish hatcheries are located on the Spring River. The first, **Mammoth Spring National Fish Hatchery**, is operated by the US Fish and Wildlife Service and is adjacent **to Mammoth Spring State Park**. The second, the **Jim Hinkle Spring River State Fish Hatchery**, is operated by the Arkansas Game and Fish Commission and located 2 miles downstream from Mammoth Spring.

From Bull Shoals to Newport, the **White River** flows through some of the most scenic regions Arkansas has to offer. The White meanders through the hills of the western Ozarks for some 300 miles before reaching Bull Shoals Lake. Boat launch facilities are located at most access points, and fishing resorts are available from Bull Shoals to Mountain View. Flat-bottomed johnboats, fitted with comfy seats, are the preferred method of fishing and viewing the scenery along the river. Several record-breaking browns and rainbows have been hooked on the upper White. Below Batesville, the White runs warmer and bass become popular targets. At Newport, the river turns southward across the Delta before joining the Mississippi River in southeast Arkansas. For White River information, call the Corps of Engineers at 870-425-2700.

✳ Towns and Villages

Eureka Springs (1-866-WISHEUREKA; www.eurekasprings.org). America's Victorian Village was named one of America's Dozen Distinctive Destinations by the National Trust for Historic Preservation. It first drew visitors to its remote Ozarks location because of its natural springs and rumors of their healing powers. During the late 1800s and early 1900s, the city became a popular spa resort, and it remains

THE BUFFALO—AMERICA'S FIRST FEDERALLY PROTECTED RIVER

Buffalo National River (870-439-2502 or 870-741-5443; www.nps.gov/buff). There are various access points. The Buffalo National River, which runs through Newton, Searcy, Marion, and Baxter Counties, became the first national river in the United States on March 1, 1972. It is one of the few remaining unpolluted, free-flowing rivers in the lower 48 states. The portion of the river administered by the National Park Service, encompasses 135 miles of the 153-mile long river. Over 100 miles of trails have been blazed to allow you to explore this river selected for federal protection. Designated horseback riding trails are located in each district of the river, and resorts and outfitters are located throughout the river region. Camping is available at most access points, and primitive camping is allowed along the water.

President Richard M. Nixon signed the legislation that put the river under the protection of the National Park Service 100 years after the establishment of Yellowstone National Park. The law begins, "That for the purposes of conserving and interpreting an area containing unique scenic and scientific features, and preserving as a free-flowing stream an important segment of the Buffalo River in Arkansas for the benefit and enjoyment of present and future generations, the Secretary of the Interior . . . may establish and administer the Buffalo National River." Behind that sentence, which set the mission for the park, were decades of debate and discussion regarding the use, ownership, and management of the Buffalo River.

Originating in the Boston Mountains, the river flows generally from west to east, traversing Newton, Searcy, and Marion Counties before flowing into the White River just inside the border of Baxter County. Although termed a national river, the park includes lands surrounding the river, as well as the river itself, giving it a total of 94,293 acres.

Since prehistoric times, the river has attracted the area's inhabitants. The first European and American settlements of the late 1820s located many of their cultural sites on land that is now included in the park. These sites range from terrace village sites, to bluff shelters once occupied by Archaic period Indians, to cabins built by early settlers.

The Buffalo River provided flood plain terraces for agricultural fields, transportation for such local industry as timbering or mining, food, and recreation. Although somewhat isolated by the terrain, the area's population fluctuated with the economy and outside influences, yet never prospered. Nevertheless, the residents who remained after World War II maintained a strong bond to the land and what had been a way of life for 150 years.

The Buffalo River and its surrounding Ozarks scenery were long admired for their beauty and potential for development. Two state parks were created along the river: Buffalo River State Park in 1938, constructed as a project of the Civilian Conservation Corps under the direction of the National Park Service, and Lost Valley State Park in 1966. The river's hydroelectric potential was also seen. With the passage of the Flood Control Act of 1938, the Army Corps of Engineers selected two potential dam sites—one on the lower portion of the river near its mouth and one at its middle, just upstream from the town of Gilbert.

The constant threat of a dam on the river caught the attention of Arkansas conservation groups and the general public, who had begun using the river for recreation or simply appreciated it as a spectacular natural resource for the state. In the early 1960s, advocates for the dams and advocates for a free-flowing stream organized for a showdown. The pro-dam Buffalo River Improvement Association, established by James Tudor of Marshall (Searcy County), and the anti-dam Ozark Society, which included environmentalist Neil Compton, emerged as the leading players in the drama.

The dam proponents aligned with the Corps of Engineers and Third District Congressman James Trimble. The free-flowing stream advocates made overtures to the Department of the Interior. In 1961, a National Park Service planning team undertook a site survey of the Buffalo River area and was favorably impressed, recommending the establishment of a park on the Buffalo River and that it be designated a national river, the country's first.

A decade of political maneuverings, speeches, and media attention—including a canoe trip on the Buffalo by Supreme Court Justice William O. Douglas—came to a head in December 1965, when Governor Orval Faubus wrote the Corps of Engineers to express his concerns and stating flatly that he could not support the idea of a dam on the Buffalo River. The corps responded by withdrawing its proposal for a dam. However, steps to establish a park along the river gained traction the following year, when John Paul Hammerschmidt assumed the Third Congressional District seat and indicated that he would support the project. Congressman Hammerschmidt and Senators J. William Fulbright and John L. McClellan partnered to introduce the first Buffalo National River park legislation in 1967. The final legislation was introduced in 1971, and in February 1972 Congress voted to establish America's first national river.

Park acreage, boundaries, and special considerations were written into the legislation. Total acreage could not exceed 95,730 acres. Hunting and fishing were allowed as a traditional use. Many permanent residents were granted an option of use and occupancy that lasted up to 25 years. Landowners in the three private-use zones of Boxley Valley, Richland Valley, and the Boy Scout camp at Camp Orr could choose to sell easements to the government instead of selling the land outright.

The first park management staff—the park superintendent, a chief ranger, and a secretary—arrived in 1972 and took up temporary office quarters in Harrison. Eventually, the park was divided into three management districts with staff in each district.

Today, the Buffalo National River is one of the leading tourist destinations in Arkansas, with park visitation averaging more than 800,000 people a year. Park headquarters are located in Harrison. Travelers can access the 135 miles of river within the park at launch points all along the river, but the US Forest Service protects its headwaters. Along with water activities, the park offers more than 100 miles of hiking trails, designated trails for horseback riding, and also includes three congressionally designated wilderness areas. As predicted in the early planning studies, the park's overall array of resources is its greatest significance. Four historic districts in the park are on the National Register, as well as individual sites depicting the cultural history of the river's peoples. The park's karst topography includes Fitton Cave, the longest cave known in Arkansas, and others that are home to endangered bat populations. Mammals range from familiar river animals, such as the beaver and raccoon, to land species such as deer, black bear, and a thriving elk herd reintroduced to the area in the early 1980s. Smallmouth bass and catfish tempt the fisherman, but more than 50 other fish species have been recorded in the river. Bird and plant populations are varied, extensive, and represent a healthy ecological system. At the center flows the undammed, free-flowing Buffalo River, fed by tributaries and springs and dramatic pour-offs down the limestone bluffs—truly, in the words of native son songwriter Jimmy Driftwood, "Arkansas's gift to the nation, America's gift to the world."

THE QUEEN ANNE MANSION IN EUREKA SPRINGS

popular for its services today. Its entire downtown district is on the National Register of Historic Places, and the list of accolades it has received for its unique sense of place could fill an Explorer's Guide of its own. While baths and spa treatments are still huge draws, the city is now nationally renowned for its art and well-preserved Victorian-era architecture. Eureka Springs is packed with attractions such as lush gardens, showy tour caves, the nation's premier big cat sanctuary, and *The Great Passion Play*, which depicts the last week of Christ's life on earth. The play has been updated through the years but remains one of the nation's most-attended outdoor dramas, and with one of the country's largest critter casts. Unique boutiques offer antiques, fine art, contemporary and vintage clothing, bells, handmade crafts, and more. A portion of history is uniquely preserved through ghost tours at the 1886 Crescent Hotel and Spa, one of several historic hotels in town. The Art Colony offers demonstrations and art for sale.

Harrison is a treasure for those who want to appreciate the unrefined splendor of the Buffalo River by day and enjoy the comforts of civilization at night. The beautiful downtown square celebrates its historic charm with colorful hanging baskets of flowers and awnings accentuating the old brick storefronts that line its perimeter. The square and a few adjacent buildings make up its National Historic District. You can get a real feel for the town by taking the Main Street Harrison Historic Walking Tour, which includes downtown parks, the historic Lyric Theater, the 1909 Boone County Courthouse, the 1914 Boone County Jail, and the 1929 Hotel Seville. Downtown Harrison also has quality restaurants, an art gallery, well-stocked antiques stores, and other retail shops. Two museums, the Boone County Heritage Museum and the Marine Corps Legacy Museum, are interesting and informative stops. Surrounding the downtown area is an urban sprawl of contemporary dining and shopping districts.

The tiny town of **Hardy**, perched on the bank of the Spring River, hosts a fascinating range of shops along the narrow main street of Old Hardy Town, from antiques to dulcimers to quilts. The annual arts and crafts show in April is well worth the trip.

Jasper's downtown square is unique because of the native rock, harvested from the mountains that surround the Buffalo River, which decorates the exterior of the businesses downtown. The Ozark Cafe on the square, if you catch them on the right day, will grill you the best burger you ever tasted. On weekends, the Ozark is the town gathering spot for live music and hospitality. Legend says that Native Americans who were given food and a place to rest while traveling west on the torturous Trail of Tears gave the town its name. Surprised by the village's warm hospitality, they named it Jasper after the stone prized for purity and strength. John M. Ross, a Choctaw Indian from Pennsylvania who is considered the founder of the town, compared the mellow color of the local stone to jasper, one of the 12 precious stones mentioned in the Book of Revelation.

HARRISON'S DOWNTOWN FEATURES ART DECO ARCHITECTURE   ARKANSAS DEPARTMENT OF PARKS & TOURISM

Mountain Home is the largest city on the Salem Plateau, no small thanks to its placement between two of the Ozarks' most important man-made natural resources, Bull Shoals and Norfork Lakes. The lakes and the White River continue to grow in importance to Mountain Home, bringing thousands of people to ground zero of the trout-fishing universe. Two of the state's finest horse ranches, Horseshoe Canyon and Stone Creek Ranch, are within 20 minutes of Mountain Home, adding to the exceptional outdoor opportunities in this area.

Mountain View is located deep in the Boston Mountains and is the home of the Ozark Folk Center (see sidebar in chapter 1). Music, crafts, and a full array of outdoor adventures await visitors to this charming community.

Pocahontas is the county seat of Randolph County, situated on the eastern edge of the Ozarks on the banks of the Black River. Its historic downtown square boasts a stately 1872 courthouse and beautifully restored buildings from Arkansas's territorial days.

✳ To See

ART GALLERIES **Eureka Fine Art Company** (1-866-715-7800; www.eurekafineart .com), 78 Spring Street, Eureka Springs. Open daily 9–6; later hours for special events or by appointment. This is the largest gallery in the region, at over 10,000 square feet.

The full-service gallery includes works from local Eureka Springs artists as well as nationally and regionally known artists. Custom framing and design services available.

Keels Creek Art Gallery and Winery (479-253-9463; www.keelscreek.com), 3185 East Van Buren, Eureka Springs. Open Sunday through Tuesday noon–5, Wednesday through Saturday 10–6. An open and airy Spanish-style building with 12-foot ceilings houses this award-winning winery. The spaciousness allows an open feel for the art. Guests can relax in the wingback chairs by the two massive stone fireplaces or sit in the enclosed patio, where the motif is accented by furniture made from old wine barrels. The gallery represents 17 artists, some local and some regional. The winery has a tasting room that is open to the public and a retail area stocked with over 80 Arkansas wines, the largest inventory of native wines in the state.

Quicksilver Gallery (479-253-7679; www.quicksilvergallery.com), 73 Spring Street, Eureka Springs. Open Monday through Saturday 10–5. A hands-on exhibit of beautiful musical instruments on the lower level includes instruments you have seen before and some you haven't—strumsticks, gongs and chimes, brass Tibetan singing bowls, and the melodious-sounding Freenotes, an offshoot of xylophones—and they are available for you to play. Explore unique art, including one-of-a-kind wall tapestries, wildlife watercolors, photographs, artist-made jewelry, limited edition prints, pottery (rustic, hand-thrown pieces fired in a wood-burning kiln, gold- or platinum-drenched porcelain, and raku fired with ostrich feathers) in a variety of shapes and glazes, and numerous works in wood and metal.

Susan Morrison Signature Gallery (1-800-522-9634; www.susanmorrison.com), 60 Spring Street, Eureka Springs. Open Monday through Saturday 10–6, Sunday 10–5. This gallery is the only place you can buy new original drawings by nationally acclaimed landscape and wildlife artist Susan Morrison. Susan considers her art to be part of her mission to protect wildlife, and she captures the true essence of each animal she portrays. "I work in pen and ink and Prisma colored pencil in life size. The detail becomes more textural, the color more powerful, and the end effect, at times, monumental," she says. She is also a poet, author, and environmentalist. She will frequently be found visiting guests at the gallery between 10 and 6 on Saturdays. Archival-quality, framed, original life-sized drawings, hand-enhanced giclée prints, lithograph prints, poetry, and Susan's books are available for purchase.

Zarks Gallery (1-877-540-9805; www.zarksgallery.com), 67 Spring Street, Eureka Springs. Open daily 9:30–5:30, usually later on Friday and Saturday. Zarks represents over 125 local, regional, and national artists. The main focus is on American hand-blown art glass, fine silver and gold jewelry, along with sculpture and two-dimensional works. In addition, the gallery is the showcase for the work of "The Studio," a collaboration of artists established in 1970, and one of the oldest studios in Eureka. Zarks has been written up in articles in numerous national publications, including *Craft Report, American Style, Southern Living, House & Garden, Midwest Motorist, New York Times,* and others.

MUSEUMS **1901 Gavioli Chapel** (1-877-933-0003), 80 Mountain Street, Eureka Springs. Call for hours. In June of 2006, noted preservationists Marty and Elise Roenigk purchased this historic chapel and began using it not only as a wedding chapel but also as a museum for special pieces of their world-renowned mechanical music collection. One such piece is their Gavioli Fairground Organ, which has 59 keys, 210 pipes, and is 15 feet wide and 11 feet tall. This ornate mechanical orchestra, which plays everything from festive turn-of-the-century dance tunes to sweet, melodic traditional wedding songs, is the interior focal point of the chapel. The organ is so spectacular that the Roenigks renamed the historic structure Gavioli Chapel. Free admission.

Aviation Cadet Museum (479-253-5008; www.aviationcadet.com), 542 CR 2073, Eureka Springs. Open Wednesday through Saturday 10–5. This museum is dedicated to the men who built the air arm of this nation's defense forces: bombardiers, navigators, observers, and pilots from the Army Air Corps, US Air Force, Navy, Marine Corps, and Coast Guard, as well as all those on the ground who were an integral part of the total force. It is the location of the only public-use airport in Eureka Springs, Silver Wings Field, which carries an identifier of 5A5. Static displays contain an F-105-G and F-100-F. Free admission, excluding special events.

The Bible Museum (1-800-882-7529; www.greatpassionplay.com), 935 Passion Play Road, US 62 East, Eureka Springs. Open May through October, noon until *The Great Passion Play* begins. Come here to see over 10,000 Bibles in 625 languages and dialects. The museum has a large collection of parchments and artifacts, including an original page of the Gutenberg Bible, plus old and rare Bibles. Admission is $12 for adults; $7 for kids 5–12; and free for kids under 5.

Boone County Heritage Museum (870-741-3312; www.bchrs.org), 124 South Cherry Street, Harrison. Open Monday through Friday 10–4, March through November; Thursday only 10–4, December through February. The Boone County Heritage Museum is located in Harrison and sponsored by the Boone County Historical & Railroad Society, a nonprofit organization devoted to the preservation of the county's historical heritage. Hundreds of collections and exhibits on three floors include a railroad showroom, genealogy records and library, Civil War exhibit, Mountain Meadows Massacre collection, Veterans of Foreign Wars (VFW) collection, medical room exhibit, an old post office, and much more. See the website for details. Admission is $2 for adults, free for kids under 12 if accompanied by an adult.

Eureka Springs Historical Museum (479-253-9417; www.eurekasprings.org), 95 South Main Street, AR 23, Eureka Springs. Generally open Monday through Saturday 9–4, Sunday 11–4. During winter, December through February, the museum closes on Monday. Before strolling down the quaint Victorian streets of Eureka Springs, step back into time and walk through the town's very colorful history. The museum, built originally as a private residence in 1889, serves as a downtown visitor center and is both educational and entertaining. The museum houses a fascinating collection of personal items, local artwork, home furnishings, photographs, letters, other ephemera from Eureka's early settlers, and a genealogy department. Displays change seasonally, so come often for a fresh new look into Eureka Springs' past. Self-guided tours are $5 for adults and $2.50 for children. With a reservation, you can add a costumed guide for $8 per person with an eight-person group. Local historian Sondra Torchia books tours of the city through the museum; reserve your tour for $17.50 per person.

Frog Fantasies Museum & Gift Shop (479-253-7227; www.mizfrogspad.com/frog_fantasies.htm), 151 Spring Street, Eureka Springs. Open Monday through Saturday 10–5. Miz Frog loves all things froggy, and this museum proves it. She has gathered frogs in every shape, size, and color in over 60 years of collecting. A gift shop featuring only frog items is available if you want to add to your collection, too. There are over 7,000 pieces displayed in this museum. Frog Fantasies was named a Rand McNally Best of the Road pick for 2007.

Marine Corps Legacy Museum (870-743-1682; www.mclm.com), 127 Rush Street, Harrison. Varied hours; call before visiting. Founded and maintained by two retired Marines—father and son—the Marine Corps Legacy Museum is an impressive volunteer effort. It displays the history of the Marine Corps from 1775 to present day in a chronological sequence. It is the only comprehensive Marine Corps museum in the central United States and the only private comprehensive Marine Corps museum in the country. In May 2007, it was featured in *Leatherneck* magazine. With 46 operational

MARINE CORPS LEGACY MUSEUM

theme displays, the Marines are represented in almost every period of history. You will appreciate hearing the history of this branch of the armed forces from these committed alumni.

Maynard Pioneer Museum & Park (870-647-2701), AR 328 West, Maynard. The museum is open May through September, Tuesday through Saturday 10–4 and Sunday 1–4. The park is built around a nineteenth-century log cabin relocated from nearby and restored to represent an 1800s rural family home, complete with period furnishings, textiles, and household implements that would have been found in a typical Ozark foothills farmstead or home. The cabin was about to be demolished in 1979 when several Maynard citizens elected to move it. They disassembled it, labeling each piece, and reassembled it at its current location. In 1982, an annex was added to house other artifacts. A second cabin was moved to the park in 1999, illustrating pioneer-days worship and education as a combination church and one-room schoolhouse. The museum also has many pictures, newspaper clippings, and historical documents, making it ideal for genealogy studies for people from that area. Also on the grounds is a park with three pavilions, BBQ pits, playground equipment, and four RV hook-ups. Every September, Maynard's population of 381 increases by 4,000 to 8,000 due to its annual Pioneer Days Craft Fair and Festival. Free admission.

Randolph County Heritage Museum (870-892-4056; www.randolphcomuseum.org), 106 East Everett Street, Pocahontas. Open Monday, Wednesday, and Friday 10–4, Tuesday and Thursday 9–4:30, Saturday 10–1. Located on the historic Pocahontas Court Square. Using permanent and transitory exhibits, lecture presentations, interactive exhibits, and other informational programs, the museum is a living forum linking the present day to Randolph County's rich and varied past. Remember the rocking horse you had as a kid? The original Wonder Horse, invented by William Baltz of Pocahontas, is displayed here. Baltz built the first Wonder Horse—named for Arkansas's former nickname of the Wonder State—for his own children by removing the rockers from a rocking horse and suspending the horse from springs held by a wooden framework. Free admission.

CULTURAL SITES **Blue Spring Heritage Center & Gardens** (479-253-9244; www .bluespringheritage.com), US 62 West, Eureka Springs. Open daily 9–6, March 15 through Thanksgiving. Historic Blue Spring, which was a stop on the Trail of Tears, pours 38 million gallons of water each day into its trout-stocked, vivid blue lagoon. There is evidence of an old mill powered by the spring and other remnants of a community centered on the water. With exquisite arrays of plants and flowers, this site has served as a tourist attraction since 1948. In 1993, some 33 acres were transformed into the Eureka Springs Gardens. A decade later, the rich history of the land was blended with the beauty of the gardens and renamed the Blue Spring Heritage Center & Gardens. Artifacts, old photos, a historic film spanning the significance of the Blue Spring site, and walkways through the natural world all await visitors. View the historic film, stroll the garden paths, and visit the prehistoric bluff shelter, which is listed on the National Register of Historic Places. The gardens demonstrate crops, plants, flowers, and healing herbs you will find in the Ozarks. Only seeing-eye dogs are permitted, so ensure your pets are comfortable in your vehicle if you bring them along. Admission is $7.25 adults, $4 students 10–17, free for kids 9 and under.

    Celestial Windz Harmonic Bizaar (479-253-5288) 381 AR 23 South, Eureka Springs. Open Monday through Saturday 10–5. Eureka Springs loves art and music and artists and musicians, so it stands to reason that sometimes they all come together. Wind chime artist Ranaga Farbiarz erected the world's largest tuned musical wind chime in the parking area of his gallery, Celestial Windz Harmonic Bizaar, just south of Eureka Springs. He employed some unusual tools to pull it off—a bucket truck and a 100-foot-tall oak tree. The top of the Celestial Windz world record chime is the roof of the tower

THE CHRIST OF THE OZARKS STATUE IN EUREKA SPRINGS

built in the center of the Harmonic Bizaar gallery. Its dimensions are 8 feet tall by 6 feet across. For the purposes of documentation, the chime was erected in the large oak tree, utilizing a full-scale replica of the tower roof. The interior tower is now the permanent home of the world's largest wind chime. As the centerpiece of the Harmonic Bizaar, it is available for free public viewing and listening during regular gallery hours.

One of my favorite stories about Eureka Springs is told by Richard Davies, director of the state's parks and tourism agency. He says that there are two inane questions people ask all the time, one being "Is the Christ of the Ozarks statue natural or manmade?" (The second question, for those who want to know, is "Do you plant the diamonds at the Crater of Diamonds State Park?") The white mortar figure of Jesus Christ is seven stories tall and weighs almost 2 million pounds. The statue is one of five giant statues of Christ in the world and one of only two in North America. It was sculpted by Emmet A. Sullivan and funded by the Elna M. Smith Foundation of Eureka Springs. Standing on a foundation of 320 tons of concrete with reinforcing steel, the statue was built to withstand winds of 500 miles an hour and has a 2-foot rectangle in the top of the head for pressure equalization in case of a passing tornado. The face itself is 15 feet long. The arms, with a spread of 65 feet between fingertips, suggest the crucifixion. The representation of Christ was built completely by hand, constructed of 24 layers of white mortar on a steel frame. The robes and hair were sculpted by workmen on scaffolds who built an elevator so that they could reach the higher segments of the statue. The statue was dedicated on June 25, 1966, although the folds of the robe took an additional three weeks to complete. Visible from a distance of 20 miles, the silhouette of Christ of the Ozarks appears to be a large white cross. It is visible from most anywhere in the area, particularly in winter, and from the rooftop deck of Dr. Baker's Lounge at the Crescent Hotel.

Eddie Mae Herron Center (870-892-4433; www.herroncenter.org), 1708 Archer Street, Pocahontas. Open Monday through Saturday 10–3, but it never hurts to call first to make sure someone's there. This center is more than a museum; it is also an education center, a community center, and a heritage and culture center. It preserves

FAYE JONES'S THORNCROWN CHAPEL IS A POPULAR WEDDING VENUE

ST. ELIZABETH'S CATHOLIC CHURCH   ARKANSAS DEPARTMENT OF PARKS & TOURISM

nearly 200 years of African American history in Randolph County, Arkansas. Through photographs, displays, books, and the spoken memories of the people who grew up around the old building and now care for it, the center works to tell the story of the African American past in the county, preserving that heritage for future generations of the local community and any visitors lucky enough to pass this way. It is housed in the former St. Mary's Church/Pocahontas Colored School, an unadorned, one-room frame building constructed in 1919, and was named for Miss Eddie Mae, who taught at the black school from 1948 to 1965. The center's Black History Month activities are widely recognized as the most comprehensive in the state.

St. Elizabeth's Catholic Church (479-253-2222), 30 Crescent Drive, Eureka Springs. Open 24/7 year-round. Listed in *Ripley's Believe It or Not*, this church is the only one in the world that is entered through the bell tower. It began as a chapel that Richard Kerens built in memory of his mother. According to a 1907 article in the *Arkansas Traveler*, the chapel was completed in 1906. Kerens was one of the builders of the Crescent Hotel and also donated the land for the Carnegie Library. Eventually, he built St. Elizabeth's Catholic Church, which was dedicated in 1909. The church is connected to the chapel and replaced the Catholic Church that was on Fairmont Street. Free.

Thorncrown Chapel (479-253-7401; www.thorncrown.com), 12968 US 62 West, Eureka Springs. Open April through November, daily 9–5, occasionally closing at 3:30 p.m. for special events; March and December, 11–4. Closed January and February. This majestic glass and wood-beam chapel nestled in the Ozark Mountains was designed by Arkansas native E. Fay Jones, a nationally honored and recognized architect. The chapel was chosen in 2001 as one of the top 10 buildings of the twentieth century by the American Institute of Architects. It also won the institute's Design of the Year for 1981 and Design of the Decade for the 1980s. This stunning chapel is the perfect place to give thanks for Nature's abundance as she joins you for a seat at the altar. You are welcome to come out for services, held on Sundays at 9 a.m. and 11 a.m., April through October. During November through the third week in December, there is one service at 11 a.m. Services last approximately one hour and include inspirational music and biblically based preaching.

HISTORIC SITES **Rush Historic District** (870-741-5443; www.nps.gov/buff), AR 14 South, Yellville. Open daily 8:30–4:30. Watch the video about this 1,300-acre zinc-mining town dating from the mid-1880s to the mid-1930s. The site has hiking trails with interpretive exhibits. Often referred to as a ghost town, the site along the Buffalo River is now protected by the federal government.

✳ To Do

FISHING **Bear Creek Springs Trout Farm** (870-741-6031), 350 DeVito's Loop, Harrison. Call for an appointment. The Ozarks is trout country, and if you have kids or you are looking for a sure thing, try Bear Creek Springs Trout Farm. Kids love watching the water boil as these beautiful rainbow trout work into a frenzy while trying to hop on your hook! No license is required and there is no limit. Bait and tackle are furnished, and your catch can be cleaned and packed on ice. You only pay for what you catch.

GOLF **Big Creek Golf Club** (870-425-0333; www.bigcreekgolf.com), 452 Country Club Drive, Mountain Home. Call for current course hours. In 2008, this 200-acre course received a five-star rating by *Golf Digest* for the third consecutive year and was rated first by the publication in several categories. It has been rated the number one public-access course by a leading Arkansas business publication for four years straight. The diversity of the hole layouts makes this 7,320-yard, 18-hole course challenging and

CATCHING DINNER AT BEAR CREEK SPRINGS TROUT FARM

enjoyable. The 15,000-square-foot clubhouse includes a fine dining room, a casual grill and bar, a fully stocked pro shop, and men's and women's locker rooms. The club also has two tennis courts and a large resort-style pool. Twilight rates are $55 after 1 p.m. and $45 after 3 p.m. Greens fees are seasonal; summer rates for play are $69 weekdays, $79 weekends and holidays. Appearance counts—no denim, guys must have collars and sleeves, ladies must wear appropriate casual tops, and golf shoes must have non-metal spikes. The club sells libations, so please leave yours at home.

Mark Martin Museum (1-800-566-5561; www.markmartinmuseum.com), 1601 Batesville Boulevard, Batesville. No, your GPS isn't off, it is located within a Ford dealership; what seems at first an unlikely locale makes terrific sense once you are drawn into its exhibits. This state-of-the-art facility features six exhibits built around, and featuring, pivotal vehicles driven by Martin during his stellar career. The multimedia displays mix interviews and race footage with film spoofs and a mock music video, creating an experience that is both informative and entertaining whether you are a Mark Martin fan, NASCAR aficionado, or just traveling with one. Centered among murals are the vehicles: the No. 6 Viagra Coca-Cola 600 win car, the '90 Folgers Thunderbird, the No. 60 Winn-Dixie Busch car, the 2005 IROC car that Martin used to win his record fifth championship, and the '89 Stroh's Thunderbird. Several helmets and historic fire suits, trophies, and other memorabilia are also on display. A retail area stocks souvenirs featuring Martin and the NASCAR logo. Take advantage of an opportunity to explore Batesville, the second-oldest town in the state, rich in history and often listed among the best small towns in the country by national travel and retirement guides. Its place on the shores of the White River fueled the town's economy, from the steamboats that motored goods on its surface to the world-class fish hiding in its clear depths. Explore its history by visiting one of its museums, touring its historic downtown, or driving residential areas populated with examples of architecture from every decade since the 1840s. Call for admission times and prices.

SAILING **Castaway Sailing on Beaver Lake** (479-684-9339; www.castawaysailing .com), US 62, Eureka Springs. There is just no topping the experience of gliding across the sparkling waters of Beaver Lake sailing aboard the 34-foot *Defiance*. All charters are private and include a licensed professional captain. Schedule a leisure trip for your group or learn to sail. Appointments are available March through November. Eagle-watching tours and corporate team-building charters are available year-round. Reserve by the hour, half day, or full day. Private hourly charters are offered at scheduled times and cost $25 per person per hour, with a $125 minimum. Half-day charters are also scheduled by appointment and are $20 per person per hour, with a $150 minimum. Call for a special rate for a full-day (10–5) charter.

SPAS **Gryphon's Roost Day Spa & Gallery** (1-877-807-5667; www.gryphonsroost.com), 137 Spring Street, Eureka Springs. Gryphon's Roost is about inner and outer relaxation. Beautiful art and a peaceful environment almost seem to fill a void left in the mind once the massage soothes the body. The private, secluded outdoor hot tub with beautiful views is offered with and without massage ($55 for half-hour soak and half-hour massage). Or you can substitute the soak in the tub with time in the cedar and stained-glass sauna. Couples' facilities are also available. Aromatherapy massage, herbal body wrap, facials, skin care treatments for men and women, and reflexology are part of a head-to-toe menu of pampering from which to choose. Gryphon's Roost also offers an extensive selection of salon products for purchase in their gift shop, including essential oils (used in aromatherapy massage); stone elixirs; essence lotions; music for relaxation, meditation, and inspiration; as well as books on health, healing, and spirituality.

New Moon Day Spa and Salon (800-599-9772), 75 Prospect Avenue, Eureka Springs. Open Sunday through Thursday 9–6, Friday and Saturday 9–7. New Moon is located in the garden level of the historic Crescent Hotel. Elegance and history add to the tranquil environment of this full service, modern salon that offers a full range of spa and beauty treatments. Facials, massages, body treatments, peels, microdermabrasion, teeth whitening, and mud wraps are just a few of the services offered here. Spa guests are welcome to make a day of it by taking advantage of the sauna, hot tub, gardens, pool, and relaxation area on-site. Check the website for spa specials with, and without, lodging at the hotel included.

Serendipity Day Spa & Salon (870-204-6650), 205 West Ridge, Harrison. Open Monday through Friday 9–5, with evening appointments available. Serendipity Day Spa is a full-service salon and spa just one block from the Hotel Seville. Located in a Victorian-era home, the layout, design, and craftsmanship on the interior provide the perfect complement to spa services. Serendipity Day Spa & Salon offers manicures and pedicures, hot stone massage, Swedish and deep tissue massage, facials, waxing, and makeup. Call for pricing and special promotions.

Spa at Grand Central (479-283-4376; eurekagrand.com/spa), 37 North Main Street, Eureka Springs. Services and techniques include full-body massage, paraffin dips, muscle tension release, facials, essential oil delight, herbal wraps, reflexology, and Body Glo. A full-service hair salon specializes in custom cuts and color, and will gladly see you without an appointment. Their line of salon products, made locally, is available for purchase in their gift shop. Grand Central also packages lodging at the Grand Central Hotel with spa services that will let you save a little money on both. They offer a two-night stay in a Royal Suite that includes two 1-hour massages and two half-hour moisturizing facials for $525, including taxes but not gratuity.

Suchness Spa Rituals (479-253-2828; www.suchnessspa.com), 63 Spring Street, Eureka Springs. Located in the historic New Orleans Hotel in downtown Eureka Springs, Suchness has a definite New Age emphasis in the services they deliver. Their menu includes the signature Suchness Massage, Crown Chakra Lightwork, Thai Herbal Steam and Lotus Shower, Glow Rituals, Body Cocoon Rituals, Facial Ritual, and Hands and Feet Ritual. They can even provide a minister for wedding services if needed.

TOURS *Belle of the Ozarks* (1-800-552-3803; www.estc.net/belle), 354 CR 146 (Starkey Park at end of Mundell Road), Eureka Springs. Open seasonally May through October, sailing daily (closed Wednesday) at 11 a.m., 1 p.m., and 3 p.m. The *Belle* also schedules an additional evening cruise at 6 p.m., Memorial Day through Labor Day. The 75-minute cruise on this excursion boat will take you on a 12-mile cruise around scenic Beaver Lake while the ship's captain fills you in on the sights you see and the area history. The tour includes several local landmarks: Beaver Dam, Indian burial grounds, the Lost Bridge area, White House Bluff, a submerged homestead, and a 200-acre game preserve. Eagle watch cruises are added during the month of October. Admission is $17 for adults and $7.50 for kids 12 and under.

Eureka Springs Ghost Tours (479-253-6800), 44 Prospect, Eureka Springs. Office opens at 7:15 p.m., tour begins at 8 p.m. Tickets are available 30 minutes prior to tour time. It is widely reported that Eureka Springs has a fairly strong contingent of out-of-body residents who like to make their presence known. In fact, the television show *Ghost Hunters* kicked off their fall season a few years ago with their investigation of the Crescent Hotel. It included their first-ever footage that seemed to show one of these ethereal residents in the former morgue of the hotel. Tours are conducted by two mediums who have also conducted paranormal investigations of the hotel. Tickets for the Crescent Hotel tour are $18 for adults and $7 for children 5 and under. A second tour

GREERS FERRY DAM WAS DEDICATED BY PRESIDENT JOHN F. KENNEDY IN 1963

of the City Cemetery is also offered. Tickets are $15 for adults and $7 for kids under 5 (kids under the age of 16 must be accompanied by an adult).

Eureka Springs & North Arkansas Railway (479-253-9623; www.esnarailway.com), 299 Main, AR 23 North, Eureka Springs. The train runs Tuesday through Saturday, April through October; departures are at 10:30 a.m., noon, 2 p.m., and 4 p.m. (provided a minimum number of passengers is onboard). Trains also run on Sundays on Memorial Day and Labor Day weekends. From the first rumble of the engine and clanging of the bell to call boarders, it's an exciting adventure and the ultimate nostalgia trip right down to the last blowing of the horn. On the Excursion Train, you can chat with the conductor and crew while switching operations are explained. The collection of vintage rolling stock at ES&NA is one of the Ozarks' largest, and the authentic railroad memorabilia here re-creates the turn-of-the-century era and gives you a taste of how it was when rail service brought the first visitors to Eureka Springs in 1883. A ride on the rails is both fun and educational for the whole family. Passage for adults is $12; kids ages 4–10 are $6; kids under age 4 (with accompanying adult) are free.

Ghost Tour—Downtown Eureka Springs—Basin Park Hotel (1-800-643-4972; www.basinpark.com), 12 Spring Street, Eureka Springs. Tours are offered Tuesday through Saturday at 8 p.m. The paranormal tour of the Basin Park Hotel and downtown Eureka Springs provides a unique history lesson into what was once a bustling Wild West town. The Haunting Tales of Downtown Eureka Springs and Ghosts of The Basin Park Hotel tour is a chance to learn more about the many tales and fascinating stories of the history of downtown Eureka Springs as well as possibly witness and/or capture our next ghost story on film. Tickets are available at the front desk of the 1905 Basin Park Hotel located in the hub of downtown Eureka Springs at 12 Spring Street. There are no reservations, so come early because space is limited. Still and video cameras are encouraged. The tour is $15 per adult and $7 for children under the age of 9. The tour begins inside the 1905 Basin Park Hotel and continues to Basin Spring Park and along historic Spring Street.

Southern Pride Carriage Tours (870-749-2665), Crescent Hotel, 75 Prospect Avenue, Eureka Springs. Days and hours vary with season. Spring and fall, tours are scheduled Thursday through Monday at 5 p.m.; summer tours start at 6 p.m. All tours are subject to cancellation due to bad weather. Enjoy old-fashioned carriage tours of historic Eureka Springs in a charming white carriage pulled by draft horses. Based at the Crescent Hotel, tours last approximately 30 minutes.

✳ Green Space

Pivot Rock and Natural Bridge (479-253-8860; www.eurekasprings.org), 1708 Pivot Rock Road, Eureka Springs. One of the more interesting geological features in Eureka Springs has been around for so long that it has attained historic status—as an attraction! Pivot Rock is one of several unique natural formations at Pivot Rock Park, located on Pivot Rock Road off Highway 62 West in Eureka Springs. First developed as a tourist attraction more than 100 years ago, the park features paved pathways winding through unique rock formations and the beautiful natural mountain scenery of the Ozarks. According to legend, however, the deep ravines and caves of the park attracted a different kind of visitor during the years after the Civil War. Tradition holds that this was one of the many hideouts of the outlaw Jesse James and the James–Younger Gang, the notorious band of Old West train and bank robbers. One bit of advice: the walk out the paved trail to Pivot Rock is a bit strenuous, so take your health into consideration before you make the attempt. Also, for some reason some visitors find the park a little hard to find, so—as the signs say—just make sure you follow Pivot Rock Road ALL the way to the end.

Quigley's Castle (479-253-8311; www.quigleyscastle.com), AR 23 South, Eureka Springs. Open April through October, 8:30–5; closed Sunday and Thursday. This fascinating family home, built in 1943, is listed on the National Register of Historic Places. Quigley's Castle is the dream home of Elise Quigley (1910–84), featuring her perennial garden of over 400 varieties of flowers. The garden paths wind around secluded benches, a lily pond, and birdbaths, up to her home that she beautifully covered with stones she'd collected since childhood. Tropical plants grow in the natural soil of the first floor and brush the ceiling of the second. A butterfly, fossil, crystal, arrowhead, and glassware collection encompasses an entire wall in a second-floor bedroom. Elise's grandchildren conduct tours of the home and will gladly share the story of how this unusual place came to be. Admission is $6.50 per adult. Children 14 and under with a parent are free.

✳ Wild Places

Fred Berry Conservation Education Center on Crooked Creek (870-449-3484; www.fredberrycec.com), 851 Conservation Lane, Yellville. One of four Arkansas Game and Fish Education Centers, open Monday through Friday 8:30–4:30. The 421 Ozark acres that constitute FBCEC lie in a 2.75-mile crook of Crooked Creek just above Kelley's access. The property, a former dairy farm, is now the site of a joint conservation education project between the Arkansas Game and Fish Foundation and the Arkansas Game and Fish Commission. The Creek Bottom Trail, a 2.5-mile loop on the floodplain, provides easy access to the creek for fishing or wildlife watching. The Woodland Edge

LUNKER LABS—ARKANSAS'S NATIONAL FISH HATCHERIES

Thirty-five states in the country hold 70 national fish hatcheries; Arkansas is home to 3 of them: Mammoth Spring, Norfork, and Greers Ferry. Arkansas's role in the conservation, protection, and enhancement of the fish population nationwide is key. Arkansas is the systems leader in trout production and has the only Gulf Coast striped bass facility in the world.

Mammoth Spring National Fish Hatchery (MSNFH), located in Mammoth Spring, was the first national hatchery established in Arkansas, dating back to 1903, making it one of the oldest in the country. Mammoth Spring is the seventh-largest spring in the United States and the largest in Arkansas. The hatchery is involved in the restoration of paddlefish, sturgeon, walleye, smallmouth and largemouth bass, bluegill, and Gulf Coast striped bass—the only captive spawning population in the world. Annually, the MSNFH is responsible for stocking an average of 40,000 paddlefish, 2,500 sturgeon, 400,000 walleye, 100,000 smallmouth bass, 100,000 largemouth bass or bluegills, 5,000 freshwater mussels, and 2 million striped bass.

Norfork National Fish Hatchery (NNFH) is a cold-water facility located near Mountain Home on the Norfork River. Norfork Dam (completed in 1944) and Bull Shoals Dam (completed in 1951) increased the need for this hatchery, which was established in 1955 and opened on August 15, 1957. NNFH is the highest-producing federal hatchery and the largest trout hatchery in the country. Annually, it released more than 2 million rainbow, cutthroat, and brown trout.

Greers Ferry National Fish Hatchery, another cold-water facility, is located in Heber Springs and was established in 1965 to mitigate the Greers Ferry Dam's impact on the Little Red River. Cold hatchery water comes from 100 feet below the reservoir surface and has an average temperature of 44 to 56 degrees. Flowing through the hatchery at 15,000 gallons per minute, the water is ideal for raising rainbow and brook trout. Annually, 1 million trout are released for stocking, with an average of 182,000 released back into the Little Red River.

Trail is the newest addition. The 1-mile loop is wheelchair accessible for 0.6 mile. Call for additional trail information. Birding and butterfly checklists are available at the on-site education building. Free.

Ponca Elk Education Center (870-861-2432; www.poncaeec.com), AR 43, 0.25 mile from intersection with AR 74. Open Thursday through Monday 10:30–4:30. Elk are one of the largest members of the deer family in North America, and many of us associate this animal with western states. However, the eastern elk was a native of the Natural State. Unfortunately, this subspecies disappeared from our state after 1840, and for almost a hundred years, a bugling elk could not be heard throughout the hills of Arkansas. Between 1981 and 1985, elk were reintroduced to the Buffalo River area and have become one of Arkansas's most successful reestablishment programs. The center houses an exhibit area focusing on elk ecology, wildlife, and area information. The building also contains classrooms for school and civic group use. It is an excellent Watchable Wildlife area with large shaded decks with bird feeders and an Ozark stream behind the center. Free admission.

CAVES **Blanchard Springs Caverns** (1-888-757-2246; www.fs.usda.gov/osfnf), Blanchard Springs Caverns is located 15 miles northwest of Mountain View off AR 14. Open daily 9:30–6. It should come as no surprise that in a land reported to hold over 4,500 caves, a king of caves would be found, and Blanchard Springs Caverns is definitely it. Dubbed by *Life* magazine as "one of the most extraordinary finds of the century," this living cave is constantly in the process of formation. Two paved, lighted

THE ARKANSAS SAFARI—TURPENTINE CREEK WILDLIFE REFUGE

Turpentine Creek Wildlife Refuge (479-253-5841; www.turpentinecreek.org), 239 Turpentine Creek Lane, Eureka Springs. Open every day except Christmas 9–6; winter hours are 9–5. Turpentine Creek is my favorite place in all of Arkansas. This 450-acre rescue facility houses over 120 big cats, plus a host of other animals, providing a lifetime home and refuge. The management and staff who rescue, rehabilitate, and then care for these animals are basically volunteers who live on the property. You will never see healthier or happier animals as you will see here. There is a sound called chuffing that tigers make when they are happy that is similar in nature, if not the same sound, as a cat purring. Only the newbies aren't chuffing here, and when they do, it is considered an important benchmark in their recovery. Education of humans is an important element in the refuge's mission, as humans create the necessity of a lifetime sanctuary to protect these animals. Tigers are social creatures, and once they bond with humans they will long for human contact for the rest of their lives, so release back into the wild is not really in their best interests. One of the refuge's founders, Tanya Smith, tells a story of one of the first cats rescued by her father and their attachment to each other. Her dad's health didn't let him visit the refuge for over a year, but once the tiger heard his voice, he bawled for his attention.

Turpentine works constantly to raise money for more habitats to house new neighbors, but an ever-growing list of animals in desperate situations means their work is never done. A compound near the visitor center houses bears, lions, and the younger cats. A small petting zoo here has a pot-bellied pig, goats, and sheep. The natural habitats are beyond the compound, spread over a lush hillside where many of the animals walk on natural turf for the first time in their lives. Each animal's biography is posted outside their enclosures, including details of their rescue in many cases. Check out Turpentine's website for endearing videos of the release of various cats into their new habitats. You can also keep up with the refuge's twins, Mack and B. B. King, born here in summer of 2008 when the refuge rescued their mother. I was lucky to be in the first public group to meet the little guys; their eyes were not even open at the time. They are much bigger now, but I still recognize them from that first day. Visit this refuge, and I will bet you dollars to doughnuts you will also be enchanted with them and their work. They can use your help; annual operating expenses exceed $1 million, making fund-raising a critical issue for their ability to survive. You can adopt a cat and keep up with them year-round and help support their care. A gift shop sells the refuge's annual calendar and various cat-related gear. You'll be chuffing yourself by the time you leave. Admission for adults is $15; kids, seniors, and military get in for $10.

trails, one of which is handicapped accessible with assistance, are open to visitors of all ages. Led by knowledgeable Forest Service guides, the tour winds through water-carved passages that include an underground river and the world's largest flowstone. The Wild Cave Tour is available by special arrangement for more adventuresome explorers. The spring itself pours out of the mountain into Mirror Lake, a great place to fish for rainbow trout. Nearby is a short, scenic walk to the falls where all water exits the caverns. This is one of the prettiest spots in the Ozark National Forest and not to be missed.

Three tours are offered. The Dripstone Trail takes you through the Cathedral Room, which is the size of three football fields, and the Coral Room, where pure calcite, or calcium carbonate, makes up limestone. The Discovery Trail navigates the routes of the early explorers, passing through their campsites. Before you leave, discover the colorful Ghost Room and the giant flow-stone, one of the largest on earth. The Wild Cave Tour is for the true adventurer. Explore undeveloped sections of the cavern's middle level. Climb steep slopes, crawl on your hands and knees, pass under low ceilings, and travel through red clay. End your tour at the Titans, a group of spectacular columns that you'll have to see to believe. The caverns are also the site of one of the most moving Christmas pageants in Arkansas, Caroling in the Caverns. Blanchard's Cathedral Room is the site for traditional folk Christmas music, its natural acoustics providing the perfect accompaniment for a hauntingly beautiful performance. Rates for the Dripstone and Discovery tours are $10.50 per adult and $5.50 for kids 6–15. The Wild Cave Tour is $75.50 per person with a $25 nonrefundable deposit. Tickets to Caroling in the Caverns performances are $17.

CAVING IN THE OZARKS

Cosmic Cavern (870-749-2298; www.cosmiccavern.com), 6386 AR 21 North, Berryville. Open daily 9–5 spring, fall, and winter; 9–6 summer. Cosmic Cavern, at 64 degrees, is the warmest cave in the Ozarks. Tours are offered every 25 minutes in spring and summer, and every 45 minutes in winter and fall. You will see two bottomless cave lakes during your 75-minute tour, with one having cave trout in the clear, dark waters. The first lake, South Lake, has had trout in it for nearly 50 years. Some trout have gone blind and most have lost their color. The bottoms of these lakes have yet to be found. Cosmic Cavern has been named as one of the top 10 show caves in the United States, so don't forget your camera, as there are several photo opportunities throughout the cave. During the tour, you can see the newly discovered Silent Splendor area, which has been hailed as a must-see in Arkansas. It houses one of the longest soda straw formations in the Ozarks, measuring over 9 feet! As you journey along the inspected and safe walkways, you will see many unique and beautiful formations of stalactites, stalagmites, flowstones, soda straws, helictites, cave bacon, draperies, and many other speleothems along the cave routes. Among the awesome cave formations you will also get a chance to see a rare and threatened salamander, the Ozark blind cave salamander. Admission for adults (ages 13 and up) is $14; children (ages 5–12) are $7.50; 4 years and under are free.

Mystic Caverns (1-888-743-1739; www.mysticcaverns.com), AR 7 South, Harrison. Seasonal hours vary, so call ahead. Here you have two of the most spectacular caves in the Ozarks—Mystic Cavern and Crystal Dome Cavern—at one location. Although their entrances are only 400 feet apart, Crystal Dome was discovered more than 100 years after Mystic. Guided tours begin in Mystic and retrace steps early settlers first took in the 1850s. Crystal Dome showcases an 8-foot-high dome in pristine condition, a rock museum, and a gift shop. You get quite a price break if you purchase tickets to both: adults (13 and older) $14.99 each; kids (ages 4–12) $6.99. Tickets for one cavern are $12.99 for adults and $5.99 for kids.

Onyx Cave (479-253-9321; onyxcaveeurekasprings.com), US 62 East, Eureka Springs. Call for hours and rates. This small show cave located about 6 miles east of Eureka Springs has been a tourist attraction since 1893, making it the oldest show cave in Arkansas. While it does not contain true onyx, it does have a kind of flowstone called cave onyx, which has a similar appearance. During the nineteenth century and the beginning of the 20th, many caves were named Onyx Cave, which makes it difficult to keep them straight. Tours are not guided but are given by headsets, which receive short-range FM transmissions from small boxes that alert tourists to chambers and rock formations such as Friendly Dragon, Witches' Fireplace, and the Lion's Head. Since the cave has only one public opening, visitors must exit the cave the way they entered. The cave stays at an average temperature of 57 degrees Fahrenheit year-round. Most of the cave is not toured.

PARKS **Bull Shoals-White River State Park** (870-445-3629; www.arkanasstateparks .com/bullshoalswhiteriver), 153 Dam Overlook Lane, Bull Shoals. The visitor center is open daily 8–5, with extended hours during spring and summer months. Talk about prime real estate. Arkansas's seventh state park, Bull Shoals-White River State Park, is sitting on a sweet spot between two of Arkansas's most prized recreational assets, its namesakes: Bull Shoals Lake and the White River. The US Army Corps of Engineers built 2,256-foot-long Bull Shoals Dam in 1951 as part of a massive damming project on the White, an effort to institute flood control on the river and generate power. Bull Shoals Lake is a fortuitous recreational by-product of that flood relief system.

The James A. Gaston Visitor Center's vantage point overlooks the lake, the dam, and the river, providing the perfect outdoor classroom for interpretation about all three. Interpretive exhibits are featured throughout the lobby, gift shop, Johnboat Theater, and Exhibit Hall, a 1,720-square-foot area filled with images of the river, lake, and dam. These state-of-the art exhibits and the video presentation in the theater tell about the histories and fisheries these renowned waters hold. The center also includes an observation tower, gift shop, two classrooms, and park offices.

The 732-acre park has lakeside and riverside facilities. The lakeshore section is a day-use area with picnic tables, a playground, and the 1-mile Lakeside Trail. The main section of the park is on the river below Bull Shoals Dam. It features campsites for tent camping or recreational vehicles, bathhouses, a sanitary trailer dump station, picnic areas, a pavilion, playgrounds, trails, a gift shop, a boat ramp, and a trout dock offering supplies, equipment, and boat, motor, and canoe rentals. Park interpreters conduct several programs from the shores of the lake and the river when telling the area's story. You can take a 90-minute johnboat float trip on the river, a party barge tour, or an interpretive canoe or kayak tour. Rates for the johnboat tour are based on the number of people in the boat. Party barge tours are $8.50 per adult and $4.50 per child. Kayak tours are $15 for adults, while kids glide for $7.50 each. You can also rent watercraft for independent exploration at the park's marina. If you have your own motor or really strong arms, a motorless boat is $38 for a half day and $48 for the whole day. Add a motor for about $60 per day more. Paddle the park's shoreline in a canoe ($20/day) or kayak ($25/day), or float the river for $55 a day. That includes your shuttle back to the park. The trails concealed within the Ozark landscape that surrounds the park beckon to mountain bikers, so the park kindly rents mountain bikes by the hour ($6.50) and the day ($33.50), and a few options in between. Camping opportunities along the river are abundant; the park's 103 campsites run the gamut of lodging available in an Arkansas state park. Starting at the top, Bull Shoals has three of the Rent-an-RV ($85) packages; one Rent-A-Camp package ($40/day includes use of a platform tent, two cots, camp stove, cooler, and light), and every class of campsite from AAA ($34/day) to the bare-bones sites with no hook-up ($13/day).

Davidsonville Historic State Park (870-892-4708; www.arkansasstateparks.com /davidsonville), 7953 AR 166 South, Pocahontas. There is a mystery that surrounds old Davidsonville. Established in 1815, the town included the Arkansas Territory's first post office, courthouse, and land office. It is known that the town's decline was a result of being bypassed by the Southwest Trail, a critical commercial artery that meant life or death to fledgling towns. But what is not known is what caused its remaining residents to leave behind personal effects that were in perfect condition. Today, archaeologists are uncovering remarkable finds of streets, foundations, and objects that tell a fascinating story of life on the Arkansas frontier following the Louisiana Purchase. Park exhibits and interpretive tours provide information about this important frontier town. Fishing is a major activity here today. The park borders the Black River (boat launch ramp) and a 12-acre fishing lake (no launch ramp), offering a barrier-free fishing pier, fishing boats (trolling motors only), pedal boats, and canoes. Anglers may also choose from the nearby Spring and Eleven Point Rivers. Facilities include 30 campsites: 12 Class AAA ($34/day), 8 Class A ($27/day), and 10 tent ($13/day) sites; picnic areas; two standard pavilions (screened); playgrounds; four hiking trails, including a self-guided walking trail though the old town site; and a visitor center with exhibits and a gift shop.

Lake Charles State Park (870-878-6595; www.arkansasstateparks.com/lakecharles), 3705 AR 25, Powhatan. This recreational park rests on the banks of 645-acre Lake Charles. The spring-fed lake in the Ozark foothills offers a good opportunity to snag bass, crappie, bream, and catfish in a peaceful setting. Pitch your tent at one of 57 campsites (22 Class AAA and 35 Class B), or take advantage of the convenient RV or cozy yurt that is permanently set up and equipped for roughing it the easy way. The Class AAA sites are $34/day and the Class B sites are $22. Within walking distance are picnic sites, hiking trails, a standard pavilion (screened with ceiling fans), launch ramp, swimming beach, and playground. The visitor center's gift shop offers gift items, camping supplies, and snacks. Boat (and kayak) tours of the lake are led by park interpreters who will point out the plant and wildlife native to the area. Ninety-minute self-guided tours have also been mapped out for you for the price of a kayak ($10/solo, $15/ tandem). Boat tours are $7 for adults and $3.50 for kids; guided kayak tours are $10 for adults and $5 for kids.

Lake Leatherwood Park (479-253-7921; www.cityofeurekasprings.org), 532 Spring Street, Eureka Springs. This city park offers 1,600 acres of Ozark Mountain countryside with an 85-acre spring-fed lake, hiking, picnicking, walking trails, playground, camping, RV full hook-up, cabins with kitchenettes, and a small marina for boating, canoes, and paddleboats. Pets are welcome. The lake is formed by one of the largest hand-cut native limestone dams in the country. The dam and several structures at the park were built in the early 1940s by the WPA and are listed on the National Register of Historic Places. Open March 1 through mid-November.

LAKES **Bull Shoals Lake** (870-425-2700; www.swl.usace.army.mil/parks/bullshoals /index.html) and the White River below its dam are synonymous with fishing in Arkansas. There are 19 developed parks around the shoreline that provide campgrounds, boat launches, swim areas, and marinas, and the 60,000 acres of public land surrounding it provide a variety of other opportunities. The US Army Corps of Engineers project, located in north-central Arkansas on the Missouri-Arkansas state line, enjoys a wide reputation for lunker bass fishing along with its twin, Lake Norfork, just to the east. Bull Shoals Dam was completed by the US Army Corps of Engineers in 1951. It is the fifth-largest concrete dam in the United States. Including the portion located in Missouri, the lake totals some 45,500 surface acres, with almost 1,000 miles of rugged shoreline open to visitors.

The parks developed on the lake's shore have both camping and picnicking facilities. There are grills, firewood, tables, and drinking water at the picnic sites. Commercial docks on the lake have boats, motors, and guides for hire. Waterskiing and swimming are popular at Bull Shoals, as is cruising the hundreds of miles of lake arms and coves by motorboat or sailboat. Scuba divers come to Bull Shoals from many states to enjoy their sport in the blue water.

Greers Ferry Lake (501-362-9067; www.swl.usace.army.mil/parks/greersferry), Heber Springs. At the foot of Round Mountain in the beautiful Ozark Mountains of north-central Arkansas stands Greers Ferry Dam, which formed the lake when it was completed in 1964. The lake and dam were dedicated in 1963 by President John F. Kennedy, his last public appearance before the fateful trip to Dallas. With over 30,000 acres of water surface, the lake serves as a playground for all kinds of water sports. The 18 parks on the shoreline provide modern campgrounds, boat launches, swim areas, and marinas. Greers Ferry Lake offers great walleye fishing and excellent crappie fishing. In fact, every game fish native to the state has been stocked in the clear waters of the lake by the Arkansas Game and Fish Commission. A rainbow trout hatchery is in operation and furnishes the trout for stocking and fishing in the lake and below the dam in the Little Red River. Record fish catches are a common occurrence at Greers Ferry, which abounds in game fish such as bream, channel catfish, rainbow trout, and largemouth and white bass.

Norfork Lake (870-425-2700; www.swl.usace.army.mil/parks/norfork) offers more than 550 miles of shoreline and some 22,000 acres of outdoor recreation options. There are 19 developed parks that provide plenty of opportunities for camping and water sports. Developed parks offer campsites that range from rustic to modern, with electrical hook-ups, playgrounds, group picnic shelters, designated swimming areas, and boat-launching ramps. Fees are charged for the use of some facilities. With wide-open, breezy stretches for sailing and quiet, secluded coves for skiing and swimming, the clear and uncrowded waters of Norfork are ideal for scuba diving, attracting divers from throughout the central United States. The wooded and undeveloped shoreline allows for ample room to enjoy the hills and hollows. Concessionaire-operated marinas provide boat and motor rental, fuel, and other related supplies and services. The Robinson Point National Recreation Trail and the Norfork section of the Ozark Trail enable nature observers and photographers to view the Ozark Mountains through the change of seasons. You can fish for all varieties of freshwater game fish in the lake, which is fed by the North Fork (also called Norfork) River and its tributaries. Bass, walleye, crappie, bream, and catfish all make their home in its waters. The oldest of Arkansas's large man-made impoundments, Norfork has consistent variety in its fishing. Lake Norfork contains one of the best striped bass fisheries in Arkansas. The lake is stocked annually, and stripers over 40 pounds are commonly taken. Many in the 30-pound class are caught every year.

The clear, blue water of 53,000-acre **Table Rock Lake** (417-334-4101; www.swl.usace .army.mil/parks/tablerock) extends from Branson, Missouri, to Eureka Springs. The US Army Corps of Engineers, which built and manages the lake, operates 13 campgrounds adjacent to it. Full-service marinas, fishing guides, and resorts are numerous. Resort rentals, a golf course, and other recreational amenities are available at Holiday Island near Eureka Springs.

✳ Lodging

WESTERN SALEM PLATEAU

BED & BREAKFAST INNS 5 Ojo Inn Bed & Breakfast (1-800-656-6734; www.5ojo .com), 5 Ojo Street, Eureka Springs. This upscale, historic bed & breakfast is situated on a large 1-acre wooded lot in the heart of Eureka Springs. This inn is well known for its three-course gourmet breakfasts and luxurious amenities. All rooms are elegantly appointed with period furniture, private baths, cable television, in-room refrigerators, coffee-makers, and high-speed Internet access. Nine rooms are equipped with two-person Jacuzzis; seven have fireplaces. You also have use of the outdoor hot tub on the inviting deck around the inn, and complimentary drinks and snacks. Wedding and other packages are available. Rates are seasonal and based on the day of the week, but generally range from $119–195 a night. The Tree Top Suite, which is billed as the largest B&B suite in town, has a sitting area, one bedroom, two baths, Jacuzzi, and fireplace, with rates ranging from $165 in off-season to $195. $$–$$$.

1884 Bridgeford House Bed & Breakfast (1-888-567-2422; www.bridgeford house.com), 263 Spring Street, Eureka Springs. Bedandbreakfastinn.com proclaimed this the best place to stay in Eureka Springs. Nicknamed "The Painted Lady," the 1884 Victorian inn has five guest rooms and is listed on the National Register of Historic Places. Located in the silk stocking district of Eureka, the Bridgeford's neighborhood is a favorite with walkers because of the stunning Victorian homes and gardens that line the street. Each of the inn's rooms features a private bath, private entrance, and cable television; some have Jacuzzis and fireplaces. A four-course gourmet breakfast is served daily, and freshly baked treats will be in your room in the afternoon. The inn's private decks afford beautiful views of Eureka Springs. $$–$$$.

Angel at Rose Hall Bed & Breakfast (1-800-828-4255; www.arkansasinn.com), 46 Hillside Avenue, Eureka Springs. This AAA Four Diamond award-winning, 7,000-sqare-foot Victorian mansion's romantic decor and spectacular condition make it a favorite with brides looking for an intimate setting for their wedding. The inn's spacious rooms are beautifully decorated with period antiques. King Jacuzzi tubs, fireplaces, balconies, and designer linens add to the pampered services for which this inn is known. Each room has its own elegant style, featuring king-sized beds, fresh flowers, and stained-glass windows. A full breakfast is served, and the inn's concierge service will gladly book shows, spa services, or just provide local directions and recommendations. Lodging packages are posted on the inn's website. This immaculate inn is located in the historic district of Eureka Springs. Rates are both seasonal and based on the days of the week you book. A premier king suite ranges between $165 and $219 a night. $$–$$$.

Arsenic and Old Lace Bed & Breakfast (1-800-243-5223; www.eureka springsromancebb.com), 60 Hillside Avenue, Eureka Springs. Luxury amenities in a romantic Victorian Queen Anne–style mansion make this inn a favorite for honeymooners. Each of the inn's five guest rooms has a private bath, whirlpool tub, private veranda, cable television, complimentary snacks, and fireplace. A gourmet breakfast from one of the inn's elegant menus will make you want to book another night. The inn can arrange golf privileges for you if want to hit the links while in town. An intimate parlor is a perfect site for nuptials. This inn does accept pets, but they need a reservation, too, before you travel. Room rates range from $115 to $259 nightly. $$–$$$.

1881 Crescent Cottage Inn (1-800-223-3246; www.1881crescentcottage inn .com), 211 Spring Street, Eureka Springs.

This bed & breakfast has four rooms with Jacuzzis. The beautiful property is part of Arkansas's political history as well as the town's. It was the home of Gen. Powell Clayton, first governor of Arkansas after the Civil War. Rooms are based on season and range from $109–149. $$–$$$.

Call of the Wild Bed & Breakfast (479-253-5841; www.turpentinecreek .org), 239 Turpentine Creek Lane, Eureka Springs. For a lodging experience unlike any other in the state, Turpentine Creek Wildlife Refuge has a purrfect opportunity for you. Stay on the grounds of America's premier big cat sanctuary and enjoy the wild sights and sounds of your feline neighbors. These lodging facilities vary from large, spacious rooms ($125) with oversized garden tubs and great views of the cats to a quaint, secluded tree house ($150) with its in-the-trees ambiance. Completely unique in the state is the Safari Lodge, with five cabins ($150/night) all decorated with fantastic art and adorned with incredible views of the mountains. Each cabin has its own theme corresponding with different regions of Africa—Congo, Kilimanjaro, Kalahari, Serengeti, Okavango. The Safari Lodge also has an incredible outdoor gas firepit along with an upscale hot tub. For those who travel with their second home on wheels or want to tent camp, Turpentine has an RV park and campground available, too. Amenities include electric, water, and sewer hook-up; picnic tables; and fire rings with grills attached. The cost is $25 (price does not include admission to the sanctuary). $–$$$.

Flatiron Flats (1-800-421-9615; www .eureka-net.com/flatiron), 25 Spring Street, Eureka Springs. Eureka Springs is packed with interesting architecture. In fact, a suburban ranch would stick out like a sore thumb in this town. But one candidate for most unusual structure, as well as the most recognizable building in town, is the Flatiron. Its triangular face, wedged between Spring and Center Streets, is truly ground zero in historic

downtown. Balconies on the Flatiron overlook both streets and are perfect for viewing the numerous parades (literally dozens annually) that wind their way around both sides of the building, offering you not one but two opportunities to enjoy your bird's-eye view. Your room is elegantly decorated with luxury linens, king beds, two-person Jacuzzi tubs, and fruit and wine baskets. As with all of Eureka lodging, rates are both seasonal and based on day of the week. Call for updated rates, but you can expect to spend between $125 and $175 per room. $$–$$$.

Heartstone Inn Bed & Breakfast (1-800-494-4921; www.heartstoneinn .com), 35 Kingshighway, Eureka Springs. This is a full-service luxury bed & breakfast located on the historic loop with six suites, three rooms, and two cottages, all with private baths and entrances. It offers a full gourmet breakfast at a private table, Jacuzzis, fireplaces, cable TV/DVDs with complimentary movies, Wi-Fi, golf privileges, afternoon refreshments, extensive decks and a gazebo, and off-street private parking. Small weddings can be arranged, and there is a massage therapy studio on the property. $$–$$$.

3 Oaks Country Bed & Breakfast (1-866-362-5722; www.3oaksbb.com), corner of AR 7 and Devore Road, Harrison. This B&B is a plantation farmhouse with three guest rooms nestled on 23 acres atop Kirk Mountain in the beautiful Ozark Mountains. At 3 Oaks, you will appreciate the down-home hospitality, hearty breakfasts, and peacefulness of country living. All bed & breakfast guest rooms have private bath and queen-sized bed, TV/VCR/DVD/CD, and clock radio. There is a parlor on the main floor where you can relax, read, and listen to music, or choose a movie from the extensive library. There are two verandas and an enclosed back porch to enjoy the beautiful Ozark hills and clean air. Room rates are based on the accommodations, as well as the season, ranging from $89–119 during the peak seasons to $69–99 during slower months. $–$$.

Queen Anne House (1-800-419-9907; www.queenannehouse.net), 610 West Central Avenue, Harrison. The Queen Anne House is an elegantly restored two-story Victorian home just blocks from Harrison's town square. A romantic ambiance permeates the property, with its gingerbread trim, stained-glass windows, beautiful gardens, large wraparound front porch with rockers, enclosed glass solarium, ornate fireplace, and period antiques. There is a 56-inch high definition TV with movie library in the parlor, high-speed Internet in the lobby, wireless Internet throughout the property, and free local calls. Guest rooms include either an infinity spa hot tub or claw foot tubs and showers. A traditional, hearty Southern breakfast is served daily. Complimentary evening desserts and beverages are provided. Several different price points for lodging are available, with and without breakfast. You can get a room for $35 without breakfast, all the way up to $125 per night for a luxurious three-room suite that includes it. Log on to the website or call the inn for details. $–$$$.

CABINS AND COTTAGES **Beaver Lakefront Cabins** (1-888-253-9210; www.beaverlakefrontcabins.com), 1234 County Road 120, Eureka Springs. These luxurious cabins have everything you could possibly want in a lakefront cabin, not to mention a mansion in your hometown. The cabins are elegantly decorated with custom cabinetry, trim, and doors, luxury linens, and that million-dollar view. Cabin amenities include romantic Jacuzzis for two overlooking the lake, 42-inch HDTVs, his-and-hers terry robes and slippers, complimentary DVD library with over 500 movies, fully equipped kitchens, pillow-top mattresses, continental breakfast provided daily, and free Wi-Fi. Walk-in showers with full-body massage showerheads, surround sound home entertainment systems, and

radiant floor heat are just a few of the cabins' elegant details. The property also offers upscale amenities you won't find just anywhere. An indoor, heated fishing area with underwater lighting will help you catch fish rain or shine, night or day. Complimentary pedal boats, a swim deck, and a covered picnic area are yours to enjoy on the lake. A 20-foot deluxe pontoon barge is available for rent if you want to venture farther offshore. Guests are also invited to take advantage of the challenging golf course at Holiday Island nearby. Cabin rates are seasonal and range from $200–245 a day off-season to $245–295 in-season. $$–$$$.

Beaver Lake Cottages (1-888-701-8439; www.beaverlakecottages.com), 2865 Mundell Road, Eureka Springs. These luxurious lakefront cottages feature contemporary, airy floor plans on the wooded shoreline of Beaver Lake. Each has a king-sized Sleep Number bed, glass and marble shower, TV with complimentary satellite and DVD player plus free library, Jacuzzi for two, and fireplace, and is very well equipped for housekeeping. Your cabin will come with all towels, linens, dishes, pots, pans, cooking spray, salt, pepper, sugar, sugar substitute, coffee, nondairy creamer, tea, hot chocolate, paper towels and napkins, full-sized kitchen appliances (including microwave, coffeemaker, toaster, mixer, and propane BBQ grill), candles and bubble bath for the Jacuzzi room, firewood and firewood starter (fireplaces closed May 15 through September 30 or first frost), and in-room phone for outgoing calls only. For your first night, they also provide beverages (your choice of wine or sparkling juice) and snacks, and for your first morning a continental breakfast of juice, pastries, and coffee. The seasonal daily rates range from a one-bedroom with Jacuzzi for $160–240 to a two-bedroom for $220–280, with various packages in between. $$–$$$.

Livingston Junction Cabooses & Depot (1-888-87TRAIN; www.estc.net /cabooses), 927 CR 222, Eureka Springs.

Livingston Junction Cabooses are recently restored, renovated, and decorated to create unique, cozy, comfortable, and nostalgic lodging. Each caboose has its own private driveway—fashioned to look like a railroad bed—and an outdoor hot tub on a large deck with outdoor furniture, a grill, and a hammock. The name Livingston Junction combines the name of the hollow viewed down below the cabooses and the intersection where the original railroad from Seligman, Missouri, headed south to Harrison and beyond. It spurs off to historic Eureka Springs. That same spur is used by the Eureka Springs & Northwest Arkansas Railway excursion train, so you can hear the steam engine chug. In the fall and winter, get a bird's-eye view of the railroad bridges and railroad junction. The cabooses rent for $95 a night. $$.

Rogue's Manor at Sweet Spring
(1-800-250-5827; www.roguesmanor .com), 124 Spring Street, Eureka Springs. Smith Truer, the rogue behind the manor, is a true Renaissance man if there ever was one. There is a wall-sized mural in the lounge at his restaurant depicting Smith and local celebrities in Middle Age garb, and Smith seems as suited for that era as this one. Elegant details are thickly layered throughout the decor of all his properties, and the bed & breakfast inn upstairs from the restaurant is no exception. Nooks and crannies mingle with vaulted ceilings for an interesting backdrop for fine antique furnishings. Fine dining is just downstairs, including steak, seafood, and BBQ. The four suites at Rogue's Manor each have a unique theme, a whirlpool tub for two, individual climate control, cable television, coffeemaker, and decks and balconies overlooking historic Eureka Springs, with in-room dinner and drinks from the restaurant available. Room rates range from $80–135 weekdays to $125–200 on weekends. Special event rates and packages are posted on the website, along with detailed descriptions of each of these original rooms. $$-$$$.

Texaco Bungalow & Bungalette
(1-888-253-8093; www.texacobungalow .com), 77 Mountain Street, Eureka Springs. A couple of the village's unique lodging options are the Texaco Bungalow and Bungalette, a renovated vintage 1930s art deco–style service station with two separate rental units. The Texaco Bungalow is located at the intersection of Mountain and White Streets in the historic residential district—within easy walking distance of fine restaurants, spas, and carriage rides. The former garage bays now compose the Bungalette. The rate for the Bungalow on weekend or single weekday is $139 a night. Two or more weekdays are $99 a night, excluding holidays or special events. Rates at the Bungalette are $99 a night weekends or single weekday. For two or more weekdays, rates are $79 a night. You can also rent both cottages for couples, girls' outings, or family for $209 a night. $$-$$$.

Treehouse Cottages (479-253-8667; www.treehousecottages.com), 165 West Van Buren, Eureka Springs. Six different units, each with its own decor and amenities, are suspended amid the canopy on the hillsides of Eureka Springs. All of the tree houses are more than 22 feet off the ground and have a stunning view of the beautiful surrounding forest. There are two unique locations: one is within walking distance of the beautiful downtown Eureka Springs historic district; the other is aloft in a pine forest just a mile away. In addition to the tree houses, there is also a two-story guest cottage that overlooks a terraced flower garden and features a hot tub on the deck. The rate is $145–165 per night, every night, year-round. Some of the room amenities include fresh flowers, complimentary snacks and beverages (including their famous homemade bread), champagne and chocolates for honeymoon and anniversary guests, fine linens and Egyptian cotton towels, and a free movie library for your enjoyment. $$-$$$.

HISTORIC HOTELS **1886 Crescent Hotel & Spa** (1-800-342-9766; www.crescent-hotel.com), 75 Prospect Avenue, Eureka Springs. Overlooking the entire Victorian village of Eureka Springs, the 1886 Crescent Hotel & Spa is a must-see in Eureka Springs. The all-encompassing view from Dr. Baker's Lounge is unmatched. Aside from the Christ of the Ozarks statue, there is no landmark that symbolizes this town as much as this hotel. It was lovingly restored when Marty and Elise Roenigk purchased it in 1997, pouring more than $12 million into its initial makeover. Before his tragic death in the summer of 2009, Marty Roenigk continued to invest in bringing the hotel back to its original splendor. A devoted preservationist, his legacy can be found all over the state, including War Eagle Mill, the Basin Park Hotel, and the Gavioli Chapel. Located in the historic district, which has more than 100 restored Victorian shops, restaurants, and galleries, the hotel retains its nineteenth-century character, from the Victorian-style Crystal Dining Room to the bold colors and antique furnishings in its guest rooms. The Governor's Suite is a truly unique offering among the luxurious options available. It consists of two spacious bedrooms with elegant furnishings and luxury beddings. A Jacuzzi bath will help you relax after a day of shopping or outdoor recreation. A balcony off the sitting room of the suite overlooks the garden and St. Elizabeth's Cathedral below. The resort boasts 12 acres of meticulous gardens, walking trails, and unsurpassed mountain views. Jacuzzi and penthouse suites provide the luxury of the grandest resorts, while the hotel has a wide offering of premium doubles, premium kings, and king balcony rooms. Fine dining is available in the award-winning Crystal Dining Room. Premium rooms are $149 a night; the Governor's Suite is $299. $$–$$$.

New Orleans Hotel & Spa (1-800-243-8630; www.neworleanshotelandspa.com), 63 Spring Street, Eureka Springs. The New Orleans Hotel offers the finest in luxury and elegance; it features king or queen beds, luxury baths with water jets, coffee service, and in-room refrigerators with sodas and bottled water. A small meeting room and reception area is available. Built in 1892, at the end of the Victorian era, the hotel reflects the charm and history of Eureka Springs as much as any place in town. The downtown location puts visitors on one of Arkansas's most popular walking and shopping streets. The entire downtown shopping district, including the New Orleans Hotel, is listed on the National Register of Historic Places. Suchness Spa is located on-site. Call for seasonal rates; standard rooms start at $99 per night. Spa and couples packages are featured on their website. $$.

Hotel Seville—An Ascend Hotel Collection Member (1-866-660-7136; www.hotelseville.com), 302 North Main Street, Harrison. This immaculately restored hotel has a polished entrance, upscale guest rooms with quality furnishings, LCD televisions, well-lit desk and work space, high-speed Internet (wired and wireless), and business services that remind you that you are in the twenty-first century. The immaculate decor and elegance that surround you make it hard to deny you are in a luxury hotel. What you may forget is that you are in the heart of the Ozarks, miles from a major metropolitan area. In addition to all the other great comforts and amenities, all rooms at the 1929 Hotel Seville include a continental breakfast ($–$$). The main hotel has 42 guest rooms and a Presidential Suite with parlor, wet bar, balcony, glass shower with dual heads and bench, and whirlpool tub. The suite annex adds 14 executive suites with seating area pullouts, multiple televisions, and finely appointed furnishings. This is the place in Harrison where locals gather to celebrate important milestones and marry off their kids. The historic hotel is adjacent to the downtown business district. John Paul's Restaurant & Gathering

Place, where the locals gather, is located in the hotel's lobby. Rates range from $71 for a standard room to $155 for a suite with a kingsize bed. $$–$$$.

RESORTS **Dinner Bell Ranch and Resort** (1-800-684-3324; www.dinnerbellranch andresort.com), 4462 County Road 302, Eureka Springs. Located on 140 peaceful and relaxing acres in the beautiful Winona Valley in the Ozark Mountains, all the new cabins are decorated with the cowboy and horse lover in mind. Each cabin at the Dinner Bell Ranch and Resort has its own theme and is complete with full kitchen, including dishes, coffeemaker, toaster, and glassware. You will also find a TV, a fireplace for cozy winter months, and an 8-by-30 deck to enjoy the dogwood trees blossoming in spring and the colorful fall foliage in autumn. Enjoy fresh homemade biscuits and muffins delivered to your door every morning. Kids and pets are more than welcome at the resort. Although smoking is not permitted in the cabins, the large covered deck on your cabin is available. Rates are $139–149 per night for two; kids 12 and under stay free. Horseback rides for both experienced riders and beginners are available. $$–$$$.

Horseshoe Canyon Ranch (1-800-480-9635; www.gohcr.com), AR 74 West, Jasper. Horseshoe Canyon sits on the most beautiful piece of land in the state, taking your breath away as you crest the hill at its gates. A western dude ranch with trail rides, hiking, and canoeing (in-season) on the Buffalo National River, Horseshoe Canyon is an outdoor playground for kids and adults alike. Your horse will be chosen with your particular needs in mind, so you can relax and enjoy each ride. The large bluffs surrounding the ranch inspire awe in all riders. As you ride through or past the wooded areas, chances are good that you'll catch a glimpse of some wildlife; deer, and turkeys are among the creatures seen regularly. There's also a possibility of coming up on a herd of Ozark Mountain goats kept to help out with the 350 acres of yard work. The ranch features guest amenities that include a hot tub, swimming pool, and fishing pond, as well as activities like rock climbing, shooting, campfires, cookouts, and a children's program. Sleeping arrangements consist of 13 log cabin units that can accommodate families ranging in size from two through seven. The larger cabins have an enclosed bedroom with a queen bed and a loft with a queen and two twins, or four or five twins. There are two ADA units that also have queen hide-a-beds. Horseshoe Canyon bases their rates on the season, and daily and weekly rates are offered. In high season, cabins are $205 a day for adults, $1,095 per week. Kids stay for $160 a day, $865 a week. Nonriders get special rates of $170 per day, $920 per week. They have a three-day minimum during summer months. Rates include cabins, three excellent meals each day, maid service, children's program, canoeing (in-season), and lots of horseback riding, rock climbing, and all other ranch activities. $$–$$$.

Lost Spur Guest Ranch (1-800-993-7605; www.rent-a-ranch.net), 8148 Lost Spur Road, Harrison. This is a pet-friendly rent-a-ranch with a log lodge. Bring your horses and fishing gear. The Lost Spur ranch is a unique 116-acre facility that is available for short-term rental (six nights). When you rent the ranch, you have total occupancy. The log lodge will sleep eight people, and there are eight 10-by-12 stalls in a semi-enclosed barn. There is a large corral and miles of seldom-traveled country roads for beautiful, peaceful horseback rides. The air-conditioned lodge features a great room with a fireplace, and just off the great room is a full kitchen and a 12-by-54-foot covered porch with gas grill. Ranch rental is based on the number in your party: one to four guests, $1,750/week (six nights); five to eight guests, $150 each per week. Horses are also available for $20 per night per guest. $–$$.

HORSESHOE CANYON RANCH IN JASPER

EASTERN SALEM PLATEAU

BED & BREAKFAST INNS **Old Ferry Road Bed & Breakfast; River Creel Cottage** (870-431-4446; www.oldferryroadbb .com), 706 Old Ferry Road, Lakeview. This luxury inn is located between the White River and Bull Shoals Lake on 300 wildlife-filled acres in the Ozarks. If you are there to fly-fish, there is a library with fly-tying station and plasma TV, along with a game/media room with billiards and projection TV. All guests enjoy a full breakfast, private baths, wireless Internet, complimentary refreshments, and evening dessert. $$–$$$.

The River Reel Cottage ($250/night) is only four lots upstream from Gaston's resort. It features two bedrooms, a well-appointed living and dining area, full kitchen, washer and dryer, screened porch, luxury hot tub, TV, telephone, and tree-shaded decks leading to private walk-in access to some of the best trout fishing in the nation. Room rates vary from $89–159 nightly, depending on the room you choose. $–$$.

Country Oaks Bed & Breakfast (1-800-455-2704; www.countryoaksbb .com), 17221 AR 9, Mountain View. Jerry and Carole Weber relocated to Mountain View from California because they fell in love with the mountains and the people. They designed and built a beautiful country Victorian home with more than 3,000 square feet of porch wrapped around it that are perfect for visiting and relaxing. The Webers are well suited to the art of innkeeping, being hospitable, well-traveled, and truly interesting company. My first night at the inn, I spent three stimulating hours with them on their front porch, eating Tommy's Famous Pizza, watching the sun set, and listening to how they fell in love with Mountain View and wound up in this pastoral setting. The main house has five large guest rooms, each with private bath. A second structure, the Carriage

House, was added a couple of years later and has three additional rooms, and parlors and sitting areas with games, television, and a library of books. There are also some decent-sized fish in the 6-acre private lake for catch and release fishing. Jerry has blazed over 2 miles of hiking trails on the property, which will help you work off the tasty country gourmet breakfast the Webers serve in their spacious dining room every morning. Jerry makes the best smoothies anywhere. Room rates range from $100–135 nightly. $$–$$$.

The Inn at Mountain View (1-800-535-1301; www.theinnatmountainview .com), 307 Washington, Mountain View. This AAA-rated bed & breakfast is on the National Register of Historic Places, but the 11 guest rooms offer today's amenities, all with private baths, air conditioning, and wireless Internet. Each overnight stay at The Inn at Mountain View includes a full country breakfast served with farm-fresh country eggs, but if you find yourself hungry throughout the day, a guest pantry with refrigerator, teas, and home-baked snacks are yours to use. This rustic Victorian inn has common areas that offer a big-screen satellite television with DVD player, pool table, and games. A business center with Wi-Fi, a fax machine, and a conference room will let you maintain contact with the cold, cruel world, and a waterfall garden will help you escape it. Room rates range from $96 a night for a standard room to the Garden Suite for $145. $–$$.

Wildflower Bed & Breakfast on the Square (1-800-591-4879; www.arkansas-inn.com), 100 Washington Street, Courthouse Square, Mountain View. This circa 1918 Craftsman-style inn has six guest rooms and suites, each with private bath, queen and king beds, ceiling fans, and cable TV. Corporate rooms are available for business travelers, with phone, data port, and work area. There is free wireless Internet. Wildflower's full buffet breakfast in their sunny dining room is a great way to fuel up for a day of sightseeing or enjoying the Ozark outdoors. Each day the inn features a different hot entrée made with rich golden eggs from a local farm. You will be served fruit, hickory-smoked bacon or ham, savory sausage, fluffy biscuits, and homemade sausage gravy. The buttermilk waffles and pancakes are light and fluffy, and the muffins and sweet breads are made from scratch. Be sure you try the homemade rhubarb sauce, plus delicious jellies and spreads made in Arkansas. Room rates, based on the room you select, range from $85–135 with nice discounts for midweek bookings. $–$$.

CABINS AND COTTAGES **Buffalo Camping, Canoeing, and Cabins** (870-439-2888; www.gilbertstore.com), 1 North Frost Street, Gilbert. These fully equipped cabins are located near the historic Gilbert General Store. Buffalo Benjamin's Cabin ($275/night for 1 to 4 people; additional $20/night for additional guests) sleeps up to 10 and includes a hot tub and fireplace; River Cabins #5 and #6 ($200 per night for 1 to 4 guests) sleep up to 7, and each includes a fireplace and a spa tub for two; the Gilbert Cabins ($85 per night) are duplexes and sleep up to 4 each; Caroline's Cottage ($200) sleeps up to 10; Mother Moore's ($200) hosts up to 12; Cousin Hayley's ($100) holds up to 5. All are within walking distance of the Buffalo National River; canoeing and rafting trips are available. This outfitter services the Middle District of the river. This section is classified as Class 1 whitewater, which is the easiest and suitable for beginning canoeists. If this is your first trip, they will be happy to give you some basic canoeing instruction. Shuttle fees are based on the length of your float and number of people in your group; call for a price. Rafts rent for $25/day, kayaks are $30/day, and canoes rent for $45/day. The campground has tent sites, and some RV sites with hook-ups are available, too. Tent sites are $7 per person; RV sites are $25 per couple. $–$$.

YOU GO FISHING, SHE GOES CATCHING

His Place Resort (1-866-435-6535; www.hisplaceresort.net), 89 Chamberlain Lane, Cotter. Owners Steve and Julie Raines have equipped this resort with everything you need for a thrilling, relaxing, and memorable fishing trip on the legendary White River: boat rentals; tackle shop; guided fishing trips; fully equipped housekeeping units (all have river views except for #8 and #9); covered riverside pavilion; nature trail; camping area; wildlife watching; and mountain bike rentals. While this is all great, the real treasures here are Steve and Julie. Not only are they full of interesting river stories and fish tales, they are exceptional anglers. Julie is the self-proclaimed Trout Diva, and she writes a fun blog for their website. These two are fishing the river every day—because they love it. Dale Douglas, one of the hired guides who books out of the resort, can spot a trout from 200 yards away and follow that by casting 10 yards upstream from them. The resort has different sizes and price points for lodging to fit your needs and budget. On two separate trips with them, we landed two trout worthy of forced release (accompanied by souvenir pin and certificate) in less than three hours on the first trip. The second trip was not marked by trophies but by the size of the stringer. We caught more than 17 really nice trout in less than half a day. We stayed in a cozy little cabin on the river. The smaller units hold 2 people ($80/day weekdays, $90/day weekends), and the largest holds up to 11 ($245/day weekdays), with sizes in between. Each unit has a charcoal grill for cookouts and is no smoking/no pets for your comfort. Licensed, professional, insured fishing guides know where the trout are for spin fishing and fly-fishing. A fully stocked fly and tackle shop plus a helpful heads-up on the preferred menu for the day are good support for your self-guided trip. Johnboats with motors, canoes, and kayaks are available for rent from their private boat dock. A little note to ladies: His Place Resort is wildly popular with guys about to get married, and you can meet some pretty cute single guys who are along for the celebration. Makes you want to take up fishing . . . girlfriends' getaway, anyone? $–$$

TROUT DIVA JULIE RAINES

3 Rivers Outfitters (870-856-4945; www.3riversoutfitters.com), 400 Church Street, Hardy. In Hardy, 3 Rivers Outfitters offers lodging and outfitter services on the Spring River and has a number of different lodging opportunities. The Couple's Cabin has a full-sized bed, bath, refrigerator, coffeemaker, cable TV, and deck for $60 per night for two adults. The Eagle's Nest is perched atop the 3 Rivers Outfitters Hill with sweeping views of the surrounding mountains. It has two rooms with a queen-sized bed and a full-sized sleeper sofa, bath, microwave, refrigerator, coffeemaker, cable TV, and a deck with a grill for $79 per night for two. The Cedar Cabin is situated along the banks of the beautiful Spring River and has a full kitchen, bath, two bedrooms, deck, and cable TV for $159 per night. The resort's luxury offering is The Heron Cabin, with its king-sized bed, full kitchen, bath, cable TV, and futon sleeper sofa for $160 a night. Float trips range in duration from two to eight hours and have several different put-in points on the Spring River. Canoe rental rates range from $20–38; kayaks are $24–35. $–$$.

Little Red River House (501-375-7767; www.littleredriverhouse.com), outskirts of Heber Springs. Little Red River House includes a main house and a bunk house, both with fully equipped kitchens, baths with showers, natural rock fireplaces, decks with grills, TVs with cable and DVD, plus full access to the dock and the river. Seasonal pricing varies; rental rates range from $275 for a two-night stay to $700 a week. Pets are welcome, with their own rate and deposit. Boat rentals are $100, and you are on your own for gas. $$–$$$.

RESORTS **Gaston's White River Resort & Restaurant** (870-431-5202; www .gastons.com), 1777 River Road, Lakeview. Gaston's White River Resort is one of the foremost resorts on the White River, capable of enticing a travel writer to stop in midstory for a vacation day on his own dime. Known for first-class amenities, Gaston's has no fewer than 12 different types of accommodations. They range from a standard room with two double beds for $85 a night to the two-story River Villa cabin with 10 bedrooms, 10 bathrooms, and large kitchen/dining/den area for $1,186 per night. The glass-enclosed restaurant is on the riverside and offers some of the most creative trout dishes you will ever eat. It provides three meals a day for resort guests. Breakfast is buffet style ($10) and served from 6–10 to ensure you can get on the water early or sleep late—your call. The lunch menu is offered from 10–5, so you can grab a snack no matter when you get off the river. The menu includes sandwiches, soups, and plate dishes like chicken-fried steak, with prices averaging $11 per person. The dinner menu features steaks, seafood, and, of course, trout prepared more ways than Bubba could name for Forrest Gump. Prices average $25 per entrée, topping out at $39 for the restaurant's acclaimed filet mignon. A seasonal swimming pool, tennis court, hiking/nature trails, lounge, gift shop, private air strip for fly-in guests, and high-speed Internet complete the resort's amenities. $–$$$.

Lindsey's Rainbow Resort (1-800-305-8790; www.lindseysresort.com), 350 Rainbow Loop, Heber Springs. Lindsey's has cozy rustic log cabins and a camping area. Each cabin has an equipped kitchen with range top, refrigerator, and sink; a sitting/dining area with cable TV; private bathroom; and is situated on or near the Little Red River. The campground has full RV hook-ups with cable TV, picnic tables, and hot showers. A modern trout dock with trout fishing pier, bait, tackle, snacks, and gifts all but put the fish in your boat for you. Boat and motor rentals and guide services are available. Pot O' Gold Restaurant lets you dine beside the river on prime rib, steaks, catfish, sandwiches, and an extensive list of appetizers. The restaurant will also pack your lunch for you for fishing trips, and

THE SHORELINE OF THE RED RIVER AT LINDSEY'S RAINBOW RESORT

then prepare your catch with all the fixings when you get back. There is a large swimming pool and a playground for small children. Cabins have one to four bathrooms and one to four bedrooms; some have fireplaces and Jacuzzis. Rates for cabins are seasonal and based on amenities, ranging from $75–192 a night. $–$$$.

Puddin' Ridge Farm (1-800-633-8166; www.puddinridge.com), 3050 Brownsville Road, Greers Ferry. This resort offers a country farm vacation experience with convenient access to area amenities, plus farm animals and a private fishing pond. Puddin' Ridge has a lot of lodging options from which to choose: deluxe cozy cabins at the Farm or the Cove, and two lakefront homes. All are located on beautiful, clear Greers Ferry Lake in the heart of the Arkansas Ozark foothills. Cabins at the Farm have

fireplaces, Jacuzzis for two, decks overlooking the woods, kitchenettes, and gas grills. They will run you $110–125 a night. At the Cove, the Lizard Trail Lakefront House sleeps 10 to 12 people, with three bedrooms, fully equipped kitchen, living room (with queen sleeper sofa), screened porch with futons, washer and dryer, and wood-burning fireplace. It is $200/night double occupancy. $$–$$$.

Red Apple Inn (1-800-733-2775; www .redappleinn.com), 1000 Club Road, Heber Springs. Red Apple Inn's original design was meant to remind one of a Spanish villa. The furnishings were acquired while traveling Europe to give the inn an Old World charm. Each room is unique in style and furnishings. Fireplace rooms have king or double beds, with some rooms offering a balcony or patio. Suites consist of two separate living areas, with a king bed dominating the sleeping room and the living area holding a sofa, chairs, and television. They both open onto a natural breezeway, and one suite has a private balcony. A whirlpool tub makes bath time spa time. Free wireless Internet access is available in all guest rooms. The restaurant at the inn is one of Arkansas's favorites for fine dining. The dining room is situated for lovely views in several different directions overlooking the lake, the landscaped patio, or the pleasantly shaded breezeway. It has been hailed in *Southern Living* magazine and specializes in delicious European fare with a Southern accent. Top off your meal with an elegant flaming dessert or the famous Sticky Pudding Cake. As with all of Arkansas's resorts, rates at Red Apple Inn are seasonal, ranging from $80–95 for deluxe rooms to $110–130 for suites. Vacation homes are also available for rent through the inn, starting at $300 a night. Condominiums on the property have one to three bedrooms and range from $160–250 a night. $–$$.

Shepherd of the Ozarks (817-310-0280; www.shepherdoftheozarks.com), Harriet. Maps are downloadable from the website, or call for directions to this rural destination. Shepherd of the Ozarks (SOTO) has the most unusual group lodging you will find in the state. It's not really about the amenities, though they are numerous. At SOTO, it's all about the lodging. Nestled in this wilderness setting are six luxurious log cabin–style lodges varying in decor and size to sleep from 6 to a group of 400 people. All of them include kitchens, meeting rooms, private bedrooms, and bunk areas. Massive rock fireplaces, rocking chairs on the porch, and comfortable beds invite you to come away for refreshment and relaxation. Listing the amenities just doesn't do them justice. Creatively designed with artistic handmade detail, the cabins have secret bedrooms where children can hide away for their own space. There is one cabin with a fireman's theme that has an impressive display

of uniforms, fireman's hats, and a full-sized antique fire truck downstairs. All of its rooms are upstairs and incorporate the theme in handmade lighting and accessories. If you need to make a quick exit, there's a fire pole from the sleeping area to the downstairs floor. SOTO is also popular with groups because of the amenities on its 460 acres. If it is active adventure that you want, SOTO has a high ropes challenge course, wilderness paintball, laser tag, and a cliffhanger swing (per person rates). Horseback riding on scenic trails is available year-round ($10 per hour). The Animal Arcade has lemurs, wallabies, llamas, and deer that are fun to pet and feed and watch. There's a tame buffalo named Buford you can pet. The lodges vary in decor and size, and floor plans and photos will help you decide the one that best fits your needs. SOTO is great for groups, with sleeping areas tucked throughout the lodges. Firehouse Lodge sleeps 53; Indian Bluff Lodge sleeps 25–53; Big Creek Lodge sleeps 30–77; Wilderness Lodge sleeps 60–61; Cedar Lodge sleeps 15–39; Mini-Lodge sleeps 14–15; and the Hideaway Lodge sleeps 12. The Buffalo Center has 20,000 square feet for meetings and includes a full-service dining room, 500-seat auditorium, a loft for smaller gatherings, and four lodge rooms. Call for rate information for the lodging of your choice. $$–$$$.

Stetson's Resort (870-453-8066; www.stetsons-resort.com), 906 County Road 7002, Flippin. The beautiful log cabins are located on the White River and can accommodate up to 10 in the five-bedroom, four-bath unit. All cabins have a great room with wood-burning fireplace, satellite television, and fully equipped kitchens. If you have come to the White River, you have come to fish. Guided fishing trips, boat, and motor rentals are available to ease your passage to the river. A swimming pool is also on the property for guests' use. Weekend rates range from $160/night for a one-bedroom, one-bath unit to $720

THE HORSE WHISPERER OF THE OZARKS

StoneCreek Ranch Resort (1-888-203-7433; www.stonecreekranchresort.com), 626 Circle B Lane, Mountain Home. StoneCreek is number two on my list of all-time favorite Arkansas destinations, and that is only because Arvell and Karry don't have as many horses as Tanya and Scott have tigers. Arvell is a true-blue, genuine horse whisperer. I have seen him take a four-year-old, unbroken mare and lay two fingers on her hip and gently guide her direction. Did you know that every horse has an emergency brake? They do, and he will show you how to use it and eliminate the source of 95 percent of the fear most people have when they step on a horse. Arvell will teach you the right way to approach a horse to ensure that the animal is not afraid of you and show you how to recognize the gentle eye the horse will give you once you have passed its test. And it all happens on the smartest horses on the planet— cutting horses lovingly coached by Arvell himself. Accelerate your ride with gentle pressure with your shins, or stop on a dime with a slight pull of the reins and shifting your seat back in the saddle. I watched a seven-year-old German girl cut a calf from its herd without the need to learn the English language. (The story behind Arvell and Karry's move to the Ozarks is a book in itself, and I will let them share it with you themselves.)

Two fully equipped, two-bedroom cabins sleep up to six each. But my favorites are the two guest rooms in the Barn Loft that overlooks the indoor arena. It lets you visit your horse in its stall at any time, and the sound of them whinnying peacefully in their stalls below makes a nice lullaby at night. You also have access to a full kitchen and dining area. Activities include indoor riding in the arena, outdoor riding, trail riding, and the cutting horse experience for the adventuresome. Pets are allowed by special prior arrangement. There is world-class fishing on the nearby White and North Fork Rivers, and water sports packages are available. StoneCreek has two deluxe cabins that sleep five to seven people in two queen bedrooms and one futon in the living room, plus one full bathroom. Price is $150 per night, with a three-night minimum for the first four people. The Barn Loft ($120 per night, two-night minimum) also sleeps four to six people and has two queen beds, one bunk bed, a full private bathroom, and a full kitchen. Eight Cowboy guest rooms in the Lodge sleep two and have their own plumbed vanity, sharing a toilet/shower with the adjoining room. All lodging includes use of a large lounge, dining room, conference area, full kitchen, and an indoor activity room with basketball and table tennis.

a night for a five-bedroom, four-bath cabin. Weekday rates average 10 percent cheaper. $$–$$$$.

✽ Where to Eat

WESTERN SALEM PLATEAU

EATING OUT **Café Soleil** (479-253-2345; www.cafesoleilrestaurant.com), 3094 East Van Buren, Eureka Springs. Open Tuesday through Saturday 11–9, Sunday 10–9 (brunch until 2 p.m.). This is simple, elegant dining in a relaxed atmosphere with a menu featuring a fusion of international and contemporary American cuisine along with a surprisingly diverse selection of vegetarian offerings. The Chicken Soleil is a sure bet with roasted chicken breast, pine nuts, dried tomatoes, spinach, and goat cheese for $16. The freshly baked bread is also something you must try before your meal. Entrées range from $5 to $20. $–$$.

Casa Colina Grill & Cantina (479-363-6226), 173 Main Street, Eureka Springs. This upscale Mexican restaurant is located in an 1890s-era home on the top of Planer Hill in the Eureka Springs historic district. The menu features fresh traditional Mexican cuisine in an elegant yet relaxed atmosphere. The decks, porches, and dining rooms are further enhanced by the acres of natural wooded surroundings. Specials of the house include skewers of grilled steak with guacamole and mango salsa, Aztec boudin, and blackened red snapper with pineapple salsa. They have full beverage service and some of the best margaritas this side of the Rio Grande. Entrées range from $25–35 per person. $$–$$$.

DeVito's of Eureka Springs (479-253-6807; www.devitoseureka.com), 6 Center Street, Eureka Springs. Open for dinner daily except Wednesday 5–9, brunch Saturday and Sunday 10:30–2. Authentic Italian cuisine voted the best in Arkansas (Readers' Choice Award, *Arkansas Times*). Located on Center Street in historic downtown Eureka Springs, DeVito's offers intimate dining in beautiful surroundings. The restaurant has been recommended twice by the *New York Times* and *Southern Living*, and has appeared in *Gourmet* and *Bon Appetit*. It is moderately priced, with most entrées between $15–20. $$–$$$.

DeVito's Restaurant & Trout Farm (870-741-8832; www.devitosrestaurant.com), 350 DeVito's Loop, Harrison. Open for dinner Monday through Saturday 5–9. This is the original DeVito's family restaurant that started the culinary legend. This restaurant also features Italian cuisine with homemade pasta and toasted ravioli. The fresh seafood dishes, including the smoked trout pâté appetizer, are local favorites. My friend, who happens to be an Alfredo aficionado, proclaimed DeVito's sauce to be the best she's ever tasted. I couldn't resist the trout, and what can you say about fish that was swimming that day? Fresh and flaky, perfectly prepared, and served by one of the best waiters who has ever served me. It's not hard to imagine that a trout farm would have an extensive menu of dishes featuring the fish, and DeVito's is no exception. It's great fun to call ahead and catch your own trout at the on-site trout farm. Entrées range from $15–25. $$–$$$.

Ermilio's Italian Home Cooking (479-253-8806), 26 White Street, Eureka Springs. Ermilio's uses family recipes from northern and southern Italy, and serves them family-style to throngs of diners who wait on the porches of the restaurant for their reservation. Pick your pasta and made-from-scratch sauces like Aunt Millie and Uncle Sal used to make. You might want to walk from your hotel or B&B, as temptations like homemade Italian cream cake and tiramisu are not to be missed. Step away from the calorie counter for the duration of your meal. Ermilio's is located on the historic route near the Crescent Hotel. Entrées average about $20 per person. $–$$.

Gaskins Cabin Steakhouse (479-253-5466; www.gaskinscabin.com), AR 23 North, Eureka Springs. Open for dinner Wednesday through Saturday 5–9, Sunday 5–8. Call for winter hours in December, January, and February. This outstanding restaurant is housed in an authentic log cabin built in 1864 by one of Eureka Springs' first settlers—the well-known bear hunter, John Gaskins. It is the oldest standing property in Carroll County. Featuring famous prime rib and 21-day aged steaks, seafood, and chicken with generous portions and a romantic setting, Gaskins Cabin Steakhouse is a wonderful choice for any occasion. Entrées range from $17–30 per person. $$–$$$.

John Paul's (870-741-2321), 302 North Main Street, Harrison. Open Tuesday through Saturday 3–10 p.m. for dinner. The Hotel Seville's restaurant, John Paul's, is the place to see and be seen. A classic neighborhood grill, the restaurant offers big burgers, hearty appetizers, and fun food, while diners also enjoy one of the few places in the county that serves cocktails. Decor is true to the proud history of Arkansas, with its most famous political statesman, John Paul Hammerschmidt, as its namesake. The menu is casual all day and features several fine dinner entrées after 5 p.m. Tap beers, burgers, appetizers, and specialty drinks served by employees in sharply pressed and appropriate uniforms complement the atmosphere. Entrées are extremely good values, topping out with a hand-cut 12-ounce rib eye that is grilled, blackened, or dry-rubbed and served with your choice of potato and the vegetable of the day for $18. $$–$$$.

Local Flavor (479-253-9522), 71 South Main Street, Eureka Springs. Open various hours; call to make sure they are open. Eclectic menu ranges from burgers to grilled salmon and oven-baked Brie; Sunday brunch features eggs Benedict, huevos rancheros, and omelets. Entrées start at $10 and range up to $25. $–$$.

Myrtie Mae's Homestyle (1-800-552-3785; www.myrtiemaes.com), US 62 West, Eureka Springs. Open weekdays 7–8:30, weekends 7–9. Myrtie Mae's is a relaxed, casual restaurant with a lovely view of the valley. Located in the Best Western Inn of the Ozarks, Myrtie Mae's has been a tradition for many Eurekan visitors for decades. Breakfast, lunch, and dinner are served daily. The Sunday brunch menu features traditional Southern entrées: Ozark fried chicken, baked catfish, and steaks, as well as an extensive soup, salad, and fruit bar. All-you-care-to-eat lunch buffets are offered on Tuesday and Thursday. A children's menu is available for kids under 12. Try their signature muffins and possum pie. Breakfast dishes run between $5–10 per plate; lunch runs from $6–12; and dinner entrées start at $10 and top out at $20. $–$$.

Mud Street Espresso Café (479-253-6732; www.mudstreetcafe.com), 22G South Main Street, Eureka Springs. Open Monday through Sunday (closed Wednesday) for breakfast 8–11 and lunch 11–3; open Friday and Saturday evenings for desserts, coffees, and spirits. This charming café was featured in *Southern Living* magazine for its food, but its decor is worth a trip all by itself. Exposed brick and hand-painted theatrical curtains will have your eye roaming and resting

FRESHLY BAKED BREADS AT NEIGHBOR'S MILL BAKERY AND CAFÉ IN HARRISON

on a 360-degree visual feast. Burgers, chicken breast sandwiches, hot and cold sandwiches, wraps, soups, and salads are some of the many tasty menu choices that make Mud Street a favorite lunchtime spot in Eureka Springs. Entrées range from $7–15. $–$$.

Neighbor's Mill Bakery & Café (870-741-MILL; www.neighborsmill.com), 1012 US 62-65 North, Harrison. Neighbor's features whole wheat ground on a 100-year-old gristmill to make handcrafted American hearth breads and crusty European breads. Breakfast features French toast and pastries; lunch includes hot and cold sandwiches, focaccia pizzas, homemade soups, and salads; the dinner menu has expanded to include pasta. Gourmet coffee, tea, and espresso drinks are available. $–$$.

New Delhi Cafe (479-253-2525), 2 North Main Street, Eureka Springs. Open daily 8:30 a.m.–2 a.m. New Delhi serves

Euro-style deli daily; it also has a great espresso bar on weekdays. The Friday through Sunday buffet featuring authentic East Indian foods contains all your favorites. New Delhi also hosts some great musical acts on weekends. Some of the Indian dishes are ridiculously cheap, starting at $3. You can get a nice sampling of their many dishes and a doggy bag for less than $15 per person. $–$$.

Rogue's Manor at Sweet Spring (1-800-250-5827; www.roguesmanor .com), 124 Spring Street, Eureka Springs. Rogue's Manor is one of my favorite restaurants in the state. Owner Smith Truer is from Oregon, and his Pacific Northwest contacts make for high-quality and extremely fresh menu items right here in the Ozark Mountains. Two-bite oyster shooters and fresh sea bass are almost commonplace on Smith's diverse menu. The Victorian structure with turrets and gables translates into multiple dining rooms for intimate dining, no matter how packed the restaurant might be. The lounge is especially cozy, with richly upholstered leather wingback chairs and a glass wall that reveals a well-lit waterfall just outside. It is very hard to pick a favorite here, but I have decided that I want to be buried in the potted Montrachet ($13) on the appetizer menu, so it is definitely worth mentioning. Entrées range from fettuccini Alfredo ($13) to the hand-cut aged beef porterhouse steak for $68. Rogue's offers specialty desserts; the menu changes regularly, but if it's offering a chocolate mousse, order it. Even if they have to pack it up to go for you. The lounge at Rogue's is one of the best places in town for a cocktail, too, with bartenders who make their own simple syrups for mixers. They know how to properly pour an Irish coffee, too. Rogue's Manor has been recognized by every travel publication to pass through this area, and a few cuisine magazines like *Bon Appetit*, too. $$–$$$.

Rowdy Beaver Restaurant & Tavern (479-253-8544; www.rowdybeaver.com), 417 West Van Buren, Eureka Springs.

This nonsmoking, full-service tavern offers casual dining in a family atmosphere, with a separate outside deck and patio for smoking patrons. Rowdy's diverse menu offers an option for every palate: pasta, pork chops, BBQ, mahimahi, tilapia, burgers, and salads. If that wasn't enough, a Southern menu was added, too. $–$$.

Sparky's Roadhouse Café (479-253-6001; www.sparkys.net), 147 East Van Buren, Eureka Springs. The menu is eclectic American with hamburgers, nachos, and quesadillas. Sparky's has excellent soups made fresh daily. A large screened-in deck with ceiling fans in the back is a perfect place to unwind after fishing or shopping or feeding the tigers at Turpentine Creek. Entrées range from $10–20. $–$$.

EASTERN SALEM PLATEAU

178 Club (870-445-4949), 109 Central Boulevard, Bull Shoals. Open for lunch and dinner Tuesday through Saturday 11–9; open Sunday 9–8. The extensive menu includes something for everyone. For those with a sophisticated palate, calamari, escargot, and scallops will satisfy their need for fine dining. More casual diners will find that an extensive selection of burgers, nachos, chicken livers, and sandwiches are also available. $–$$.

Anglers White River Resort (1-800-794-2226; www.anglerswhiteriver.com), intersection of AR 5, 9, and 14, Mountain View. Open in summer, Sunday through Thursday 11–8, Friday 11–9, Saturday 7–9, Sunday 7–11 a.m. Winter hours are Wednesday and Thursday 11–7, Friday and Saturday 11–8, Sunday 11–3:30. This fishing resort is located in the Ozarks on the White River and Sylamore Creek. If the rustic exterior didn't say fishing/hunting to you, once inside the taxidermy will make the point. The restaurant features American-style ribs, steak, catfish, and BBQ. It is located five minutes from the Syllamo Mountain Bike Trail; no pets are allowed inside the restaurant, so leave Fido in the cabin. Better yet, take him a doggy bag—at $15 per person for lunch or $25 for dinner, you can afford to take a little home. $–$$.

Brenda's Sale Barn Café (870-892-0240), 706 Townsend Drive, Pocahontas. This is not the place to take your vegetarian friends. Brenda's is located in a real live sale barn—a place where cattle ranchers meet to conduct business—and the menu reflects a deep appreciation for the product. Country-folk carnivores know that these places are among the best for the finest and freshest beef around. Brenda's is no exception, and from her Southern-style breakfast to steaks cooked to order, you know that all of these regular customers you see are there because the food is great. If you like chocolate gravy, go for breakfast; Brenda's has the best I have ever eaten anytime or anywhere. Breakfast runs about $7 each off the menu. Lunch and dinner run the gamut, but expect an average of $20 per person. $–$$.

Parachute Inn Restaurant (870-886-5918), 10 Skywatch, Walnut Ridge. Open Tuesday through Thursday 8–2. Part of this restaurant is now housed in a reconfigured Southwest Airlines Boeing 737. The interior has been restored to give it the original Southwest look, and the seats have been adjusted to fit the tables. Store your coats in the overhead bins. The Parachute Inn serves Southern homestyle cooking and seafood that is head and shoulders above your typical airline fare. It has been featured in *USA Today*, the *Dallas Morning News*, *Splash News* (Great Britain), and on ABC. Entrées average $15–22 per person. $–$$.

Tommy's Famous . . . A Pizzeria, Inc. (870-269-3278; www.tommysfamous .com), AR 66 (West Main Street) at Carpenter, Mountain View. Open Tuesday through Saturday 11–9. Tommy's serves Memphis-style ribs, hand-tossed pizza, and homemade pesto, drawing people here from hundreds of miles away and earning accolades from local media, *Southern Living*, and *National*

Geographic Traveler. Awarded *Arkansas Times*' best pizza in northeast Arkansas every year since 1996. Family owned and operated since 1991, Tommy's is known for their ribs, but the calzones and pizza are also excellent. From the cooked-daily hickory-smoked BBQ, baby back ribs, and beans to the homemade coleslaw, each entrée has quite a following. The 5-pound Fatboy and veggie pizzas are perennial best-sellers. Go with a lot of people and practice your sharing skills. Expect to spend between $10 and $20 per person, without alcohol. $–$$.

✳ Entertainment

Free Music in Basin Spring Park (479-253-2586; www.eurekasprings.org), Basin Spring Park on Spring Street in historic downtown. Free performances in Basin Spring Park are held every Friday and Saturday from noon to 6 p.m. and Sundays from noon to 4 p.m. You will be amazed at the talented artists you find performing around this spring. Headliners from local clubs will frequently put in a set in this historic park right in the center of town, with the music serenading shoppers and diners throughout downtown.

Eureka Springs City Auditorium (1-888-855-7823; www.theaud.org), 36 South Main Street, Eureka Springs. This little auditorium is a real favorite with a lot of the nationally known performers who make it a point to include it when they go out on the road. I once worked on a movie that was filmed in Eureka Springs, *Pass the Ammunition*, about a televangelist who was just a wee bit shady, and his set was at the Aud, as it is affectionately called. The movie ends with the Aud in flames—fortunately, it was only a movie. The Aud offers an intimate setting with clear and distinctive acoustics. With the balcony and main floor, it seats 984. The auditorium has a long history of attracting stars; the first performance in the facility was John

Philip Sousa and his 67-piece band. The auditorium was the dream of Mayor Claude A. Fuller, who pushed construction in 1928. He aimed to fill the needs and expectations of visitors who desired the most current entertainment available while visiting the Victorian town known for its beautiful scenery and soothing springs. It continues to attract big names such as John Prine, Alison Krauss, Emmylou Harris, Béla Fleck, and Willie Nelson.

Escape Room 13 (479-308-8624; www.escaperoom13.com), 13 North Main Street, Eureka Springs. Open 10–10 daily. This family friendly activity is suitable for anyone from eight to 80 years of age. Eureka Springs is a town with a rich and vibrant history from which the creators of Escape Room 13 have drawn upon when crafting their mysteries. The 1822 Eureka Springs bank heist is revisited, and visitors are challenged to solve the case with clues, secret messages, and hidden passages. Tickets for the one-hour experience are $25 per person. Group discounts are also available.

Fun Spot (479-253-7548), 3173 East Van Buren, US 62 East, Eureka Springs. Very varied hours; call ahead or stop if you see they are open, which it seems like they always are, except during church. This family entertainment center has go-carts, bumper boats, miniature golf, batting cages, and an arcade. It's a great outing for restless dads and children who are tired of watching Mom shop.

Imperial Dinner Theatre (870-892-0030; www.imperialdinnertheatre.com), 1401 AR 304 East, Pocahontas. Open Friday and Saturday; dinner is served at 6:30 p.m., show starts at 7:30 p.m. A Sunday matinee serves lunch at 1, with the curtain going up on the first act at 2. This family-oriented dinner theater is in the charming atmosphere of the renovated 1930s Imperial Theatre. One of my favorite things about the Imperial is that it features a multigenerational resident acting company, which includes actors

ages 7 to 80. The Imperial also has a studio for the arts that offers classes, workshops, and summer camps in all areas of fine arts. Tickets for dinner and the show are $25 for adults and $20 for students. You can also go and just see the show for $15 per adult and $10 per student.

Jimmy Driftwood's Barn (870-269-8042), 19775 AR 5 North, Mountain View. Open Friday through Sunday from 7 p.m. until they close her down. Jimmy Driftwood is a local legend in these parts, and if you are in Mountain View for the music, his barn is a must-see for you. Local musicians play country, bluegrass, and gospel music year-round.

Lyric Theatre (1-888-283-2163; www.thelyricharrison.org), 113 East Rush Avenue, Harrison. This is a beautifully restored theater with a somber beginning. It opened the day after the stock market crashed in 1929, so it failed to receive the fanfare it might otherwise have. Soon after it opened, a painter came by and offered to paint murals on the walls in exchange for a place to stay and a little food and money. The vibrant scenes he left on the Lyric's walls will rival any performance on its stage, yet the artist's name is not even known. There are a number of events held here each year; check the website for performance and ticket information.

The Great Passion Play (1-866-566-3565; www.greatpassionplay.com), 935 Passion Play Road, Eureka Springs. The season runs May 1 through October 24; show times are based on sunset and posted on the website. An unforgettable and inspiring performance enjoyed by more than 7 million people from all over the world for over 35 years. The script has been updated within the past few years, as has the music. A cast of hundreds performs amid historically accurate stage settings; *The Great Passion Play* brings to life the thrilling, epic drama surrounding Christ's last days on earth and his death and resurrection. Performed in a stunning 4,100-seat panoramic outdoor amphitheater, *The Great*

Passion Play features state-of-the art sound and lighting effects and original music in a dramatic two-hour presentation. The story is told with a huge cast in a ginormous way: the colorful spectacle of the marketplace, the pageantry of the chariots and camel caravan, and the hustle and bustle of the crowds as they go about their daily activities drawing water from the well or herding their sheep through the streets of Jerusalem. You can join the cast if you are one of the first four to ask; call before you travel just to be safe if it is important to you. People come from all over the country as a pilgrimage just to be a part of the greatest story ever told.

Opera in the Ozarks at Inspiration Point (479-253-8595; www.opera.org), 16311 US 62 East, Eureka Springs. The view from Inspiration Point will make you want to do a Julie Andrews and burst into song. If you're like me and can't carry a tune in a suitcase, you can still enjoy Opera in the Ozarks; it presents three fully staged operas as part of an annual summer opera festival featuring outstanding young artists. The theater has roof coverage for the audience and stage, and open siding similar to the Santa Fe Opera. Check the website for performance and ticket information.

Ozark Mountain Hoe-Down (1-800-458-2113; www.theozarkmountain hoedown.com), 310 East Van Buren, Eureka Springs. Open daily except Tuesday; closed most of December and a lot of November, so check the website if you are traveling during those months. The Hoe-Down Gang performs contemporary, country, Cajun, pop, and gospel entertainment. Ticket prices are adult $21.50; senior $20.50 (62 and over); military $17.50.

Stone Drive In (870-269-3227; www.stonedrivein.net), off Highway 87 North near the water tower, Mountain View. Open Friday through Sunday, shows start at 8:45 p.m. Good old-fashioned family fun reigns in Mountain View. The Stone Drive In plays first-run movies

beneath the starry skies of this hamlet in the Ozark mountains. Children 12 and under are free; over 13 years of age are $5. Rain or shine, the show goes on.

✳ Selective Shopping

Antique Warehouse (501-745-5842; www.antiquewarehouse.com), US 65 and AR 110, Botkinburg. Open Monday through Saturday 9–5, Sunday noon–5. The largest antique inventory in the country is stashed in 12 buildings, encompassing more than 90,000 square feet of warehouses, shops, and showrooms.

Arkansas Craft Guild Gallery (870-269-3897; www.arkansascraftguild.org), 104 East Main Street, Mountain View. Open Tuesday through Saturday 9:30–6. This retail shop features both fine art and handmade, traditional, and contemporary crafts by some 300 Arkansas artists who are members of one of the oldest craft guilds in the mid-South.

Black River Beads & Pottery (870-248-0450; www.blackriverbeads.com), 213 East Broadway Street, Pocahontas. Open Monday through Thursday 10–5, Friday 10–4, Sunday noon–5; closed Saturday. Located on the historic courthouse square in downtown Pocahontas, Black River Beads & Pottery features the work of James and Amanda Tinker, as well as the other local artists they promote in this shop. Handmade glass beads, stoneware pottery, hand-poured soy candles, and unique gifts are stocked in stunning displays. Each bead is individually crafted, and many original jewelry pieces are also available. If you are looking for jewelry for a special occasion or outfit, they will be glad to work with you to design a one-of-a-kind piece. The shop carries the work of several local artists.

Crystal Waters (479-253-0222), 7 Basin Spring Avenue, Eureka Springs. Generally open daily 11–5, occasionally later for special events. Crystal Waters specializes in Arkansas quartz crystals, and this shop has everything you need to create sanctuary in your life. Shelves are stocked to the brim with crystals and gemstones from around the world, incense, candles, jewelry, and art—an eclectic blend of nature and nurture. Located on the stairway directly across from Basin Spring Park, you can also book a tarot reading with a medium through the shop.

Iris at the Basin Park (479-253-9494), 8 Spring Street, Eureka Springs. This shop is located on the street level of the Basin Park Hotel and stocks beautifully handcrafted items created by talented local artists. They also carry a nice selection of art glass pieces and Judaica.

Earl's Antique Mall (870-425-8578), 3328 Highway 62 West, Mountain Home. Open 10–5 daily. Earl's Antique Mall is one of those stores where you are likely to find something you want even if you are just window shopping. If you can't find something in their 11,000 square feet of shopping space, then you just aren't trying. Forty room and 77 display cases break down the massive inventory into well organized clusters of gifts, antiques, and collectibles.

Quicksilver Gallery (479-253-7679), 73 Spring Street, Eureka Springs. Open Monday through Friday 10–5. This gallery features the works of over 120 local, regional, and nationally known artists. There is no shortage of one of a kind items when every item is handmade. Tapestries, wildlife watercolors, photographs, limited edition prints, pottery, and jewelry are displayed on two levels in the heart of downtown Eureka.

Shelby's (870-741-5309; www.shopshelbys.com), 215 North Main Street, Harrison. Open Monday through Saturday 9–5. Shelby's is a 7,500-square-foot freestanding establishment that's been in business since 1976. Kitchen utensils and gadgets, bath and beauty products, server ware, and dozens of other household products are available both in their store and online.

White River Pottery (870-425-2164), 397 Remington Circle, Mountain Home. Seasonal hours; call before visiting. This craft store features hand-thrown pottery and the work of local artists.

✳ Special Events

April: **22nd Annual Ozark UFO Conference** (501-354-8158; www.ozarkufo.com), Inn of the Ozarks Convention Center, Eureka Springs. It makes sense, if you think about it, that a town like Eureka Springs, with so many spectral citizens, might also attract a couple of aliens, too. Who more likely to embrace otherworldly visitors than those accustomed to supernatural ones? If you just want to believe, or if you consider Mulder and Scully to be folk heroes, this is a good conference for you. Lectures are offered throughout by nationally known authorities on various aspects of UFOs. There are usually between 9 and 10 speakers, plus vendors of books, tapes, and DVDs on all aspects of UFOs. Anyone with an interest in the subject should attend. Admission: $45 in advance, $50 at the door.

May: **Syllamo's Revenge Mountain Bike Challenge** (870-269-8068), Mountain View. More than 50 miles of awesome mountain biking through the beautiful Ozark Mountains, Syllamo's Revenge is rapidly gaining popularity with mountain bikers around the country. Unlike many mountain bike trails that have a limited area for trail construction, the Syllamo Mountain Bike Trail stretches over thousands of acres of the Ozark National Forest, offering riders changing scenery and beautiful views of the White River and Sylamore Creek Valleys and the Ozark Mountains.

September: **Off the Beaten Path Studio Tour** (870-269-4103; www.offthebeatenpathstudiotour.com), at 25 artists' studios within 30 miles of Court House Square in Mountain View. This is a unique opportunity to visit the private working studios of artists and craft artisans and see firsthand the distinctive work created by these artists. The tour includes potters, jewelers, painters, photographers, metalworkers, wood turners, weavers, bead makers, and more. The studios are open Friday and Saturday 9–6, Sunday 10–4. There is also an artists' reception on Friday evening. Admission is free for the studio tour, but call the chamber of commerce for information about the reception.

October: **Annual Beanfest & Outhouse Races** (870-269-8068; www .yourplaceinthemountains.com), Courthouse Square, Mountain View. More than 1,000 pounds of pinto beans are cooked in huge iron kettles around the courthouse square. Folks come from all around, armed with their secret ingredients and the determination to stir up the best batch of beans. Later the most outrageous race in the country takes place as outhouse racers are pushed down the course by teams vying for the coveted gold toilet seat.

Artisans Market on the Square (www .artisansmarketonthesquare.com), Courthouse Square, Mountain View. The Artisans' Market at Beanfest takes one of Arkansas's longest-running festivals and combines it with two of the Ozarks' finest resources—artisans and craftspeople. The result is a fun-filled weekend featuring folk music, folk cuisine, and fine arts and crafts. Definitely worth the trip! The festival is held the last weekend of October. Market hours are noon–5 Friday and 9–4 Saturday. Handmade fine contemporary arts and crafts, heritage arts, and folk art are featured. Admission is free.

November: **Annual Ozark Folk Festival** (479-253-2586; www.eurekasprings .org/folk), Basin Spring Park and the Eureka Springs City Auditorium, Eureka Springs. This is the oldest continuously running folk festival in the country. Eureka Springs continues to draw the world's best folk musicians to venues throughout the Victorian village. An updated list of events and performers is maintained on the website. Admission varies by the venue, with many free performances on the street.

INDEX

Park, 243; Onyx Cave, 242; Opera, 263; Ozark Mountain Hoe-Down, 263; Pigeon Roost Trail, 221; Pivot Rock and Natural Bridge, 238; Quigley's Castle, 238; Shaddox Hollow Trail, 222; Southern Pride Carriage Tours, 238; spas, 235–36, 249; St. Elizabeth's Catholic Church, 233, *233*; *The Great Passion Play*, 229, 262; tours, 236; Turpentine Creek Wildlife Refuge, 240; UFO conference, 264

Eureka Springs & North Arkansas Railway, 32, 237

Eureka Springs City Auditorium, 261, 265

Eureka Springs Ghost Tours, 236

Eureka Springs Historical Museum, 229

Eureka Springs Historic Downtown Walking Tours, 221

F

fall color, 28, 68, 80

Family Pie Shop, The, 32, 58

Fargo Agricultural School Museum, 48

Faulkner County Museum, 131

Fayetteville, 188; Ale Trail, 26; All Seasons Trail, 186; Beaver Lake, 203, *204*; Belladerm, 200; bicycling, 24; Bikes, Blues, & BBQ Motorcycle Rally, 29, 30, 218; Boston Mountains Scenic Loop, The, 186; Botanical Garden of the Ozarks, 198, *199*; Carnall Hall, *202*, 205, *206*; Clinton House Museum, 25, 192; Dickson Street Entertainment District, 215; drive-in, 27; Emelia's Kitchen, 210; farmers' market, *217*; Glo Limited, 201; Headquarters House Museum, 192, *193*; Herman's Ribhouse, 210; Joe Martin Stage Race, 24; Lights of the Ozarks, 218; nightlife, 215; Pratt Place Inn & Barn, 207, *207*; spas, 200; The Farmers Table, 210; University of Arkansas, 30, 194; Walton Arts Center, 195; White River, 187

Fayetteville Arts Festival, 188

Fayetteville Confederate Cemetery, 197

Fayetteville Visitor Center, 194

Felsenthal National Wildlife Refuge, 90, 106

festivals: Ale Trail, 26; Annual Beanfest & Outhouse Races, 265; Annual Camden BPW Barn Sale, 119–20; Annual Ozark Folk Festival, 265; Annual Tontitown Grape Festival, 218; Arkansas Blues and Heritage Festival, 78; Arkansas Folk Festival, 40; Arkansas.com, 23; Bentonville Film Festival (BFF), 188; Bikes, Blues, and BBQ, 26, 28, 188;

bluegrass, 26; Blues Festival in Helena, 31; butterfly festival, 25; Camden Daffodil Festival, 91, 119; Cardboard Boat Festival, 28; Fayetteville Arts Festival, 188; Great American Beer Festival, 118; Harvest! Festival, 118; Hot Springs Documentary Film Festival, 150, 152; Jonquil Festival, 93; King Biscuit Blues Festival, 26, 28, 62–63, 84; Lights of the Delta, 64; Loose Caboose Festival, 83; National Chuckwagon Race Championships, 28; Old Fort Day Rodeo, 159; Opera in the Ozarks, 31, 263; Ozark Mountain Bike Festival, 38; Pinnacle Mountain State Park, 109; Pioneer Days Craft Fair and Festival, 230; Portfest, 28; Racing Festival of the South, 28, 138; Riverfest, 29; Southwestern Regional Ballet Association Festival, 116; T Tauri Film Festival & Movie Camp, 62; Toad Suck Daze, 151; The Unexpected, 11, 161; Wildwood Music Festival, 118; Wine & Food FEASTival, 118; Wings Over the Prairie Festival, 49, 63–64

fishing, 29; Anglers White River Resort, 260; Arkansas River, 157, 159; Bar J Ranch, 114; Bear Creek Lake, *70*, 78; Bear Creek Springs Trout Farm, 234, *234*; Beaver Lake, 247; Beaverfork Lake, 129; Big Lake National Wildlife Refuge, 52; Brinkley, 48; Bull Shoals Lake, 227, 243–44; Cache River National Wildlife Refuge, 52; Caddo River, 127; Crooked Creek, 238; Crowley's Ridge State Park, 79; Davidsonville Historic State Park, 243; Dry Run Creek, 223; Earl Buss Bayou DeView, 77; Felsenthal National Wildlife Refuge, 106; Greers Ferry Lake, 244; Guide Services, 136; Highway 27 Fishing Village, 146; His Place Resort, 253; Jim Hinkle Spring River State Fish Hatchery, 223; Kings River, 222; Lake Atalanta, 203; Lake Austell, 80; Lake Bailey, 174; Lake Charles State Park, 243; Lake Chicot, 48; Lake Conway, 129; Lake Dardanelle, 157, 158, 160, 170; Lake Devil, 209; Lake Dunn, 80; Lake Frierson State Park, 79; Lake Maumelle, 90, 111; Lake Ouachita, 128, 131, 139; Lake Poinsett State Park, 80; Lake Village, 48; Lake Wilhelmina, 130; L'Anguille River, 70; Lindsey's Rainbow Resort, 254; Little Red River, 222; Mammoth Spring National Fish Hatchery, 223;